# Christian Social Ethics
## in a
## Changing World

## VOLUMES IN THIS SERIES

# Christian Social Ethics
## in a
## Changing World

*An Ecumenical Theological Inquiry*

*Edited by* JOHN C. BENNETT

ASSOCIATION PRESS · NEW YORK

SCM PRESS · BLOOMSBURY STREET · LONDON

Christian Social Ethics in a Changing World

---

First Printing April 1966
Second Printing June 1966
Third Printing October 1966
Fourth Printing April 1967

*Library of Congress catalog card number: 65-10118*
*Publisher's stock number: 1587*

 72

PRINTED IN THE UNITED STATES OF AMERICA

# PREFACE

In 1962, the Central Committee of the World Council of Churches authorized the Department on Church and Society to begin preparations for a world conference to be held in 1966. The theme that was finally selected was "Christians in the Technical and Social Revolutions of Our Time." The department was also requested to undertake such preparatory studies as would help the conference in considering the central issues for Christian social ethics in contemporary society. In 1963, the Working Committee of the department recommended the preparation of four books of essays on the following subjects:

    I. *Christian Social Ethics in a Changing World*
    II. *Responsible Government in a Revolutionary Age*
    III. *Economic Growth in World Perspective*
    IV. *Man in Community*

We are pleased to commend these books to Christians around the world, and we invite them to share with us their reactions and opinions on the issues raised therein. Although the books are primarily intended as preparatory reading for the 1966 conference, it is hoped that they will also be used for discussion in local and regional groups, after the conference as well as before.

Not since the Oxford World Conference on Church, Community and State, in 1937, has there been a similar worldwide effort to rethink Christian social responsibility. The study volumes for that conference dealt largely with the theological issues of social ethics within the context of the churches' encounter with the challenges of that time. Since then, new technical and social revolutions have overtaken societies all over the world; and new issues of social ethics have arisen as the churches have responded to them. This first volume deals with the theological problems of social ethics as such, while the others concentrate on relating theological insights to the actual problems of Christian responsibility in the contemporary situation of world political, economic and social change.

These symposia do not pretend to represent the full range of viewpoints held within the ecumenical fellowship on these questions. This is impossible in the space of four volumes on such large themes. The aim is rather to reveal the wide range of attitudes and opinions held, giving special attention to new and challenging points of view.

The responsibility for the structure and content of these volumes is shared by the international editorial committees, which met in 1963 and 1964 to prepare the outline of each book and to review the first drafts of the contributions; by the chairman or editorial conveners of these committees, who have since become the editors of the books; and by the staff of the Department on Church and Society, who necessarily had to undertake the large part of the detailed editorial work and correspondence. Each writer remains responsible for the content of his contribution.

We are grateful to all those who have contributed to the volumes and to those who have commented on the essays in draft form. We acknowledge with appreciation the contribution of the Church and Society staff—Professor Mauricio Lopez, the Reverend Thomas Okuma and, in particular, Miss Margaret Sinclair, one of the early workers in the Universal Christian Council for Life and Work, who forsook her retirement for three months to assist us in preparing the manuscripts for publication. We depended throughout on our secretarial staff, Miss Audrey Smith, Miss Christa Stalschus, Miss Judith Brown, and Miss Karin Hoek who typed the many drafts of these manuscripts.

M. M. THOMAS, *Chairman*
Working Committee
Department on Church and Society

PAUL ABRECHT, *Executive Secretary*
Department on Church and Society

World Council of Churches
Division of Studies

# CONTRIBUTORS TO
# THIS VOLUME

DR. JOHN C. BENNETT (Editor). President of Union Theological Seminary, New York City; participant in ecumenical deliberations on social questions since World Conference on Church, Community and State, Oxford (1937); leader in discussion on Church and Society at World Council of Churches assemblies: Amsterdam (1948), Evanston (1954) and New Delhi (1961); member of the Working Committee of the Department on Church and Society. Author of many studies on social ethics. (United Church of Christ)

PROFESSOR RICHARD SHAULL Professor of ecumenics, Princeton Theological Seminary; pioneer in Church and Society studies in Latin America; a younger theologian appealing especially to the new student generation. Author of *Encounter with Revolution* and many articles and essays. (United Presbyterian Church)

PROFESSOR ROGER MEHL Professor of philosophy and ethics, University of Strasbourg; a leader of ecumenical thought in France. Author of many books including *La condition du philosophe chrétien* (1947); *De l'autorité des valeurs* (1957); *Société et amour* (1961); *Du Catholicisme romain* (1947). (Reformed Church of France)

PROFESSOR HANS-WERNER BARTSCH, TH.D. Director of the Seminary for Evangelical Theology of the College for Education at the Johann Wolfgang Goethe University, Frankfurt. Editor of the seven-volume series *Kerygma und Mythos* and author of many other theological and biblical studies. (Evangelical Church of Germany)

DR. NICOS A. NISSIOTIS, TH.D. Associate director, Ecumenical Institute, Chateau de Bossey, Switzerland; Greek Orthodox lay theologian; one of the WCC observers to Vatican Council II. His writings include *The Problem of Faith in Kierkegaard and Modern Existentialists* (Athens, 1956); *Theology as a Discipline of Knowledge and as a Doxology* (Athens, 1962); and *Philosophy of Religion as Philosophical Theology* (Athens, 1965). (Greek Orthodox)

REV. BRUCE REED Director, Christian Teamwork, an evangelical action group, with headquarters in London, that is developing new forms of ministry to workers and others in modern urban setting. (Church of England)

PROFESSOR WILLIAM H. LAZARETH Dean and professor of systematic theology at the Lutheran Theological Seminary, Philadelphia; representative of the Lutheran Church in America on the Faith and Order Commission of the WCC. Author of *Luther on the Christian Home; A Theology of Politics;* and *Protestant Churches and Reform Today.* (United Lutheran Church in America)

PROFESSOR H. D. WENDLAND Rector, University of Westphalia; professor of Christian social science and director of the Institute for Christian Social Science at the Westphalian Wilhelms University at Münster. Author of numerous studies on the church in modern society, including *Die Kirche in der modernen Gesellschaft; Botschaft an die soziale Welt; Einführung in die Sozialethik.* (Evangelical Church of Germany)

REV. PAUL ABRECHT Executive secretary, Department on Church and Society, Division of Studies, World Council of Churches; secretary of the section on social questions at the Second WCC Assembly at Evanston (1954) and the Third WCC Assembly at New Delhi (1961). (Baptist)

CANON LOUIS JANSSENS Professor of moral theology, Catholic University of Louvain, Belgium. (Roman Catholic)

REV. ADEOLU ADEGBOLA Principal, Immanuel College (United Theological Seminary for Western Nigeria); one of the leading young theologians of Africa; organizing secretary of the All-Africa Youth Conference, Nairobi (1962); chairman of the WCC's Youth Department. (Methodist)

DR. GONZALO CASTILLO CÁRDENAS Executive secretary, Commission on Presbyterian Cooperation in Latin America. (Presbyterian)

DR. J. RUSSELL CHANDRAN Principal of the United Theological College, Bangalore, India; during 1964-1965, Henry W. Luce visiting professor on world Christianity at Union Theological Seminary, New York City. Contributor to the publications of the Christian Institute for the Study of Religion and Society. (Church of South India)

PROFESSOR J. M. LOCHMAN Professor of systematic theology and philosophy at the Comenius-Faculty, Prague. Author of several publications, including *Religious Thought of the Czech Enlightenment* (2 volumes); *Theology and Philosophy; Theology and History of Religion;* and *Importance of Historical Events for Ethical Decisions.* (Evangelical Church of Czech Brethren)

DR. HARRY ARONSON Docent of ethics and philosophy of religion, University of Lund, Sweden. (Lutheran Church of Sweden)

PROFESSOR ROGER L. SHINN William E. Dodge, Jr., professor of applied Christianity and dean of instruction, Union Theological Seminary, New York City. His writings include *Christianity and the Problem of History* and *Life, Death and Destiny;* editor of *The Search for Identity: Essays on the American Character;* a leader in Christian social action movements sponsored by the National Council of Churches, U. S. A., and his own church. (United Church of Christ)

PROFESSOR N. H. SÖE Professor of theology, University of Copenhagen; participant in many ecumenical discussions on social ethics, including assemblies of Amsterdam, Evanston and New Delhi. Author of *Kristelig Etik* (5th ed., 1962); *Religionsfilosof* (2nd ed., 1963); and other studies. (Lutheran Church of Denmark)

PROFESSOR JOSEPH FLETCHER Professor of social ethics, Episcopal Theological School, Cambridge, Mass.; also external professor of theological ethics, Harvard Divinity School. His recent publications include *Morals and Medicine* (1954); *William Temple: Theological Portrait* (1963). (Episcopalian)

DEAN WALTER G. MUELDER Dean, Boston School of Theology, Boston University; observer, Vatican Council II; active participant in ecumenical studies both for Faith and Order and for Life and Work; participated in the discussion on social questions at the WCC assemblies of Evanston (1954) and New Delhi (1961). Author of *Religion and Economic Responsibility; Institutionalism and Church Unity;* and other books and articles. (Methodist)

REV. EMILIO CASTRO Pastor of the Central Methodist Church in Montevideo, Uruguay; licentiate in theology of the Evangelical Theological Seminary; postgraduate studies in Basel, Switzerland; secretary of the recently formed Commission for Evangelical Unity in Latin America.

# CONTENTS

## PART II

### Theology in Ecumenical Social Thinking

## PART III

### The Function of the Church in Changing Societies

# FOREWORD

by JOHN C. BENNETT (United States)

THIS volume will introduce the reader to much fresh theological thinking about social ethics. It is a response to a new situation in the church and to new problems in the world. The theologians who have dominated the theological thought of previous ecumenical conferences are not generally represented here; these authors are, for the most part, new voices on the ecumenical level. All the chapters come out of a deep concern for the social implications of Christian faith and theology, and for the responsibility of the church for action on the frontiers of social change. This is not a mere collection of chapters, since many of the authors have met together for discussion and mutual criticism before completing them.

One clear difference between this volume and all previous books of the same type is that parts of the worldwide Christian community are represented here for the first time. When the plan for the volume was first discussed, the phrase "enlarging the conversation" was often used. The preparation for previous ecumenical conferences was done chiefly by Protestant thinkers in the older churches of the West. The ethical problems discussed were those of the older nations. Even the reports of the Evanston Assembly in 1954 have been criticized as reflecting too much the experience of Christians who live with established political and economic systems. The New Delhi Assembly of 1961 represented a movement away from this traditional orientation, but it provided no opportunity for much discussion of the theological issues raised by the social responsibility of Christians and churches.

In this volume, one writer is from the Eastern Orthodox Church. Three writers reflect the experience of Latin American Christians. One more is from Africa, and another is from Asia. One is from eastern Europe. Two other writers represent types of theological thought that have played little part in the ecumenical conversation: the neo-Evangelicals, who have often been suspicious of the emphasis on "social action" in the thought and work of the World Council of Churches, and a very fluid group of theologians who have been influenced in a central way by Rudolf Bultmann. The critic may say that in neither of these cases do we provide a pure specimen of the type, if such exists! We are glad to welcome a Roman Catholic author.

Another new aspect of this volume in the library of ecumenical theology is that there is a new mood in most of these chapters. It is a mood of greater hope for man's historical future than has often been present in ecumenical circles, certainly a mood that is ready for radical changes. Some of the chapters emphasize the necessity or the reality of social revolution. There is the mood of expectancy in churches in new nations that have only recently achieved their independence. The lines between the ideological West and the ideological East are much less hard, and it is possible for theologians on both sides of this ideological dividing line to talk with each other in a more relaxed way than has been the case since the beginning of the Cold War. The tragic experiences of National Socialism, of the Second World War and of Stalinism, which were shadows over ecumenical theological thought for years, now seem far away, and the prosperity of western Europe may have more influence on theology than theologians like to admit. Americans have long been influenced in this way by relative prosperity, and they may now be somewhat chastened as they face the new problems of the affluent society and the conflicts related to their nation's international role, especially the war in Vietnam.

I have said that there is a change of mood. There are numerous tragic failures to overcome particular conflicts between nations; there are civil conflicts and stalemates that do not have any end in sight. There are profoundly frustrated revolutions in some places and distorted revolutions in others. The optimism of the days of the Stockholm Conference in 1925 and the ideological confidence of more recent periods are no longer possible. Yet there are grounds for expectancy and even for hope. There has been some melting of frozen positions. The fear of nuclear destruction remains, but it is vaguer and less inspired by the fact of conflict between the two major nuclear powers. There is a fluid situation by which one feels less imprisoned than was the case with the world that the churches confronted from Amsterdam (1948) to New Delhi (1961). Theologians are inclined to see the human in man reasserting itself in spite of all the conflicts and the oppression, even in spite of much brainwashing. I speak of this to emphasize what is new in this book. The reader will find no new theological pattern to which he can give a label. But he will find new accents reflecting a world that is being transformed, a world in which much that seemed theologically profound at another time may now seem less relevant.

# PART I

## REOPENING THE DEBATE ON THE THEOLOGICAL FOUNDATIONS OF SOCIAL ETHICS

# I

# REVOLUTIONARY CHANGE IN THEOLOGICAL PERSPECTIVE

by RICHARD SHAULL (United States)

As we have become increasingly aware of the dynamic nature of society today, ecumenical social thinking has focused on *rapid social change*. Technology has emerged as the central factor, in a close and unusual relationship with other elements. The technological revolution developed in the West as a consequence of a fundamental change in man's understanding of reality and of the social order. At the same time, the spread of technology seems to accelerate this shift to a functional and secular attitude and to make imperative the development of new and more flexible forms of institutional life. In *Christianity in World History*,[1] Professor A. Van Leeuwen insists that this is part of an irresistible historical process in which traditional "ontocratic" [2] patterns of life are being shattered. All orders of society are losing their sacral character and are now open toward the future, to be shaped as man wills. At the same time, the author discerns a growing tendency toward the emergence of messianic movements dedicated to the liberation of man from all that enslaves and dehumanizes him.

---

[1] London: Edinburgh House Press, 1964.

[2] By "ontocratic," PROFESSOR VAN LEEUWEN means having an understanding of reality in terms of a total order of harmony between the eternal and the temporal, the divine and the human. The divine order is identified with nature and society, especially with the state conceived of as the "embodiment of cosmic totality." All structures of society are given a sacred character; they dare not be tampered with or changed.

Given the fluidity of a dynamic society, we should now be witnessing gradual progress toward the shaping of new social structures, which would offer a greater degree of justice and well-being to the depressed classes of the world. Thus far, however, this has not happened to any significant extent. Over against the discovery that society can be changed stands the fact that those who most benefit from the present situation have tremendous economic and political power and are willing to go to almost any length to preserve it. Entire classes and races of people have discovered that their suffering is not inevitable and have thus awakened to a new hope for a better life. But this hope has not been fulfilled. Institutions structured for a stable society have failed to adjust to the new order and are in crisis. Economic development, industrialization and the rapid growth of large cities, the population explosion and other factors have raised new problems, which they are unable to meet creatively; especially in the developing nations, this technological progress has often tended to increase the misery and insecurity of the poor, provide even greater opportunities for the few to profit, and leave the masses in greater insecurity than before. The process of secularization has undercut traditional concepts of authority, but new patterns of relationships have not yet evolved. In the midst of rapid social change, the uprooted masses discover the extent to which society has deprived them of their selfhood and left them in a state of alienation. In these circumstances, mass movements become the way by which they acquire a new identity as they participate in a struggle to shape a new society.[3]

We are thus confronted by a new and unprecedented polarization between those who have enjoyed the benefits of the status quo and those who are most anxious to change it. Our world is divided sharply between the rich and the poor nations; and in each country, a struggle is taking shape between those groups, races and classes who have awakened to their inferior position and those who are reluctant to make way for a new order. Consequently, it would seem that *social revolution* is the primary fact with which our generation will have to come to terms.

---

[3] ERIC HOFFER, commenting on the Negro revolution in the United States, writes: "Mass movements are often the means by which a population undergoing drastic change acquires a sense of rebirth and a new identity." *New York Times Magazine,* Nov. 29, 1964, p. 109.

Except in Latin America, the anticolonial struggle has now passed its peak; but the struggle of the poor and weak nations for an opportunity to participate more fully in international life and to have a more equitable share of the wealth of an interdependent world has only just begun. In developing and developed nations, the revolution of the dispossessed is still in its early stages. The Negro revolution in the United States now occupies the center of attention; it may well trigger similar upheavals among other under-privileged racial and economic groups, especially in large urban centers. The tremendous concentration of economic and political power in a few hands, which has occurred in our modern tech-nological society, will sooner or later lead to revolutionary de-mands for greater participation on the part of many groups of people. There are signs that this is already taking place in some of the communist countries; it may not long delay in western Europe and America. All around the world, a sort of revolution is brewing among young people, which may take on increasing significance in the years ahead.

If the analysis above is correct, it will be on the frontiers of revolution that many of the major issues of humanization and dehumanization will be decided in our modern world; it will be on these frontiers that those most concerned for the well-being and for the future of man will find themselves involved. This will be true not only for those young people—from both the privileged and underprivileged classes—who discover that their responsibility for their fellowmen leads them to participation in revolution, but it will also be true for those in positions of power in the established order who understand the world in which they are living and feel com-pelled to work for change. If we hope to preserve the most impor-tant elements of our cultural, moral and religious heritage and to contribute to the shaping of the future, we cannot remain outside the revolutionary struggle or withdraw from it. The only path of responsibility is the one that passes through it toward whatever may lie ahead.

For most of us, this will not be easy. Our past experience and training have not prepared us for this type of struggle. Many of us are too closely identified with the status quo to understand or participate freely in a revolution against it. Moreover, we are surrounded by evidences that revolution is a highly ambiguous phenomenon. It represents a passion for justice and for the liberation of the oppressed, but it also releases great forces of destruction and leads to new forms of injustice. Vast numbers of men and women have struggled and sacrificed their lives for the sake of a new society; all too often, the order that is established after the revolution has spent itself is not very different from the previous one. Movements that succeed in awakening the masses and invite them to participate in the use of public power often lead to destructive fanaticism and end up by depriving them of power. New centers of power are indispensable if change is to be brought about, but, in a revolutionary situation, it is impossible to predict how this power will eventually be used. The unselfish commitment of the young revolutionary to the service of his people is one of the most hopeful developments in the modern world, but this very attitude may lead him to exaggerate the rightness of his cause, as well as the injustices on the other side, and to close his eyes to aspects of reality that must be taken into account if the revolution is to achieve its goals.

If revolution is to be our destiny, we are challenged to find new categories of thought about social and political questions, and a new perspective on the relationship between stability and change. We are confronted by the need to develop communities of thought and action, on both sides of the major revolutionary struggles, that will search for solutions and work for reconciliation in the midst of tension and conflict.

Our major political movements do not offer much ground for hope. Conservative ideologies cannot understand the problem, much less meet its challenge; liberal ways of thinking do not seem to fare much better. The liberal, who works for *orderly* change in a world in which he can perceive signs of continued progress toward a better society, may be quite at a loss when confronted with the reality of a revolutionary upheaval. Marxism stands alone in its attempt to understand revolution as essential to the creation of a more stable and just society, and, in some parts of the world, it is the supreme symbol of hope for those who long for a new day. Yet after it comes to power, alters the structures of society and institutionalizes a new order, the situation changes. Then, the very ideology that provided the dynamic for revolution gets in the way of a creative response to the problem of order and change.

In this situation, has Christianity any contribution to make? Religion has traditionally given a sacral character to the institutions of the status quo and has thus been a major factor in preserving them against the forces of revolution. In the West, Christianity has been so closely identified with the established order of Christendom that it has tended to play the same role. In the face of revolutionary upheavals, the great temptation for the church is to become the rallying point of all who fear change.

At the same time, the breakdown of Christendom and the process of secularization have undercut the authority of the church, transferred this task of saving the status quo to new secular ideologies and movements and thus set the church free to be once again a revolutionary force.[4]

Moreover, as small groups of Christians become involved in revolutionary struggles, they discover in the Christian heritage resources for thought and action of which they were not previously aware. If these resources are available, we should give a certain priority to the type of study and research that will work them out and put them at the disposal of those who are now moving toward involvement in these areas. We indicate below some lines which may deserve further investigation.

### Toward a Theological Perspective on Revolution

If we look at our history in the light of biblical history, we may feel quite at home in the midst of revolution. There are several strands of biblical thought that may justify such an affirmation:

1. *The fact that God is both the Creator and Ruler of all spheres of nature and of society.* These are temporal realities ex-

---

[4] For an interesting discussion of this thesis, see the paper by B. Morel: "L'Avenir du ministère de l'Eglise dans un monde en voie de sécularisation," *Bulletin du Centre Protestant d'Etudes,* Geneva, XIV, 4, June, 1962. Taking as his starting point a recent discussion, in anthropology, of the role of *interdit* and *transgression* in the social sphere, he suggests that the task of preserving certain *interdits,* formerly exercised by the church, has now passed to secular institutions, and that the church is now called to be a force of *transgression* against the limitations imposed by such restrictions.

isting to serve God's purpose for *man;* therefore, they can and must be used and changed in line with that purpose. Throughout the Bible, there is a strong eschatological emphasis, which stresses the dynamic nature of God and the fact that his action in history is moving toward a goal. It is this which has led Professor Van Leeuwen to conclude that the biblical attitude toward the world has made our modern revolution both possible and inevitable. It has desacralized all institutions and awakened a concern for the reshaping of human life.

2. *The revolutionary character of biblical messianism.* From the first pages of the Old Testament, it is evident that God's rule over the nations and over Israel constantly runs into difficulties. His redemptive action means judgment, which is, at the same time, a new beginning. The scattering of the nations at Babel (Genesis 11) is followed by the calling of Abraham (Genesis 12), who will be the instrument for their restoration. In Israel, those most sensitive to the divine activity are convinced that he is tearing down in order to build up (Jeremiah 1 : 10), that he breaks the power of the oppressor in order to establish his justice.[5] As H. Berkhof puts it, "The Gospel introduced . . . a revolutionary God, whose 'righteousness,' according to the Psalms and the prophets, means that he lifts up those who are bowed down and humiliates the oppressors." [6]

In this atmosphere of revolution, the Messiah is the central figure. He arises after the house of David has been destroyed, as a shoot out of an apparently dead trunk. In Isaiah especially, central attention is given to his role as a political revolutionary, an emphasis that breaks forth in the New Testament in the Magnificat (Luke 1 : 50–53). In the life, death and resurrection of Jesus, the messianic theme of destruction and restoration finds new meaning and focus.

3. *The dynamic historical character of God's action.* Israel meets and knows God in the midst of her history, in her involvements in political crises and complex social and cultural problems. In the Incarnation, this God relates himself once and for all to man within a dynamic process. As God's action in the world aims at its

---

[5] See I Sam. 2 : 1–10; Ps. 9, 72, 146.
[6] *The Doctrine of the Holy Spirit.* Richmond, Va.: John Knox Press, 1964, p. 102.

transformation, the coming of Christ and the work of the Holy Spirit release new and disturbing forces in history that affect the process itself. As the influence of Christ grows, old stabilities are swept away, and the struggle for humanization moves to new frontiers; at the same time, new threats appear, and the forces that resist Christ become stronger and more manifest. Along this road, there can be no turning back; those who would participate in God's work cannot seek refuge in old ways nor draw back from the front lines because the situation is becoming increasingly dangerous. For it is in this struggle that the battle for the future of man is being waged; it is in the midst of apocalyptic events that we perceive signs of imminent victory (Luke 21 : 28).

## The Augustinian View of Social Change

The history of Christian thought does not provide us with many theologians of revolution. Augustine stands out across the centuries. Living as he did at the time of the collapse of the Roman Empire, much of his thought, especially in *The City of God,* deals with questions similar to those which face us today. As Professor Charles Cochrane has shown,[7] the trinitarian dogma provided him with a foundation for thought and action precisely at those points where classical culture had failed. Taking as his starting point a "principle" *beyond* nature and history, which was nevertheless at work *in* nature and history and which was capable of being apprehended there, he was able to take account of "being and movement in the universe" [8] in a new way. Trusting in a divine sovereignty at work in and through an "order of causes," Augustine was able to admit the impossibility of finding a satisfactory rational relationship of these causes to each other. And, at the same time, he sought new clues to an order, which, though not fully perceived, was nonetheless present. Convinced that the Logos of Christ, revealed in Scripture, was the ultimate reality in human life and history, he could think and act on the conviction that "each and every occurrence in the manifold of events bears wit-

---

[7] *Christianity and Classical Culture.* New York: Oxford University Press, 1940.
[8] *Ibid.,* p. 456.

ness to the activity of God." [9] It was this "principle of intelligibility," according to Professor Cochrane, which was capable of "saving the reason as well as the will," [10] for, in the working out of it, the rich diversity of human experience was pulled together in a meaningful configuration, and the historical process was seen as full of meaning and purpose.

Those who looked at the world in the perspective of the Logos of Christ as its "creating and moving principle," perceived that personality was as central in the historical process; crisis and change became meaningful. Historical events were seen as occurring along a line set by the dynamic reality of God's Providence, his bringing in of his Kingdom, the work of the Holy Spirit in the world and the movement of history toward its final goal. Along this road, two cities coexist. In constant conflict with each other, they are also "inextricably intermingled . . . in the concrete reality of history." [11] Both these cities are striving after one thing only, *peace,* which Augustine defined as "the tranquillity of order." [12] The peace of the eternal city, which is constantly permeating and transforming the city of man, is that of a "perfectly ordered and harmonious communion of those who find their joy in God and in one another in God." [13] But the peace of the earthly city, which is an attempt to develop some sort of order among men motivated by self-love, is a temporary, partial and unstable peace. It is an order that is always being established in the midst of conflict, in which men must often wage war for the sake of peace, and in which the divine judgment upon human pride and self-centeredness means that, from time to time, certain structures of society must be reformed and, in some cases, must collapse. [14]

This Augustinian perspective, with its wealth of insight into the meaning of events and the nature of responsible action in a revo-

---

[9] *Ibid.,* p. 480.
[10] *Ibid.,* p. 384.
[11] *The City of God,* X, 2.
[12] *Ibid.,* XIX, 13.
[13] *Ibid.*
[14] Speaking of the Romans who were upset by the crisis of the empire, Augustine says, "If they only had sense, they would see that the hardships and cruelties they suffered from the enemy came from that Divine Providence who makes use of war to reform the corrupt lives of men." *The City of God,* I, 1.

lutionary world, provides a basis for political realism that recognizes both the importance and the ambiguity of political action. The political struggle forms an essential part of the life of the earthly city and contributes to the renovation and reconstruction of human life in community, but not to its regeneration. For the Christian, the vortex of the social struggle has a very definite attraction. It is there, at the heart of the commingling of the two cities, that both the inevitable destructiveness of human self-love and new possibilities for social reform and for new structures of human relationships are exposed. Thus, the decline and collapse of the old order is not necessarily a disaster; it may well be the one way by which the divine purpose for a more just human order can move forward.

Among the theologians, Professor Paul L. Lehmann seems to have gone furthest in exploring Augustine's thought about the action of the triune God in history and has provided a number of theological categories for dealing with revolution; and, not surprisingly, there is, among those who are involved in revolutionary struggles, a certain interest in his thought. Professor Lehmann contends that it is only in Christianity that history is understood as a compound of stability and change, decay and fulfillment, in such a way that change is seen as the prelude to authentic stability, and decay as the occasion for fulfillment. This unusual perspective is the result of God's revelation of himself as "I will be who I will be," the God whose "moving strength" is at the heart of events and whose action must be understood by looking to the future, more than to the past.[15] But, for Professor Lehmann, it is primarily the messianic tradition and imagery of the Bible that provide the real clue to what is going on in the world. Here the focus is on the "political character" of God's activity, by which he is creating the conditions for human fulfillment in interrelatedness in the world.[16] The Messiah is the bearer of God's new deliverance where all human possibilities are played out; his purpose goes forward as he tears down in order to rebuild (Jeremiah 1 : 10; Luke 1 : 46–55).

---

[15] See his development of this theme in "The Dynamics of Reformation Ethics," *Princeton Seminary Bulletin*, XLIII, 4, Spring, 1950, pp. 17–22.
[16] See his *Ethics in a Christian Context*. New York: Harper & Row, 1963. Especially Ch. 3.

He is the Incarnate Son of God, "the humanization of God for the sake of the humanization of man." [17]

The Messiah was also crucified: It is only God's program, not man's, that offers the road to human fulfillment, a fulfillment that comes through judgment and reconciliation. The church is a sign and foretaste of this possibility present in the midst of life. When it is faithful to its Lord, the church incarnates this "passion for and vision of human deliverance and fulfilment"; [18] its disobedience contributes to the creation of a messianic vacuum, such as is evident today.

For Lehmann, revolution must be understood theologically, for it is set firmly in the context of God's humanizing activity in history. As a political form of change, revolution represents the cutting edge of humanization. We must therefore look to the revolutionary process if we hope to understand the dynamics and direction of change. But, in this context, revolution is the bearer both of signs of fulfillment and of symptoms of decay. The Christian looks for stability on the other side of change; he is therefore free to be fully involved in the revolution. At the same time, his understanding of what is going on there obliges him to work constantly for reconciliation.

## The Role of the Christian Koinonia in the Revolutionary Process

As a consequence of the self-invalidation of Christianity and the increasing dominance of a secular mentality, especially among revolutionaries, Christians cannot speak to the revolution by means of systematic theological treatises on the nature of the divine activity. What is now called for is rather the presence on the frontiers of revolution of communities dynamically involved in the struggle for humanization and engaged in a constant running conversation with their biblical and theological heritage. Such koinonias will find it easier to raise questions than to provide answers, and their voice may sound weak over against that of political ideologies. To the degree that they are faithful to their heritage, they will live in sharp

---

[17] PAUL L. LEHMANN, *Ideology and Incarnation.* Geneva: John Knox House, 1962, p. 24.
[18] *Ibid.*

tension with the revolutionary movements in which they participate or with the established order of which they are a part. And yet it is precisely this type of existence that may contribute something to the deepening of insight, the recovery of purpose, the rebirth of courage and the work of reconciliation among Christians and non-Christians alike. Certain concrete issues reveal that the possibilities are these:

1. *The dynamics of the revolutionary process.* Christians, and many others, especially of the middle class, are upset and confused when confronted with the reality of revolution. Although identified with the status quo, they see certain injustices around them and want to work for reasonable and gradual changes in society. They may even be enthusiastic about revolution in its early stages. But they find themselves confronted by a dynamic process which they cannot understand, and which leads those on each side to assume more radical positions. As attitudes become more extreme and actions more excessive, the Christian may find himself attempting to expose the exaggerations of both groups but unable to identify with either of them. Thus he soon finds himself far from the front lines of the struggle and ignored by all.

At this point, a radical theological reorientation would seem to be called for. The God who is tearing down old structures in order to create the conditions for a more human existence is himself in the midst of the struggle. It is his presence in the world and his pressure upon those structures which stand in his way that constitute the dynamics of this process. God has taken human form in the concreteness of historical life and has called us to follow this path if we are to be the salt of the earth and the light of the world (Matthew 5 : 13–14). In this context, the Christian is called to be fully involved in the revolution as it develops. It is only at its center that we can perceive what God is doing, understand how the struggle for humanization is being defined and serve as agents of reconciliation. From within this struggle we discover that we do not bear witness in revolution by preserving our purity in line with certain moral principles, but rather by freedom to be *for man* at every moment. It is also in the midst of this situation that we who have been silent and inactive in the face of suffering and injustice are made to see our guilt and accept the judgment that has come upon us. If our failure to act in the past is responsible for this radicalization of the revolutionary process, we can accept our guilt and work for reconciliation only as we are free to participate in movements in which we have lost the right to be heard and in which our sincerity may now be called into question.

Here we also face *the nature of the revolutionary process itself.* The forces of reaction often tend to ignore or underestimate the dynamics of this process; the revolutionaries consider it as an inevitable law of historic necessity. Especially since the time of the French Revolution, revolution has been understood as a series of tremendous events following a destined course beyond human control. Hegel's philosophy of history may well have been greatly influenced by his reflection upon these events, and Marx gave definitive formulation to this deterministic view.

In a Christian perspective, the revolutionary process is a reality that we dare not ignore, but it loses its character of determinism and inevitability. As Augustine interpreted history in the light of God's sovereignty over an order of causes, so the Christian understands events in a revolutionary situation. He is free to attempt to understand what is happening by analyzing the concrete social, economic and political realities, while remaining sensitive to the direction in which things seem to be moving. The dynamics of the process is determined not by some inevitable law of history, but by the interworking of God's pressure for change and man's response to it—by trying to stop it, or by absolutizing the revolutionary struggle or by taking concrete steps toward a more just society. The development of the revolution will thus be determined by the way in which those on each side of the struggle respond to the pressures for a more human society, as it takes shape in the "providence of God and the confusion of men."

2. *Stability and change.* In the Christian perspective, order is the order of humanization as it is made visible in the *koinonia;* it can be established only in and through the renewal and transformation of structures, even though such changes bring with them also new possibilities of dehumanization. A crisis in any social structure does not necessarily endanger the well-being of those who live in it; it is more likely to be a new opportunity for a richer life, espe-

cially for those groups whose well-being has been ignored. In a world that operates this way, the past can be preserved only as it is constantly being transformed. Efforts to save our heritage by enclosing it in rigid institutional forms of a former era can lead only to its repudiation.

In this context, men and women discover new possibilities for creative thought and action in the midst of revolution. Those who are closely identified with the established order may be free to recognize the judgment upon their way of life, accept the loss of privileges in the interest of their neighbor and look for new opportunities of fulfillment, even for themselves, as the new order takes shape around them. They may be able to take initiatives in bringing about changes in their society, thus opening the way to a more gradual and less violent transition.

Likewise, the revolutionary may discover that he should not make an idol of revolution. The overthrow of the old order will not automatically bring about a more just society. That can come only as the result of an intensive effort that works toward the shaping of the new out of the concrete material given in a specific situation. Moreover, in the long run, the new order will be an instrument of humanization only if it, too, is open to change. A revolution will be able to move toward an approximate realization of its objectives only if it develops a type of institution in which self-criticism and sensitivity to dissatisfaction are built into its very structures. It is this fact that modern revolutionaries, dominated as they have been by a mistaken understanding of the historical process, seem singularly unable to comprehend. It is hard to find examples that match Thomas Jefferson's reaction to the news of Shays' uprising: "God forbid that we should ever be twenty years without such a rebellion."

Moreover, in the Christian community, we have certain clues to the type of structure that is most clearly in line with God's work of humanization. Revolutions today are basically struggles for justice. But, in God's world, justice and reconciliation belong together. The enemy must be taken seriously. This does not necessarily imply that a two-party political system must be preserved in all circumstances nor does it imply that the nerve of revolutionary action must be cut by endless and fruitless search for an agreement on a program that satisfies all groups in society. It does mean openness toward those whose criticisms expose our rationalizations and our mistakes, and constant efforts toward reconciliation of conflicting interests and restoration of broken relationships. In the *koinonia,* human fulfillment comes through growth to maturity in interrelatedness. Thus, only as a person has the opportunity to participate in the life of his community and in the decisions that shape his destiny, can he be fully human.

3. *The new revolutionary order and the kingdom of God.* The conservative of the established order may be aware of its limitations, and even of its injustices; what he tends to ignore is the dynamics of history. The revolutionary, on the other hand, is sensitive to the dynamics of the historical process; his temptation is to trust in the power of man to build a completely new order and to solve all problems that may arise.

The kingdom of God always stands over against every social and political order, thus exposing its dehumanizing elements and judging it. At the same time, the Kingdom is a dynamic reality; it is "coming" through the work of him who is restoring the nations (II Isaiah) and in whose good time the kingdom of this world shall become the kingdom of our Lord and of his Christ (Revelations 11 : 15). Thus, a particular crisis of structures may be the result of God's relentless pressure; and the Christian may perceive, in certain situations, a relative coincidence of direction of the revolutionary struggle with God's humanizing action in the world.

When this occurs, we are confronted with forces that will shape the future, and in relation to which our obedience must be defined. Guidance for such discernment cannot come from a philosophy of history or a political ideology, but only from participation in a community that, orientated by God's revelation, is also involved in the world where he is at work. For those who have eyes to see, this coincidence of direction will be found not only in the crisis of structures of a feudal or bourgeois society but also in the struggle for humanization in those orders established by revolutions today. In the perspective of the Kingdom, involvement in revolution means living in a state of tension that can become a creative force. The new order of society is a "gift." It comes in the midst of, and in spite of, our limitations and failures. What is of ultimate signifi-

cance is the fulfillment of human life in a new context of relationships. For this new order, a change of structures in society is essential, but it is only one element in a larger process of humanization.
Thus, we can participate fully in the political struggle at the same
time as we recognize its limitations. We can be open to unexpected
possibilities of meaning and fulfillment, which may come at any
moment, even when our most strenuous political efforts seem to
suffer complete defeat. Each new experience of community points
to the Kingdom toward which we are moving, but in which, even
now, we participate in a partial way.

4. *Thought and action orientated toward the future.* In our dynamic society, the categories of thought on which we rely for
understanding are soon outmoded, the shape of the problems we
confront is constantly changing, and our methods of dealing with
them can become inadequate almost overnight. Those who are
bound to the past become victims of fear and frustration, and men
who have offered creative leadership at one moment may discover that they are suddenly unable to meet the new challenge before them. Even those who contribute to the establishment of a
new society may betray their cause because they are not free to
think and act in the new situation, which their own revolution has
created.

In spite of our traditional ways of thinking, Christian faith does
look at the present in the light of the future; and the future, brought
into the present, provides a unique perspective of understanding
and becomes an explosive force. As we respond to the God who is
moving ahead, we find ourselves directed toward "the shape of
things to come." This action of God is hidden to a certain extent,
but we need not, for this reason, formulate a world view that
affirms the absence of God or the absurdity of history. Trusting
that every moment of history is shaped by the divine activity, we
can await the manifestations of God's action along the road toward
the future. This understanding of reality saves the reason by freeing it from the tendency to absolutize its systems of thought and
from the pretension to omniscience and infallibility. At the same
time, it grounds our efforts at understanding upon an order of
truth which is not necessarily logical, but which is determined by
the providential ordering of God, partially apprehended by faith

in the midst of concrete historical reality. Along this road, the reason is free to seek new patterns of society not according to some social dogma or utopian dream, but by a realistic apprehension of the possibilities of change and development that open up as we move from one stage to another in the revolutionary struggle. What matters at each stage is not the success or failure of a specific project, but the way in which, in success or failure, the struggle for humanization moves to a new level.[19] To the degree that we participate in a community that is present on the frontier and lives by this hope, we shall be able to meet the breakdown of present structures without fear and act in a way that points to the shape of things to come.

### Orientation for Ethical Decisions

The Christian in a revolutionary movement finds himself surrounded by a variety of groups and ideologies, each of which has specific proposals for the creation of a new society. Has Christian faith anything to say about the shape of the new structures that are to be established after the collapse of the old? This question, central in all Christian ethical reflection today, takes on new importance in a revolutionary situation for at least two reasons:

1. The revolutionary finds himself caught up in an accelerated process in which he is confronted, at every moment, with a new configuration of facts and events. All schematic definitions of ethical responsibility tend to hinder him from dealing with concrete reality. In fact, it is in the revolutionary struggle that the attempt of modern secular man to formulate a new conception of reality and find a new basis for ethical decisions has a special appeal.

2. In the midst of revolution, life is insecure, the shape of the future is unclear. The struggle for a new order takes place in the

---

[19] Interesting examples of this are provided by the civil-rights struggle in the United States. A small group of Negro and white students organizes a sit-in at a few lunch counters in an Alabama city. They do not accomplish their immediate objective, yet they spark off a movement that affects the entire country. Other similar efforts fail, but they do lead to the adoption of civil-rights legislation by Congress, which changes the pattern of race relations at many points.

midst of opposition, repeated failures and the constant appearance of new threats of dehumanization. For the revolutionary, the ethical question is not merely that of a logical definition of a new order; what he most needs is an understanding of the revolutionary process that orientates his struggle for change in the direction of the future and provides a context of hope and trust in which he can make wise decisions.

In the face of these demands, it is not surprising that the natural-law tradition, with its rational definition of cosmic order and its attempt to formulate general principles for an ideal society, breaks down. What may not yet be so evident is that our ecumenical studies, to the degree that they depend upon this tradition, may prove irrelevant. To speak only of the situation I know most directly, in Brazil, the rapid social change studies were widely used until we confronted a revolutionary situation. Then we discovered that those most involved were turning elsewhere for orientation.

Professor Hendrik Van Oyen, in his paper on "Fundamental Problems of Evangelical Social Ethics," [20] suggests why this was so. He finds that our ecumenical studies have preserved the unresolved tension in Anglo-Saxon Christian social thought between "the Calvinistic ideal of the rule of the Kingdom of God over the whole creation" and "the claim of natural law as a cosmic order of life, in other words, the ideal of reason." [21] Many of our more specifically theological statements have followed the first line; our definitions of structure, the second. Useful as the latter has been, it is questionable whether this logical enterprise can deal effectively with the concreteness of the revolutionary process or with the increasing demands to give sufficient attention to the knowledge of the specialist in the formulation of ethical goals.[22]

---

[20] *Background Information,* World Council of Churches: No. 32. Feb., 1964, pp. 1–9.

[21] *Ibid.,* p. 3.

[22] This unresolved tension, with its consequences, is evident especially in the Evanston Report. The introductory statement ends thus: "Our hope in Christ does not offer technical answers or specific solutions which statesmen and experts have not found. But in the context of Christian faith, we gain new insights into our dilemmas and ways to overcome them." Rather than pursuing this line, the report then moves into anthropology and natural law, defining a responsible society, which provides "a criterion by which we judge all existing orders and at the same time a standard to guide us in the specific choices we have to make."

Where, then, can we seek answer to the question regarding the shaping of structures in a revolutionary situation? In Brazil, among certain groups, there has been a decisive shift toward a contextual ethic, the starting point of which is a "theology of messianism" rather than a theological anthropology together with a modified natural-law theory. As Professor Lehmann describes it, a theology of messianism focuses on what God is doing in the world to make and keep human life human. This divine action follows a line indicated by the doctrines of providence, the kingdom of God, and eschatology, as well as by the third article of the Creed, regarding the activity of the Holy Spirit in the church and in the world. Along this road, every situation in which the Christian finds himself called upon to live and act is an expressionn of the commingling of the two cities, which continues throughout history. In this process, the pressures of the redemptive God upon the earthly city and the constant encounter and conflict between the two constitute the context in which men strive for order and peace in the world. In Lehmann's words:

The complexity of the actual human situation ... is always compounded of an intricate network of circumstance and human interrelationships bracketed by the dynamics of God's political activity on the one hand and God's forgiveness on the other.[23]

If this is the nature of the reality with which we are dealing, the proximate good for which Christians or non-Christians strive cannot be defined in terms of principles and precepts; it is, rather, a question of relationships and acts that point to the opportunities for human fulfillment, which God opens up at a particular time and place, on the road to the future. Guidance for the shaping of structures cannot be provided primarily by any general, rational set of values, but by participation in the *koinonia,* where—through word, sacrament and interrelatedness—the concrete shape of God's humanizing work in the world is becoming visible.

The basic issue is not whether the Christian can formulate certain values with which the non-Christian can agree as a basis for common action. It is, rather, whether or not the Christian is able

---

[23] *Ethics in a Christian Context*, p. 141.

to perceive and respond to fundamental dimensions of reality, which Christian and non-Christian alike should take into account in making ethical decisions. In every situation, there are certain aspects of worldly reality that can be understood and analyzed only by the sociologist, the political scientist or the economist. But none of these disciplines is able to capture the full dimensions of this reality. This real world, in its concreteness, has been accepted, is judged and is being reconciled to God. In the midst of the full complexity of this situation, God is creating the conditions for the fulfillment of human life. Only as these elements of reality receive attention, alongside the technical, can proximate goals be realistically defined; only in the light of the ultimate toward which it is moving can the penultimate be properly understood.

## The Christian Contribution to Revolutionary Goals

What, specifically, are the elements at the center of God's humanizing activity in the world? One of them is the fact of forgiveness, which sets us free to act for our neighbor; free to see the ambiguities of the situation, as well as of our own motivation, and still move ahead; free to participate fully in a struggle involving conflict and the risk of violence, injustice and the power of self-interest, and there know that the power of sin is broken; free to perceive that when the human situation is falling apart, God is picking up the pieces and putting them together again. Another basic element is justice, the recognition that God's order is being established on the other side of change, as structures are shaped that defend those classes and groups in society that have no power and can count on no one to defend them. A third is reconciliation, which occurs in the midst of struggle and hostility as all perspectives are transformed through the encounter and reconciliation of differences.

If Christians are able to deal competently with reality in full openness to these dimensions, their presence could make a significant difference in the definition of proximate goals. Their participation will be a constant reminder that, at every point, the crucial issue is what is happening and what is likely to happen in human relationships. They will recognize that revolutionary structures can contribute to this goal only as they provide all classes and groups in society with an opportunity for increasing participation in the shaping of the life of the community, the economic order and the nation. They will make evident that the most adequate goals are those which are worked out in dialogue with the widest variety of ideologies and with those technically competent in many different aspects of the problem. They will recognize that only those structures open to change and renewal can serve the well-being of man in a dynamic society such as ours today. Most important of all, they should bring into the situation a basic attitude of trust and hope and a creative imagination for handling the facts, which are manifest because the absoluteness of the technical has been broken and each situation is seen in the light of the goal toward which it is moving.

In the revolution confronting us, the real test of any theological and ethical perspective will be its ability to recognize fully the importance of the insights of the expert and to contribute something in the dialogue with him. Recent writings of Professor Denys Munby provide a basis for further reflection on this question. In his book, *The Idea of a Secular Society*,[24] and in an essay, "The Importance of Technical Competence," [25] he contends that the size of our society, the wide variety of situations in it and the fact of rapid social change make it impossible to find much help in any set of principles or values. We live in a world in which there is no longer any image that reflects generally accepted common ideals. If we want to get anywhere in solving our problems, we must study the diverse aspects of reality with the tools provided by the various scientific disciplines: "It is only possible to discover the truth about men in society by the patient application of complicated techniques to the empirical facts." [26]

Has a Christian ethic, then, anything to contribute to the definition of goals? Professor Munby would urge caution at this point: "Men do not always act according to facts, but it remains, nevertheless, surprisingly true that, in a large number of cases, once the

---

[24] London: Oxford University Press, 1963.
[25] In *Essays in Anglican Self Criticism,* D. M. PATON, ed. London: SCM Press, 1958.
[26] *Ibid.,* p. 47.

facts have been elucidated, the appropriate action almost inevitably follows." [27] This may be true as far as it goes. But the technical mind all too easily acquires a very restricted idea of just what the "facts" are and forgets that the technical is ethically ambiguous. As a phenomenon of the commingling of the two cities, it points toward the ethical and contributes to the dehumanization of man. The technical is concerned with knowledge and power, and power is both "gracious" and demonic. Unless the technical analysis of reality is confronted constantly with a witness to the dimensions of that reality, which may escape the technician, we face a very dangerous situation in the society.

Professor Munby is always dealing with the technical in the context of Christian faith. His deep concern for the well-being of man, his relative optimism about the human enterprise and his confidence in the redemptive activity of God in the world all have a decisive influence. He is an economist, but he looks upon worldly reality in terms of an Anglican sacramental theology.[28] But, if a creative dialogue is to develop between the expert and the theologian, our reflection on these problems in ecumenical circles must give more attention to the terms of the discussion and explore further the lines suggested both directly and indirectly by Professor Munby.

It is our contention that a contextual theology and ethic offer creative possibilities at this point. When technical insight is set in the context of the humanizing activity of God, it makes sense to affirm that once the full facts are known, the appropriate action will follow. Along this road, it may be possible for theology to move into the center of the current struggle—rather than being, as is so often the case, a burden or an irrelevant factor for those who are involved in the secular world—and thus "assume its servant-critical function through which all the sciences may be summoned once again to their authentic humanistic occasion and promise." [29]

---

[27] *The Idea of a Secular Society,* p. 26.
[28] *Ibid.,* pp. 89–91.
[29] PAUL L. LEHMANN: "The Formative Power of Particularity," *Union Seminary Quarterly Review,* XVIII, 3, ii, March, 1963, p. 318.

# 2

# THE BASIS OF CHRISTIAN SOCIAL ETHICS

by ROGER MEHL (France)

THE idea that society is governed by its own system of ethics is a recent one. For a long time, it was thought that social life was no more than the sum of relationships between individuals and that in consequence, social ethics was no different from personal ethics; that the same virtues needed to be cultivated in both domains. The good husband and father would, as a matter of course, be the good citizen, the social man par excellence. In this way, the extension of the individual ethic into the social sphere resulted in an authentic social conservatism.

It is undoubtedly to the credit of the different socialist movements and ideologies that they have brought out (even at the price of indifference to the individual ethic and the virtues of the private citizen) the original character of social ethics and have shown that it cannot be reduced to the norms of the individual conscience. Whereas the spontaneous movements of working-class rebellion in the nineteenth century were apt to be directed against individuals, scientific socialism, and especially Marxism, went beyond this superficial analysis. Karl Marx brought out the fact that alienation not only attacked the worker but, under other forms, the employer himself; that it was consequently useless to bear a grievance against the employer as an individual; and that the "goodness" of the owner would not fundamentally have changed the condition of the worker, but that the social system itself needed to be changed. In other words, socialism discovered that the chief problems of social ethics are problems of structures. These are objective realities, which evolve in accordance with their own laws. It is possible to make a scientific study of them. The consequence of this discovery was the setting up of a science of social structures—sociology. Individual decisions and good will have no power over social structures. The social measures adopted in the second half of the nineteenth century by the Protestant employers of Mulhouse did not prevent and could not have prevented the social disturbances that arose a few years later. The improvement of human relations within a firm depends certainly upon good will, human contacts and generosity; but it is puerile to suppose (as Moral Rearmament still does) that this change of atmosphere is enough to resolve social problems if the problem of the transformation of structures —a problem going far beyond the range of one firm—is not squarely faced.

The discovery of a specific social ethic that could not be reduced to the individual ethic filled the Christian conscience with dismay. It is easy to understand why. The biblical message is addressed fundamentally to the individual: Whether it is a question of faith, that is to say, the personal relationship of trust that unites the believer to Christ, or of repentance, the new life starting from baptism, or of regeneration as the result of justification by grace alone, it is always the individual who is addressed. The New Testament contains a highly developed personal ethic (although, in the Pauline epistles, moral exhortation is always subordinated to dogmatic teaching concerning the great work of God in Christ), but it could be described as showing indifference to social problems. Christ refused to adopt any view in relation to the political problem, which aroused passionate interest in some of his contemporaries (the political problem is, in itself, only the most superficial and episodic aspect of the social problem). He was usually far removed from the Zealots, a party to which certain of his disciples manifested an attachment. The famous words "Render unto Caesar the things which are Caesar's and unto God the things which are God's" has much more theological than political significance. It means that the demands of political authority, the lawfulness of which is not contested, are, and must remain, limited to a very precise domain and must not trespass upon the infinite demands of God. Jesus thus warns us not to confuse the order of the state with the divine order. Christianity has in fact introduced into history a relativization of the political order, whereas Greek thought had believed in a close relationship between the state and the cosmos—the expression of the ultimate and undoubtedly divine order in the universe. Henceforward, the relationship of man with God escapes from the control of the state; and it is better to obey God than men. The trial of Jesus, as Schlier and Barth have well shown, takes for granted, especially in the Johannine version, a certain conception of political authority. Not only would Pilate have no authority over Jesus if it were not given him from on high, that is to say, if the political order bore no relation to the creating, preserving and redeeming work of God; but even more, in the behavior of Pilate himself, it appears that the magistrate has the possibility of doing what is right in a sinful world. Pilate lets this possibility escape him, but that is a personal failing on his part, probably to be explained either by his character or by his rather uncomfortable political situation; in any case, this personal shortcoming does not prove that political authority is not instituted by God and is not ordered for good. Thus the teaching on authority that Paul gives in Romans 13 is not a kind of innovation in the setting of the New Testament. Paul systematizes a teaching that is in direct reference to Christ's attitude. The authorities must not be regarded by Christians as realities that they could ignore. They have their place in the redemptive plan of God; they are destined by God to ensure to men the setting of a peaceful existence, where honesty is encouraged and evil repressed. They are a sign, ambiguous, like all signs, of the mercy of God toward all men. They witness to the fact that God has not left his sinful creation without protection from the prince of this world. Within this unjust world, a provisional and relative justice is possible.

But it will also be noticed that the text of Romans 13 envisages a function of the state that concerns especially what we should call penal justice; that is, a justice the essential object of which is to repress individual transgressions and crimes (theft, murder, and the like). There is no allusion to what we call social justice, the problem of the distribution of wealth, of social classes and of the structures of society. Paul has no intention of going beyond the given concrete situation that presented itself to him: The political authority of those days had little social function and hardly penetrated what we call social life. At most, it went so far as to distribute food to the poor when necessary. But its principal function (apart from the military and diplomatic functions to which the New Testament does not allude) was to maintain order between individuals by repressing misdemeanors and crimes of an individual nature. When it happens that Paul encounters a problem of social structure (the condition of women or of slaves), it is evident that his fundamental preoccupation is in no sense to modify the established order: Within the established order and without calling it into question, Paul seeks to transform individual relationships, because he is speaking to men who have entered through faith and have been led by the Holy Spirit into a new life, in which the relationship of brotherhood must be expressed. Thus Paul sends the fugitive slave Onesimus back to his master, but the master must welcome him and treat him as a brother in Christ not only *kata pneuma* but also *kata sarka,* which means that Philemon must consider Onesimus as a well-loved brother not only in the communion of worship and eucharist but also in daily life. But the question of liberation, in the political and social sense, does not arise, although a juridical procedure for such a liberation did exist.

All these remarks tend to the following conclusion: It is vain to search the New Testament for precise norms of, or even directives for, a social ethic, and it is easy to understand the embarrassment of the Christian conscience when, aroused by the social movement that did not come to birth within itself, it is yet obliged to take up this challenge of the modern age.

We may outline two typical reactions of the Christian conscience, neither of which gives us a satisfactory answer.

### The Answer of Pietism

The first may be called pietistic, although its audience goes far beyond the framework of historic pietism. It consists quite simply of ignoring the problem or of putting it onto other shoulders. Basing its argument on the fact, true enough in itself, that the gospel is addressed to the individual, it holds that the church's sole task is to preach the good news of man's reconciliation with God. The gospel has only one meaning: It proclaims that in Jesus Christ we have peace with God, that our sins are forgiven and that by resting in Christ we have the certainty of salvation and of eternal life. All the rest, including political and social action, is vain agitation. This pietism has found sure support in the Lutheran theory of the two kingdoms. The church's sole mission is the preaching of salvation through the cross of Christ, that is, the gospel. Any other activity belongs to the domain of law. If the church, because of the hardness of our hearts or in order to lead us to repentance, must teach the law, this is not its *opus proprium* but, on the contrary, its *opus alienum*. The organization of the state in conformity with the prescriptions of the law (of the decalogue and natural law) belongs exclusively to the magistrature, and the church must limit itself to recalling its people to submission to the magistrates, as long as these do not interfere with the preaching of the gospel. Even the external and temporal organization of the church is the domain of the magistrature. Let us then not ask the church to intervene in the political and social world. It would be playing the wrong role. Moreover, it has no means of doing so, for, like Paul, it would know only one thing, Jesus Christ and him crucified. The world's injustices, the state's political and social errors, must be borne with complete patience, in the certainty that God governs the world and that he even uses sinners for the good of those who love him. God will re-establish all things at the end of time. The kingdom of God and his righteousness are thus purely eschatological values and the Christian must not ask himself if he can already set up signs of this Kingdom, analogies of this Kingdom, in the world of today.

This attitude, largely abandoned by Lutheranism today, is to be criticized on two counts. It can be criticized from the sociological point of view, for it rests upon the idea of a radical separation between man as an individual person and man as a social being. It corresponds to a sociological situation where it was possible to draw effectively a fairly clear dividing line between private and public life. Today, this dividing line has become entirely problematical. The decisions made by public authority in matters of education, security, health and the incidences of civilization affect us deeply in our individual lives. It is the private man himself who is called to be a citizen and to engage himself in social action. But we must, above all, submit this conception to a theological critique. What does it make of the New Testament affirmation of the Lordship of Christ glorified over the church and over the world? How can this Lordship be seriously proclaimed if we do not try to show it forth in our behavior in the world? How can the expectation of the Kingdom be anything but purely sentimental and abstract if we do not believe that this Kingdom that is coming toward us rests already all its weight upon the present time, giving rise here and there to signs of renewal, banishing all forms of injustice? In this conception, eschatology finds itself bereft of all ethical significance. For the experience of the sects should warn us that all eschatology thus amputated becomes mythical and only feeds dreams of the millennium. At a deeper level still, we may ask whether, when we claim that the gospel is only the Word of God insofar as it is concerned exclusively with our salvation in Jesus Christ and the gift of eternal life, we are not in fact whittling down the biblical message. For this man to whom salvation is proclaimed is not only a religious subject, he is the whole man with his social dimension, the creature to whom God has given power over the whole creation, who is also called by the will of God to dominate and consequently to organize the world. Is it possible to admit that the salvation that is proclaimed to him does not concern him in his totality, in the multiplicity of his undertakings? Does not the dissociation of gospel and law compromise the unity of action of the trinitarian God? That, thanks to the gospel, man is no longer under the domination and condemnation of the law, is an incontrovertible statement, and it is essential to affirm the end of the rule of the law that produces sin and condemnation. But this law remains, nevertheless, an expression of the holiness of God. Is it not precisely the task of the Christian, when he has been freed by receiving the promise of grace, to make use of this sovereign liberty in order to seek to re-establish a living and concrete link between the gospel of grace and the law recovered through grace? The sphere of law is precisely the sphere of our temporal and social life, and this sphere cannot and could not conceivably remain unaffected by the eruption of new life and the expectation of the new heaven and the new earth.

## The Problem of Biblicist Ethics

The second attitude consists of taking the Word of God seriously and seeking to apply its demands in all spheres of individual and social life. There is certainly no objection in principle to this. Everything depends upon the manner in which it is carried out. Very often it produces a biblicism that consists of using a certain biblical quotation or group of verses and immediately deducing a rule of action therefrom. Calvinism is not immune to this reproach. When Calvin, in his *Ordonnances ecclésiastiques,* attempts to model the organization of the Reformed churches on a norm of organization that he claims to find in Scripture, and affirms that the four ministries are in a sense an article of faith, he is guilty of this naïve biblicism and is in danger of transforming the gospel into law: When, not without some ingenuity, we deduce the right to work and the right to private ownership from Genesis 2 : 15, we make the same mistake. When the Lutheran Künneth justifies from biblical quotations the right and duty of the state to impose the death penalty, he loses sight of a fundamental distinction between the biblical kerygma itself, centered upon the redemptive work of Christ, and the historical and sociological conditions that constitute the *Sitz im Leben* of the biblical writings. When we read Romans 13 and conclude that the Christian has no other duty in the state beyond the one duty of submission to the established authorities, we are guilty of the same confusion. Christian pacifists also are sometimes guilty of naïve biblicism when they use quotations to try to persuade us that the Bible forbids the Christian either to participate in any war or any kind of military service. I do not say that their thesis is false (this is not the place to discuss it), but that the method they use to establish it is debatable. How can one honestly claim that the decalogue commandment "Thou shalt not kill" meant for Israel the refusal of military service and the defense of the chosen people? How can one maintain that the words of Jesus, "All those who take the sword shall perish by the sword" (Matthew 26 : 52), spoken in a very definite context and in manifest connection with the events of redemption, were intended as a prohibition of military service? Many more examples could be given.[1] Concrete precepts relating to a definite, given situation are not transformable into universally valid rules, especially in the field of social ethics. Generally, moreover, and having regard to the silence of the New Testament on social problems, those who adopt this attitude seek their inspiration in the Old Testament. It is easy to extract one or even several systems of social ethics from these books. But, as is perfectly normal, they are stamped with the seal of relativity. They concern a traditionalist society, with simple and paternalistic structures, a society that was essentially agrarian, sometimes seminomadic and pastoral. What analogy could be drawn between such a society and our complex, urbanized, industrialized, democratic societies? The Christian church will make a positive contribution to our age only if it takes care to speak for the society and civilization that are ours. It condemns itself to total ineffectiveness, it even make itself ridiculous, when it puts forward an ethical system that does not apply to the existing social structures—not that ethics should be confined to being a pure reflection of these structures; indeed, it should rather be working to transform them, and should certainly not be conformed to the present century. But it should take them into account; it should make clear their contradictions and their injustices and look inside these structures for the cracks where a change might take root.

The criticisms of the two attitudes examined lead quite naturally to a formulation of the scriptural and christological basis of social ethics. Even if this ethic does not differ fundamentally in its content from that which non-Christians might formulate for themselves, we must by no means leave on one side the theological and christological motivation of this ethic. We cannot follow in the path of the social encyclicals of Pope John XXIII, which, on the pretext of universal validity, attempt to base their recommendations upon natural law. For one thing, this concept is highly inconsistent; it was in the name of natural law that the Roman Catholic Church upheld for centuries the law of individual ownership, gave its approval to a certain measure of socialism and de-

---

[1] Cf. GUNNAR HILLERDAL: *Kirche und Sozialethik*. Guetersloh, 1963.

clared the necessity, within limits, of the collective organization of production. If the natural man, as evidenced in Romans 2 : 14–15, was not left by God without moral discernment, then this above all makes dialogue and agreement for practical objectives possible with him. But this discernment, the existence of which should rejoice Christians, should in no way lead them to despise the "discernment of spirits" that is given them in faith in Christ the Lord. Moreover, if it is true that the language of natural law makes the dialogue between Christians and non-Christians possible, Christians cannot allow that the object of their faith, Christ the risen Lord, to whom all power has been given in heaven and upon earth, is not of far more concretely universal relevance than a concept formulated by reason. Lastly, they cannot separate social action from witness. For the greatest service that Christians can render to the world is to make known to it the good news of salvation. It is because of the reality of this salvation that every act of mutual aid and service takes on its full meaning, as is well shown in the great passage of Matthew 25. Far from compromising the disinterested character of social service, witness, on the contrary, guarantees it more effectively than any human ideology. To proclaim him who was the suffering servant, who being rich became poor, is to set the seal of disinterestedness upon social service. For this reason, a Christian social ethic must never hide its motivations, even though, at the level of action, respect for the conscience of non-Christians may require discretion in expressing them.

## The Kingdom of God as the Motivation of Social Ethics

What are these motivations? We have seen that contrary to Bossuet's thinking, we cannot draw a political system out of Holy Scripture; similarly, we cannot deduce a social ethic from Scripture without transforming it into a book of principles. We must certainly take Scripture as our starting point, but we must understand it as it demands to be understood. Scripture does not present us with immediately usable ethical values but with a fundamental demand bound up with the redemptive work of Christ. It tells us that God in Christ has made all things new and requires us to share in this transformation of the world. It announces the imminence of a Kingdom, in the light of which we can no longer accept the perpetuation of injustice, tyranny and war. We can say with Hillerdal that the Scriptures give us a new vision of the world and a new conception of man. This formula is accurate, provided we make it clear that it is not concerned with cultural phenomena that have their place in the long series of visions of the world and conceptions of man that characterize the ideological evolution of humanity. What is unique and irreplaceable in the New Testament conception of man and history is not only that it opens up a future and confers upon the man who lives in Christ a complete freedom to enlist himself in this wide open future (after all, Marxism could claim that it also opens a way into the future of man) but also that this future is already present: The Kingdom is not only at the end of time, but in Christ it has drawn near to us, it has been in the midst of us and, through the present Lordship of Christ, it continues to come close to us; it already exercises a kind of attraction upon our history; it breaks the established order, the established injustice, and calls us to take part in the great renewal of history. It is possible that the "fathers" of the Stockholm Life and Work Conference (1925) used the notion of the Kingdom of God with the intention of cutting short all theological debate in which christological and ecclesiological differences had appeared insoluble. It is nonetheless true that they were right in setting this idea of the Kingdom at the heart of their ethical thinking. Without it, the new New Testament conception of man is not complete: The justified man who has been given peace with God through grace, and to whom God has given fellow humans, is also the man who shares in the active expectation and dynamism of the Kingdom. For this reason, he cannot be satisfied with the assurance of salvation that is given him in faith in Christ, as though, once he had received this assurance, all would be well. On the contrary, because of this assurance, he finds himself integrated in the *militia Christi,* in this people on the march who expect the Kingdom.

We say rightly that the people of God *expect* this Kingdom. They do not create it or build it. But they are in the service of God who builds it. Because of the radical novelty of this Kingdom, the Christian cannot be content with either equilibrium or compromise or with the real injustices that still mark human history. He is perpetually engaged in a struggle against all the ways in which man is enslaved by nature or by man. He lives fully (in different ways, depending on his personal choice) the great human adventure of liberation by means of technology and the organization of a more brotherly state. Unlike Hillerdal, I see no objection to using the words of Karl Barth: "Conscious of the lordship of Christ over the church and over the world, conscious of the permanent imminence of the kingdom, the Christian seeks to realize analogically in society and in the state what Christ manifestly realizes in the church which is his body: a new brotherhood." The term "analogically" here seems to us to be perfectly in keeping. There cannot be identity between the church and the world, because the church alone knows its Lord and lives by his grace and his forgiveness. But, if it is true that the law is only one face of the gospel, this law, which will find expression in the search for solidarity, fraternity and service, can be an analogy of the gospel in the world, a sort of shadowy gospel; that is, a gospel robbed in the eyes of the world, but not for the Christian of its premises.

There is one particular point upon which, with Paul Ricoeur,[2] I should like to insist, because it shows so clearly the solely analogical character of the Christian's social action. The law of Christ is love, and love in its fullness and truth always shows itself in a *personal encounter,* within a personal relationship. Love knows no mediation. That is why Christ came into the world to meet men and to establish a personal relationship with them. That is also why, within the community of the church, the personal relationship must always come before the juridical and administrative type of relationship. But modern society itself could not be satisfied with a purely personal expression of love and mutual help. In place of the person-to-person relationship, which may be called the short or direct relationship, it substitutes the long or indirect relationship; that is to say, it organizes systems of mutual help, of social security, of social services, which function anonymously and in which the personal relationship no longer plays more than a supplementary role. The sick, the old, the poor, victims of social injustice, de-

---

[2] "Le Socius et le Prochain," *Histoire et vérité*. Paris: Editions du Seuil, 1955.

serted children are helped not by personal initiative but by virtue of legislation of universal application. It is only in the practical working of this legislation that the personal relationship can, here and there, discreetly recover its true value. Technique wins over the personal act of sympathy and love. This is the price of efficiency. And yet the direct and the indirect relationships are not entirely heterogeneous. It is because I love my own children that I cannot but wish for the setting up of an efficient system for the care of other children. Obviously, to speak absolutely, it would be preferable for every unhappy or abandoned child to be taken care of and adopted by a family. But, if we had to depend on this kind of initiative, how many children would find themselves left to their own devices? It is therefore necessary that the state undertake the organization of institutions for the reception of neglected or deserted children. But the state can also correct the too-anonymous, too-impersonal element in the system: It can set up, according to the prevalent method today, a multitude of small houses for ten or twelve children and entrust the responsibility for them to a married couple. In this way, the anonymous nature of the long or indirect relationship can be corrected. This example clearly shows that the social order can become a figure, a parable, an analogy of the order of love that is the law of the Kingdom. It is precisely because they must be concerned with the construction of such analogies of the Kingdom that Christians must engage themselves wholeheartedly and with complete devotion in the social action suggested to them by secularized society. Their knowledge of the love with which they themselves are loved will give them this inventive genius, this creative imagination, which will enable them to work unceasingly for the correction and improvement in a personal sense of the techniques of social action.[3]

In acting in this way, Christians are not, as Hillerdal believes, in the sphere of natural law, but rather in the sphere of the gospel, and their action has a christological foundation, even if it is exercised in the framework of an entirely secularized society.

---

[3] I am unable to understand the unjust criticisms leveled so harshly against Paul Ricoeur's thesis by JACQUES ELLUL in his book *Fausse présence au monde moderne,* Paris: Librairie Protestante, 1963.

## The Search for Analogies of the Kingdom

To build up these signs or analogies of the Kingdom in the world, to manifest concretely the Lordship of the head of the church over the world, Christians must invent, with the liberty that is theirs (but, of course, at their own risk) *models of action*—political and social plans that can give real coherence and effectiveness to action in the various fields. Western Protestantism has often found models of this kind in the ideas of democracy, socialism and the welfare state. But these ideas are charged with an ideological content that has often distorted their meaning. Moreover, these concepts lend themselves to use in various directions. Democracy is pleaded both by those who favor a political organization inspired by economic liberalism and by those who would set up a totalitarian dictatorship.

So we must be grateful to the World Council of Churches, especially since the Evanston Assembly (1954), for having launched the idea, so rich in possibilities, of the responsible society. Precisely because of the reconciliation of which they have been the beneficiaries, of the brotherhood in Christ that has been revealed to them, Christians can desire only a society the structures of which give to every man the possibility of assuming his responsibility for other men, in which every man is called through its various institutions to be his brother's keeper. The idea of a responsible society appears to us to be the analogical transcription in the secular world of the brotherhood of the gospel. It is its cipher. It excludes equally the type of individualist society that is based simply on *free competition* and profit-seeking and the type of authoritarian society that is *entirely enclosed* in the meshes of plans laid down at the top. It gives a meaning to temporal existence. This meaning cannot be economic expansion alone, nor technological progress, nor the accumulation of wealth, for, all these things, which have an undeniable value, have meaning only when they provide man's opportunity to assume responsibility for his neighbor and so to become fully human. The concept of the responsible society includes the idea of a finality of political and social action.

It appears to us to be in this respect infinitely superior to that of the *common good,* which was favored for centuries by the Roman Catholic Church, and which, the church claimed, derived from natural law. On the one hand, the common good has a content that is difficult to determine. In fact, it has always been presented as a kind of balance between the interests and prerogatives of individuals or of social groups. To maintain this equilibrium, society must remain static, everyone must stay in his place, the social hierarchies must remain stable. The common good has thus been the screen for social conservatism. Admittedly, the modern technocrats tell us that we can determine the common good scientifically, that the fair distribution of income and the drawing-up of a plan of production and social investment depend upon statistics and science. All economic and social planning requires a certain number of options that are of an ethical nature. Science cannot tell us whether investment in heavy industry in the nonaligned countries should have priority over investment in the modernization of agriculture and rural and semiartisan industry. There is a choice there that depends upon ethical imperatives. And it is precisely in order that this choice shall not be made by the central political authority alone, on the advice of technocrats, that we need to set up the structures of a responsible society. The common good is not to be found in an unchangeable factor of natural law, nor in a scientific calculation. It must be worked out through decisions taken within the community by men and groups of men desirous of exercising their responsibility in service. The common good that the papal encyclicals make into a kind of absolute rule has a purely formal character.

On the other hand, the idea of the common good does not involve a *purpose*. Or rather, it indicates as its sole purpose the (relative) prosperity of all. Without doubt, in a world in which two thirds of mankind are undernourished, the increase of production and the balanced distribution of this production are ideals not to be despised. They are even imperatives of indisputable urgency. Nevertheless, especially in the wealthy societies of the western world, it is fitting now to ask, bluntly: For what purpose do prosperity, abundance, expansion, a higher standard of life exist? Does the purpose of human society consist in ensuring that everyone can satisfy his primary needs (food, clothing, housing) and his secondary needs (health, security, culture, leisure)? Beyond these objectives should we not aim at a more brotherly society, a more intense social solidarity, the responsibility of each for the other? In short, should we not now have in view not only a society whose needs are satisfied but a responsible society, in which everyone is called to exercise his responsibility and has the real possibility of doing so? If we turn away from this objective, all that remains, especially in an expanding society, is the creation of new needs, the multiplication of needs. It is the duty of Christians to offer both to the capitalist world and to the communist world a social purpose with an ethical content. Originally, Marxism did this; but to judge from the speeches of the former Soviet Premier, Mr. Khrushchev, in polemic with the Chinese Communists, plenty of goulash has become the criterion of a true communist society. Affluence, security and comfort cannot be the only purpose of temporal society for Christians.

For this society is itself under the Lordship of Christ. His promise to renew all things applies also to modern society. The secularization of modern life certainly makes it more difficult to perceive the purpose of modern society. It is the task of a Christian social ethic to emphasize that purpose afresh. The Christian ethic can do this only if it preserves its vision of the *eschaton,* that is, if it remains fundamentally christological.

# 3

# A NEW THEOLOGICAL
# APPROACH TO CHRISTIAN
# SOCIAL ETHICS

by Hans-Werner Bartsch (Germany)

THE events of the past three decades have led to a lively discussion of Christian social ethics, but, at the same time, owing to the need for immediate, concrete decisions, they have put difficulties in the way of any new reflection on its theological and biblical basis. The churches of the ecumenical movement have been short of time, so to speak, because the decisions demanded of them had to be made at once. Thus, it is understandable that for instance, the contributions of German theologians to the ecumenical discussion in the early years of the national socialist state kept to the traditional doctrine of the "created order" or "preserving order" of God.[1] Hence the Christian's attitude toward the state came to depend on an evaluation of the quality of the state in question: "For the ethical evaluation it depends what kind of state is totalitarian, i.e. *to what end* it makes a total claim." [2] Thus, it became possible to condemn Soviet Russia on the one hand for its collectivism, as endangering "personal life in society and therefore

---

[1] Cf. GERHARD MAY: "Der Totalitätsanspruch des heutigen Staates und das christliche Freiheitsverständnis," *Totaler Staat und christliche Freiheit.* Geneva: 1937, p. 117. Cf. also P. ALTHAUS: "Totaler Staat?," in *Luthertum,* 1934-35.
[2] P. ALTHAUS: "Zum gegenwärtigen lutherischen Staatsverständnis," *Die Kirche und das Staatsproblem in der Gegenwart.* 2nd ed. Geneva: 1935, p. 7.

the possibility of Christian life," [3] while in regard to conditions in Germany (1937) the total claim of the state was regarded as an antithesis not to Christian freedom but to the "totality of sin." [4]

Compared with this, it was an advance when H. D. Wendland, during the same period, explicitly opposed a "doctrine of the best state or ideal state" and pointed out that the state always stands "as a creation and order of God under the divine commandment of *righteousness.*" [5] Here, it is true, the Lutheran view of the state is not questioned in principle, but it is certainly placed in a perspective that makes the total claim of the state impossible in practice.

Even the deliberations of the Oxford Conference (1937) were fundamentally unable to get beyond a "basic Christian view of the state": "The state has a divine sanction. Its authority and its dignity are based upon this fact." [6] What is today regarded as the basic error of theological works on the state was at that time adopted in every instance as the basic position, and only its exposition was in dispute.

A new exegetical starting point was, however, apparent as early as 1934, in Martin Dibelius's essay, "Das soziale Motiv in Neuen Testament." [7] Although Dibelius starts from the message of Jesus and, in so doing, from his eschatological proclamation, it is easy to draw from this the conclusions for an exposition of the ethical injunctions, beginning with the primitive Christian message of the

---

[3] MAY: *op. cit.,* p. 125.

[4] *Ibid.,* p. 117. This verdict may be excused on the ground of an optimism that was understandable in 1937, however grotesque it now seems after what has happened in the name of this "last barrier against the dissolution of all created ties" (*ibid.*). But it is necessary, in view of all the concrete decisions that were repeatedly required, to recognize the weakness that came of failing to discuss, and to question, the theological basis.

[5] H. D. WENDLAND: " 'Christliche' Freiheit, kreatürliche Freiheit und totaler Staat," *Totaler Staat und christliche Freiheit,* pp. 151ff.; quotations from pp. 172f. Wendland rightly attacks both "any accommodation to a political world-view by way of compromise" and any identification of the bourgeois state of the nineteenth century with the "true" or the "proper" state.

[6] J. H. OLDHAM: *The Churches Survey Their Task (Kirche und Welt in ökumenischer Sicht),* report on the Oxford World Conference on Church, Community and State. Geneva: 1938, p. 257 (p. 132).

[7] First published in the first study volume *Kirche und Welt* with the title "*Kirche, Bekenntnis und Sozialethos,*" Geneva: 1934, pp. 9ff., now in the volume *Botschaft und Geschichte,* I, 1953, pp. 178ff. The quotations that follow are according to this latter collection of essays.

Kingdom that is come in Christ. "The gospel is not a social message, but it functions as a social demand." [8] Since the gospel as an eschatological message calls for decision, its demand has absolute actuality. Behind all its demands stands the view of the coming kingdom of God. Hence, we must expect not a program that seeks to order the world anew "but watchwords for all ages. And these watchwords are only special forms of the one eschatological call to repentance; they are meant to bring the hearer—then as now—to understand his own position before God." [9]

The decisive step that Dibelius thereby took in the realm of exegesis was to include the ethical demands immediately in the eschatological message. The primitive Christian exhortation, the treasure house of the ethical injunctions in the New Testament, is no longer regarded as having grown up independently alongside the preaching but is directly related to the preaching and taken up into it. Hence, the social demand that arises from the gospel is included with everything else when the starting point is said to be: "This society of sinners, in all its solidarity, is now overtaken by the proclamation of the *divine grace,* authenticated by Jesus in word and deed." [10] And it is on that basis that the command to love our neighbor is to be understood: "The *basis of all Christian love* is thus *God's love for the sinner.* The Christian has no longer any right to exalt himself above his brother. The love of God shines through him; he responds to God's love in loving his brother." [11] Thus, all Christian action is as much a "sign" of the kingdom of God as was Jesus' healing and help. If we begin by laying the foundation of social behavior in this way, it is exegetically no longer possible to base obedience to earthly powers on some peculiar character inherent in them. The Christian's behavior toward his neighbor is already, apart from any intraworldly orders, determined by the fact that it is to be a proof of the love of God experienced in Christ.

---

[8] *Ibid.,* p. 181.
[9] *Ibid.,* p. 183.
[10] *Ibid.,* p. 194.
[11] *Ibid.,* p. 195.

The warning against overestimating and isolating such cardinal passages as Romans 13 was further expounded by Dibelius in his essay "Rom und die Christen im ersten Jahrhundert." [12] If this exegetical pointer was not immediately followed up, it was due partly to the pertinacity and significance of the Lutheran tradition, especially within the evangelical theology of the German-speaking world, but also to the fact of the church struggle in Hitler's Germany. In that context, it was natural not to deny the state a priori any peculiar dignity, leaving it, as it were, to its own devices, but rather to point to the peculiar dignity of the state that Lutheran teaching recognizes and, on that basis, to summon it to its particular responsibility. It is in that context that the famous fifth thesis of the declaration of Barmen (1934) is to be understood: "That according to God's appointment the state has, by the threat and the exercise of force, to care for justice and peace." In repeatedly making the same statement the basis of declarations by the church and by theology today, we overlook that in its historical context this thesis was calling those who held the power of the state to their responsibility and was restricting the right to the exercise of unlimited force, which those in power claimed. The aim of the thesis, therefore, was not to provide a metaphysical foundation for the power of the state but to limit that power by deriving the exercise of power from justice and law.[13] If we want to make use of this Barmen thesis today, we must not ignore that fact. The historical meaning of the thesis calls for an interpretation today that keeps its purpose in view, but not for a renewal of the attempts to give the power of the state a metaphysical basis in some appointment of God.

## The Contemporary Trend of Christian Social Ethics

The political and ideological divisions of the divided world have raised anew the question of the right theological foundation for social and political ethics; and the development of nuclear weapons

---

[12] In *Botschaft und Geschichte,* II, 1956, pp. 117–228.
[13] Cf. H.-W. BARTSCH: "Die neutestamentliche Verkündigung zu dem Verhältnis des Einzelnen zum Staat," in *Neues Ethos und Friedensordnung,* 1960, p. 34.

into means of mass destruction has cast doubts on the general, comprehensive charter that the state received when it was conceded the right to exercise power.

It is true that because of the problems of our day, theological studies have been intensified, and the abundance of literature, both on the exposition of Romans 13 and on the general question of Christian behavior in social and political life, is almost beyond compass. Yet the derivation of the state's power as divine appointment remains the basis of all the reflections, which are shaped by the modern problems.

In a paper read to a church fraternal (meeting of pastors), in Wuppertal in 1957,[14] Ernst Wolf takes as his starting point an interpretation of the statement that "all power" is concentrated in the Lordship of Christ, giving it a christological relation to the disempowering of the demonic powers, and thus freeing the Christian "to 'accept' the state in its 'worldliness' as a task for *human* action in obedience to God's command." [15] This systematic grounding of the "worldliness" of the state, and the rejection of any theological grounding of the state, are an extension of the christological view of the state that Karl Barth had advanced.[16] The obedience is no longer seen as founded on a peculiar quality belonging to the earthly power but as an expression of the faith which confesses Jesus Christ as Lord and which therefore sees him as Lord of the individual's relation to the state.

At the pastoral discussions in Wuppertal, five theses were agreed upon as a basis for discussion, the first and third of which concern the theological ground of the Christian's relation to the state:

1. We must turn resolutely away from the path of seeking to answer the question of the standing of the Christian in the political sphere by outlining a "theological doctrine of the state" concerning the nature and purpose of the state, with the aim of being able to deduce from that the individual ethical injunctions. . . .

---

[14] WERNER SCHMAUCH and ERNST WOLF: *Königsherrschaft Christi*, Theol. Ex. NF 64, 1958.

[15] *Ibid.*, pp. 23f.

[16] BARTH: *Christengemeinde und Bürgergemeinde*, 1946. E. WOLF's further development of Barth's view implies at the same time a correction of it, in that what he supplies is precisely not a christological ground for the state, but a christological ground for the attitude of the Christian toward the civil powers.

3. The traditional and self-evident appeal to *Romans* 13 cannot be maintained in an unprejudiced exegesis. *Romans* 13 does not formulate a doctrine of the state, nor does it summon to subjection at any price, but it does commit the church to a co-responsible loyalty towards the actual political power of the moment—a loyalty determined and limited by the love of God and the expectation of his kingdom. Behind this loyalty stands the faith that Jesus Christ has overcome the powers of this world (Eph. 1 : 20f.), so that they cannot harm the disciples of Christ. That of course does not take the disciples of Christ out of the world; rather, they are claimed by their lord with their whole earthly life and called into the being of Jesus Christ for the world. The church of the disciples exists as such only by practising the obedience of faith in the overcoming of the world by surrender to it.[17]

A decisive step beyond this point was taken in the "theological declaration" of the church fraternals on the atomic threat to the world, issued in 1958, in Frankfurt. There we read:

The new life brought by the gospel of Jesus Christ includes within it the active co-responsibility both of the church and of the individual for the preservation of human life, and therefore also for the *instituting of human judicial orders, which is made possible by the patience of God.* The Christians' co-responsibility for the state consists in using the proclamation, and the action which accords with it, to remind those who wield the power of the state of their entrusted task of preserving human life, to help them in the completion of their task and to protect them from the misuse of their power. Christian faith acknowledges *the state to be a means used by God in his grace* towards preserving the life of the men to whom the gospel is to be preached until the end of time.

In observing this co-responsibility we must declare: The inclusion of means of mass destruction in the execution of the state's threat and exercise of force can take place only in factual denial of the will of the God who is true to his creation and gracious towards man. Action of such a kind cannot be upheld by the Christian. The attitude of neutrality in this matter, which we perceive to be sin, is irreconcilable with confessing Jesus Christ. To seek a theological justification for both leads to false doctrine and abrogates the will of the triune God.[18]

The difference as compared with other and earlier church statements on the same set of problems is to be seen in the subtle change that takes place in the characterizing of earthly power. Instead of

---

17 SCHMAUCH and WOLF: *op. cit.*, pp. 65f.
18 Quoted according to the first official cyclostyled copies. My italics.

the civil power that comes by divine appointment, this declaration speaks of the institution that is made possible by the patience of God. And, when the declaration goes on to speak of the state as a means used by God in his grace, it implies a decisively new interpretation of Romans 13 : 4: "For he is the minister of God to thee." Another declaration, produced in 1960 by a study group of the church fraternals, with the title "Die Christen und ihre Obrigkeit," [19] is equally unequivocal:

Holy scripture teaches us that all men who are responsibly engaged in the state and the political community are to be seen as *tools in the hand of God,* quite apart from any consideration of the way in which they attained to their superior offices. We do not in any state live outside the sovereignty of God. The Christians of East Germany can therefore no more refuse recognition to the authority of their government than the Christians of West Germany can to theirs.

Christians, like all citizens of the state, are called to take a responsible share in the tasks of the state in both parts of Germany, and on either side "to seek the good of the city.". . . Christians take part in all efforts of the state which serve the well-being of men. Since, however, the persons in offices of authority are constantly exposed to the temptation to misuse their power, it belongs to the Christians' responsibility to remind them of their task, to pray for the right use of the means of force in their hands, to repudiate demands and measures which are contrary to the will of God, and if need be to establish by suffering a visible token of the fact that Christians seek to obey God rather than men.[20]

Short comments are added that explicitly stress what is already clear from the wording, namely, that an effort has been made to interpret Romans 13 for the problems of today. Hence, "tool" as a description of the responsible magistrate is a still more pointed interpretation of Romans 13 : 4, and the whole chapter is seen not as a definition of the nature of the state but as a definite application of the statement "that we never live outside the sovereignty of God" to the relation of the Christian to the state. In the second paragraph, Romans 13 : 8 is primarily in mind: "He that loveth his neighbour hath fulfilled the law."

---

[19] The declaration, along with what led up to it, and the discussion provoked by it, has been published with the title *Christen und Obrigkeit im geteilten Deutschland,* by G. HEIPP and H. RÜCHER, Ev. Zeitstimmen, Vol. X/XI, 1962.

[20] *Ibid.,* pp. 17f. A third paragraph follows with concrete advice.

These brief statements, although closely related to the problems of a divided Germany, provide a new theological foundation of political ethics in that instead of inquiring into the nature of the state, to derive therefrom the necessary ethical injunctions, they understand the state in the context of the commandment to love our neighbor.

We could mention many other theological studies that are concerned with social and political ethics.[21] Here, however, we have to inquire into the theological basis and go on from there to see the special problems of the Christian's behavior toward the state and in the social sphere generally, in the light of the fundamental question of criteria of conduct. The relation of social ethics to the command to love our neighbor, at which we then arrive, is suggested also by the course indicated for our study.

## The Basis of New Testament Social Ethics

If we look for the theological basis of a Christian social ethic, and if, with this question in mind, we turn to the ethical injunctions of the Bible, we have first to inquire not into the material content of these injunctions, but into their structure. We therefore ask: (1) Whence do we derive the injunction to be obedient to the superior powers? We must break with the old traditional idea that the basis is to be seen in the nature of these powers, in their metaphysical dignity. We ask (2) about the party toward which the Christian's action in these injunctions is directed and (3) about the purpose this action is to serve. All three questions are directly interconnected. If the party toward which the Christian's action is directed is the institution of the state, an anonymous order, the ground for the required obedience must perforce be seen in the

---

21 E. KÄSEMANN discusses the principal literature up to 1959. Cf. further *Christusbekenntnis im Atomzeitalter?*, published by E. WOLF and others, Theol. Ex. NF 70; BARTSCH: *Der Staat ist nicht der liebe God. u.a. Vorträge*, 1962; G. JASPERS and J. YODER: *Christen im Ost-West Konflikt*, Ev. Zeitst. VI, 1961; H. BETHKE: *Was gilt der Mensch im Atomzeitalter*, Ev. Zeitst. VIII, 1962; H. TREBLIN and H. WEITBRECHT: *Christusbekenntnis-Friedenszeugnis*, Ev. Zeitst. XV/XVI, 1963; E. WOLF: *Ordnung und Freiheit, zur politischen Ethik des Christen*, Unterwegs XIX, 1962. A picture of the parallel problems in Japan is given by M. MIYATA: *Der politische Auftrag des Protestantismus in Japan*, Ev. Zeitst. XVIII, 1964.

peculiar dignity of this institution, and the purpose of the obedience in obedience itself, in the fulfilling of the command. Our mistrust of the conclusions that have resulted from such a view of the structure of the biblical injunctions must lead us to cast doubts on the structure as thus understood.

Wolf's rejection of a christological ontology of the state as the goal of the New Testament injunctions [22] means, first of all, a different conception of the direction of the injunctions. The same change of view, however, was already apparent in Dibelius's essay on the social motif in the New Testament, when he insists that the Christian's action must be understood as a response to God's love, and the ethical demands as "special forms of the eschatological call to repentance." [23] The actuality of this call takes concrete form in the ethical demands that concern the relation of the Christian to his neighbor. If we are not to see the institution of the state as thereby eliminated, we must understand it in terms of, and in the light of, our neighbor. We must see the relation of the Christian to the superior powers only as a special form of the relation of the Christian to his neighbor.

But that must not lead to an institutionalizing of our neighbor, and thus to a revival of the old question, Who is my neighbor? (Luke 10 : 29). This question must be answered not by a constant, statically valid concept, but with a dynamically valid concept wherever my action is directed toward a man.[24] Dibelius has pointed out that in Jesus' answer to the scribe in Luke 10 : 36, the static concept of neighbor, as found also in the tradition quoted in Matthew 5 : 43, is changed into one that is dynamically conceived.[25] This change is shown above all by the verb in the sentence, "Which of these three do you think *became* neighbour to him who fell among the thieves?" True, it is possible here, too, to understand "to have become" in the sense of "to be" (was), but the verb points at all events to the fact that the neighbor relationship is not something that exists apart from the active event, but is constituted by the event. We become a neighbor by virtue of the

---

[22] See Note 21.
[23] Cf. Note 7 in this chapter.
[24] DIBELIUS: *Botschaft und Geschichte,* I, p. 197.
[25] *Ibid.*

fact that action or claim establishes a relation.[26] Likewise, the command in Matthew 5 : 44/Luke 6 : 27, 35 to love our enemies is not to be understood as a command that expects more of us than Leviticus 19 :18. Rather, it breaks through the static concept of neighbor, which limits it by contrasting it with the concept of enemy: No one *is* my neighbor on the ground of some ascertainable quality, but everyone *becomes* my neighbor by virtue of the fact that by my action or speech I enter into a relation with him, or that by a request, a claim, or by what he does, he has entered into a relation with me.

It should be clear that by such a concept of neighbor we cannot mean an institution; and that therefore the state, too, when it is interpreted in terms of this concept, is not to be regarded as a special category of neighbor, but that the actual coming about of the state's demands and regulations constitutes a neighbor relationship on each occasion. It is likewise, then, clear that the command to be obedient to the political powers is subject to the criterion of the commandment to love our neighbor. As compared with the position of the Reformers, that means a change. They made obedience to the state subject only to the restriction that it does not bind us to sin: *Itaque necessario debent christiani oboedire magistratibus suis et legibus nisi cum iubent peccare; tunc enim magis debent oboedire Deo quam hominibus. Actuum 5.* [27] But now there is an active possibility of testing the duty of obedience according to the criterion whether the regulations, the state's law, serves our neighbor—the neighbor, moreover, to whom the regulation in question relates, who is affected by the action demanded by this regulation.[28]

The fact that in the New Testament, too, the "superior powers"

---

[26] We cannot enter here into the discussion on the parable of the Good Samaritan. We would only point out that the classification of the parable in the category of example stories comes of still maintaining a static view of our neighbor. Cf. BARTSCH: *Wachet aber zu jeder Zeit,* 1963, pp. 96ff.

[27] Confessio Augustana, XVI, *Die Bekenntnisschriften der evangelisch-lutherischen Kirche.* Deutsch. Evang. Kirchenausschuss: 1930, p. 69.

[28] We would merely point out what would have been the result of that for the Christians' attitude to the Nazi state's laws concerning the Jews. Today it means a critical scrutiny of all laws or official regulations that affect other persons or groups of persons, as is most obviously the case with the *apartheid* laws of the Union of South Africa.

are understood in this personal, dynamic way is clearer from I Peter 2 : 13ff. than from Romans 13 : 1–7, in that in I Peter 2 the demand to "be subject" is made not in regard to an anonymous institution but in regard to those who confront the citizen as the representatives of the superior power: the king, the premier, the governors. Moreover, at the beginning of this exhortation stands the simple, comprehensive clause: "Be submitted to every human ordinance because of the Lord" (2 : 13). The only possible translation is: "Be subject to everyone (= every human creature) for the Lord's sake." [29] The clause reminds the Christians that their attitude toward their neighbor, that is, to everyone they meet, is to be that of service, subjection. The exhortations of I Peter give concrete illustration of this fact in the relation to the representatives of the civil power (2 : 13–16), in that of the slave to his master (2 : 18–20) and of the wife to her husband (3 : 1f). At the end of the epistle, the admonition is taken up again and illustrated in terms of the relation of the young to the old (5 : 5). Incidental confirmation is provided by a large number of manuscripts, which, by introducing the verb "to be subjected," have taken up the clause that introduced the exhortation of 2 : 13 and related it again to the congregation: "All of you be subject one to another, and be clothed with humility." What this attitude means is shown by Paul in I Cor. 9 : 19: "For because I am free from all men, I have made myself everyone's slave."

## The Meaning of Ethical Injunction in the Gospel

We conclude, therefore, that the exhortations never direct the Christian to institutions but always to persons with whom he has entered into a relation that has made them his neighbors. Hence, we must see the ground of the injunctions of social ethics in the command to love our neighbor. But now we have to go a step further and inquire into the place of this commandment in the gospel. The much-discussed question of the relationship of law

---

[29] Although the translation is still maintained "seid untertan aller menschlichen Ordnung" (revised Luther text of 1956), or, "Submit yourselves to every human institution for the sake of the Lord" (N.E.B.), no authority has been found to justify this translation. Cf. FOERSTER, *ThWNT*, IV, col. 1034.

and gospel, which, for the present range of problems, was particularly significant in the German church struggle, has to be subjected to exegetical scrutiny in the light of the connection between the ethical injunctions in early Christian exhortation and the primitive Christian message.[30]

The early Christian exhortations, both in the apostolic epistles and in the gospels, are generally understood to be a product of a church that, in the process of consolidating its position in this world,[31] required for its existence rules by which to measure its conduct. We, however, are seeking the factor that governs the exhortations in a relation between the primitive Christian message and the admonitions. That such a relation existed, that the exhortations did not grow up independently, solely out of the needs of the church, is shown by the place the exhortations occupied in the earliest Christian tradition. While parenetic collections were later handed down as parts of the primitive Christian catechism and are understood even within the gospels as instruction for the church, we find, for example, in the Sermon on the Plain in Luke 6, a collection of parenetic sayings that is identified as a genuine sermon by the situation in which it is placed in the gospel. It has long been recognized that the Sermon on the Mount, in Matthew 5 : 7 was regarded as instruction for disciples. The hearers are the disciples, and the situation of the sermon on a mountain means not only a parallel with the proclamation of the law on Mount Sinai (Exodus 20) but a separation of the narrower circle of hearers from the multitude that had earlier surrounded Jesus (Matthew 5 : 1). The conclusion, however (Matthew 7 : 28f.), enables us to

---

[30] Barth's study, *Evangelium und Gesetz* (Theol. Existenz heute, XXXII, 1935), and the Lutheran counterpolemic that followed it can be used to show the importance of the question in the harmful effect of this neo-Lutheran formulation of the doctrine of law and gospel on the decisions of the church struggle. Cf. the article "Evangelium und Gesetz, dogmengeschichtlich," by E. WOLF in RGG3, II, cols. 1519ff., with copious references to the literature.

[31] Thus E. GRÄSER, *Das Problem der Parusieverzögerung in den synoptischen Evangelien und in der Apostelgeschichte*, 1957, p. 217, takes the stronger emphasis on the ethical and parenetic motif to be the mark of a later time in which the nonoccurrence of the Parousia was already taken into account. But this view of the exhortations is, in practice, already presupposed in BULTMANN: *Geschichte der synoptischen Tradition*, 2nd ed. 1931, pp. 362ff., in the chapter on the editing and composing of the gospels.

see that this account of the situation was the creation of the evangelist, and that what was originally assumed in the tradition was,
on the contrary, a genuine preaching situation into which Matthew
fitted the complex of teaching. This genuine sermon situation is
maintained, on the other hand, in Luke 6. There the situation in
which Jesus is with the twelve on the mountain (6 : 12–16) is
distinguished from the sermon on the open plain, where the multitude now gathers to hear him (6 : 17f.).[32] The change of place
and of hearers, however, marks a change in the significance of the
sermon. Whereas the Sermon on the Mount provides instruction
for the church, the Sermon on the Plain is understood as missionary preaching addressed to all. There is a shifting of accent here:
the missionary preaching as eschatological proclamation changes in
the tradition, as a result of the change of audience, into instruction,
catechism.[33] But now, if we find in the Sermon on the Plain a
collection of parenetic sayings, which, because of the situation and
audience, must be recognized as missionary preaching, we have in
the first instance a formal proof of what transpires also at the end
of the Sermon on the Mount: that collections of parenetic sayings
originally also have their place within the proclamation. We therefore have to ask what relation the ethical injunctions bear to the
proclamation. The very form of the Beatitudes proves the Sermon on the Plain to be preaching (6 : 20f.), insofar as direct
speech means an immediate offer to the hearers.[34] The poor, the
hungry and the weeping are, on the basis of the word now spoken
to them, that is, in the eschatological situation of the proclamation,
pronounced blessed. The "woes" that follow heighten by contrast

---

[32] I have given the detailed basis of this analysis in my essay "Feldrede
und Bergpredigt," *Entmythologisierende Auslegung*, 1962, pp. 116–24.
H. CONZELMANN, *Die Mitte der Zeit* (3rd. ed. 1960, p. 38), overlooks *this*
contrast between the situation on the open plain and that on the mountain
when, with no grounds, he sees the motif of the open plain as parallel with
that of the sea and assumes verging on the "abyss" to be constitutive for
the sea motif. Yet the sea motif is not by any means peculiar to Luke,
but is in Mark 4 : 1, likewise the place of missionary preaching.
[33] J. JEREMIAS has shown this, e.g., in the case of the parable of the lost
sheep (Matt. 18 : 12ff./Luke 15 : 3–7) and in the case of the parable of
delivery to the judge (Matt. 5 : 25ff./Luke 12 : 58f). Cf. *Die Gleichnisse
Jesu*, 2nd ed. 1952, pp. 19ff.
[34] Contrary to BULTMANN, *op. cit.*, p. 114, cf. my argument referred to
in Note 32, *op. cit.*, p. 119.

this eschatological situation. Against the dark background of the "woes," the eschatological offer of salvation stands out.

The exhortation proper (6 : 27ff.) and the ensuing admonitions to love our enemies and to refrain from judging merely expound the one admonition that arises directly from this offer—to attest our acceptance of the offer made in the Beatitudes by showing love to our neighbor. In doing this, the hearer becomes a son of the highest (6 : 35) because he thereby accepts the offer that has been made to him. That brings us to the same ground for the ethical injunction to which Dibelius referred: "The love of God shines through him." Then, however, the action is no longer understood as an independent decision that follows on faith or grows out of it as a second act, but, in showing love toward his neighbor, the believer attests his faith, his acceptance of the offer made to him in the proclamation. Without action of this kind, he has not accepted the offer; for, without such action in love, he is not a son of the highest. Correspondingly, in Luke 6 : 35, God's action in judgment is the criterion by which the Christian's action is to be measured—not, however, in the sense that it could now be proved in intraworldly terms that this is the action that is right and obedient to God but in the sense that faith lives in action of this kind, which corresponds to the gracious judgment of God.[35] The injunctions of the Sermon on the Plain are therefore unintelligible if separated from the eschatological proclamation and the immediate confrontation with the *eschaton*. But that makes clear that the social motif is not something supplementary to the proclamation of the gospel, but that it is vital to faith itself, in that faith requires, as an indispensable element in its life, the confrontation with the neighbor to whom it testifies.

We see clearly this immediate relation of the proclamation of the gospel to the injunctions of social ethics when we inquire into the understanding of ourselves which we are offered in the Beatitudes and which is expressed in carrying out the injunctions. In the Beatitudes, we are offered eschatological salvation—the oppor-

---

[35] This becomes especially clear from a comparison with the parallel in Matt. 5 : 45, in that there God's action within the world, the shining of the sun on both evil and good, is the norm, and the Christian is required to show like action in this world.

tunity to know that we are under the grace of God, no longer dependent on our own possessions or achievements but dependent exclusively on that grace now offered to us. This offer is made at the last minute; for what we are now offered is God's grace in judgment. If the hearer accepts this offer, he attests this new understanding of his own existence by addressing himself in love to the man whom, according to a static neighbor relationship (which is overcome in this way), he formerly regarded as his enemy. In so doing, he attests that he no longer sees himself as threatened by this man's enmity. He attests the same understanding of himself by lending to the man from whom he can expect nothing back, since he thereby proves that he is not dependent on what he has lent. And he attests the same understanding by refraining from judging, by speaking the forgiving word, because he knows that, in the judgment of God, he does not depend on the fact that he is relatively better than his neighbor through his own achievement. This forgiving word springs, of necessity, from his faith, as the fruit on the tree (Luke 6 : 43f.). To do what Jesus says (6 : 46) means, therefore, to accept this offer and to act accordingly.

The admonitions of social ethics no longer stand as law alongside the proclamation of the gospel; they are nothing but an invitation to faith, to the practical exercise of this faith in our action toward our neighbor. If action thus has its goal in the attesting of faith, in the reflecting of the love of God received in the proclamation, then the Christian's action itself becomes a piece of attestation— proclamation—of the gospel. We can also see this goal of Christian action in the further development of primitive Christian exhortation. Men are to see our "good works" and praise God for them (Matthew 5 : 16; I Peter 2 : 12). Wives are to win their non-Christian husbands by their conduct (I Peter 3 : 1f.). This is the meaning of the metaphor about the light of the world and the salt of the earth (Matthew 5 : 13–16; Philippians 2 : 15).

We need only to deduce the consequences as they apply to the present situation at any given moment if we wish to discover what is ethically required. It is, above all in social matters, no longer a matter of formal obedience to divine commandments, which is satisfied with formal proof of whether a particular ethical demand has been fulfilled or transgressed. The question whether a Christian may or may not do this or that cannot be answered formally. Rather, we must always be concerned to ask whether in this action or that we have attested the love of God received from Christ. The personal view of the institutions makes this question possible and necessarily excludes the opposite view. I cannot attest the love of Christ to an anonymous institution. I can only express formal obedience. But if it is also the neighbor who encounters me in the institutions, then I must ask the question that is implied at the starting point of the ethical injunctions in the New Testament, how do I rightly attest the love of God?

## The Consequences of Eschatological Urgency for Christian Social Ethics

This consequence can be clearly illustrated in the much-discussed problem of the death penalty. The ground for it is rooted one way or another in a metaphysical, institutional view of the state, the dignity of which is manifested in the right to exact this penalty.[36] If, however, we ask about attesting the love of God to the man toward whom the action of passing the judgment and exacting the penalty is directed, then the question is, Can the death penalty attest the love of God to the man who is to be executed? And the answer must necessarily be the one that Barth gave in a discourse on the care of convicts: "The death penalty is ruled out by the fact that the killing of a criminal could be a proclamation of the unrestricted sovereignty of the state. . . . Besides, it must in principle be said of the death penalty that it can never be a way of caring for the evildoer." [37] With the collapse of all argument about the peculiar dignity of the state or of parallel institutions, and of all legalistic and casuistic interpretation, the question of the injunctions of social ethics and their interpretation is very much simpli-

---

[36] Thus, already in Martin Luther's "Larger Catechism" (see Note 27, op. cit. p. 606), and from there this argument has remained in Lutheran theology to this day (ALTHAUS, W. KÜNNETH). On this point and what follows, cf. BARTH: Kirchliche Dogmatik, III, 4, 1957, pp. 499ff., and the article "Todesstrafe" in RGG3, VI, 1962, cols. 921ff.

[37] Stimme, XII, 1960, cols. 571f. It is noteworthy that in the discourse reproduced here, Barth explicitly revokes the possibility of a death penalty in exceptional cases, which he had conceded in KD III.

fied. I no longer have to ask whether the demand that, say, society makes upon me, is right. All the factors which derive from the institutional character of the state (country, home, honor, freedom) and which are so often invoked no longer require examination. What constitutes the civil authority is theologically of no significance since, in every institution that makes its demands on me, my neighbor in one way or another encounters me. It is not the rightness of the demand that I have to examine; I have only to ask what kind of behavior, in the face of this demand, attests my faith and hence my love to the man who encounters me. This bears out Dibelius's view of the parenetic statements in the New Testament: that they are watchwords, actualizations of the call to repentance. Thus, in the first instance, I have to ask not what is materially demanded of me in these injunctions but in what way the faith of those who first heard this exhortation would attest itself in the action demanded; and I have to take over the relation between faith and action that is seen in the demand of the New Testament for that age and transfer it to my own decision today.

That does not prevent the Christian today from picturing for himself what he understands by the state. The state would at once appear at the same level as all the other forms of community that the Christian, and therefore theological ethics, can picture. But this picture can be acquired only empirically as the sum of my experience of the ways in which my neighbor encounters me in the several actions of the state. In that way, we shall arrive at ideas of the state that draw a relative distinction between a good and bad order. We shall arrive in the same way at an idea of the different social relations, and we shall be able likewise to make relative judgments here, also.[38] But we shall never make such ideas and judgments absolute or clothe them with theological dignity.

Let me conclude by putting the proposed view to the test in the light of the exegesis of Romans 13 : 1–7. In this passage, Paul is taking over a piece of preformed exhortation from hellenistic Judaism. Thus by no means is it a theological argument of his own. The observation that the section can be removed without difficulty,

---

[38] Cf. the picture presented on the basis of young theologians' experiences of factory work by HORST SYMANOWSKI and FRITZ VILMAR: "Die Welt des Arbeiters," *Antworten*, II, 1963.

and that looked at, then, in detachment, it gives no indication of being a piece of Christian exhortation, misled earlier textual criticism to the assumption that in this passage we have an insertion that has its origin in the favorable disposition of the Roman Church, under Clement of Rome, toward the state. The problem is generally solved today not by textual criticism but by literary criticism, by assuming that Paul is not using his own formulation here. Rather, he is giving the Roman Church the instruction to keep unhesitatingly to tradition as far as standards of conduct are concerned. That, however, already implies an explicit rejection of any peculiar position of the state that could require the state to be ordered according to Christian principles.[39] It also means taking over what is given as the ground of the obedience that this traditional exhortation demands: The civil powers are ordained by God. In contrast, however, to the possibility of a revolution for the sake of Christ, this grounding does not mean that we assert a peculiar position of the state, but that we reject the possibility that the Christian within the power of the state could be beyond the power of God. In other words, we reject any possible demonizing of the state, and the Christian is assured that even in the hands of the pagan civil power, he is not beyond the reach of the goodness of God. When we then call those who wield the power of the state "servants of God" or "ministers of God," we do not imply any peculiar commission, and therefore peculiar dignity, but we are referring to what they in fact are, whether willingly and knowingly or not. The Christian need not fear them when he is doing right, although he must certainly fear them when he is doing wrong; for God can use them to punish, as he once used Nebuchadnezzar to punish Israel. There is no question of God's giving a commission to the holders of the civil power. Finally, Paul sets the whole passage within a double bracket, which is provided first by the command to love our neighbor, which in 12 : 1f. and 13 : 8 determines

---

[39] J. SCHNIEWIND had already emphasized this in his lectures on Romans in the winter semester of 1936–37. I take the following sentences from my own notes: "It is only said that we must not create a revolution for the sake of Christ. It does not reject any revolution at all." Just as opposition may be necessary to call the bearer of power to order, *i.e.*, to the service of our neighbor, so, as a last resort, a revolution may also be necessary for the sake of our neighbor.

what the traditional teaching means; and second, by the eschatological conclusion in 13 : 11ff. If 13 : 8 makes it plain that what precedes it is to be understood only within this central commandment and as its actualization, then the eschatological bracket subjects the factors previously mentioned to the eschatological qualification that the superior powers are the forces that *still* exist but whose power, in reality is broken. This eschatological qualification must not be neutralized again by explaining it away as a bygone and nonbinding peculiarity on Paul's part, due to his expectation of a near end. If the message of the gospel is an eschatological message, all intraworldly factors come within this qualification. The fact that the Christian approaches the things of this world from the angle of "having as though we had not" (I Corinthians 7 : 29 ff.) has not been canceled by the fact that the Parousia has still, after two thousand years, not taken place. Christendom needs to be repeatedly reminded that this attitude has its ground in the eschatological expectation which cannot be abandoned and which no passage of time can relativize. Yet, at the same time, it is this eschatological orientation that gives the ethical injunctions their supreme urgency. Every encounter with my neighbor that makes demands upon me is in fact, at the same time, the last opportunity to attest my faith. The eschatological expectation that leads to that result is in fact only the practical way in which I acknowledge that I am at the exclusive disposal of God—an acknowledgment that leaves me not a moment as my own. What is true of the hearing of God's Word (Psalms 95 : 7f.=Hebrews 3 : 7f.)—that each time it has to be recognized as the last time—and what Martin Kähler said of preaching—"Let me preach as if I should never do so again. . . ."—is therefore correspondingly true of the Christian's conduct. That is what gives the ethical injunctions their urgency. That urgency is bound up with the freedom that comes of the fact that all factors and forces within the world have lost their peculiar dignity, whether demonic or theological. I encounter no one anywhere but the neighbor to whom the love of Christ directs me.

# 4

# CHURCH AND SOCIETY IN GREEK ORTHODOX THEOLOGY

by Nicos A. Nissiotis (Greece)

It is difficult to analyze the relationship between church and society in Orthodox countries today because of the tremendous variety that prevails, not in interpretation of the Orthodox concept of
world and society but in the political and social systems in eastern
countries. Moreover, eastern theology has never crystallized its
teachings in order to suggest a Christian sociology or to inspire a
Christian social order. There are, therefore, many different Orthodox approaches to the relationship with society, and none can
claim to express the genuine Orthodox attitude. The change in the
political scene and the breakdown in the majority of Orthodox
countries of the idea of Christendom make this task even more
difficult, if not impossible. In this paper, therefore, we shall seek
only to analyze some fundamental characteristics of Orthodox theology and tradition that might suggest a possible approach to the
problem of relationships between church and society. We shall also
discuss the situation in one Orthodox country, Greece, which is of
particular interest as an eastern country that is completely involved
in a western type of industrialization and secularization.

## Appraisal of the Situation

It is unfortunate that after long ecumenical cooperation, one still
encounters extravagant criticisms and unthinking analyses of the
theological reasons why societies have been shaped in different

ways in East and West. In particular, some western analyses of the specific causes of the "negative" attitude of the eastern churches to social problems are ill-informed. It is no longer possible, for instance, to regard eastern mystical theology as a deviation from authentic evangelical Christianity and as a negative spiritual power that has hindered developments in social ethics. It is true that eastern spirituality centers on personal edification, which, to some extent, disregards the common good and the world's striving for welfare, but it is wrong to study Orthodox spirituality only in this perspective, as it is expressed by the monastic ideal of the East. To regard eastern mystical theology only as a negative spiritual power for social action is to ignore its main characteristic, which is to be found in the creative dynamism of the regenerating power of the Holy Spirit. True monasticism gives life to the people of God, pointing at the same time to the end of history and to the second coming of Jesus, when he will meet his own people. Monasticism is the missionary church going out into the world, possessing nothing, being a living witness to the second coming of the Lord. A western theologian can see in monasticism a failure to value the world and the social order, a transhistorical interpretation of the Christian message. It is true that for historical reasons after the fall of the Byzantine Empire, monasticism in Greece and the Near East withdrew from this missionary, outgoing activity. But, for all those countries under the domination of non-Christian powers, it remained the unique hope of preserving not only the Christian faith but their cultural and national inheritance as well.

Eastern theology sees in the monastic spirituality a legitimate and necessary maximalism; but the whole Orthodox Church is centered on the family principle of society, and lives according to principles that, rightly applied by a local church, help Orthodox Christians to relate themselves directly to all forms of social life. Where it can act openly, Orthodoxy tries not merely to sanctify all common undertakings in family, social, economic and political life, but to penetrate all these and to prepare every citizen to become a responsible member of the community. There is no doubt that Orthodoxy seeks to express both the communal and the individual aspects of faith—"communal" in the sense of the group encouraging personal responsibility and not mere collectivism.

The contemplation and vision of the glory of God is another maximalism of Orthodox spirituality, but it would be totally wrong to identify this attitude with passivity in the social field. On the contrary, the eastern doxology is the continuous thanksgiving of Christians who receive, through the church, the gifts that God gives to the whole of his creation, recapitulated in Christ and regenerated by the Spirit. Doxology is not simply contemplation or a visionary illusion; it is dynamic participation in the glory of God, as revealed in Christ and in his church, making possible continually renewed action in this world.

It is in this light that we must understand the dynamism of Byzantine literature and art. The West has hitherto been somewhat reluctant to appreciate the contribution of Byzantine civilization—its culture, its political and artistic achievements—to the European Middle Ages and post-Renaissance development and has often criticized the whole of Byzantine civilization on the basis of one of its elements—caesaropapism in state-church relationships, the so-called Constantinian era, or, worst of all, Byzantine monasticism seen from a very limited perspective. It has failed to discern behind these façades the positive contributions of the church: giving rise to new nations, restoring old ones and leading peoples to a totally new approach to national and communal life.

Criticism, if it is to be objective, must recognize a certain dualism in Orthodoxy's approach to the meaning of the world and its theological significance. On this point (which we shall discuss in more detail in the next section of this chapter), I would only say here that eastern theology has never adopted either of the theories that have been the basis of most western Christian social thinking: neither the Thomist understanding of order in creation preserved absolutely after the fall, which provided the framework for the ethics of natural law; nor the extreme Protestant understanding of the world after the fall as totally corrupt, and which provoked the response of liberalism. The debate about natural theology has remained quite foreign to eastern theology. This may be regarded as its weak point, but, at the same time, it gives it flexibility in all the situations in which Orthodoxy has to live and survive.

As a result of this equivocal theological attitude, Orthodoxy has been unable (it is true) to shape a "social gospel," a definition of its relationship with the state, such as the doctrine of total separation, or the two-realms theory or even the system of the "Constantinian era" as it is understood by the West. All these forms of relationship are open but relative possibilities for the Eastern Church. They are applied today in many different ways in the Orthodox countries and by the Orthodox of the Diaspora, without the unity of the autocephalous churches being threatened, because of this very flexibility that eastern theological presuppositions provide. But none of them can claim to express *the* Orthodox attitude to *the* problem of the relationship with state and society. Therefore, the Orthodox have no social systems and no fixed Christian theories regarding social relationships, no theological doctrine of work and profession or sexual ethics, no closed chapter on birth control, no guiding principles of industrialization, no theological appreciation of the modern secularization. The church is not here to suggest norms which would be applicable everywhere and which would give rise to a single form of technical civilization or culture. Another reason is the fact that for the Orthodox, the Bible is not a code of guiding principles for social action. The wisdom of the Bible is relevant only for those who already live within the spiritual reality of the Christian community, the church. Therefore, one has to experience one's discipleship from within the church in the service of the world, and then the biblical message for regenerating society can be revealed and understood. Otherwise, social action will lead to a one-sided and limited interpretation of the world, because the biblical picture of the world and of society is a richly varied one, showing how the church can live in all kinds of situations, but without identifying any as authentically and absolutely Christian.

I pose the problem in this way in order to show that Eastern Orthodoxy is, of its essence, continually open to new developments in every situation in the modern world. For Orthodoxy, there is no one sociological system to be applied in all situations where Orthodox churches are facing modern societies, either of the western type or in socialist, communist or Moslem countries. In the next section, I shall try to explain why Orthodoxy should never formulate a Christian doctrine about social relationships but should maintain its comprehensive and flexible position.

## The Theological Basis of the Relationship
### Between Church and Society

This open Orthodox attitude to all forms of relationship between church and society is based upon some fundamental theological principles. In Orthodoxy, there is a dualistic concept of the world, embracing both positive and negative elements, which has deep roots in the biblical conception of cosmos. On the one hand, its positive and optimistic view of the world explains the Byzantine tendency to achieve harmony between church and state, and church and society, as well as the Orthodox understanding of man and its qualitative interpretation of the catholicity of the church. On the other hand, its recognition of the tragic element of history, of the disintegrating effect of the sin of man and the constant threat of secularism to the church, explains Orthodox theology's hesitation to adopt a fixed form of Christian social ethics that would be valid for all situations. Orthodox optimism regarding society may be explained as follows:

a. Positive theological teachings about the world are to be found in almost all the patristic writers as well as in Orthodoxy today. The Orthodox Church ascribes primary importance to the triumphant Johannine presentation of the victory and Lordship of Jesus and his light over the darkness of the world. Its ecclesiology insists that in him who is the Head of the Body, the church, everything in heaven and in earth is recapitulated (Colossians 1 : 19). It is also the church that tries to see the world within its martyrdom, the cruel historical reality through the event of the Resurrection.

Because it is centered on the risen and exalted Lord, Orthodoxy regards this world as a prelude to the final victory, which gives a glory to everything already in this world. The understanding of the world as exalted because of the Cross, and especially the Resurrection, enables us to see every human condition as potentially transfigured and regenerated by the certainty of the eschatological victory and the sure, triumphal return of the risen Lord of all. The Holy Spirit is at work in history, as another Creator after the Resurrection, giving new life, restoring the fallen creature to his Creator. On this theological basis, nature is not to be separated from grace. There is no opposition between the divine grace given in Christ Jesus and the world as an existence restored to him by the Paraclete. The Orthodox theology of the Holy Spirit overcomes the dualism between nature and grace by filling the gap between fallen nature and the risen Christ within nature. The Resurrection reveals the working of the Holy Spirit, who has always been present and active from the beginning of creation and is so now in an apocalyptic sense, as a power of the *eschaton* already present in time by anticipation, reflected and apprehended by man within history. The Orthodox eschatology becomes in the Holy Spirit and the ecclesia a historical Parousia that transcends the world by giving it supreme value as the unique scene where the salvation of man is worked out. All historical realities, even those that appear to be disastrous, are understood in Orthodox pneumatology as one more victory of the risen Lord in his Spirit, once they are experienced through the church community of all ages, recapitulating in itself by faith the whole cosmic reality.

b. The Eastern Church's understanding of man is consistent with its cosmology. Western theologians are sometimes shocked by its anthropology, regarding it as a very optimistic and emotional evaluation of human existence. They object that Orthodoxy makes an easy leap from the broad understanding of the incarnation and resurrection of Christ to humanity as a whole, by teaching an anthropology that is full of ontological affirmations about the glory of redeemed man raised with Christ Jesus. But western critics have criticized eastern anthropology for its ontological affirmations without understanding the kind of ontology it is. When the fathers and modern Orthodox theologians basing themselves on the patristic writings, speak of the *theosis* of man, using phrases like that of St. Athanasius, "God became man so that man might become God," it should not be thought that these affirmations are trying to define the new nature of exalted man by an easy, generalized application of the mystery of incarnation to all men who believe in him. *Theosis* here refers to the possibility that the believer may return to his original relationship of communion with his God in order to recapture his true humanity and establish a right relationship with his fellowman in all realms of social life. *Theosis* in patristic thought is in no way a static, ontological idea or affirmation of the divinization of man, but it points to the final goal, to the possibility opened by faith for a man to act in this world as a new creation, transcending the normal conduct imposed by fallen nature and its laws. In this optimistic anthropology, the notion of *theosis* draws the attention of the saved man to his final purpose, which coincides with the central event of the gospel, the risen Lord in his church, and not with any abstract concept of resurrection.

c. This cosmology and this anthropology have meaning for the Orthodox only if they are experienced within the fellowship of the historical ecclesia.

No one alone can have an optimistic view and evaluate correctly the historical situation of the world. Christian hope is not an individual experience any more than faith is. Everything depends on participation with the militant people of God in the Body of Christ. In this community, the whole world is reflected as transfigured, giving us a foretaste of the final fulfillment of the world in history. The church, not viewed simply in its institutional aspect of a single congregation, but as the divine presence of the Paraclete, is the main microcosm, the center and the axis of all history. The church cannot be separated from the world; it is its very heart. It is implanted precisely at the center of the historical reality, of which it is both the origin and the end. This is the qualitative sense of catholicity (*sobornost* in Russian), which produces the geographic reality of the church.

This optimistic view of man and of the world makes Eastern Orthodoxy aware of its historical responsibility and helps it to maintain a concern for all human conditions. But this is not the whole truth; if it were, then some of the accusations of Monophysitism would be justified. Unfortunately, some Orthodox theologians today are not always careful to present the other side of the Orthodox attitude regarding world history and society. We risk, therefore, arriving at a superficial concern for human life, introducing an unbridgeable gap between the exalted Christ and the cruel historical situation in which we are inevitably involved.

## The Orthodox View of History and the World

It is perhaps for this reason that Orthodox worship can become an end in itself, when it should be a springboard for social action.

At three additional points, we can summarize the second dimension of Orthodoxy. Although they are separated here for the sake of a clear presentation, they are, in fact, inseparably bound together.

1. Eastern Orthodoxy has always emphasized the importance of history against all kinds of radical existentialism, which see history simply as a sequence of successive moments without inner coherence. Orthodoxy sees in history a judgment of the living God. The eastern tradition, in accordance with the teaching of the Old Testament prophets, regards the life of this world as the unique opportunity to respond to the glory of the revealed God and to act accordingly. The acts of man as a historical being are inseparable from his faith in Christ Jesus as the center of history, not only in the church but particularly in daily life. History is not a narration about acts of God, nor is it an apocalyptic sign of things to come at the end of time, but it is the theater where God is in action; hence, the fight with the principalities of this world cannot be ignored.

Historical realism does not mean accepting passively the historical situation as a priori good or bad. Orthodox patristic thought and modern theology insist that the primary task of man is to act through the *charismata* of the Holy Spirit not only as a separate individual, to transform and regenerate himself, but within church and society. The Orthodox fathers went so far as to speak of synergy with God in perfecting his creation, during the eighth day of creation that is human history. What they meant was that, in history, the Christian believer has to become a factor in the shaping of the new creation and the new world according to the victorious message of the gospel. Orthodoxy is therefore very wary of accepting any easy theory of moral order inspired by the natural law, which would speak of a deposit of *justitia originalis* remaining untouched by sin after the fall; and it is equally opposed to any new appearances of natural theology in modern times that see and affirm the Holy Spirit acting and God present in all human relationships and social revolutions, without discriminating between good and evil in history. The eastern tradition requires every member of the Body of Christ to play his part in the present historical situation, always dynamic and flexible, because it is acting in the image of Christ, that is to say, through the love of God, which takes the lead. In this way, the Christian can never remain a detached spectator of the given order or of God's action, simply affirming the presence of God. He must make out of his Parousia, his presence, a *parresia,* a bold action, a peaceful revolution, in all situations. Christian participation in historical reality is therefore the fight of the victorious Christ with the principalities of this world, which have been defeated, though they still hold sway. At first sight, this confident expectation does not appear to yield social action; it combines patience and hidden dynamism with martyrdom and withdrawal from the world to make mankind realize that at the heart of the world, God has established the communion of saints. History has no other center in which it can find its deepest meaning, its *raison d'être* and its final purpose, than this humble, weak, suffering community in its midst, which is judging the world by its martyrdom.

2. In the eastern tradition, anthropology is expressed in terms of the sinner redeemed by Christ. The *theosis* of man is the result of his continual repentance. Orthodox theology has insisted on the fact that our humanity assumed by Christ is the humanity of the Divine Logos, therefore the purified humanity, which (as the historical person, the Jesus of Nazareth) he presents sinless to God the Father. Orthodoxy never professed, therefore, by analogy with the manhood of Jesus, any general idea of Christian humanism based on the goodness of man. Orthodoxy does not create by *theosis* the anthropology of an optimistic humanist, disregarding sin or accepting it as a simple disorder. For the Orthodox, sin is rebellion against God and a breaking away from his communion. Sin is man's actual condition in revolt against the plan of the Creation. Sin is the cataclysm from which no one can escape and of which the saints have more experience than sinners. It is in Christ and through the work of the Holy Spirit in the church that one grasps the tremendous dimensions of sin, because there it is revealed to be a sin of relationships and never the abstract concept of a sinful nature. Sin is always a sin against my neighbor, revealing my apostasy from God, breaking communion with him and with man. This can be grasped only if one becomes a member of a Christian community where individualism is defeated. Orthodoxy has always maintained, in its effort to embrace the whole world

and to sanctify it through the church, that sin is the element which the fall has brought into all human relationships and which tends to disintegrate the whole creation, whose motive power and purpose is *koinonia* in love. It is the deep sense of this reality that led the greatest spiritual leaders of Eastern Orthodoxy, though maintaining the principle of concord with the state and a positive attitude to the world, to retire from it and become monks, hermits and *startsi,* in order to rouse it from its self-complacency. Their action has a double significance: Without splitting away from the church, which is acting in the world and sanctifying societies, they point to the spiritual danger and the disintegration; they prefer to become silent witnesses of the need for man to be watchful before the principalities of this world. Their example is not to be followed as a rule of Christian behavior, but it is a necessary exception, challenging a theocratic state and any kind of easy concord between church and society, and recalling that the church cannot have a simple, direct and full relationship with all kinds of society. A certain distance is always implied, even when the church identifies itself with a given situation. It is in the world but not of the world. For a church to be in the world does not mean losing its own sanctifying role and becoming a social club or a social system working for the welfare of mankind. If it does that, the church betrays its mission to help society become real communion by bringing to it the uncompromising judgment of God.

3. Eastern Orthodoxy sees the church as under a continual threat from its secular environment and directly affected by it. Orthodox ecclesiology has nothing to do with any kind of ecclesiastical triumphalism. The promise of Jesus that the gates of hell should not prevail against the church has never been understood in the East as foretelling a glorious life of the church in this world, uniting political and religious authority in a hierarchical structure. On the contrary, eastern ecclesiology has expressed in theory and experienced in practice the tragic situation of the church between heaven and earth and the human condition in this world, of the Eastern Orthodox churches fighting to survive and maintain the faith in the most difficult historical circumstances. Political protection or persecution, as well as secularism in the form of theism or antitheism or indifferentism, always confront the church, not as a

counterpart to it, or an opponent, but as something rooted in the world in which the church exists and whose existence is shaken when the church tries to proclaim the gospel of God's great victory in history.

We should never forget that this world is not yet fully under the direct rule of God, but is under the principalities and evil powers; and the church, as the Body of Christ, proclaiming his Lordship, cannot undertake evangelism and mission without immediately clashing with the powers of this world. The church's diakonia is inseparably united with martyrdom. *Martyria* and resurrection, in the sense of the Acts of the Apostles, is, for the eastern tradition, almost identical with martyrdom, when the good news of the gospel penetrates the world where this church exists. It is, therefore, a great error to regard the life of the Eastern Church, as western criticism has repeatedly done, as the place where mystics, *startsi* and Hesychasts, as "aristocrats" among the chosen people of God, try to enjoy in peace and quiet the glory of the risen Lord by withdrawing from the historical scene and caring only for the salvation of their souls and the spiritual growth of the individual transfigured in the Holy Spirit apart from the world. There is some truth in this; but, first, this is not the whole of Orthodox spirituality; and, further, this spirituality is never to be understood and practiced as separation from the world. Orthodox spirituality finds its highest expression as a diakonia in the world based on an awareness of the importance of life in the world and in the service of the world.

This kind of ecclesiology maintains an open attitude in the relation between church and world in general and church and state, or society, in particular. It is not a simple theocratic vision of the church, which sees everything "possessed" by its sanctifying action, exemplified in countries where the Constantinian era and the idea of Christendom still prevail. Nor does the church use this "open attitude," with its qualitative sense of catholicity, as a hidden way of monopolizing the world. This would be greatly to misunderstand the Orthodox ecclesiology and its relationship with all aspects of national, social and economic life in countries where it is still the "official religion of the nation." It would be equally wrong to think that the Orthodox visualize the whole of a secularized and atheistic society as potentially already saved and invited by Christ to become members of his Body.

Behind this "open attitude," and inspiring it in all Orthodox churches, is another aspect of its ecclesiology, which actually precedes it. It is that the church is neither instrumental in the mystery of salvation nor an external support of the faith of the individual. The church is the *oikodome,* the building where God the Paraclete acts, perfecting it by framing it together, and thus continually re-creating the *koinonia,* the communion of the faithful, the center of the world.

This basic ecclesiological element signifies that to be a Christian means becoming an active member of a new *koinonia* by the act of God. It means to pass from the state of *individuum* to that of a *persona,* or better, of a "personal being," a man in and for the others, for the wholeness. An *individuum* as *a-tomon,* believing in Christ but outside a church communion, cannot easily be called fully a Christian. The vertical individual confession of faith, God-man, which regards the church as secondary, as a necessary social organization, leads to a sectarian, individualistic view of society and introduces all kinds of separations between nature and grace, and grace and law. The vertical relationship with God in a living faith is to be found in its horizontal manifestation with others in the communion of the Holy Spirit, which cannot be separated from the institutional aspect of the church, its visible reality here and now.

A person, *prosopon,* in the eastern tradition, is not the *individuum.* It is the opposite of the subjective ego. It is the *individuum* in movement toward another *individuum;* together in the Spirit, they become members of his communion. In the Orthodox tradition, you may not use the term "person" in the humanitarian, romantic or idealistic understanding of the word, as a subject having its own personality grounded in distinctiveness. "Person" in the Orthodox tradition must, I think, be understood as "personal being," which can be defined only on the basis of its relationship with the other members of the church community. "Personal being" means that its individuality springs only out of the reciprocal movement of love, which leads to the interdependence of men in Christ, brought together by the Paraclete. This togetherness is established by God in this world, in this history of ours, as one unshaken, unbroken community of men. It is a real, visible community, with structure and institutions, which are not to be regarded as a necessary evil or as external instruments added by men to the invisible act of God. These structures cannot and should not be separated from the essence of God's revelation in time and the establishment of his community in the world. They are the outcome of the energy of the Spirit and they are quickened by his *charismata*.

It is evident that this ecclesiology has its roots deep in the efforts of the eastern tradition to penetrate the mystery of the triune God. The fathers of the Orthodox Church never made the distinction between the essence and the will of God that we find in the post-Augustinian tradition in the West. From the very beginning of the development of the trinitarian theology in the East, there was the effort to escape from a static understanding of the nature of God. Revelation was thought of as a movement from within the incomprehensible nature of God, and the gap between essence and will was breached in the East by the energy, or rather the "energies," of God. These energies were thought of as flowing into the world for its redemption and re-creation. It is always a movement from a center out of love to incorporate all alienated elements of the created and fallen humanity. This "energetic" approach to the most difficult problem confronting the human mind signifies that God is not one person, resulting out of the three persons, but a personal being in three hypostases, distinct but inseparable, united in the movement that springs from one and the same essence, flowing out into the whole world. The Orthodox ecclesiology tries to reflect this primary event. The ecclesia is the window through which one can get a glimpse into this mystery and, at the same time, act as a new gathered community in and for the whole world.

It is therefore of basic importance that an individual or a group, facing a specific problem, should act together with the other members of the ecclesial community. An individual decision on any social problem can never fully express the will of Christ. Nor can the decision of a group isolated from the rest of the universal church fully express this will. All sectarian attitudes are excluded, especially when the church acts in society. The social witness of the church, apart from this solid ecclesiological basis, is going to produce new division in its own body.

This kind of ecclesiology excludes every tendency of conformism with a given social structure. It is wrong to think, as some non-Orthodox seem to, that an acceptance and affirmation of existing sociological patterns is implied when the Orthodox speak of the church as a microcosm, trying to incorporate everything in the Body of Christ simply by sanctifying it. Orthodox ecclesiology does not accept the secular order without criticism of injustice. Without separating church and world, and stressing the transcendent reality of the church in the world, as well as its holiness and sacramental nature, it allows the church to identify itself with the world, sharing all aspects of family, social and national life, yet on guard against every danger of conformism. The Orthodox ecclesiology can lead the church to a realistic solidarity with the suffering, the poor, a nation fighting for its freedom, in which laity and clergy are equally responsible; but not for a moment does the word that it preaches in this situation imply a passive acceptance of the given patterns of economic, social and national life. If that were to happen, then at a particular moment of history, certain people have wrongly interpreted Orthodox ecclesiology. That is why the Orthodox Church, with very few exceptions, has never become a class church or a church centered on principles dictated by secular authorities, including, for example, the imposing of a uniform system of education for priests; (note that, in Greece, only 25 per cent of the priests are theologians). It means, also, that the church is totally involved in the daily life of the people, at the center of family and social life and, at the same time, clearly distinguished from it and not in danger of conformism. It means that the Orthodox preachers (lay and clerical) must learn that the solidarity of their church with the world around them does not mean withdrawal or a sacrifice of the prophetic element of the Word of God; on the contrary, the Word of God is expected through this solidarity to console, but also to judge, criticize and renew the social patterns with which the church is, by its nature, in solidarity.

We therefore arrive at the following conclusions about the Orthodox understanding of responsible society:

1. The Orthodox view of church and state is not a system that

necessarily leads to either theocracy or caesaropapism. The so-called system of "friendly relationships" denotes only the good will of the church to the political authorities, an openness and a concern for their problems and a spirit of sacrifice for the spiritual up-building and the material welfare of the citizens of the nation. In no sense does this mean that the church must sacrifice the prophetic element of its ministry or its critical attitude to political leaders who are abusing their authority.

2.  This ecclesiology does not look upon the world as a new creation in which people inevitably pass from the state of individualistic existence to personal, conscious, responsible existence; rather, the new creation is the result of mission, evangelism and the active presence of the Christian community and its members. In Orthodox ecclesiology, all men are united to join the Christian community by participation in word and sacrament and thus begin to realize that their whole being and life in the world are an offering to God for the sake of the whole of society in which they live. Scientists and sociologists, in particular, perform to some extent a parapriestly action in the humanity redeemed by Jesus. It is something very basic for a man to live both as a member of the Christian community and as a responsible member of a secularized society; but, for Orthodox thought, the meaning of such a situation does not come about automatically, without the man's act of repentance and his perpetual nourishment by the sacraments and the experience of the reality of church life. An Orthodox would say that where this happens, he becomes in society a *parresia,* the presence in bold action of the church in the world.

3.  What lies behind this attitude is a kind of acknowledgment of God and his Word that I regard as a presupposition of any theory of knowledge; it is the reception of God's gifts in the church and, through the faith of the church, for life in the world. It means that everything we have and achieve and offer comes from God in Christ through the Spirit. Before the scientist begins his research or the sociologist his analysis of the constitutive elements of a society, they have to realize that the divine activity of giving places us all in an attitude of reception. Hence, Christian action in society is to help man in all social situations to see what is human and what is inhuman, what belongs in the gift of God and what he has

given for the sake of the whole body of his society. In discriminating thus, the church must always preach the absolute priority of the divine, saving judgment over the human application of the possibilities of nature for development and progress.

## The Present Relationships Between Church and Society

We have already seen that, for the Orthodox Church, there are a great variety of possibilities in the actual relation of church and society, by reason of the many social and political contexts in which the church is now living; and when we come to discuss the type of relationship that the West usually describes as Christendom, or the Constantinian era, we can do so, again, in terms only of Greece.

The idea of Christendom, which, in Greece, identifies national life not only with the Christian faith, but more specifically with Orthodoxy, is not just a system suggested either by the political authorities or by the theologians and church leaders but is the result of the church's leadership in all realms of social, political and national life during long periods of its history of struggle to survive under the threat of foreign dominion. It seems, therefore, natural and logical today to argue that a Greek is an Orthodox and belongs to the state church; and, although the existence of small religious minorities and of other confessions is tolerated, for a Greek to belong to a non-Orthodox church is a curiosity. Greece still sees confessional unity as the backbone of her national identity. Particularly since the Second World War, the friendly relationship is accepted not only between state and church but also between the church and social and family life. Although there are signs that this peaceful relationship may be threatened, the church appears to remain the center around which social relationships have to be built and from which spiritual power must come. According to Orthodox doctrine, it gives the nation, through religious education, its spiritual basis and preserves the continuity of a people who believe themselves to be heirs of a long tradition. It is the expression of Greek Christian culture, which unites the national and the Christian heritage. In the same way, it is unthinkable that a family can be founded outside the church through a civil marriage; and, as a rule, a new factory or office is blessed by the priest at a special service of inauguration. Further, there are special services for all important social events, not only on a single occasion but repeated as a token of the sanctifying presence of the church in the midst of her own members. Church life, therefore, is interwoven with all aspects of secular life, even where this is only a generally accepted habit.

However, we are experiencing today, and are likely to experience more acutely in the coming decades, a kind of silent emancipation, though there are no signs yet of the type of laicization and anticlericalism found, for instance, in France. Some observers believe that in many respects, the friendly relations are only an external form without content. But, on the other hand, Orthodoxy has always been careful, in matters of social development, political change and scientific progress, never to give cause for a violent reaction or revolt of the secular world. The church never intervenes by condemning this or that political party or this type of secularism or that scientific doctrine and has never presented countersystems through a Christian political party or a Christian type of science or a Christian sociology; this would make a clash inevitable. Flexibility has hitherto preserved the Church of Greece from setting itself up as an opponent of secular ideologies, social programs or scientific theories. It is also true that Greece, liberated from the Turkish yoke only in modern times, has not yet experienced the type of secularization that is found in many countries of western Europe; consequently, the church has not so far felt the necessity to react. For the theological reasons already explained, I doubt whether the Orthodox Church will ever become involved, as have the western churches, in ideological, sociological and scientific struggles. It is strange but true that although enjoying friendly relations with every kind of secular environment, and especially with the state, the Church of Greece has maintained a careful distinction between the holy and the profane and consequently understands the limits of its evangelism and action.

It is true that the church is the center of society, that it sometimes has to speak clearly, to criticize social injustices and political extremism and to fight a conservatism that hinders the reform of the structure of a patriarchal society; but, again, such criticism on the part of an Orthodox Church will never, I believe, become a radical revolutionary reaction against the prevailing order, and the church will never try, through a particular ideology, to promote one final solution to current problems. We face today a delicate situation, where the church is called again to preach prophetically the judgment of God, to the right and the left, offering God's grace for renewal to all, and offering it in a far broader sense than it has done in the recent past: as power for daily life, for a Christian faith that is applied in professional activity, for a spirituality that is expressed by acts of service and in social action.

Greece is of particular interest since it is a country with an ancient church tradition, where the church, being typically Eastern Orthodox, tries to preserve unchanged the inherited tradition, its "values and ideals," while suffering, at the same time, deeper penetration by western secularism than any other country of eastern Europe. The continuance of this Orthodox tradition is challenged almost daily by the great majority of the young generation, especially among the intellectuals. Alienation from church life and from its particular duties is growing. Regular attendance at services, fasting and confession are not treated with hostility but with an indifference that is familiar in the western countries. Though the basic pattern of relationships between church and society has not changed fundamentally, a certain shaking of the foundations is taking place, silently and gradually. They call attention to specific problems that are becoming acute for the church today.

1. *Secularism.* If secularism means giving absolute value to the objects of the world as the means of achieving the greatest possible welfare of the individual and of the group, modern Greece has to face a strange problem. This type of secularism was born within a culture that had emphasized the value of material goods and the natural environment. It is the result of an activism, in and for the world, that seeks to achieve higher levels of production and to raise the individual's standard of living. To some extent, it is the result of a western Christian "spirituality." In many respects, one can speak of this secularism as an illegitimate offspring of applied Christianity in the western Christian inheritance. When this type of secularism penetrates a typically Orthodox country like Greece, it causes a great spiritual revolution, convincing young people of

the collapse of an era and a way of life that only their grand-parents lived. They feel frustrated by religiosity, which seeks to gather everything under the lordship of a divine power, which comes to the believer through missionary activity and is expressed in an irrational way, centering on the miraculous. At present, the distinction between religiosity and Christian faith does not yet seem clear to the younger generation or to the intellectuals. This will come, of course, but it is doubtful whether the distinction will be made on the basis of western Protestant writers like Bonhoeffer. What interests us at the moment is the way in which the church maintains and renews its relationship with the new Greek secular society. This is extremely difficult, because the church authorities still operate according to the idea of Christendom, expressed by the words, "Let the young people come to the church: It is their church."

The Greek Orthodox can say in self-criticism that they are not altogether ready to go out into the secular world, and that they must wait for people to come in.

Furthermore, the era of an ethics of admonition by a spiritual father is definitely over for the majority of young people in Greece. It has to be replaced by the presence, among the secularized people and in solidarity with them, of devoted young Orthodox, who struggle with them and study with them the problems of the new Greek society. This cannot be done unless one admits that secularism is not a necessary evil, causing total alienation from the church. In the Greek situation of today, this new approach can be a motive for renewal and purification of inherited religious formalities, which, within a secular environment, are tested and proved to be secondary and unimportant.

2. *The inequality in the sharing of the benefits of industrialization.* Greece was fundamentally an agricultural and maritime country: from ancient times, it has always been a poor country, importing some basic foodstuffs. In its present form, it came into existence after 1830, liberating and adding new parts until 1920, and so it is a relatively new state. If we consider also the catastrophe of 1921, when this new state with 4,500,000 people had to receive and assimilate 2,000,000 more people expelled from Asia Minor,

starting their life from nothing, we have a clear picture of the difficult beginning of the national economy.

The most acute problem, since the time of liberation from the Turks, and especially today, is the transition from an agricultural type of economy, which proved insufficient to satisfy the needs of the increased population, to an industrial economy. Industrialization raises a great problem because the country lacks raw materials. The Second World War devastated 80 per cent of the country's resources. Moreover, it would be difficult to establish a national economy of a socialist type in Greece. In this situation, though one cannot speak of capitalism, one is tempted to speak of "plutocracy," where a limited number of people plan an economy that allows profiteers to flourish. I would dare to add that this is true also in political and scientific life: We have too much individualism and too many "clever people" fighting to get more and more, while the majority do not have enough. The situation creates great uneasiness among the majority of the younger people. As the economic inequality becomes more evident, the thirst for social justice becomes stronger and receives very radical expression.

A church that tries to keep its continuity with a nation that in turn owes its unity and survival largely to this church, hesitates to break through and share this anxiety fully. There is also the difficulty that many of the mature members of the Church of Greece accept the church's passivity in this respect, because they are used to thinking of the church as a place of withdrawal, a place of holiness and religious devotion. In comparison with the West, there are few who request an intervention from the pulpit, and there is fear of those who attempt to formulate a Christian social policy. But it becomes increasingly clear to the younger generation of theologians, as well as to many devoted Christians in some of the lay movements, that the Church of Greece must speak and act boldly, because there is no other spiritual force with the power to convince the country of the need for radical economic change and for equal opportunities for all. And this is because the Church of Greece has succeeded in remaining in close contact with the poorer classes and the workers, rather than with the intelligentsia. The Orthodox faith has never been socially exclusive, and the church has fully shared the martyrdom of a weak nation.

This sharing in the sufferings of the people is seen, first of all, in the poverty of the married clergy, especially in rural areas, where most of them still work at a secular job in order to earn a living. The church thus remains in solidarity with the poorer people. The rich and the intelligentsia should not be excluded from responsible church life, but the great need of the moment is for the framework of Greek society to be changed by a peaceful co-operation between the vital elements in the church and genuine movements for improving social justice.

The Church of Greece, through its bishops, clergy and devoted laymen, is in the vanguard in the relief of poverty and suffering, especially when disaster strikes. During the hard years of war and foreign occupation, the Church of Greece took the lead in almost all the relief organizations. The parishes, too, have a relief program for the benefit of their poor members, and there are many orphanages and old people's homes in different dioceses. Yet all these activities are based on the old conception of providing first aid, through regular almsgiving, in parochial committees for social work, without a planned policy that would help Greeks, as members of their own church, to contribute in a generous way to a social program. Such a policy, together with a strong appeal for radical social reforms in Greece, must definitely come into existence in the near future if the church is to maintain living links with society today.

3. *The revolutionary age and nationalism.* It is not surprising that the danger of a social explosion always remains imminent in Greece. Unfortunately, in the Civil War after the Second World War, the forces of the left were impelled by political motives rather than by social concern to reverse the traditional social policy. They would say, of course, that had they dominated the political scene, they would have introduced radical changes; but once it became clear that these reformers were concerned more for domination than for reform and had no social program designed for the Greek situation with respect for personal freedom, their rebellion ceased to be regarded as promising a real social change. The worst effect of this violent uprising in the years after the war, when this small nation was struggling to recover from its difficulties, was to make

all kinds of progressive movements easily suspect by those who struggled to maintain the old patterns.

It is also true that after the war, the government introduced many changes, especially better organization in social relief and welfare programs and measures in favor of economic stability. However, we still are, today, far from the economic changes needed to meet the threat of revolution and disorder. The revolutionary tendencies are apparent in the voting for the parties of the extreme left by people who are in no way ideologically associated with them. People need spiritual guidance and help to form a strong, inspired social movement that will bring fundamental change without using violence, if that is at all possible.

On the other hand, the younger generation in Greece is becoming nationalistic. This has developed since the Second World War and is expressed in demanding better treatment for Greece by her western allies, because she alone among the eastern European countries fought faithfully in the whole war. Because of the Cyprus question, it is a common feeling in Greece that something has gone wrong in international politics, whereby Greece has suffered injustice. We cannot discuss here the rights or wrongs of this opinion, but it clearly gives rise to a dangerous new nationalism. This is of special concern to the Church of Greece, since it has always been at the head of all movements involving national action, particularly where it concerns parts of Greece still under foreign dominion. The non-Greek Orthodox has difficulty in understanding this, although to the great majority of Greeks it appears obvious and reasonable. We feel we must accept this heritage of nation and church, which produced the struggle to recapture our freedom and preserve through the centuries faith against invaders.

Yet it is also apparent that the church has to lead this nationalism in new directions, helping the young Greeks to understand that national ideals can no longer be limited to the interests of one nation alone, and that today there are no national problems or goals that do not have international implications. The main characteristic of our age is that it is becoming more and more universal, international and ecumenical, and the Church of Greece bears an enormous responsibility in redirecting historic Greek national feeling to the service of international understanding and peace. If the church is to have a dynamic and efficacious impact on our society, it must give particular attention to three aspects of our social structure:

1. The new complexities in the life of the state during the transition from the patriarchal, traditional structure to the secularized type of society will require us to reinterpret carefully church and state relationships. The church has to see that the "friendly relationship" now implies a certain distance and a bold and constructive criticism. If the pattern of the Christian nation is to be maintained in Greece, it must undergo serious and frank criticism. The beautiful surface of unity must be examined realistically.

2. Another dangerous tendency is that of easily accepting an unbroken continuity between the wisdom of the classical Greek antiquity and the Christian Orthodox era of Byzantium and of modern times. I mean by this the theory according to which ancient Greek wisdom—Plato's philosophy in particular—had a preparatory role to play in bringing the Gentiles to accept the Christian gospel. This idea of "Greco-Christian civilization" can inhibit self-criticism and lead to a superficial understanding, which does not analyze critically the history of the church, establishing an easy continuity and idealizing the past. This continuity can be of great service, provided that one always considers seriously the element of discontinuity, the failures and shortcomings both of Greek philosophy and of the different Greek theologies that try to maintain this unity in an uncritical way. It is the duty of the church and its theology in Greece today to lead the campaign for such a historical critical analysis and to refuse to allow any kind of self-sufficiency to continue in the future.

3. The idea of Christendom is still very much accepted and endorsed in Greece. Again, this is a façade, which, as in many western countries, may conceal many deviations in the interpretation of the true Christian message in the modern world. It must be said, however, that the idea of Christendom in all Orthodox countries, especially in Greece, differs from that found in western countries, because the laymen in Greece are never regarded as secondary church members. Although we are often confronted with abuses from both the hierarchy and the laity, the danger of clericalism does not exist, at least at the moment. The church, not only

in theory but also in practice, is a *pleroma* of clergy and laity to-gether. Actions by some individuals should not lead the observer to conclude that this balance has not been maintained in recent years. There are clear instances to show that in critical moments, the people of God are thought of in their wholeness; the members are absolutely interdependent, and the priesthood does not have absolute authority over the laity. But, here again, the church has to alert its members and defeat a kind of hidden "despotism" by arousing in all a sense of responsibility for the life of the church, reminding them especially of their role in the modern world.

## The Action of the Church in Society

In conclusion, I make some general observations, lest the west-ern reader should jump to false conclusions, expecting church ac-tion at the same level and by the same methods to which he is accustomed. In Greece, a systematic, social action of the church will be possible. But it will be impossible to place Greek society, even in its most secularized form, "outside the church," as some-thing with a separate existence, *vis-à-vis* the church, as a foreign element having no connection with its life. This is not because the split between church and society in Greece has not yet oc-curred; even if it does happen, as in other "Orthodox" countries, the church will maintain its belief and its vision and will try to act as the center of society, embracing all its members, regardless of the measure and loyalty of their faith. The separation is not im-posed by the church. When separation occurs in Orthodox coun-tries, it is through the will of a particular state. The church should never introduce a separation between sacred and profane or ec-clesial and secular, since the church lives for this world and in the heart of this world. In situations where others have introduced separation, its main object is to incorporate everything into the Body of Christ by a *martyria,* which is more powerful when it in-cludes martyrdom.

This is something authentically Orthodox, which one can still see in other Orthodox countries, where the split has occurred vio-lently and bloodily. The church is the place into which, through the grace of God, all must be gradually incorporated. Everybody is potentially saved, especially when he has received the grace of baptism. The church is responsible for keeping the continuity of its eucharistic, sacramental center, by radiating grace in all directions in this world, which is Christ's, raising barriers between itself and modern society. But the vision and the movement toward society are always *from within* the church to the surrounding circles; the church is the center of the world and bound to it through the grace of God. Therefore, from the point of view of the church, there is no opposition to the world as alienated from it. It is the predominance of love in the church that must keep the contact with the world, and shape the relationship anew in different situations; the church is always ready for service, trying to bring everything under the Lordship of Christ and restore it. The Orthodox do not, therefore, distinguish between the institutional aspect of the church and its social activity but should speak of the responsible Orthodox laymen with the clergy, as one body, in the service of the society of which they are members, acting, if necessary, in a revolutionary or radical way, as I have tried to describe.

Let me draw three final conclusions: First, although the Orthodox hesitate to speak about a Christian social action, in the form sometimes found in the West, it is evident that social activity as a worldly spirituality *is fully possible in Greece and very necessary*. The practice of many priests and lay movements has proved that it can be one of the major preoccupations of the Orthodox Church when it is free to act in society.

Second, with the rise of the modern type of social relationships and the reorganization of social and economic life, the Church of Greece must pass from unsystematic social assistance, based on good will to answer emergencies, to systematic social action. Yet it must not become one more social movement alongside others; rather, it must be the ground on which all the other social movements and programs can gain new impetus, new inspiration and true spiritual content. It would be catastrophic in an Orthodox country for the church to appear to produce further divisions of groups and parties.

And third, the Orthodox Church, with the freedom and flexibility it enjoys, through the absence of any definitive positions laid down in canon law, encyclicals or confessional statements on the detailed questions of personal relationships, especially of sex and family, should be ready to acknowledge a necessary pluralism in ethical behavior in modern society. This does not mean that the church's morality should be ambiguous and that it should adopt a "Christian ethical pluralism." Here we approach the most delicate problem of our study, and we should not confuse the issue by maintaining that, because the church is for everybody, it must remain silent and cease to accord absolute value to the God-given charismatic community of the saints. The church should not seek to domesticate God as though, in his love, he simply served people in their given social relationships. The loving Christ is truly the lover of men, but when men have come to understand him also as their supreme judge. Without *metanoia* there is no possibility of maintaining a true and living relationship between Christ and man in modern society. The manhood, the humanity of Jesus is sinless: This signifies the movement of the Christian toward ethical perfection in today's society. Although sinful, he strives to become sinless, purified and strengthened by the Spirit.

The duty of the church is not simply to serve society or to acknowledge the automatic presence of Christ in society. The presence of Christ in society will clearly be seen only when the church calls everybody to be incorporated into the Body of Christ and to reinterpret in action—which distinguishes the human from the inhuman—his particular daily work as a service to the whole of society. We are in agreement with the evangelicals that the church is an extroverted movement, with the distinction that we maintain that the church is a solid building of God, has a center that is given in history by the Holy Spirit and is expressed through the prophetic teaching of his Word, radiating from his real presence in baptism and the eucharist. We agree with them that there is a "worldly spirituality," but it should always be the result of a rebirth through the baptismal waters and the eucharistic blood in the One Apostolic Church. Then, through the service of the Christian in society, these two flow out, and this should make all social action the fruit of the Spirit and the doing of the Word of God.

This essay in no way seeks to deny the value of any kind of sincere effort in social work by non-Orthodox churches. There are truly great deeds and a rich thought and activity by these churches, in the face of which the Orthodox churches must pause, with admiration and in thanksgiving to God. This treatise is intended only to show how the Orthodox can contribute their own ecclesiological basis to the social thought and actions of the church. This can have a certain importance, particularly when we try to approach the vital problem of church and society in a new and more ecumenical perspective. Orthodox ecclesiology not only does not hinder ecumenical social thinking, but it quickens it by showing its dimension as an interchurch diakonia that flows out of the one unbroken community of Christ among his churches into the world as the one undivided *martyria,* in action, to manifest his Lordship over all and in all.

# 5

# BIBLICAL SOCIAL ETHICS: AN EVANGELICAL VIEW

by BRUCE REED (United Kingdom)

By "ethics" we mean the reflective consideration of the foundations of moral behavior in human society. The term "social ethics" implies that we are concerned with something more than individual morality. One of our greatest difficulties in elaborating principles of social ethics is that we do not naturally see a man in the context of his social relationships, and so ethical questions tend to become questions of individual morality.

Unfortunately, modern methods of evangelism frequently reinforce this outlook instead of transforming it. Those who are converted feel themselves to be over against the rest of the world. For the purposes of earning their living, they must be involved in the world, but for the purposes of carrying on their Christian life, they see themselves as separated from the world and accept no responsibility for its behavior. This can lead to the idea that a man's soul is distinct from the rest of his personality, which leads to the devaluation of large areas of life: art, culture, politics—and social ethics. The tragedy is that the converted Christian is often willing and eager to place himself under obedience to Christ, and yet the context in which he has heard the gospel preached prevents him from correctly interpreting so many of Christ's words. In his attack upon the "social gospel," the evangelical frequently denies the validity of social ethics for the Christian, and is consequently unable to see the way God is acting in every situation and area of human activity.

## Personality and Community in the Bible

In the Bible, personality is conceived corporately. An isolated individual is hardly a man at all. To find fulfillment as a person means to be involved in a community and to participate in its life. As G. Ernest Wright says: "In the Bible we possess, not a description of the development of true individualism after the pattern of modern humanism, but instead a portrayal of the true relationship between the individual and the community in which the true nature of both is revealed.[1] A man's soul, or self, was thought of as extending through all his relationships, so that his clothes, possessions, family, tribe and nation *were* he. His neighbor *was* himself, so that to love his neighbor was to love himself, as the second great commandment states, and his neighbor's death diminished him (cf. JOHN DONNE: ". . . any man's death diminishes me, because I am involved in Mankinde. . . ."). The story of Achan illustrates this. In order for Achan to be punished, not only the man himself but his family, animals and property had to be destroyed; if any of these had remained, Achan would have lived on, because they were he. The conception also had its positive implications. One man's blessing spread to the whole community around him and to succeeding generations. This is the meaning of the explanatory clause in the second commandment (Exodus 20 : 6).

As Wright says, this view of personality enhances the individual's worth and responsibility and makes social ethics a subject of vital importance. How is life in community possible, when, as it were, the souls making up the community "overlap"—when every action may diminish the being of another? The biblical answer is that life in community is made possible by an agreement or covenant, expressed in laws to which all subscribe. The laws are appropriate to the particular circumstances of the community and make clear the rights and obligations of each member of it.

## The Thesis of This Chapter

We are, more than ever, conscious that we cannot "read off" laws from the Bible, because our society is so different from the

---

[1] *The Biblical Doctrine of Man in Society,* p. 28f.

communities of the Old and New Testaments, is changing so rapidly and is so diverse. The complexity of life today makes it impossible to formulate universal principles or laws, but this apparent disadvantage has forced us to investigate our presuppositions for action in the world more thoroughly.

In this essay, we propose to expand the following thesis: God is active in all situations, and, in those involving moral issues, he is at work as King. He is to be encountered existentially in the persons and processes of life situations, and he is working through them toward a just resolution of the moral issues. Therefore, if we can discern what God is doing in the situation, we can learn how we should behave.

### Awareness of the Activity of God

This thesis implies that we believe (1) that God is the Living God; (2) that God is actively working out his purpose for mankind through every situation; (3) that a just resolution of a moral issue is one way in which God works out his purpose; (4) that we must use all our resources to ascertain the reality of the situation, that is, its truth; (5) that we have the gift of the Holy Spirit to lead us into the truth; (6) that the result of this will be a call to obedience—in other words, that when we discern what God is doing, we are called to cooperate with him; (7) that God accepts us as we are, with our limitations and powers, and will not call us to do what is beyond us.

This can be illustrated by reference to the way Christ behaved. He showed his concern for the well-being and destiny of all men; but, contrary to the expectation of his contemporaries and probably ours, he did not lay down a detailed program of behavior. On the contrary, he did not talk about man in general but loved men and women as he found them. Social ethics for Christ arose out of concrete situations, and the gospels are a collection of such situations. For our purposes, one of the most significant is the story in John 5, in which he is criticized for healing a paralyzed man on the Sabbath Day. He says: "My Father has never yet ceased His work, and I am working too. . . . In truth, in very truth, I tell you, the Son can do nothing by Himself; He does only what He sees the

Father doing: what the Father does, the Son does" (John 5 : 17, 19, 20). Jesus is saying that his responsibility is to be obedient to the Father. But his father does not communicate to him through principles or general commands, but by acting in and through the situation in which Christ is involved, and calls for Christ's obedience in acting out before men what he sees the Father doing in reality.

At least two points crucial for this study can be derived from this biblical passage:

1. Jesus says: "My Father has never yet ceased His work . . ." Therefore, there is no situation where it is not relevant to ask, What is God doing? The true distinction between the sacred and the secular is not related to God's activity but to man's faith. What we commonly call a secular situation is one in which we are unable to discern God working. The Old Testament prophets could show that events such as the birth of a baby, a political revolution, the return of displaced persons, civil war, prostitution or an epidemic were significant from a religious [2] point of view. In themselves, these events were hardly more significant than the news in today's papers. But, because there was somebody who was able to see God working in these situations through the people involved in them, whether Jews or Persians, pagan kings or godly priests, they were able to address their own communities and tell them how to respond, namely, to repent, to be courageous, to flee, to fight, to believe or to wait. These events are recorded in the Bible, not as if they were special, but rather as case studies through which we can learn to interpret our own "here and now."

2. The theme of Jesus' reply to the accusations of the Pharisees is that he is not under judgment from them but answerable to the One who sent him. Because he is aware of the nature of his responsibility to God, of the reality of the "here and now," and of God's activity in that situation, his relationship with God is "absolute." That is, there is nothing further to be said about that relationship than is being said precisely now. Therefore, he is absolutely certain of where he stands in relationship to God.

This is why Jesus can say: "I cannot act by myself, I judge as

---

[2] I despair of finding a better word.

I am bidden, and my verdict is just because my aim is not my own will but the will of Him who sent me" (John 5 : 30). His authority to judge is by virtue of his obedience: "As Son of Man, He has also been given the right to pass judgment" (John 5 : 27).

The implication of this for social ethics is that it is possible to have social ethics, to give guidance for human behavior that is appropriate to the situations in which men find themselves. These social ethics, however, are not founded on a program but on obedience to a God whose name, "I am that I am," reveals him to be the God of the "here and now." The Bible, the history of the church and the life of Christ, gives us clear interpretations of the way God has acted in history; these enable us to draw conclusions as to how he may be acting in any situation. These same channels also indicate the way men have sought to respond to this action of God through obedience, and they give us a clue as to the kind of obedience required of us. The pitfall appears when we reduce these insights to a new law, which substitutes fantasy for reality and arrogance for faith.

How, then, do we discover what God is doing? Our task parallels that of the prophets. Each of them sought to declare God's activity to his contemporaries. Each of them saw God's role in history as threefold:

First, they proclaimed that God as *Creator* initiated and sustained the world; second, that there would be a summing-up, a Day of the Lord, when God would reveal himself to all men for what he is all the time—*Judge and King;* and third, that he has intervened in history as *Redeemer* of a people who would, through his constant renewal, more adequately witness to his character. Their purpose in referring to these acts of God was to make their hearers aware that God was at work in the same way in the here and now: "The prophets not only see God as active in past salvation events which are remembered and recorded, they claim that his hand is also *and equally* at work in the events of their own day...." [3] The New Testament underlines these three modes of God's behavior and declares that the work of God in Christ, through his incarnation, life, death, resurrection and ascension, and

---

[3] NORMAN PERRIN: *The Kingdom of God in the Teaching of Jesus.* Philadelphia: Westminster Press, 1963, p. 161. His italics.

through the coming of the Holy Spirit to the church, supersedes the deliverance of Israel from Egypt as the unique and normative act of God as Redeemer (see Stephen's speech, Acts 7).

Man responds, consciously or unconsciously, to these activities of God with different roles to meet different situations in his life. In relation to God as Creator, man acts as worker, for example, as parent, explorer, technologist, and toolmaker, and God continues his creative acts through man in this role. In relation to God's work as King and Judge, man takes the role of king, illustrated, for example, by mediator, evangelist, friend and pastor. This may be illustrated as follows: In a manufacturing department in a factory, on the production line, one could see God at work as Creator, and men in their roles as workers; in the works manager's office where a shop steward is arguing over a wage claim, one could see God at work as King and Judge, and man in his kingly role; where a workman is trying to sort out a personal problem with his fellow workers, one could see God as Redeemer and man in his priestly role.

The justification for the statement that social ethics is related to the work of God as King and Judge will be provided by the examination of the concept of kingship that follows. Though not denying that God is at work in other ways in situations involving ethics, we shall follow the example of the prophets, who found that reference to one particular mode enabled them to talk about God meaningfully in relation to particular events.

## The Kingly Role

God exercises his kingly role in the world by giving authority to men and women to act as his agents. "Then God said, 'Let us make man in our image, after our likeness; and let them have dominion over the fish of the sea, and over the birds of the air, and over the cattle, and over all the earth, and over every creeping thing that creeps upon the earth' " (Genesis 1 : 26). Gerhard Von Rad expounds the meaning of the word image in this way: "Just as powerful earthly kings, to indicate their claim to dominion, erect an image of themselves in the provinces of their empire where they do not personally appear, so man is placed upon the earth in God's image as God's sovereign emblem. He is really only God's representative, summoned to maintain and enforce God's claim to dominion over the earth." [4]

In human groups and communities, God gives authority to kings and rulers (Romans 13 : 1–7) to help them to live and work together and to achieve their goals. To those who have a kingly role of this kind, he gives power and resources to carry out their tasks.

The Old Testament king is, in a sense, a type of all those who are in positions of leadership or authority: Study of the Hebrew conception of kingship helps us to understand in theological terms the responsibility of anyone in authority and how God works through him.

The Old Testament idea of the king was, in most respects, similar to that of the surrounding nations. On the one hand, he was the embodiment of God. His anointing signified his setting apart as God's servant (I Kings 3 : 7–9) and his endowment with the Spirit of God (II Samuel 1 : 14–16; cf. Isaiah 11 : 2). The enthronement psalms speak of the king in terms that almost identify him with God (see Psalm 132 : 11–18; Psalm 20 : 6–9). On the other hand, he was the embodiment of the people. Lamentations 4 : 20 speaks of the Lord's Anointed as "the breath of the people's nostrils." His death in battle meant the defeat of the entire nation. When he did that which was right in the eyes of the Lord, for example, Asa, the people were righteous; when he did evil in the sight of the Lord; as did Ahab, the people were also unrighteous.

The welfare and peace of the whole people depended upon him. He carried on the task of the judges like Gideon and Samson, defending the people and leading them into battle against their enemies, and also administering justice to the people themselves. He was specifically charged in the book of Deuteronomy with maintaining justice and seeing that those who had been deprived of their rights were restored to them.

The failure of successive kings to do this led the prophets to describe the functions of the ideal king. Isaiah 11 : 2–5, for instance, illustrates the effect in kingly responsibility of the fact that the spirit of the Lord shall rest upon him. Here the king is seen as acting righteously in restoring power to those who are power-

---

[4] *Genesis: A Commentary*. Philadelphia: Westminster Press, 1961, pp. 57f.

less. He is God's agent on behalf of the deprived to enable them to take their rightful place in the community. Thus, he maintains justice, and judges the poor with righteousness. In Chapter 32 : 1–8, we have a further description of the ideal king. Here he not only protects the people—he "will be like a hiding-place from the wind, a covert from the tempest"—but also acts as judge, unmasking those who plot to deprive those in need.

The king is seen as using his power rightly when he restores to the deprived, the weak and the needy that power that is theirs by right as citizens of Israel, and also when he takes power away from those who have amassed it by depriving their brother and exposes them for what they are. When a king does this, he "reigns in righteousness" and "executes justice."

This conception of kingship lay behind Jesus' proclamation that the kingdom of God was being established in his own words and acts. When John the Baptist asked whether Jesus was "he that should come" (Luke 7 : 19), a kingly title, Jesus' response was to cure "many sufferers from diseases, plagues and evil spirits, and on many blind people he bestowed sight." He then told the messengers to go and tell John what they had seen and heard. Here was a decisive demonstration that he was the king, restoring power to the powerless. He told the Pharisees that if he cast out demons "by the finger of God," then the kingdom of God had come upon them (Luke 11 : 20). In John's gospel Jesus performed "signs" by making up deficiencies—lack of wine (John 2 : 11), lack of sight (John 9 : 3), lack of health (John 5 : 9) and lack of food (John 6 : 14, 15). When he provided food, the multitudes rightly perceived that this was a kingly function (John 6 : 15). This power could also be delegated by Christ to his followers: "When you come into a town and they make you welcome, eat the food provided for you; heal the sick there, and say: 'The Kingdom of God has come close to you'" (Luke 10 : 8, 9).

In this way, the kingdom of God comes among men (see Luke 17 : 21), but this is obvious only to a few, and Nicodemus was not one of them (John 3 : 3). There must be some disclosure by the Holy Spirit if a man is rightly to interpret these acts of Christ as signs of the kingly rule of God.

The kingly role of men and women in society can now be understood more clearly. The authority of all who exercise power, irrespective of their Christian faith or lack of it, is from God (Genesis 1 : 28; Colossians 1 : 16). The fact that they may misuse this power or be deluded about its origin (Matthew 4 : 24; II Thessalonians 2 : 3, 4) makes no difference. The purpose of this power is that through it they may help those they represent to achieve their goals and may maintain justice among those over whom they have been placed. It is therefore the responsibility of those in authority to be concerned for social justice, and God is constantly working through them to secure that end.

The increasing alienation in modern life has made us more conscious of those who are deprived—the hungry millions, the mentally ill, the homeless, the aged, criminals, drug addicts and displaced persons. The state, whether acting through its designated authorities (parliamentary representatives), its qualified experts (social workers, probation officers, doctors, architects) or self-appointed agencies (like our relief and refugee societies and housing associations) takes up a kingly role in relation to those in need.

Injustice in society cannot always be attributed to an easily identifiable ruler. One of the consequences of the complexity of modern society and the interdependence of its members is that power is widely distributed among shareholders, consumers, voters and workers. Those who are concerned about evils in society that cause dehumanization and suffering frequently feel that they are up against faceless, impersonal forces with which they are powerless to deal. They are bewildered, because when they confront those who appear to have definite responsibility for the prevailing injustice, they often find pleasant people who seem themselves to be victims of the system.

These impersonal forces seem to have a relationship to the principalities and powers of the New Testament. The fact that man has fallen under their domination is a result of his disobedience, which has caused him partially to lose his dominion in the world and to come under the control of demonic structures, personified by Satan, "the prince of this world."

Those in authority have to make difficult decisions, which affect the well-being of others, and to arbitrate in situations where no course of action is open that will be wholly just to all concerned. Delegating responsibility to others implies readiness to take the consequences of their failures. In these and other ways, the kingly role involves tension and suffering (the diaries of Dag Hammarskjold illustrate this fact).

The king is also the servant of his followers, the shepherd who lays down his life for the sheep (John 10 : 11; see also Mark 10 : 45). When the leader is prepared to endure suffering for the sake of those he represents, God may work through him as Redeemer as well as King, creating new possibilities for justice in situations where no just outcome seemed possible (see Isaiah 52 : 13—53 : 12).

The necessity of the one who takes the kingly role to expose himself to rejection and suffering is particularly clear in the case of attacking impersonal forces in society. Those who are contributing anonymously to the unjust situation must be forced to recognize their personal responsibility for it; this can be achieved only by the "king" exposing himself as a person. Those who demonstrate against nuclear weapons or racial discrimination may be looked upon as making an opportunity for personal action and exposure in a situation where no effective action seems possible. But the onlooker of the march is forced to ask himself, What is *my* attitude toward the hydrogen bomb or toward racial discrimination? The supreme example is that of Christ, who defeated the principalities and powers by allowing them to crucify him (I Corinthians 2 : 8; Colossians 2 : 15). Christ's death looks like defeat but is, in fact, the moment of judgment on the principalities and powers and upon Satan himself (John 16 : 11).

We have seen that God acts as King in the world through the agency of men and women exercising different kinds of authority. But the world at large does not recognize his hand in what they do or the coming of the Kingdom in the results of their work. This is because no human authority represents God perfectly. To some extent, we all abuse the power that we have: (1) We fail to recognize that our power has been given to us by God to carry out his purposes; (2) we abuse our power by using it for our own limited ends; this inevitably results in injustice to other members of society; and (3) we turn our power against God by using it to confuse the truth and conceal reality and by exploiting emotions like fear, dependence and hate, to build barriers to the love of God.

Because God's image has been defaced in this way, he has set up his image again by sending Christ who "reflects the glory of God and bears the very stamp [image] of his nature" (Hebrews 1 : 3). "He is the image of the invisible God" (Colossians 1 : 15). In his coming, the Kingdom of God drew near (see Mark 1 : 14f.), so that men had further opportunity to recognize God's kingship. Because man's disobedience disqualified him from proclaiming the kingship of God unambiguously, it was only through his obedience to the point of death that Christ won, on behalf of man, the right to have all things in subjection under his feet (Hebrews 2 : 9).

The church, as the Body of Christ, has the responsibility of making God's kingship known where it is not acknowledged. This does not mean that the church's authority nullifies that of all those who have kingly roles in the world. On the contrary, the church is in a position to perceive that God is at work through all these authorities. Conversion and baptism into the church do not give anyone a short cut to skill as a social worker, or schoolteacher or works manager. But, as a citizen of the kingdom of God, the Christian may be called upon to take up a kingly role in any area of life where authority is being abused and to be the instrument of God's judgment on those in authority. This can never be an easy decision to make, since the one in authority is still God's representative. Examples of this dilemma are seen in the agonizing of the Christian Germans who plotted to take Hitler's life, in Luther's attitude to the Peasants' Revolt, and in David's attitude toward Saul.

## Discerning the Activity of God in the Concrete Situation

People who exercise different kingly roles may tend to devalue one another's work; for example, the professional social worker may regard the Christian who is seeking to help a maladjusted girl as an amateurish "do-gooder." The Christian occupies the best vantage point for evaluating these various kingly roles. He is in a position to appreciate the extraordinary diversity of ways in which God is working in the world, and he is able to respond to them in obedience, working alongside a great variety of colleagues in many different surroundings.

In his book, *The Diversity of Morals,* Morris Ginsberg maintains that the people of western Europe are bewildered because genuine moral difficulties have not been resolved by the way the Christian church has stated fundamental moral principles. He goes on to say that these moral principles "are perhaps not seriously questioned but their application to complex issues is felt to be vague and uncertain and this shakes belief in their workability" (page 4). Moreover, he maintains that "lack of accurate knowledge of the facts involved tends to obscure the ethical aspects of the problem and, in particular, to suggest greater differences of opinion regarding ethical standards than would exist if the factual issues were more clearly grasped."

Therefore, taking note of Ginsberg's strictures, we need to consider the following points in endeavoring to arrive at an ethical judgment about any situations:

1. Those in authority have received their authority from God, even though they may misuse it or deny its origin; Christians see them as already under the judgment that they will not perceive until they give account of themselves to God at the Last Day.

2. The laws that they promulgate have behind them the authority of God, even though they may be inadequate or unjust; they were formulated by sinful people and so partake of sin, but God continues to work through them. God's delegation of authority to man is genuine—man has real freedom and can use it for unjust ends. In the Cross, God accepts responsibility for the consequences of giving man this freedom.

3. God may have delegated authority in different ways to people who are involved in the same situation; for instance, in a discussion on contraception, there may be a government official, a doctor, a priest and a mother.

4. What are the boundaries of the situation under review? Are they personal, local, national or international? Who are the persons and communities involved? The precision with which these boundaries are drawn will depend upon the clarity with which we can define the human authorities concerned. These authorities must be seen as persons with feelings of love, hate, fear and anxiety,

persons who interact upon one another and upon those who are outside the boundaries of the situation.

5. In order to understand the situation, I must give full consideration to all the technical facts at my disposal. This may involve defining the boundaries in time; that is, its past history and possible future development. How far am I equipped with the conceptual tools to interpret these facts?

6. How far are my own sin and prejudice likely to cloud my understanding of this reality? Through the gift of the Holy Spirit, the Christian should be able to perceive the depths of reality more effectively than the non-Christian, but experience shows that this is by no means the case. Perhaps this is because we have not taken seriously the possibility that God is calling to us from the heart of every situation with which we are concerned.

7. How far do I accept responsibility for those in the situation? To the extent to which I am prepared to see myself as their servant, and to identify myself with all or some of those concerned and to act as their representative. The biblical term for identification in this context is "love," and James refers to the second great commandment as the *royal* law of love (2 : 8). If those in the situation accept my love, I receive power from them to act on their behalf. My love may, however, be rejected, as Christ's was: "He came to his own home, and his own people did not receive him" (John 1 : 11). To the extent that I understand that Christ by his incarnation identified himself perfectly with them, I shall, through my identification with Christ, be able to identify myself with them, whether they reject me or not. In this instance, the power I have to act, of which they will be most conscious, is from God.

8. I bring to this situation my own experience and knowledge of other situations, which now become part of my resources in the situation under discussion. Loyalties to those outside this particular situation may enable me to draw upon resources greater than myself; but they may also decrease my level of involvement and consequently my ability to resolve the moral issues involved.

9. Does this situation bear any resemblance to events in the Bible in which it is made clear what God is doing? Do passages in the Bible, which in the past have disclosed God to me, illuminate the present situation, making me aware of the Living God in it?

10. As the totality of the situation comes into clearer focus, I become increasingly aware of the activity of God through the processes and persons concerned. To the extent that I am aware of God, I shall be able to respond in obedience to him. This obedience may take various forms. It may be a decision, a judgment, the formulation of a principle, the writing of a letter to a newspaper, the passing of a law, a book or a single word.

## Ethics and Involvement

It is thus obvious that only those who are voluntarily or involuntarily involved in any situation are in a position to discern its reality and to say what should be done. The only question we can ask with any seriousness is, What must *I* do? This does not mean that we should look upon ourselves as isolated individuals knowing nothing about what other people should do, but that we cannot tell anyone else what to do before we have considered our own responsibility to act. Kant's maxim that the individual should act only in such a way that his action could be made a universal law is correct only if one adds that the law would apply only to those in identical positions. The ethical dilemma of the pacifist is not solved by letting him work in a munitions factory instead of firing the rifle the factory makes.

The writer of this essay is committed to the boundaries of his own experience. Here he becomes painfully conscious that he is only dimly aware of his involvement in many of the burning issues of modern society—the H-bomb, the color bar, endemic poverty, overpopulation. His involvement is due to identification with a wide variety of people, through whom he has been concerned at one time or another with most of the acute problems in Britain. This consultant role qualifies him to interpret social ethics as a discipline but not to take a kingly role himself in relation to many of these situations, because, as a consultant, he has no authority or power to act in them.

It makes ethical judgments tedious to say that not until someone involved in the situation is able to describe its reality and to see the way God is acting in that situation is he able to begin to formulate his own action; but we are left no other choice.

# 6

# LUTHER'S "TWO KINGDOMS" ETHIC RECONSIDERED

by WILLIAM H. LAZARETH (United States)

### *Barth's Attack on Lutheran Quietism*

Since the Second World War, Lutherans have been forced to rethink the biblical and theological foundation of their social ethics. Prompted by all the anguish of the war, Karl Barth charged German Lutheranism with social ethical bankruptcy and traced this weakness back to Luther's controversial doctrine of the "two kingdoms" of creation and redemption. In an open letter to French Protestants in 1939, he said:

The German people suffer from the heritage of the greatest German Christian, from the error of Martin Luther with respect to the relationship of law and gospel, of worldly and spiritual order and power, by which its (the world's) natural paganism has not been so much limited and restricted as ideologically transfigured, confirmed, and even strengthened.... Hitlerism is the present evil dream of the German pagan who first became Christianized as a Lutheran.

Barth went still further in a 1940 wartime letter to the Dutch Protestants. He wrote:

To a certain extent, Lutheranism has provided a breathing space for German paganism, and—with its separation of creation and law from the gospel—has allotted it something like a sacral precinct. It is possible for the German pagan to use the Lutheran doctrine of the authority of the state as a Christian justification for National Socialism, and it is possible for the German Christian to feel himself invited by the same doctrine to a recognition of National Socialism. Both have in fact occurred.[1]

Barth's position must be judged in the context of recent European theological developments. A theology of "orders of creation" (*Schöpfungsordnungen*), promoted by some influential German Lutherans in the 1930's, badly corrupted a Christ-centered interpretation of Christian ethics. It moved in the direction of idealistic philosophy, natural theology, and an autonomous primal revelation of God in creation (see Althaus, Gogarten, Hirsch). At its worst, it was twisted by the Nazified *Deutsche Christen* party to sanctify their heresies of *Blut und Boden*. They offered a pseudo-Lutheran view of orders of creation (for example, the state), which made them a "law unto themselves," sacrosanct sources of divine revelation parallel to and independent of God's normative self-revelation in Jesus Christ.

In order to salvage the realm of God's creation from such non-biblical perversions, Barth affirmed the *de facto* Lordship of the cosmic Christ over the "outer circle" of the state as well as over the "inner circle" of the church. By fusing the reigning Christ of the New Testament with the theocratic ideal of the Old Testament, he emerged with a "christocratic" ethic that seriously weakened the Pauline opposition between the law (work-righteousness) and the gospel (faith-righteousness) as competing ways of salvation.

Barth offered instead the novel hermeneutical principle: "The law is nothing else than the necessary form of the gospel, whose content is grace." [2] This conflation of the realms of justification and justice (*Rechtfertigung und Recht*) permitted him to suggest "examples of analogies and corrolaries of that Kingdom of God in which the church believes and which it preaches, in the sphere of the external, relative, and provisional problems of the civil community." [3]

Employing language strangely reminiscent of the liberal theology he originally set out to destroy, Barth justified his approach on the ground that it is part of the church's mission "to set in motion

---

[1] The full texts of both letters are in KARL BARTH: *Eine Schweizer Stimme, 1938–1945*. Zollikon-Zürich: Evangelischer Verlag, 1948.

[2] BARTH: *Community, State and Church: Three Essays*. New York: Doubleday Anchor, 1960, p. 80.

[3] *Ibid.*, p. 179.

the historical process whose aim and content are the moulding of the state into the likeness of the Kingdom of God." [4]

For most Lutherans, Barth's so-called "christological monism" represents an understandable but indefensible reaction against the Nazified *Deutsche Christen* movement. Hermeneutically, his reversed sequence of gospel-law does not permit God's new covenant in Christ to purify as well as fulfill his old covenant with Israel. Theologically, this downgrades the unique work of God the Sanctifier in the church, and works its way out in the direction of a "christological" universalism. Ethically, this also downgrades the preserving work of God the Creator in society, and works its way out in the direction of a "christocratic" clericalism. In a noble attempt to check the godless autonomy of a modern secularized state, Barth seems to have substituted Christ's *de facto* rule over the world in a "theology of glory" for his *de jure* rule through the witness of the church in a "theology of the cross."

The basic fact remains, however, that Barth has properly exposed the "soft underbelly" of Lutheran social ethics in the realm of creation. Lutherans have been far more responsible in the realm of redemption. They have rightly stressed the redemptive significance of Christ, grace, Scripture, faith and the gospel. But they have often neglected the crucial importance of the nonredemptive counterparts: Caesar, nature, tradition, reason and the law. Lutherans must quickly recapture and boldly champion the Reformer's appreciation of the "sacred secularity" of civil life, which is at once free from church-rule and yet subject to God-rule.

In brief, there is nothing so sick about Lutheran ethics that a strong dose of Luther cannot cure it! We can echo the judgment of H. Richard Niebuhr:

More than any great Christian leader before him, Luther affirmed the life in culture as the sphere in which Christ could and ought to be followed. . . . Luther's answer to the Christ-and-culture question was that of a dynamic, dialectical thinker. Its reproductions by many who called themselves his followers were static and undialectical. They substituted two parallel moralities for his closely related ethics. As faith became a matter of belief rather than the fundamental, trustful orienta-

---

[4] *Ibid.*, p. 171.

tion of the person in every moment before God, so the freedom of the Christian man became autonomy in all the spheres of culture.

It is a great error to confuse the parallelistic dualism of separated spiritual and temporal life with the interactionism of Luther's gospel of faith working through love in the world of culture.[5]

## *Luther and the Augsburg Confession*

The biblical message of salvation is, for Luther, a tension-filled unity that can be viewed from the perspective of any one of its constitutive elements. He can speak of "grace alone," "Christ alone," "scripture alone" or "faith alone" and mean, thereby, the same saving event in terms of its eternal source, historical expression, apostolic witness, or personal appropriation. In fidelity to this Christ-centered faith, Luther roundly condemned the moral and rational work-righteousness inherent in the philosophical theology of Rome in his day. Before God, reason must submit to Scripture, and works must bow to faith. In an evangelical "theology of the cross," men humbly confess that "the righteous shall live by faith" (Romans 1 : 17).

With their salvation thus assured in the unmerited forgiveness of Christ, grateful Christians are free to redirect their reason and good works toward serving their neighbors' welfare. Luther grounds his ethic in the paradoxical nature of Christian freedom, which accepts liberation from satanic bondage as the invitation to human service. All men act as their brother's keeper: willingly in faith, begrudgingly in rebellion. Since the Christian is at once righteous and sinful, his enforced service aids his self-discipline, and his voluntary service meets his neighbors' needs. Against the presumption of Roman clericalism, Luther insists that all baptized Christians be permitted the beneficial exercise of their royal priesthood in loving service to their God-given neighbors.

In opposition to all unevangelical ethics of principles, "blue laws," ideals or rules and regulations, Luther portrays the biblical pattern of a life of "faith working through love" (Galatians 5 : 6). A Christian ethic based on the "divine indicative" of God's grace

---

[5] H. RICHARD NIEBUHR: *Christ and Culture*. New York: Harper & Brothers, 1951, pp. 174, 179.

(rather than the "divine imperative" of God's law) preserves the freedom of the believer, under the guidance of the Holy Spirit through the Bible, the church and prayer, to discover anew in each situation what the will of God permits or requires of him then and there.

Biblically, Luther rooted his doctrine of the "two kingdoms" of creation and redemption in the Pauline eschatology of the "two ages" (aeons) in Adam and in Christ (Romans 5). In the Kingdom of God, the Redeemer rules all regenerate believers through Christ and the gospel by personal faith and love. In the kingdom of men, the Creator rules all sinful creatures through Caesar and the law by civil justice and order. As both Redeemer and Creator, God is at once the Lord of both kingdoms; as both righteous and sinful, the Christian is at once a subject of both kingdoms. Hence, for an evangelical theology of society, the two kingdoms must always be properly distinguished, but never separated in secularism or equated in clericalism.

In this doctrine of the "two kingdoms" of creation and redemption, Luther reaffirmed the "sacred secularity" of the ordinary tasks of the common life that serve our neighbors' needs to God's glory. Whether empowered by Christ in faith-activated love (Christian righteousness) or compelled by Caesar in law-abiding reason civil righteousness), the Christian citizen lives not for himself but for the benefit of others.

Christian social action was a major concern in Luther's own life and thought. The profound effects of the Reformation in the area of religion are common knowledge to all. What is not so well known—or, at least, not so commonly acknowledged—is the impressive social reformation that Luther's theology envisioned and even partially brought about in the common life. Here, Luther's contribution to a better world is incalculable.

This emancipation of the common life was not so popular a crusade as might be supposed. Luther's understanding of the Christian ethical life compelled him to combat the two extremes of clericalism and secularism as unevangelical. From the outset, he had to fight for the preservation of music, art and sculpture in the worship life of the church (*Against the Heavenly Prophets*). Against Roman Catholics, he had to struggle for the opening of the monasteries and the freedom of all Christians to marry and to engage in secular pursuits without endangering their salvation (*On Monastic Vows: On Married Life*). Against recalcitrant parents and lax public officials, he fought for educational reforms and the establishment of community chests to replace the illiteracy and begging so prevalent in his day (*On Keeping Children in School; Preface to an Ordinance of a Common Chest*). Against irresponsible merchants, he attacked economic injustice and proposed government controls to halt unfair commercial and labor practices (*On Trading and Usury*). Against both the reckless mobs who confused their Christian freedom with their civil rights, and the arbitrary rulers who disregarded their responsibility under God for their subjects' economic and social welfare, Luther appealed both for civil obedience and—less strongly!—for political justice in a community of law and order (*Admonition to Peace; Exposition of the Eighty-Second Psalm*).

It is true, however, that Luther did not normally conceive of the Christian's social responsibility as including transformation of the existing structures of society. In the Kingdom of God, persons can be transformed by the gospel, but in the kingdom of men, institutions can only be reformed by the law. Men are to accept the social structures for what they are (the Creator's dikes against sin) and try to act as responsible Christian citizens within them (as the Redeemer's channels of serving love). When our secular occupations among men are faithfully acknowledged to be part of our religious vocation under God, then love provides law with its ethical content, and law provides love with its social form.

For example, against those who would spiritualize marriage into a Christian sacrament, Luther protests that marriage belongs essentially to the realm of creation, and not redemption. It is therefore ruled by God's law and not his gospel, and, as such, it is one of God's temporal remedies against sin, and not a sanctifying means of grace.

On the other hand, against those who would interpret this liberating message as justification for carnal lust and license, Luther is equally insistent that marriage is rooted firmly in the creative will of God as one of his own divine ordinances. Although it is not a sacrament of the church, there is nevertheless no higher social calling in which a Christian can exercise his faith in deeds of serving love for his family and neighbors. Hence, the former monk, Luther, eventually married—a public testimony to his view of marriage and home life under God.

For Luther's social ethic, all offices and stations of life—ecclesiastical, domestic, economic, political—embody in institutional form a particular command of God's law. They are all integrated within the earthly kingdom of men as the Creator's divinely ordained bulwarks in his ongoing struggles against Satan. There is no particularly "Christian" form of these "orders." Though corrupted by sin, the "orders" are still the means by which the Creator graciously preserves his fallen world from even greater chaos, injustice and suffering.

This is why the church can "Christianize" politicians and economists, but not politics and economics. These "orders" are ordained by God to remain secular and to enjoy a relative autonomy of their own under the sovereign law of the Creator. Hence, not faith and love, but reason and justice are normative for the temporal realm of life. At the same time, however, it cannot be emphasized too strongly—against the background of the *Deutsche Christen* tragedy—that faith can illumine reason, and love can temper justice whenever Christians meet their civil responsibilities as part of their religious discipleship. Lutherans, above all, need to learn anew from Luther that it is only through the priestly service of Christian citizens and the prophetic judgment of Christian churches that the state's "sacred secularity" is saved from godless secularism.

To conclude this brief survey of the Lutheran Reformation heritage in the area of Christian ethics, we shall cite four articles from the Augsburg Confession in which Luther's restatement of the central thrust of Paul's ethic is afforded normative authority by the Lutheran Church.

On the personal level, Article IV rejects all moral work-righteousness by grounding man's salvation solely in his being justified before God for Christ's sake through faith alone. Article VI militates against any ethical quietism by affirming that this Christian faith—"a living, busy, active thing"—is bound to bring forth good fruits, and that it is also necessary for Christians to do those good works that are commanded by God for their neighbors' benefit.

On the social level, Article XVI guards against secularism by insisting that Christians are not to espouse any rigorous dualism between the "two kingdoms" of creation and redemption, but are rather to permeate all of society with personal love and social justice in the exercise of their Christian social responsibility. Finally, Article XXVIII complements this stress with a rejection of clericalism by sharply distinguishing the valid functions of the church and the state in the two kingdoms and by refusing to permit the church to make civil laws that fall properly within the domain of the state.

It is relatively easy to demonstrate the ways in which the Nazified *Deutsche Christen* misinterpreted the social ethic of Luther and the Lutheran confessions. Far more crucial, however, is the corollary challenge that now confronts those Christians who believe that Luther's social doctrine, in its essential features, is a valid restatement of Paul's eschatology of the "two ages" of Adam and Christ (Romans 5). Can we demonstrate that this is a relevant biblical answer both to the false heteronomy of the *Corpus Christianum* and to the equally false autonomy of *Nausea* and *No Exit?* Can this doctrine be "demedievalized" and sufficiently qualified so that it will help shape the daily lives of both Christians and non-Christians in a world "come of age"? The remainder of this chapter represents a halting first step in that direction.

## Lutheran Social Ethics: Christocentric Depth and Trinitarian Breadth

Evangelical Christianity embraces both a religious faith and an ethical way of life. Creed and deed may be distinguished but never separated, as faith supplies the power, and love the direction, for a life committed to the Lordship of Jesus Christ. Both are determined by the biblical gift and command of a righteous life dedicated to the love of God and neighbor. Religiously, the emphasis is placed on "the righteous who shall live by *faith.*" Ethically, stress is given to "the righteous who by faith shall *live.*" But this interaction of man's God-given faith and life constitutes an organic unity in which the Christian religion and ethic complement each other as root and fruit of the same God-pleasing tree. Faith gives life its religious meaning, while life gives faith its ethical opportunities.

Conceived of in this dynamic fashion, Christian ethics may be defined as that branch of theology that is concerned with the social activity of men as "the coworkers of God," through whom he governs the common life of society. The Christian life is essentially man's faithful re-enactment of God's loving act in Christ. It is God's love channeled through man's faithful deeds meeting his neighbors' needs.

Furthermore, it is a central affirmation of Christian theology that God rules the whole of his creation through the power of his Holy Word. This affirmation includes both the demands of his law and the promises of his gospel. By the law, God rules men as their Creator and Judge; by the gospel, he rules them as their Redeemer and Sanctifier. This means that all of God's sinful creatures are subject to his law, but only Christians—as both righteous and sinful—are responsible under God's law and gospel alike.

This divine power complex provides Christian ethics with its twofold task. On the one hand, it performs a prophetic mission by calling all of society to account for its conduct in keeping with the universal law of God (civil righteousness). On the other, it performs a priestly mission by empowering and guiding the ethical activity of Christians in their faithful practice of brotherly love and community service (Christian righteousness). By employing the double-edged sword of God's Word in this dialectical fashion, Christian ethics remains faithful to the normative pattern of Christ's ministry by judging a rebellious society from without, while at the same time serving it from within.

The peculiar characteristics of an evangelical ethic are determined by its fidelity to the ongoing activity of the living triune God. Men learn to do God's will once they are enlisted in his service against the forces of evil in this world. Created in, and in the process of being restored to, God's holy and loving image, Christians can best determine what they should be doing by first learning what God is doing. Holy Scripture clearly testified that God provides all the resources necessary for a life devoted to the faithful stewardship of his manifold gifts in keeping with his sovereign will. As Creator, God supplies the Christian life with its theater of action; as Redeemer, he provides its pattern and style; as Sanctifier, he generates its motives and power.

1. *When incorporated into the divine work of God the Redeemer, the Christian ethic is seen first as an ethic of freedom.* To be a Christian is to accept what God has done for man's salvation in the person and work of Jesus Christ. It is to receive Christ as personal Lord and Savior, acknowledging that on the Cross of Calvary, the Son of God atoned for man's sin in his stead. It is to share through faith in the blessed fruits of Christ's righteousness. These fruits center in reconciliation with man's sin-forgiving Father and in redemption from the evil forces of sin, death and the devil. The Christian is freed from rebellious slavery for a life of faithful, hopeful and loving service.

This is what it means for man to be "justified by grace through faith for Christ's sake unto good works." This is the glorious gospel message of the mighty act of God in Christ. This is the "divine indicative" of God's gracious action, which always precedes the ethical actions (or better, response) of Christian men.

This liberating power of Christian faith as a life-transforming commitment to a personal Savior—rather than to an impersonal ideology, system of thought or institutional structure—militates against any ethic that would once again subject men to the yoke of self-righteous legalism. Nevertheless, every Christian age and tradition has been tempted to deny that "Christ has set us free for freedom" (Galatians 5 : 1). Work-righteousness, whether in its moralistic form in types of Catholicism and Calvinism, or in its rationalistic version in types of Lutheranism and Anglicanism, is a perennial danger for evangelical ethics. Christians do not have "merits to earn," "principles to apply," "ideals to realize" or "rules to obey." Rather, they have a crucified and risen Lord "whose service is perfect freedom."

2. *When incorporated into the divine work of God the Sanctifier, the Christian ethic may also be viewed as an ethic of grace.* It is God and not man who generates the unselfish love that Christians try to transmit to their neighbors. It is the Living Lord himself who acts through Christians who have dedicated their lives to

becoming the willing instruments of his love. For to be a Christian means not only to accept what Christ has once done for us and our religious salvation (justification); it also means to accept what he continually does in and through us for our ethical service (sanctification). Whomever God declares righteous by grace through faith, he makes righteous by grace through love.

The Holy Spirit resides in the hearts of Christians and enables them to exercise his gifts of peace, love and joy, as regenerated "little Christs" to their neighbors. Living within the community of grace we call the church, Christians are constantly nourished by God's Word in sermon and sacrament to empower their growth in grace as new creatures in a new age. However tarnished by the forgiven sin that still remains in their hearts, the social action of Christians is acceptable to God as the "Christian righteousness" of faith active in love.

Christians, certain of the righteousness of God through faith in Jesus Christ, are free both personally and corporately to join with other men of good will—whatever their faith—in working together for more just civil approximations of the moral law of God. Such cooperation is possible in the temporal realm of "civil righteousness" because some form of God's law (however corrupted by sin) is to be found written on the hearts of all men created in his image. Through the common insights of God's general witness apart from Holy Scripture, enlightened men of all faiths can agree on many key features of personal morality and public legality. Fortunately, justice among men is not dependent on justification before God. Non-Christians who may not fulfill the spirit of God's law in faith and love are still able to obey the law's letter in reason and justice (often to the shame and judgment of more apathetic Christians). Consequently, as we shall note more fully below, Christians will find it necessary and beneficial to cooperate with all conscientious "children of light" in the ongoing struggle for peace, justice and freedom in the world.

3. *When incorporated into the divine work of God the Creator, the Christian ethic may finally be considered a social ethic.* This does not mean, of course, that the Christian has no personal responsibilities. What it does mean is that the man of faith views his personal responsibilities from the perspective and within the to-

tality of the myriad of communal commitments and relationships in which he is inevitably and inextricably involved.

God never lets man "go it alone" as a nonrelated "rugged individual." Insofar as man is righteous, he is ruled by God's gospel as one among many members of the corporate Body of Christ. It is his participation in this religious community that inspires his ethical service. But, insofar as he remains a sinful creature, that same man is ruled by God's law as he "renders to Caesar" all that is expected of him in the civil community as a loyal citizen, industrious worker, and responsible husband, parent and neighbor. Whether at church or at home, in school or factory, the Christian always finds himself living within God-preserved social structures in the midst of neighbors with concrete needs, which await his personal love and social justice. Faith incorporates our earthly occupation into our heavenly vocation through the social action of the priesthood of all believers.

Christians have not always been faithful to their dual responsibilities as citizens of the "two kingdoms" of redemption and creation. Instead of nurturing community-minded individuals and individual-minded communities, misguided Christans have often espoused a truncated ethic that has led them into either a false individualism or a false collectivism. Perhaps the former is more common to Protestant piety, in which a man often limits his ethical concerns to his own immediate, personal contacts, and permits the more impersonal social structures of the community to become "a law unto themselves," in a godless ethos permeated by secularism. On the other hand, Roman Catholic piety has sometimes encouraged a collectivistic ethos in which the institutional church and its hierarchy are permitted to dominate the temporal affairs of men in political and economic life, thereby inviting the equally dangerous evils of clericalism.

It is precisely at this concluding point that we should recall the Barthian critique of Lutheran ethical quietism. In attempting to translate Luther's theology into the twentieth century, we must never forget to shift the ethical accent, since his chief enemy was clericalism, whereas ours is secularism. Luther had to put the church back under the gospel; we must put the state and society back under God's law.

Let no one underestimate the difficulty of this mission. Yet many unnecessary obstacles might be removed at the outset if Christians would properly distinguish the gospel of redemption from the law of creation and then differentiate the law's theological function to condemn sin from its political function to promote justice. Especially in our pluralistic culture, men and women who cannot worship together under the gospel must find more ways in which they can work together under the law. In mapping out the terrain, Christian social ethicists can perform an incomparable service.

For example, is there not a "hard core" of nonredemptive morality in what Lutherans call "civil righteousness," what Calvinists call "common grace," what recent ecumenical statements call "middle axioms," what Roman Catholics call "natural law," what Jews call "social justice" and what secularists call "enlightened self-interest"? Even Karl Barth is compelled to admit, "It cannot be denied, however, that in the lists of examples [of ethical guidelines] quoted, we have more than once made assertions which have been justified elsewhere on the basis of natural law." [6] Well, as Shakespeare said, ". . . a rose by any other name. . . ."

Lutherans must now be challenged to make their contribution to this mighty ecumenical effort. Their traditional concentration on the gospel has energized a sound evangelical personal ethic: "faith active in love." But the vast realm of corporate structures and institutional life has often thereby been deprived of the normative judgment and guidance of God's law by the church's neglect of a corresponding social ethic: "love seeking justice." Though responsible for the proclamation of the whole Word of God, Lutherans have generally put much stronger emphasis on the personal appropriation of God's gospel (for politicians and economists) than on the social demands of God's law (for politics and economic life).

In short, what Lutherans need desperately today is a prophetic counterpart of the priesthood of all believers. Evangelical Christians will be reverent to God's Word as well as relevant to God's world by expressing both their priestly Yes, through faith active in love, and their prophetic No, through love seeking justice.

---

[6] *Community, State and Church, op. cit.,* p. 180.

# PART II

## THEOLOGY IN ECUMENICAL
## SOCIAL THINKING

# 7

# THE THEOLOGY OF THE RESPONSIBLE SOCIETY

by H. D. WENDLAND (Germany)

IN describing the theology of the ecumenical movement, W. A. Visser 't Hooft speaks of a "substantial consensus," in the churches that are members of the World Council, on the importance of a "responsible society." [1] Ecumenical discussions on social questions in the last few years, particularly at the WCC Assembly in New Delhi (1961) and the International Study Conference in Salonika (1959) on the problems of rapid social change have been guided by the theme of the responsible society and have developed the many concrete demands and implications that define the concept and give it substance. These meetings did not resume the discussion of the theological basis of the idea of the responsible society initiated at Amsterdam, but we must take up this inquiry again to avoid misinterpretation and to relate it creatively to particular socio-ethical demands. It is necessary to define more clearly the theological and ethical character of this concept and to clarify its meaning in relation to the dynamic society of today.

## Freedom and Responsibility

In interpreting the idea of the responsible society, it is necessary to draw certain distinctions. The first is between individual and social responsibility. Responsible society implies more than a re-

---

[1] *The Pressure of Our Calling.* London: SCM Press, 1959, p. 59.

sponsibility on the part of the individual members of that society. Individual responsibility involves merely personal ethics and leaves unresolved the question of which social spheres and which persons the individual is to be responsible for. At the same time, the individual's responsibility is limited and defined by his place in society. Therefore, we must go beyond the demand of personal ethics, and "act as responsible men." Every individual plays a variety of roles in society, as a member of a family, an industry, a trade union, an economic association, a political party and so forth. In every instance, his responsibility is limited by other co-responsible persons. The socio-ethical insight of the Reformers that the individual's responsibility is assigned to him through his "station in life" [2] is still valid. However, it has to be adapted, because the varying responsibilities resulting from the individual's many social roles are sometimes in conflict with one another. In this situation, the responsible society would be interpreted as, "Act responsibly according to the norm in the various roles that you fill in society." [3] These norms indicate the particular persons and matters for which the individual is responsible, and then indicate in which spheres and social relationships he can act responsibly.

But the opportunity to act responsibly does not depend solely upon the individual's sense of responsibility and personal commitment; it also depends upon the structure of the social institutions that assign him his place. Ecumenical use of the term "responsible society" makes it clear that it implies demands not only upon the individual but also upon institutions in society.

These institutions should be organized in such a manner that the individual is able to act freely and to live responsibly within them and with their help. In the light of the purely hierarchical structure of traditional society, this appears as a truly revolutionary demand. It implies that all institutions of society shall be built on the foundation of freedom; and it requires us "to take seriously hu-

---

[2] *Neu-Delhi, 1961: Dokumentarbericht,* deutsche Fassung (*New Delhi, 1961: Reports and Documents,* German edition), W. A. VISSER 'T HOOFT, ed. Stuttgart: 1962, pp. 110ff.

[3] OTTO HEINRICH VON DER GABLENTZ: "Der politische Auftrag der Kirche" in *Christliche Gemeinde und Gesellschaftswandel* ("The Political Mission of the Church" in *Christian Church and Social Change*), I. Beckman and G. Weisser, eds. Stuttgart: 1964, p. 217.

manism and personalism. Man is superior to every institution." [4]
Hence the rejection of every type of absolutism of any institution,
not only of the totalitarian state but also of every heteronomous
institutional structure (Paul Tillich).

The consequences of such a demand are far-reaching. Rightly
understood, this criterion of a responsible society indicates that
the process of fundamentally democratizing modern society will be
pursued in every sphere to the end. Therefore, any pronouncements about social ethics will have to take into account personal,
social and political freedom. Consequently, as the ecumenical statements on social questions testify, directly and indirectly on every
page, a Christian social ethic developed on the basis of the concept of the responsible society must be cast in a different mold
from that of Christian social ethics before the Enlightenment and
the revolutionary emancipation that followed. The earlier Christian social ethics were orientated to very differently structured social institutions: for example, those having a hierarchical basis.

This emphasis on freedom poses anew, in regard to the whole
range of social life, the question: "person-institution." Even dynamic society today has institutions that support and "unburden"
the individual, and he has to fit into these all-embracing institutions, which organize and integrate great numbers of people. Among
these institutions, the legal order is the noblest, because it integrates
all the members of a social body, though for the sociologist it represents only one particular form of social integration among others.

In a society based on the fundamental precondition of freedom,
social coordination and integration are clearly difficult, because the
traditional, sanctified authorities are no longer absolute. The monopoly of one ruling class or elite no longer exists. The power of
those who actually wield power is no longer sacrosanct. The individual is no longer the unquestioning subordinate. He is neither
merely subject to the powers-that-be nor an element within a
"higher whole" (as a romantic social philosophy used to teach).

---

[4] GERHARD WEISSER: "Das Postulat 'verantwortliche Gesellschaft' er-
kenntniskritisch und sozialwissenschaftlich erörtert" in *Christliche Gemeinde
und Gesellschaftswandel* ("The Postulate 'Responsible Society' discussed
from an Epistemological and Social-Scientific Point of View" in *Christian
Church and Social Change*), pp. 70ff., especially pp. 81f.

Nonetheless, countless individuals have to live and work together in a great variety of social relationships and roles that are remote from one another. Rational organization has developed forms of functional cooperation and of technical management of the work of society. A society of free and equal men must seek new ways of social integration and should be building and planning new institutions. Emancipation, as such, does indeed do away with the old order, in which the individual is without freedom (*Unfreiheit*), but it cannot create a new order of society by itself.

The free individual, however, does not have the freedom of an absolute ego. As the phrase "responsible society" implies, "free" and "responsible" are complementary terms. Freedom is to be conceived as responsible freedom. Whatever the situation, we are free with others and for others. The individual is defined by his relation to his fellowmen, by "being-with-others." To be a responsible person is to accept one's fellowman, to acknowledge him, to receive him into one's own person, to "respond" to him. Freedom without responsibility would no longer be the human freedom of the person but an inhuman attempt to isolate the self by repelling and rejecting one's fellowman; it would be, in fact, emancipation *from* responsibility.

Observations like these are beyond the scope of an empirical socio-scientific analysis of social groups and institutions. However, if we assert that man is called to responsible existence with others, a social ethic is possible only if the "true" relationship between man and man is presented over against all existing social orders. This recognition of the responsible bond between man and man is, at the same time, a statement about the "true being" of man: It testifies to his true destiny according to the Christian faith. An ecumenical-Christian ethic (the beginnings of which are discernible) would be impossible if it limited itself to historically and geographically confined Christian traditions and did not venture ontological-ethical statements (which, in this double sense, are also statements on "natural law"). Yet such statements are made in relation to man in society (present and future), and this historical relation distinguishes them from all allegedly "pure," timeless, ontological definitions of human existence. It is the task of such Christian ethical affirmations to assert that the "ultimate" vocation of modern man is to live with others and to serve them. Freedom and responsibility are the medium or instrument through which this humanity is expressed and through which the church proclaims the "eternal" destiny of man. Accepting the historical presupposition of social freedom and equality, the church interprets them in the light of the "ultimate" destiny of man—as God's creature, fellow worker and servant—to be the man of God.

However, the ecumenical social ethic cannot limit itself to an appeal to the individual to realize his responsibility for his fellow-man. Admittedly, such imperatives have their place in the preaching and educational work of the Christian church, all the more so since it should set an example in loving and serving others, especially all those who are in want and distress.

But there is a socio-ethical task that is far greater than the historically limited effectiveness of the churches and the imperatives applying to them. This is the formation and handing down of socio-ethical conventions that everyone in society can understand and observe, the demands of a general social ethos, binding and expressing the responsibility of all in every aspect of life.

## Partnership as an Element of Responsible Society

Such a demand is implied in the concept of partnership which finds expression today in all fields where people cooperate and which indicates an ethical necessity characteristic of modern society.[5] Partnership expresses a sense of human solidarity among people who are free and equal. At the same time, it presupposes different social positions, which are bound together through cooperation; for example, the cooperation necessary in a productive enterprise if it is to be efficient. Without some simple rules of hu-

---

[5] Cf. WENDLAND: *Einführung in die Sozialethik* (*Introduction into Social Ethics*). Berlin: Sammlung Göschen Band 1203, 1963, pp. 117ff, on the future of society; and pp. 122ff., on the responsible society.

I am using here some observations from my book, *Person und Gesellschaft in evangelischer Sicht,* 1963, pp. 34ff. The concept of partnership is a socio-ethical term used here solely as an aid in explaining the concept "responsible society." Everywhere today there is talk of partnership—in production, between employers and employees, between nations, within supranational economic bodies, and between individuals, as for instance between men and women. It is a concept that has won widespread acceptance and that shows clearly the need of our times for new principles of social order.

man behavior, social institutions cannot last, however rationally they may be organized and however efficiently they may function. The life of an institution is not shaped by its written constitution or charter, but by unwritten, recognized rules of behavior. Convention and institution condition each other. Working toward a responsible society means developing conventions through which members of society are trained to realize their responsibility for others and which will help them to understand both themselves and others as active partners who are co-responsible for the institution.

Partnership is not identical with personal responsibility or with what in German is called *Gemeinschaft* (community). Partnership is a particular form of relationship within certain given social conditions, especially those involving differences in the social position of individuals and the resulting social differentiation between them. Partnership recognizes the necessity of such differences, but it is opposed to the formation of classes; it insists, for instance, that the dependent employee shall at the same time be recognized as a co-responsible associate, that he shall be treated, legally and ethically, as a partner, and that a cooperative structure shall be developed that takes account not only of the differentiation between positions but also of the human equality of persons. Class privileges or paternalism within industry are as incompatible with partnership as is the ideological freezing of social distinctions ("class struggle"). Though social differences are a necessity in a society based on freedom, they must be integrated into legal institutions, de-ideologized and humanized. For example, women workers in industrial society must be protected by law against downgrading to second-class status as employees or workers. It is precisely this legal-ethical control of social differences that is the goal of the demand for partnership, and, for this reason, it tends toward organized cooperation and, in the service of cooperation, toward an open and continuous dialogue between the partners.

Seen from the viewpoint of the guiding concept of the responsible society, this search for partnership, originating at various points in society, should be affirmed in an ecumenical social ethic, for it is only through partnership that a responsible society can be built up. Partnership as a way of conduct for the members of society is an element of social humanity and is not identical with the brotherly love bestowed and insisted on by Christ. Brotherly love, however, should make use of partnership as a form of practicing human solidarity that will pave the way toward reducing social differences and toward cooperation between those in different social positions. By accepting the demand for partnership, the Christian ethic is meeting a deep need in our highly organized society and is answering a socio-ethical problem.

### Responsible Society as the Purpose of Social Organization

Gerhard Weisser is right in insisting that we define more accurately what we mean by speaking of the responsible society as an aim of our action. This involves distinguishing between fundamental decisions and those which are provisional and conditioned by history.

The ordering of human society does not have the "ultimate character" of the eschatological *telos* of the kingdom of God, the end toward which God is leading the history of the world and mankind. The responsible society is not the kingdom of God on earth nor even a transitory stage or a bridge on the way to it, in the shape of a "Christian society"; the responsible society is secular and historical. The responsible society must and can exist for and among non-Christians. All states and all social bodies are called upon to became responsible societies. This is a universal and "humane" demand, because it is made for the sake of man and for his human dignity, for the sake of the social and political liberty of every man in every concrete historical society, for all continents and for all social and political systems. One need not be a Christian to be convinced of the benefit, for human society, of this demand. One need not become a Christian in order to work for its realization.

Further, this demand has not the same status as the unconditional command to love our neighbor, a command as eternally valid as the gospel itself. The demand of the responsible society is not a divine command. It has certain historical bases and carries with it certain time-conditioned negations, like the protest against every kind of dehumanization and oppression of working people and against every kind of class or race domination. The socio-ethical maxim, "responsible society," is unthinkable without the whole modern movement for emancipation and enlightenment, which strives for a society based on the freedom and equality of its individual members. Even the necessary critique of this emancipation movement shows that the demand is related to and conditioned by history. On the other hand, the command to love one's neighbor, which discovers the neighbor in the "other person," was and still is valid, even in social systems where the responsible society could not even be conceived. However, the universal significance of the demand for a responsible society must be stressed, because it applies "globally" to the society of the whole world and not merely to "individual" societies of a single continent or a particular country. It is the expression of a "world-wide" humanism.

Is this distinction, between the demand of the responsible society and the absolute commandment to love, the last word on this matter? Is there no relationship between the two? The answer takes the form of a thesis: Love makes humanitarian demands and imposes humanitarian aims in the service of the welfare of all men. Ecumenical thinking shows clearly that the responsibility of the churches in and for the changing society of our day must be interpreted as helping toward the organization of a responsible society. If the church (meaning here the ecumenical brotherhood of the churches) is the advocate of man in this world, if it bears his burdens with him, if it cares for his cares, if it understands itself as a *serving* church, then, in the present situation, for the sake of man, it will insist on the responsible society as an expression of freedom and justice. In terms of the ecumenical fellowship of churches, it becomes a demand of Christian social ethics, because it must be the concern of the Christian church to help *all* men in society today to attain a truly human order of society. Love of one's neighbor includes the recognition of liberty and human dignity, because it recognizes that every man is created by God, with authority to cooperate in organizing life in this world, and called to the kingdom of God. It is love that makes *humanitas* the goal of social ethics, because it is the instrument whereby society is constantly revised and transformed in order to benefit man.

Within this society, as it is, there are indeed incalculable opportunities to love one's fellowmen; but it is precisely this love that by looking at the relationship of man to society and its institutions (state, organization of labor, and so on), evokes the demand for the responsible society and makes it the expression of its will to serve, its "social *diakonia*." This will be an historically limited expression of love, which, in other periods of history, may well be replaced by other demands. But, as far as can be judged now, the social-*critical* importance of the demand will remain "actual" for a long time to come, because it opposes man's subjugation to social and ideological forces (such as collectivism and racial hatred).[6] This approach means uniting the sober, critical realism of Christian ethics with the courage to set definite goals, "small" advances that are possible here and now.

Self-critical Christian thought will always be concerned to relate particular demands for small advances and partial solutions (such as reforms in agriculture or education or in the social and legal status of industrial workers) to the comprehensive goal of the responsible society. For all partial reforms receive their significance and norm from the ultimate goal, which is a "realistic utopia" insofar as it definitely transcends both the existing state of the social bodies and the particular demands and suggested reforms that seek to give it expression. Without this critical-transcendent character, the maxim "responsible society" would be ineffective, even meaningless. It would no longer be the pattern for the whole of society. As a result, both pessimists and pragmatists regard with suspicion this critical-revolutionary force of the not-yet-realized "utopia" of the future society. This utopia is relative and historically conditioned: It aims at a relatively better order of society, at social progress, at the abolition of social abuses and injustices; but it makes no illusory claim to absolute justice or to creating a totally "new" man or to removing all the contingencies of the historical world.

In the search for the goal of a *future* society,[7] the church and Christians have to fight ceaselessly against all forms of "unfreedom" and injustice. We must make this goal the theme of a dia-

---

6 *New Delhi* . . . , pp. 104ff., 110ff.: *Aufgaben und Möglichkeiten christlichen Handelns im raschen sozialen Umbruch* (Saloniki Report, official German edition), *Zeitschrift für evangelische Ethik*, 1960, pp. 257ff. (*Dilemmas and Opportunities: Christian Action in Areas of Rapid Social Change*) See also Note 1 above.

7 Saloniki Report, pp. 260ff., 269ff., 280ff., 294ff., etc.

logue with everyone, Christian or non-Christian, seeking thus to open the way to cooperation between churches and social groups, such as social and democratic reform movements, and perhaps even guiding this cooperation. All of us, Christians and non-Christians, churches and social organizations, need a critical norm and a definite goal for the future order of society for which we are jointly responsible and which we have to shape in such a way that all the groups within society can lead a decent human life, protected from impoverishment and oppression. We cannot formulate what should be done in individual regions or countries, for this depends on the particular economic and social state of the country concerned. On the other hand, the investigation of areas of rapid social change has shown that in these regions, there are many common needs and common problems [8] caused by the breakup of historical forms of society through technological developments and industrialization. In the face of these problems, the more the idea of comprehensive social and economic planning gains ground, the more urgently the question arises, What is the norm that will help us to decide what we are planning for?

Where the norm is freedom, limited by responsible partnership, and the commonweal of all the partners, the aim of political and social activity is neither economic prosperity as such, nor the enjoyment of affluence or power by particular groups in society. A class society is contrary to the aims of the responsible society; thus, it is a society that devotes itself solely to economic production and to the enjoyment of the resulting prosperity. An affluent society, living in plenty, or even in abundance, may well be a society acting "*ir*responsibly," because it regards mere economic achievement, the quantity of goods produced and the power of money as the supreme values and aims.

Consequently, the goal of a responsible society has nothing to do with any glorification of the "western" way of life and of the technical achievements of western civilization nor with any glorification of the absolute emancipation of the individual from all social bonds and responsibilities; nor has this goal anything to do with the illusion of an "absolute" revolution, which regards radical

---

[8] New Delhi . . . , *op. cit.*, p. 108.

negations as a sufficient basis for a new ordering of society. Western social traditions must therefore be subjected to the same critical standard of the responsible society as is applied to traditional feudalism or to any forms of modern collectivism. Only if this condition is met are we entitled to speak of the worldwide, universal importance and status of this aim; otherwise, it would prove dishonest and carry no weight, particularly in regions of rapid social change. Searching and comprehensive self-criticism on the part of the western churches and social groups is an essential precondition for the effective use and application of this guiding concept in all those areas that are going through the process of social change and political emancipation. It was rightly stated at the New Delhi Assembly that western culture is not *culture* pure and simple nor is it "Christian" culture.[9] But the *purpose and meaning* of technical and industrial civilization must be defined. Is this purpose its own justification, an absolute end in itself that needs no further justification? Or is it a means of bringing order and shape into society in accordance with the dignity of man?

The basic question today in all lands is, What is to be the position of man in the society of the future? Old and new ideologies and syncretistic social religions are offering themselves as the answer to this central question. Man's position in society necessarily involves another question, What is to be the order of society in an age of pluralism, of the differentiation and progressive expansion of organizations, particularly in a world that has been influenced by the historic attempts of socialism and communism to provide a solution? Using the goal of the responsible society, it is therefore necessary to develop more precise concepts of social order for the areas and countries of rapid social change, with special regard to their particular historical-social conditions. These concepts should indicate the opportunities that exist for shaping such an order, the possibilities, for example, of gradual democratization, or of an appropriate social policy designed to prevent the rise of a depressed proletariat, with no rights, in newly developing industrial regions and cities. Thus we must begin to plan an order of

---

9 HELMUT SCHELSKY: *Der Mensch in der Wissenschaftlichen Zivillsation* (*Man in Scientific Civilization*), Arbeitsgemeinschaft des Landes Nordrhein-Westfalen, Geisteswissenschaften Heft 96. Köln and Opladen: 1961, pp. 39ff.

society for man for his responsible freedom. The danger is that differences of social position will become frozen into a pseudo-sacral hierarchy; partnership and democracy must break through the differences and link people together without abolishing or leveling down the different positions. Even a purely functional hierarchy might cause a new class structure to develop. For that reason, democracy in the structure of institutions—the joint control of, and ordered share in, the direction and management of these institutions by the people in them—is one of the conditions for their "humanization." Social democracy in the form of widely differing institutions is the precondition for what is strictly called "political" democracy: It resists the perversion of democracy into a façade that conceals a dictatorship or total domination by a minority.

At the same time, responsible society does not demand the elimination or disintegration of rules and leadership. We know that in a democratic society there must be government by law. Responsible society has nothing to do with the illusion of a society without government, which could be organized solely through communal sentiment or, according to the claim of Christian enthusiasts, solely through love. What a responsible society demands is democratic constitution and control of the government and leadership, responsibility of those in power, and legally ordered joint control by the members of every society.

### The Responsible Society as a Postulate of Ecumenical Social Ethics

What do the image and object of a responsible society, the goal of a world-wide social policy based on a universal humanism, have to do with Christian ethics and with the "social *diakonia*" of the churches? This question must be taken up again.

It should now be clear that the presupposition for all that has been said is the awareness that the church of Christ has to evolve not merely an "ethic for Christians" valid for the "inner circle" of the congregation. The church confesses and proclaims the God who in Christ gives and offers himself to the "world," the God who has raised man and mankind to the dignity of his "ally" and his responsive-responsible partner; therefore man and human so-

ciety are committed to the care and compassionate service of the
church and are a legitimate theme of Christian ethics. If the church
was instituted not to rule men but to serve them, the Christian
ethic necessarily involves certain claims concerning the physical,
spiritual and social welfare of everyone; the church becomes the
advocate of *humanitas*. It is in this sense that the Christian ethic
formulates the principles and postulates of a Christian humanism
• that seeks to determine—in different social situations—what can
be done for the good of man. Hence, the Christian social ethic
must make demands of a general humane character, judicious and
realizable demands where they are related to social realities.

This corresponds exactly to the character and the fundamental
movement of agape as love of one's neighbor. Agape gives help
by using human, secular (for example, technical and scientific)
means in every imaginable form of social assistance. These "good
works" must meet three requirements: They must (1) do justice
to man, (2) meet people's needs and (3) be adapted to the situation. This is love's secular action. If love is *not* realized in this
way as social humaneness, then it is not really love of our "neighbor" but abstract idealism. If love does not issue in a social
*diakonia,* through understanding of the social conditions and problems that must determine any action, then it cannot perform any
true service. Without the realistic assessment of a given situation
and of the particular social status of man, love and *diakonia* become mere pious ideologies that produce pseudosolutions as harmful as the needs they were meant to meet.

By raising "humanist" demands and by advocating social-ethical
conventions in the service of men of every race and every social
group, the churches also bear in mind their own historical limitations, that is to say, their *minority position,* in large areas of the
world. They have a joint, not the sole, responsibility for social
welfare; they serve, but they do not rule. They are seeking to prove,
by social action that does justice to man, their own *ethical right to
be there*.

However, this ethical justification through practical action can
never be the "ultimate" justification for the church's world service.
This it can receive only from Christ through his grace as a gift by
means of the gospel. The church traces the origin of its responsi-

bility for man and for a truly human society back to its responsibility in the eyes of Christ, in whom God's love of the world was incarnate and who therefore commands us to love. It is from Christ himself that the church receives its function as an advocate in the service of man. Because Christ represents the restoration of man to his true nature, the church knows it is sent to serve men. The "ultimate," eschatological justification for the church's secular, humane action lies in the authority whereby Christ calls men into his church, gathers them and sends them into the world that is his "property." For the sake of Christ, the Christian church speaks humanely and ethically to men and reminds them of their calling to responsible *humanitas*. It speaks the language of the "myth of man" (his power and progress), which is the logical product of this society based on science and technology. But it also "demythologizes" this myth by destroying the utopia of a perfect society and the Promethean illusion that man could ever re-create himself into superman. Man's true greatness is that he is called to create a society fit for men to live in and to maintain it against its many enemies who do not recognize this goal and who try to suffocate it through oppression and injustice. To fight for a responsible society means to carry out this purpose within the institutions of society, which involves the ceaseless criticism, revision and reforms of their structures; to reckon with the constant tendency of this organizing and planning society to "manipulate" and "depersonalize" man through "social techniques" and to reckon equally with the tendency of all institutions to perpetuate themselves, to extend their powers and to become a law unto themselves. The guiding concept of a responsible society will have to be constantly reinterpreted to disclose the forces of perversion and dehumanization.

The ecumenical Christian social ethic must assume this task of criticizing society. It must not wait until other forces reveal society's shortcomings. For this reason, the churches must rid themselves of their inherited conservative determinism, which identifies given social structures with what is "natural" and therefore unalterable or which regards their obvious defects as an inevitable fate, in spite of the fact that history is showing day by day how changeable all social forms are, and how immense the transforming power of great social and political movements is. The conservative determinism in the church, no less than its Marxist opposite, is an ideology that conceals reality. It condones social evils that cannot be justified and tries to prevent their abolition by pointing, for example, to the sinfulness of man. The guilding concept of the responsible society, on the other hand, presupposes the changeability of social structures and the necessity for continually revising them.

Critical freedom in every direction, and awareness of anything that might bar the "way to social maturity" in the shape of "social immaturity" [10] are indispensable for an ecumenical social ethic that interprets the watchword "responsible society."

In this connection, the question arises whether the churches should not leave the task of shaping society entirely to the "mature," humanistic world, to society and its own social and political forces. Would this not prove that the church really does respect the "worldliness" (or secularity) of society and of the state? Is not the way in which we now talk of the "social *diakonia* of the church in the world" a survival of the old Christian desire to conquer the world, of an "ecclesiastical imperialism" that will only provoke new secularist and anticlerical ideologies? Have we not only half conceded and half denied the "competence" of society to organize itself and to evolve its own guiding concepts? Do we Christians talk of the problems and tasks of our society only because we are afraid of "lagging behind in the history of the world"? Do we make our comments always *post festum?*

No doubt, there are instances where Christian social thinking and speaking wrongly falls into a new Christian social ideology, and the criticism of such false Christian attitudes is one of the principal tasks of Christian theology and ethics.

Both the idea that the church needs justification for social action other than that which is found in its mission, and the idea that its social action cannot be justified because the mission of the church excludes it, are wrong. By virtue of the incarnation of Christ, church and society are joined together in mutual interdependence before, and not only after, cooperation between them is organized. Here we are dealing with a prevenient unity between church and society. The "social *diakonia*" of the church is only the historical

---

[10] RICHARD F. BEHRENDT: *Dynamische Gesellschaft (Dynamic Society).* Bern: 1963, pp. 100ff.

expression of this unity, the witness to it by word and deed; and this expression is the responsibility of churches and Christians. All Christians have received authority for active obedience within the framework of society. A church that restricted its preaching of the gospel to individuals would be contemptuous of the real man who is entwined with society in thousands of ways and who is liable to be crushed by its structures. There is no department of human life that can be withdrawn from the church's co-responsibility. This assertion does not mean that society should apply to the church to heal all its ills; the church itself is suffering from terrible distortions and ravages. Only a Christian ideology, a false concept of the church, could imagine that the church could have such healing powers. The concepts developed by Christian social teaching today are nothing but an expression of simple obedience to God's love of the world: For we are his world and his mankind, and his call goes out to all. He has made man a person and given him authority for the ordering of society, an authority that Christians share.

Though the churches do not bear the sole responsibility with regard to the ordering of society and though they are clearly not called to exercise dominion, there is no justifiable reason to release the churches from this joint concern for the society that is to come. To separate and detach the church from society would mean to despise the unity of church and society and to separate man from God; it would mean the eschatological abolition of all provisional forms of the kingdom of God, such as church or social institutions. Lutheran theology—and ecumenical social thinking—rightly protect the gospel from an interpretation that identifies it with a "social-revolutionary program" and a "legal catalogue" for the reform of society; but Lutheran theology disregards both the need for rational programs and "legal catalogues," precisely and principally in the sphere of *justitia civilis,* and also the impossibility of applying and practicing the *"primus seu politicus usus legis"* in society without a "catalogue" of social ethical demands and conventions.[11]

---

[11] *Über Legitimität und Notwendigkeit des kritisch-revolutionaren Elementes in der christlichen Ethik;* cf. ARTHUR RICH: *Glaube in politischer Entscheidung (On Legitimacy and Necessity of the Critical-Revolutionary*

Theological disparagement of the "law" in the sense of a social order encourages capitulation in the face of social evils and disregards the necessary relation of what is done in the present to the future structure of society. The theological protest against "legalism" is nowhere so out of place as here, where it is the function of reason to make good "laws," to improve the institutions of society and to create conventions that regulate, facilitate and simplify human relationships. The primary theological task here is to perceive and praise the benefit of order and, in view of revolutionary changes, the salutary effect of clear "legal catalogues." Thus the social order requires a combination of brotherly love and reason. The antinomianism of some types of traditional theology completely fails to render this moral service. That "law" in the sense of social-ethical demands for a human ordering of society does not have any *Heils Charakter,* and that these demands do not effect any "social redemption," goes without saying. But this negation is legitimate only if the Christian ethic reflects both the ethical validation and the appreciation of the secular benefits of social order and conventions.

On the other hand, the Christian expectation of the kingdom of God indicates that the secular character of social-ethical programs must be clearly recognized. The Christian ethic is far greater than human-ethical demands, for, as the church proclaims the message of Christ, it calls men to follow him in bearing the cross and suffering and to answer the eternal call to seek the kingdom of God through faith. The church proclaims this eschatological destiny of man, which radically transcends his social existence and his authority to establish a social order within this world. The social ethic expressed in human ethical demands and legal catalogues has its place in the secular age (*Welt-Zeit*) of the church which lives within and for the world. The Christian social ethic represents a necessary consequence of the message of salvation; but the Christion message is not restricted to social ethics. The responsible society cannot take the place of the kingdom of God or of the church.

---

*Element in Christian Ethics;* cf. ARTHUR RICH: *Faith in Political Decision*). Zürich and Stuttgart: 1962, pp. 96f., 155f., 179f. He emphasizes rightly that "eschatology of the Christian faith gives rise to a revolutionary humanity" (p. 96).

The gospel, however (as the whole paranesis of the New Testament shows), always assumes the form of directives and "imperatives of grace." For that reason, all social-ethical demands must be understood as commandments of grace for secular existence in society. They have to be developed as a necessary consequence of the message of salvation (*Heilsverkündigung*), as the commands of and in obedience to that love to which the church always bears witness in its preaching. The "ministry of reconciliation" includes the ministry of peace and reconciliation among men.

# 8

# THE DEVELOPMENT OF
# ECUMENICAL SOCIAL ETHICS

by Paul Abrecht (Geneva)

THE great variety and intensity of social issues all over the world, the widespread debate both within and outside the Vatican Council on Schema 13, and the preparations for the 1966 World Conference on Church and Society make this a timely moment to reflect on the present situation of the social thought of the World Council of Churches. We must ask not only what the contemporary social realities to which the churches should address themselves are but also whether the theological and ethical concepts around which our social thinking has developed still provide the best framework for understanding and interpreting Christian responsibility in the contemporary world. The latter question is raised in many different ways today, and, whatever we may say in defense of the contribution of earlier statements on Church and Society, we must accept the fact that the old formulations of the basis and aims of Christian action in society are being very sharply challenged. The amalgam of biblical truth, traditional doctrine and philosophical ideas on which the church has built its social teaching in the past has now come unstuck, and there is considerable disagreement about the nature of the biblical and theological insights on which the future action of the church can be based.

To question the adequacy of World Council social thinking raises the prior question, What is its nature and content? There have been only a few substantial efforts to explain and interpret the development of ecumenical social thinking, and the only comprehensive and noteworthy attempt has been that of Father Ed. Duff, an American Jesuit theologian and social scholar. However, his book on the *Social Thought of the World Council of Churches* was completed just after the 1954 Assembly of the World Council. Since then, there has been a great widening of interests and concerns, and some of the issues that preoccupied us at that time have receded in importance, while others, particularly the issues of social change, have become very important. It is not possible to attempt here a new and comprehensive interpretation of the development of ecumenical social thinking but only to call attention to certain aspects of its development that point to the areas where problems arise and where new thinking is needed, or is already under way.

### The Theological and Ethical Dynamics of the First Ecumenical Discussions of Christian Life and Work

It is often said that the first efforts (between 1919 and 1925) to develop a social ethics in the non-Roman churches are interesting mainly because they are the starting point for what was later to become a theologically more profound and socially more perceptive movement. It is concluded that the first Universal Christian Conference on Life and Work held at Stockholm (1925) contributed very little of lasting theological or ethical insight to the social teaching of the churches.

This judgment, however, tends to overlook or underestimate the fundamental achievements of that first effort. Like Roman Catholic social movements in the latter half of the nineteenth century and the early decades of this century, Protestant and Anglican groups struggled for years to arrive at some new formulations of the relation between gospel, church and world. The spirit of pious individualism that predominated in the churches seemed to them no true answer to the problems of the industrial revolution. Eventually, their thinking crystallized around the Christian social movement, which took as its theological and sociological basis the ideas of the social gospel. It was a prophetic movement, a movement of outrage and protest against social evils, a movement of reform and a call to action. It is useful to recall in summary form the basic presuppositions or postulates of this movement:

1. The rejection of the prevailing static conception of human nature and society, and the refusal to interpret the Christian doctrine of sin and the fall of man as an argument against working for social betterment.

2. The insistence that God is at work in the protest movement within society and that man must cooperate with him in realizing his will to establish his Kingdom.

3. The rejection of all atomistic and mechanistic conceptions of society such as were dominant in the heyday of *laissez-faire* capitalism.

4. The insistence that men are largely shaped by their social environment, and the conviction that social structures can be altered in order to promote better conditions of human life.

5. The emphasis on the role of the state and the community in regulating various aspects of social life and in developing new and more just patterns of society.

6. The concern for the solidarity of men and for equality of opportunity as a vital element in the Christian understanding of social reform and social change.

It might be said that the Stockholm Conference of 1925, in endorsing these ideas, gave a kind of ecumenical blessing to the social gospel movement, which had already gained great momentum in the United States, Britain and many countries of Europe. In later years, it has been said that this was the beginning of an Anglo-Saxon theological domination of ecumenical social ethics, but this overlooks the deep interest in Europe in Christian social ethics and the encounter with some of the insights of the social protest movements, including the ethical ideas of the socialist movement. A European Christian student leader of that time, writing his doctoral thesis on the American social gospel, observed: "In America . . . this ethic constitutes the one most important attempt made to transcend the individualistic notions of these last centuries and arrive at a solidaristic conception of social life." (VISSER 'T HOOFT: *The Background of the Social Gospel in America*, 1928, p. 65.) [1]

---

[1] However, he concludes, that ". . . The evidence so far seems to support the thesis that the social gospel does not do justice to essential elements of Christian truth and therefore does not produce a firmly rooted and abiding type of Christian life," p. 186.

And one of the most noteworthy European theological statements in support of the social gospel was based on the apparent affinity between the gospel and socialism. Harnack, in his book *Mission and Expansion of Christianity* (1908), describing the social expression of Christianity in the first three centuries, concluded:

The gospel, it has been truly said, is at bottom both individualistic and socialistic. Its tendency towards mutual association, so far from being an accidental phenomenon in its history, is inherent in its character. It spiritualizes the irresistible impulse which draws one man to another, and raises the social connection of human beings from the sphere of a convention to that of a moral obligation. In this way it serves to heighten the worth of man, and essays to recast contemporary society, to transform the socialism which involves a conflict of interests into the socialism which rests upon the consciousness of spiritual unity and a common goal.

The great work of Troeltsch on *The Social Teaching of the Christian Churches* (1907) had also opened Christian thinking to a new concern for society by showing the ethical and sociological pattern of the various forms of Christianity and their affinity for various social classes and groups.

It would be instinctive at this point to compare these developments with Roman Catholic social thinking as it emerged in the social encyclicals *Rerum Novarum* and *Quadragesimo Anno*. It might be argued that, whereas in later years, Roman Catholic thinking has had to overcome an uncompromising rejection of socialism and communism, non-Roman churches were obliged to overcome a certain sentimentality about the socialist conception of history and social change and to rid themselves of some of the illusions about man and society that a semisocialist reading of the Bible had fostered. The economic depression in the western capitalist countries and the rise of the totalitarian political systems in Europe, though strengthening the social concern within the churches, also showed the inadequacy of the theological and ethical ideas with which the church was working. A deeper theological basis was needed. This was to be one of the chief contributions of the Conference on Church, Community and State at Oxford in 1937.

## The Conception of Christian Social Ethics in the Oxford Conference of 1937

The 1937 Conference on Church, Community and State at Oxford brought into the open the debate about the theological and biblical basis of Christian social ethics. In his own description of that debate, J. H. Oldham, the chief architect of the Oxford Conference, summarized thus the three theological perspectives that were presented to the conference and that represented the different attitudes held by the leading theologians of that time: [2]

1. A Christian ethics based on "principles" derived from New Testament teaching, especially the Sermon on the Mount (representing the position of Stockholm).

2. A personal ethics of salvation—suspicious of "Christian social programmes." This view was set forth by several continental theologians. At Oxford Professor Emil Brunner had argued that "the Christian Church has no right to lay down a social programme, because it is not its business to establish any kind of system. It is doubtful whether we ought to speak of a Christian ethic at all, since an ethic means something which has an independent existence and which once for all lays down rules for the various relations of life."

3. A Christian ethics of justice derived from the love commandment. This view emphasized the prophetic mission of the church in relation to the family, the nation, the state, economics and culture. In contrast to the first position it emphasized the reality of evil and the difficulty of direct applications of the love commandment. In contrast to the second view it emphasized the need to translate love into justice and disassociate Christianity from pure individualism.

There is no evidence that the Oxford Conference formally adopted any one of these interpretations, but it is clear that the third position dominated ecumenical social thinking and writing in the period up to the first Assembly of the World Council of Churches at Amsterdam in 1948. (The influential book by Arch-

---

[2] J. H. OLDHAM: *The Oxford Conference* (Official Report). New York: Willett, Clark & Co., 1937. See pp. 27–38.

bishop William Temple, *Christianity and Social Order* (1942), may be cited as an example of writing from this theological-ethical perspective although under his particular theological outlook the emphasis on "principles" of social order was accentuated more than in ecumenical social thinking generally.)

The theological corrective that the Oxford Conference applied to the social thinking of the 1925 Conference at Stockholm is well illustrated in the Oxford report on Economic Life. It is argued that a Christian social ethic cannot be developed directly from the love commandment or the standard of the kingdom of God, since these, because of human sinfulness, are in contradiction to the world. Therefore, "in so far as the kingdom of God is in conflict with the world and is therefore still to come, the Christian finds himself under the necessity of discovering the best available means of checking human sinfulness and of increasing the possibilities and opportunities of love within a sinful world." The task of the Christian is to make use of the "principle of justice, as the relative expression of the commandment of love in any critique of economic, political and social institutions."

In opposition to some interpretations of Lutheran social ethics it is pointed out: "The laws of justice are not purely negative. They are not merely 'dykes against sin'. The political and economic structure of society is also the mechanical skeleton which carries the organic element of society. Forms of production and methods of cooperation may serve the cause of human brotherhood by serving and extending the principle of love beyond the sphere of purely personal relations."

The Oxford report illustrated this by indicating four ways in which the economic order of that day challenged the Christian understanding of man and society: (1) by its enhancement of acquisitiveness, (2) by its inequalities, (3) by the irresponsible possession of economic power, (4) by the frustration of the sense of Christian vocation.

In relation to these problems the report set forth a body of "Christian teaching" representing "the kind of guidance which it is possible to receive from the Christian faith for economic life." What followed constituted the most comprehensive and systematic review ever made by a group of Protestant, Anglican and Orthodox churches of the problems of economic life. It was specifically noted that the teaching would apply for about a decade. As matters turned out, the war shortened that period considerably, bringing with it a new concern for social welfare that was to lead to great economic changes and the rapid development of the modern welfare society and state. Thus, most of the prewar proposals of the churches for changing economic life were realized in many countries by 1945.

The need to accept a larger authority for the state in ordering economic life did not lead the participants in the Oxford Conference to overlook the dangers of the growing power of the state. The rise of nazism and totalitarian communism raised this problem very acutely. The conference defined the ultimate limit of the state as follows:

Since we believe in the holy God as the source of justice, we do not consider the state as the ultimate source of law but rather as its guarantor. It is not the lord but the servant of justice. There can be for the Christian no ultimate authority but very God.

The report also declared that in the present situation, "the widespread tendency of the State to control the totality of human life in all its individual and social aspects, combined with the tendency to attribute absolute value to the State itself," was forcing the church to reconsider its relation to the state. The conference agreed that there are areas where the social activities of church and state overlap; tensions are therefore unavoidable and solutions will vary in different historical circumstances. The report emphasized also that the church as a Christian community has a responsibility to help its members to interpret their responsibility in relation to the state.

## Developments After the Second World War— the Responsible Society

After the Second World War, ecumenical attention in our churches focused on the issues of economic welfare and justice in relation to the conflict between *laissez-faire* capitalism and totalitarian communism; and in the discussion of these topics at the first

Assembly of the World Council of Churches (Amsterdam, 1948) the theological ideas developed in 1937 at Oxford continued to serve as the basis of ecumenical social thought. In the situation where churches seemed to be presented with two extreme ideologies, the Assembly stressed that they should reject both and "should seek to draw men away from the false assumptions that these extremes are the only alternatives. ... It is the responsibility of Christians to seek new, creative solutions which never allow either justice or freedom to destroy the other." The Amsterdam Assembly concluded that it could not "resolve the debate between those who feel that the primary solution is to socialize the means of production, and those who fear that such a course will merely lead to new and inordinate combinations of political power, culminating finally in an omnicompetent State." The statements of the World Council Assemblies of Amsterdam and Evanston tended to favor a kind of mixed economy in which the "coherent and purposeful ordering of society" by government action and regulation is combined with centers of private initiative in economic life through industry, trade unions, and so on.

The term "responsible society" thus developed as an ethical concept to give expression to the search for a new and creative answer to the quest for economic justice and order. The definition of "responsible society" at Amsterdam is as follows:

Man is created and called to be a free being, responsible to God and his neighbour. Any tendencies in State and society depriving man of the possibility of acting responsibly are a denial of God's intention for man and his work of salvation. A responsible society is one where freedom is the freedom of men who acknowledge responsibility to justice and public order, and where those who hold political authority or economic power are responsible for its exercise to God and the people whose welfare is affected by it. ... For a society to be responsible under modern conditions it is required that the people have freedom to control, to criticize and to change their governments, that power be made responsible by law and tradition, and be distributed as widely as possible through the whole community. It is required that economic justice and provision of equality of opportunity be established for all the members of society.

There is no doubt that this concept was welcomed by many churches as a help in the formulation of Christian social concern in the postwar period where so many were caught up in the sterile and self-righteous anticommunist crusade that obsessed many western countries in the 1950's. But ecumenical social thought had also come under new theological critique: from those, especially the followers of Karl Barth, who wanted a clearer christological and biblical basis for Christian action in society and from some younger theologians (not necessarily followers of Barth) who argued that the Christian social ethics developed at Oxford was based on some questionable assumptions about the authority and universality of western Christendom. This critique gained increasing support as the ecumenical movement began to give serious consideration to the social problems of the new nations in Africa, Asia and Latin America and discovered the elements of cultural and ideological bias in the old formulations.

## The Christian Responsibility for Rapid Social Change

It is a somewhat sobering fact that the churches like the rest of society did not do justice to the rise of the new nations until the process of radical decolonization was well under way. There are institutional reasons which help to explain this fact. The World Council of Churches had very few member churches from Asia, Africa and Latin America in 1948; and most of the Christian concern for society in these lands was expressed through western missions and societies. Despite the great concern of western Christians they could not, generally speaking, be expected to see the need for revolutionary change as clearly as Christians in these countries.

The development of the World Council's work in this area seemed at first to require no new theological-ethical categories. But gradually it has become apparent that new theological categories relevant to the problems of revolutionary change are needed, and there have been attempts to develop a theology of Christian action in relation to dynamic secular society. We have been obliged to rc-examine our Christian understanding of history, especially of western domination of these lands, and develop a Christian interpretation of their emancipation and of thcir attempt at nationbuilding.

Christian reflection on the meaning of rapid social change in Africa, Asia and Latin America is challenging the relatively static character of much Christian social thinking in the past and other evidence of western bias. It is apparent that we have not yet discovered the theological and sociological categories that will help to express the meaning of the Christian faith for the problems of an emerging world society. Here is probably the greatest challenge to Christian thought in the coming decade.

All these considerations have produced some very sharp criticisms of traditional ecumenical social thinking; and, though it is difficult to measure the strength of this opposition, it is evident that some of our ablest younger theological minds are pressing for new theological approaches. The criticism emphasizes the legalistic and moralistic character of much Christian social thinking. It argues that much of ecumenical social ethics was developed under the influence of a Christendom mentality that was seeking to build a Christian society. These critics plead for a new existential or contextual approach to replace the emphasis on theoretical norms or standards, and to put the focus on the discoveries of Christian community in the midst of the conflicts and tensions of society. The theological arguments developed in support of this critique are very difficult to assess because so much of the attack is against views which have long since been abandoned. The criticism overlooks the fact that most ecumenical social thinking has been contextual in practice, speaking to the issues of society as they have arisen, rather than enunciating general principles valid for all times.

But the criticism is too widespread to be dismissed. And one of the important tasks in the area of Church and Society is to determine the extent to which we must revise our theological approach in the light of the new social situation and in the light also of the theological challenge that is being posed.

The theological challenge is related to the more fundamental issue: whether the thought of our churches on social questions is not still too western to provide an interpretation of the problems of revolutionary change in Africa, Asia and Latin America. This is the greatest test for the future. We see a new world emerging. Great cultures and peoples hitherto living under domination suddenly become active in a new and remarkable way in world history. What is the real meaning of this fact, and what is the Christian interpretation of this new historical dynamism? Here is the great challenge to Christian social thinking in the years ahead.

## The Future of Ecumenical Social Ethics

It will be apparent from this brief survey that ecumenical social ethics has developed according to the following pattern:

1. It is highly pragmatic. It is based on a rather limited theological consensus developed in relation to the search for theological clues to guide Christian thought on particular problems of economic and social life. This pragmatic quality has been encouraged by laymen who are impatient with theological debates that seem unrelated to the work of the church in the world.

2. Though there has been a considerable emphasis in ecumenical thought on the search for "Christian principles" for social action, this has always been qualified by an emphasis on the ambiguity of all programs for social justice. The search for "principles" has arisen in the discussion of the new and creative forms of justice that might be possible in any particular social situation.

3. There is a mounting critique from Christians in Africa, Asia and Latin America who find that much ecumenical social thinking has been too static and too defensive of western attitudes. It is argued that the examination and elimination of this ideological element is one of the primary tasks in ecumenical social ethics. Theology can help in this critical task, but theology is itself subject to the ideological and cultural trends which have formed western thought generally.

4. The strongest theological influence on Christian social ethics coming out of the new nations is one which emphasizes the action of God in contemporary history. This viewpoint tends to place a positive and optimistic interpretation on the nation-building process in Africa, Asia and Latin America. At the same time, it is a challenge to the static quality of much western Christian social thinking and to legalistic definitions of Christian action in society.

Some theologians today suggest that we give up all attempts to develop Christian programs or even a Christian social ethic because they lead inevitably to a Christian ideology. It is argued that we can only live in faith amidst the ideological tensions and the obligations to take ideological decisions. What this means in any particular situation and how it will be accomplished without establishing some criteria for such ideological involvement is not yet clear. Certainly the Christian community around the world is not yet agreed on what that ideological involvement should be. The dangers of a sentimental and uncritical optimism and activism seem just as real in the attitude of those who seek for an existential involvement in a changing society as they were in the views of those who too confidently and too theoretically outlined the pattern of Christian action in the world.

However, the sharp debate that this theological issue provokes could be a great stimulus to the further development of ecumenical social thought. Insofar as the debate reflects the Christian encounter with the movements of secularization and other spiritual and ideological forces at work in modern society it is necessary and creative.

We must face the fact that the world Christian community may in the years to come be more and more pulled apart by the ideological and social forces that divide our world and that often exert great influence also over theological points of view. This remains the constant challenge that underlies and gives importance to the ecumenical debate on social ethics.

# 9

# THE CHRISTIAN CONCERN
# FOR SOCIETY —
# A ROMAN CATHOLIC VIEW

by Louis Janssens (Belgium)

THE Christian revelation throws light on our social nature. We are
not involved in the plan of salvation as isolated individuals, but as
members of the People of God. Our unity in Christ is such that
we form a Body, of which Christ is the Head. As members of this
Body we are "open": our destiny is to love God and our neighbor
(Matthew 22 : 37–39).

Contemporary anthropology and psychology confirm that man
is essentially open by nature. He realizes who he is only through
his relationships with others. His consciousness becomes aware of
itself only if it is "intentional": it is real to itself only if it is related
to something else. From the very beginning of his life, even before
becoming conscious of himself, the child is open to his environment, and participates in what happens there. Due to his need
for affection, protection and security, he is in emotional symbiosis
with his evironment. In his emotional relationship with his mother,
the child reacts by mimicking her look, her gestures, the sound of
her voice. From his second year onward the child comes more and
more to understand the *meaning* of the words spoken to him,
the *purpose* of the objects that he sees about him, the *reason* for
the actions carried out around him.

Social relationships continue to be essential after our consciousness has been awakened. But henceforward these relationships

commit us to personal responsibility. We are no longer simply *parts* of a social whole; we are called to *take part* in the life of society. Our social nature becomes a task and a vocation that make demands on our freedom. We must consciously seek the *meaning* of our social relationships and assume responsibility for the free acts which acceptance of that meaning implies. We accomplish this mission by responding to the demands of the common good of the groups to which we belong.

That common good includes *all the requirements of life in society*. It presupposes *co*existence between persons and their groups, it is a "life together." It means also *co*operation in putting the values of the common culture into practice. Lastly, it involves *co*participation in the good things of the culture, the fruit of the cooperation and the contributions of each member.

### The Demands of Coexistence

Life in society is first of all coexistence between persons and groups of persons. This coexistence takes widely differing forms. The intimate, permanent coexistence within the family is usually much more intense than the coexistence between workers who are together only during their hours of work, or between the citizens of a country who may have nothing in common except that they live under the same political régime. Human coexistence spreads over an ever-wider area as culture advances. Today all men coexist with one another. Distance is being eliminated as communications improve. The telephone, the telegraph, the press, radio, television may bring us into closer touch with events in other continents than with the concerns of people in the house next door. Cultural exchange between areas and peoples is growing stronger and extending. Now that men have armaments capable of effecting mass suicide, they are realizing more and more that "peaceful coexistence" on the worldwide level is a question of life or death. Nations are beginning to recognize that the coexistence of all mankind is now a reality that requires a moral basis and a legal superstructure.

What is the moral basis of all human coexistence?

One of the most marvelous manifestations of our coexistence

is *dialogue*. The mere fact of being able to converse with, and to understand—each has deep significance. As soon as we enter into dialogue with someone, we both become interested in the same things or the same values, and want to exchange our ideas, our feelings, our desires and our free attitudes toward them. The dialogue reveals that the other is a person like ourselves, an *alter ego* who also reflects, feels, is free and responsible, is open to values and capable of inquiring about the meaning of his existence in the world with others. Conversation shows us that we are meeting on the same level, as equals, that we share the same human nature, the same human condition. In other words, our coexistence or our being-with-others has fundamental meaning when we see it objectively. The other person is not a means, an object in the world: he is a subject, a person, an equal, a neighbor.

Not only does the dialogue demonstrate our basic equality: it also reveals the uniqueness of each person, especially when the conversation takes the form of a discussion. A discussion should be focused on a subject of common concern; otherwise, there is always a danger that it will dissolve into a futile wordy quarrel as we begin talking about different things. The fact that we are able to come together with a common purpose demonstrates our basic equality. Discussion also implies that we are not in complete agreement about the matter under consideration, that we have different conceptions, feelings, attitudes and reactions toward it. Every person is unique, with his own constitution, temperament, capacities, and tendencies, and as he recognizes and cultivates his original gifts, he develops a character of his own.

This simple analysis of the universal phenomenon called "conversation" reveals the basic meaning of our coexistence, our being-with-others. Respect for this meaning demands that we treat everyone as a person who is both like ourselves and, at the same time, unique.

The virtue whereby we recognize and develop the full meaning of our relationships with others we call *love*. That is why Pope Leo XIII in his first great social Encyclical (*Rerum Novarum*) said that in our social relationships love must have first place. This love has two aspects: one human, the other theological.

Christ himself insisted on the demands of human love when

he said, "Thou shalt love thy neighbor as thyself" (Matthew 22 : 39). He explained it by giving us what Christians usually call "the Golden Rule": "Whatever you wish that men would do to you, do so to them" (Matthew 7 : 12). Our Lord knows how extremely sensitive we are about everything that affects ourselves and the attitude of other people to us, and he asks us to show the same sensitivity to the well-being of others. In this way Christ illumines the human aspect of love. It is therefore not surprising that we find the same "Golden Rule" among many non-Christian peoples [1] and that the Schoolmen regarded it as a first principle of natural law. Quoting Aristotle, St. Thomas Aquinas writes that loving someone means wishing him what is good: *amare est velle bonum alicui.* It is the person himself whom we love. But if our love is genuine, we shall want him to attain the perfection of which he is capable, and shall want to contribute effectively toward his doing so.

Our Lord did not confine himself to explaining the human demands of loving our neighbor. He also explained the theological dimensions: "A new commandment I give to you, that you love one another, even as I have loved you" (John 13 : 34). Brotherly love is to be an imitation of the love of Christ, which itself is the manifestation of the love that the Father has for us. It is on the basis of the Father's love for us that the Christian must discover the meaning of loving his neighbor.

Concerning the love of the Father, St. John writes: "God is love. In this the love of God was made manifest among us, that God sent his only Son into the world, so that we might live through him. In this is love, not that we loved God but that he loved us and sent his Son to be the expiation for our sins" (I John 4 : 8–10). St. Paul defined the love of the Father in the same way: "God shows his love for us in that while we were yet sinners, Christ died for us. . . . For . . . while we were enemies we were reconciled to God by the death of his Son" (Romans 5 : 8–10). That is what the Father's love is like. It *gives,* and the gift consists in the Father sending his own Son to save us. It forgives and reconciles; it offers

---

[1] J. Schmid: *Das Evangelium nach Matthäus übersetzt und erklärt.* Regensburg: 4th ed., 1959, p. 148, affirms that the Golden Rule is found in substance in: *Tob.* 4, 15; Homer's *Odyssey* 5, 188 *et seq.;* Thalès; in India; in China (Lao-tse and Kung Futse); and in Islam.

itself in love as Christ sacrificed himself for our sins. Being sinners and, therefore, enemies of God, we did not in any way deserve this love, which is, therefore, a free gift and pardon, a *grace,* a selfless and generous initiative on the part of the Father.

We shared the Father's love, for "God's love has been poured into our hearts through the Holy Spirit which has been given to us" (Romans 5 : 5). When St. Paul speaks of the fruits of the Spirit within us, he first mentions love (Galatians 5 : 22), and says that it is incomparably superior to all the other charismata bestowed by the same Spirit (I Corinthians 13 : 1–11). "Love is of God, and he who loves is born of God" (I John 4 : 7).

Because we share in the love of the Father, our love will manifest the same qualities. It will also take the initiative in giving, in forgiving and in reconciling (Matthew 5 : 23–24; 6 : 14–15; 18 : 21–35). Our love will be extended to enemies and even to persecutors, for it will be generously and freely given as was the love of the Father toward us when we were still sinners and enemies (Matthew 5 : 43–48).

St. Paul gives us a magnificent synthesis of the demands of Christian love: "Do not grieve the Holy Spirit of God, in whom you were sealed for the day of redemption. Let all bitterness and wrath and anger and clamour and slander be put away from you" (Ephesians 4 : 30–31). A Christian cannot commit sins against brotherly love —sins that are opposed to the Holy Spirit through whom the Father's love has been poured into his heart. After condemning these negative attitudes, the Apostle describes Christian love and its divine motivation: "Be kind to one another, tenderhearted, forgiving one another, as God in Christ forgave you. Therefore be imitators of God, as beloved children. And walk in love, as Christ loved us and gave himself up for us, a fragrant offering and sacrifice to God" (Ephesians 4 : 32–5 : 2).

Love, with its two aspects, human and divine, is for us the basic essential of all human coexistence. But it needs the guarantee of justice. Why?

As an appreciation of others and a desire to promote their wellbeing, love is a direct relationship between persons, a *subjective relationship*. But it is more than that. Although it is directed at an individual it reaches him effectively only through the intermediary of objective elements—through *objective relationships*.[2] Our attitude toward others remains purely subjective unless we express it by some sign: a smile, a gesture of approval, a word of encouragement, a kind act. These are material things, but they assume a deeply human meaning when they become means of expressing the human encounter in mutual love. The same applies to the desire for the other person's welfare which is part of the essence of love. It will fail to reach its object unless it is translated into tangible acts or services. Love is, therefore, necessarily a subjective relationship embodied in objective elements and relations. These subjective and objective relationships reflect our own human nature. We are incarnate spirits. Just as the objective elements of which our bodies are formed are animated by the spirit within us whose intentions they express, so our subjective relationships animate our objective relationships and are manifest in them.

The indispensable role of objective elements in our coexistence with others brings us to the heart of justice. For a long time the moralists have affirmed that relationships based on justice include an objective element, *medium rei,* and thus create objective relationships. Spiritual values are indivisible and inexhaustible. Everyone can participate in them without their diminishing and without the participation of one interfering with the participation of others. By their very nature, spiritual values unite those who share them; and conflicts in the spiritual sphere can spring only from involuntary mistakes or from the perverseness of human nature.

The same cannot be said of the material elements of our objective relationships. Material possessions must be divided among many people, and each person's share becomes smaller as the number of participants increases. The use of something by one individual excludes its simultaneous use by anyone else. The very nature of material wealth is therefore a source of conflict. It is also ambiguous: it may be used as a *means* in the service of love; or it

---

[2] Subjective culture includes the development of the different possibilities of the human personality, especially the education of the mind, the cultivation of artistic taste, the improvement of health, the refinement of an ethical sense, etc. Objective culture embraces all the creative works of man in the world, such as science, technology, art, economic wealth, language, social institutions, the political and legal order, international organization, etc.

may be an obstacle to love. It is the task of justice to solve this ambiguity in the interests of love.

Today we possess the necessary elements for defining the aim and the need for justice. The aim of justice is all those objective relationships that are indispensable to the fulfillment of love and without which the recognition of man by man becomes impossible. And in order that everyone may be treated in accordance with his human dignity, all must be faithful to the objective relationships imposed upon them by society.

It must be emphasized that justice is not static and unchangeable. Admittedly, it has a static side in that it is laid down in a code of rules which impose certain minimum requirements on society. But justice is also dynamic and progressive and must be constantly enriched. This progress is conditioned by the level of subjective culture, especially by the extent of moral education. The better prepared a person is to know and to put into practice the requirements of man's recognition by man, the more sensitive he will be to the objective elements which must characterize his relationships with others if he is to treat them as persons. It is an historic fact that the great figures in the social sphere, inspired by an inventive love, have enriched objective relationships with new values that have subsequently inspired progress in the legal order. It can, therefore, be said that justice represents within a civilization, the level of the work already accomplished by love.

Furthermore, the advance of objective culture is continually increasing the wealth available, and, consequently, the objective elements indispensable for just relationships. What becomes *socially possible* at a given moment, in view of the level of culture already reached, is, by that very fact, required by justice. In the life of a social group, the dignity of the human person is not really respected unless relationships are being enriched in the search for, and the use of, every available resource for the good of all. Justice has its source and its end in love, and participates in the dynamism of love. It is this dynamism which explains the progress in the church's social teaching. One has only to compare *Rerum Novarum* of Leo XIII with *Mater et Magistra* of John XXIII!

## The Demands of Cooperation

Between objective and subjective culture there exists a dialectic relationship in which one acts upon and influences the other. Even the most spiritual aspects of subjective culture cannot flourish without elements of objective culture. There can be no scientific education without books or laboratories, no aesthetic life without works of art, no physical culture without economic wealth. In short, the resources of the objective culture must be enlisted for the improvement and cultivation of human personality. On the other hand, the progress of subjective culture makes possible fresh acquisitions in the sphere of the objective culture. After an individual has been "formed" by the heritage of the objective culture around him, he can, through the exercise of his own natural gifts and capacities, in his turn enrich that culture. If man is to develop, he must transform the universe into a world of objective culture, which, in its turn, shapes man and helps him to attain greater perfection and to develop along new lines. Man perfects himself by perfecting the universe.

The objective culture of yesterday is the source of the subjective culture of today, which, in its turn, is a source of enrichment for the objective culture of tomorrow. The mutual exchange between objective and subjective culture through the centuries makes culture a historic reality; it also means that culture is a social reality, a fruit of cooperation.

No man on his own can create everything that is required for a truly human subjective culture. This is due in the first place to our temporal nature: we never have enough time to achieve everything. The time-factor is not our only limitation. Everyone possesses human potentialities in a limited way. This limitation of our aptitudes and capacities is reflected in our need to be helped and complemented by others. In fact, our uniqueness does not mean only that we are limited: it also means that each of us is limited in his own way; each differs from the others by reason of his special gifts. This diversity enables us to respond to and complete one another. Our diversity enables us to cooperate in the creation of the different elements of the objective culture, and the fruits of cooperation make a truly human subjective culture accessible to all. We are united in society not so much by what we have in common, as by what makes us different from one another. Our basic equality is an indispensable condition for our cooperation in society. But the real source of our joint action is our diversity.

Culture is created by human work, but not all people are able to work all the time in order to satisfy their needs. Consequently, it is the duty of those members who are able to cooperate to ensure the satisfaction of the needs of all, including those who are unable to participate in the common effort. This is part of the very pattern of our existence. Children begin life completely dependent upon their parents. They could not attain the full development which is essential to their participation in cooperation, unless during their early years their parents provided for their needs. Once the children are grown up, they are equipped to share with their parents in supporting the family. But the children have hardly reached maturity before their parents are on the threshold of old age, and are in need of more and more help. This alternation between receiving and giving is a basic law of every society. Those who are fit to work must provide for the needs of all, including those who are unable to contribute at present—children, the sick, the incapacitated, the old. And since the richness of this cooperation derives from the diversity of those involved in it, each individual must perform the function for which he is best suited. The maxim, "From each according to his ability," constantly recurs in Marxist writings. This is only a paraphrase of what St. Paul wrote to the Thessalonians (II Thessalonians 3 : 10). Collaboration for the common good involves this twofold obligation imposed by justice: on the one hand, society must mobilize the available resources so that everyone can develop his abilities and unique gifts; on the other hand, society must stimulate each person to contribute to the general cooperation in accordance with his personal capacities.

If it is true that our uniqueness and diversity form the source of collaboration and of its fecundity, then the society that reflects most adequately our social nature is the universal community of mankind. Only this universal society fully encompasses all the different kinds of persons and all the possibilities of the different nations. Again, the wealth that enables us to implement the values of objective culture is unequally divided between the different parts of the world. Every country and area possesses certain natural resources, and it is only by worldwide cooperation in the exploitation of these that the common culture can be fully developed. Economic life has become international, so that a country is on the road to ruin unless it succeeds in adapting its national economy to the needs of the world market. And what is true in the economic sphere is equally true in the scientific field: the progress of science is achieved through worldwide cooperation, and those scientists who take no interest in the research going on in other countries are left far behind. We have also recognized the necessity of worldwide cooperation for the accomplishment of our cultural mission.

From these facts a number of important conclusions may be drawn:

In the first place, these requirements of cooperation throw light on a fundamental aspect of the aid given by rich to developing countries. As we have said, diversity is the source of all fruitful cooperation, and this diversity compels individuals and nations to help and complete one another. Culture will become richer and more complete as all people increase their contribution. How many underdeveloped peoples are still incapable of making use of their valuable resources and thus of taking their proper place in worldwide cooperation! It is the duty of the rich, well-developed countries to help them to become full partners in the international collaboration. This is one of the most important aspects of scientific, economic, financial and technical assistance to the developing countries, and the rich countries must devote a reasonable share of their national income to it. The authority in an international society should even be able to impose a tax for this purpose on each of the developed countries in proportion to its income.

When people are asked the meaning of their work or occupation, they usually reply that it is a means of earning their living and supporting their families. Undoubtedly, work does have this meaning, for justice demands that those who contribute toward cooperation should also share in its fruits. However, the primary meaning of work is service to society. John XXIII stressed this in *Mater et Magistra*. But for a Christian there are more profound reasons for the dignity and grandeur of his participation in the cultural task of mankind. The first is that he knows he was created in the likeness of God (Genesis 1 : 17). The fact that man is the image of God means (in the language of the Bible) that he is God's representative, his steward. God is the Creator and Lord of his creation; as God's "likeness," man is also a creator and lord of creation, under God and in his service. The Bible adds that God gave man to have domination over the earth (Genesis 1 : 28), to "till it and and to keep it" (Genesis 2 : 15). Made in the likeness of God, man accomplishes his mission of creator and lord in his role as secondary cause and free agent, transforming the natural milieu more and more into a cultural milieu, and at the same time finding self-fulfillment. The Christian must work in the consciousness that he is cooperating with God (I Corinthians 3 : 9), that the daily task to which he devotes himself is really an *opus Dei,* and that his realization that his daily work has a religious significance is an essential element in his mission to do all to the glory of God (I Corinthians 10 : 31). Furthermore, the great commandment given by Christ to his disciples (Matthew 22 : 39; John 14 : 34–35) to which he frequently referred as a decisive criterion (Matthew 25 : 31–46) was the commandment of love.

For a Christian, love to be genuine must promote the good of others; it must be incarnate in his daily work in the human community. A Christian who does not take seriously the practice of his profession is not worthy of the name (Didache 12 : 3–5), because he is neglecting an important element in the exercise of love. On the other hand, the Christian will *live* the religious meaning of his work if he sees it as the incarnation of the most essential value of Christianity, which is *love.*

St. Paul tells us that the creation is waiting with eager longing for the revealing of the sons of God . . . because the creation also hopes to be freed from its bondage to decay and to share in the glorious liberty of the children of God (Romans 8 : 19–22). It is in the Spirit that Christ works out the future of the new creation; but we are called to humanize the world and, under the sign of the Cross, as long as history endures, to prepare the material from which the Spirit will bring forth the new earth and the new heaven. That is the eschatological meaning of human work.

Lastly, as the starting point for collaboration, we must give the fullest possible scope to free personal initiative, in both individual and group activities. This is what is meant by the principle of subsidiarity. Pius XI, in *Quadragesimo anno,* said that this principle is immutable and impregnable, and that it would be unjust to attribute to society initiatives that can be undertaken by individuals and groups. Pius XII and John XXIII also stressed the importance of this principle. The dignity of human personality demands freedom for individual initiative, for man is *a moral being,* that is, conscious, free and therefore responsible. He is autonomous and irreplaceable in the sense that his moral perfection can be enhanced or damaged only by his own voluntary acts, for which he assumes responsibility before his conscience. He has the right to exercise his personal initiative, because he is autonomous and irreplaceable in fulfilling his destiny. But the principle of subsidiarity is also a social requirement. The diversity through which members of society collaborate in the progress of culture, is enriched when individuals enjoy liberty to develop their particular possibilities. When personal initiative is stifled, diversity withers and the source of a rich and fruitful collaboration dries up.

## The Demands of Coparticipation

The immediate goal of life in society is to work out the values of the objective culture. However, it must be orientated toward a more ultimate goal: the subjective culture or personal development of every member of society.

The effective achievement of our subjective culture ultimately depends on our personal choice. To promote our scientific culture, we must educate ourselves through contact with scientific inventions and achievements. To refine our artistic taste, we must take an interest in works of art and other expressions of art. We may choose either to work at our self-improvement or to neglect it. That is the strictly subjective element in our destiny, in relation to which we are autonomous and irreplaceable.

But this personal task can be carried out only if we have at our disposal those values which are indispensable for the objective culture. And it is through our involvement in the life of society that we gain access to these values. Those who are capable must contribute to the best of their ability to the cultivation of the values of the objective culture; and these values, which are the fruit of collaboration, must be ordered and shared in such a way that everyone has access to what he needs in order to complete as fully as possible his subjective culture. The adage, "From each according to his capacities," must be complemented by another, "To each according to his needs." This maxim is also dear to the Marxist, but it is taken from the New Testament (Acts 4 : 35).

This leads us to a consideration of distributive justice, which is of primary importance today. Formerly, ethical treatises gave little space to this. Access to cultural wealth remained the privilege of a minority. How could there be much interest in distributive justice when there was so little to "distribute"? Today in the developed countries we are witnessing an impressive production of economic wealth. This wealth is clearly part of human culture, and forms the indispensable infrastructure for freeing people to interest themselves in other cultural values. The fruits of collaboration in the objective culture are becoming so abundant that through equitable "distribution," access to cultural values may become the "common good," the prerogative of everyone. In other words, the possibilities of fostering the subjective culture of each individual are constantly increasing. If we do not seize these possibilities we shall fail to respect the intrinsic meaning of the objective culture, which exists in order to serve the subjective culture; we shall also fail to recognize that since society is composed of human beings, its ultimate aim must be to see that their lives reach fruition.

It is this dynamism of distributive justice which determines the new dimension of what is called "the social question." This question has been too often raised exclusively in connection with the interests of the wage earners. It is true that the social question as such was first raised when the members of the working class, having recognized their common lot, united to gain the position due them in society. That was the viewpoint of *De Rerum Novarum* (the Encyclical of Leo XIII). But the progress of the evolved countries makes it essential that the social problem be examined in connection with the dynamic force of distributive justice: the social question will be solved as citizens not only have the possibility to undertake the task suited to their real capacities (cooperation), but also can participate in accordance with their real needs in the fruits of collaboration (coparticipation).

The social question is, therefore, not confined to the interests of a single class; it is concerned with the kind of social order which should be established in order to benefit all members of a society. This is stressed by John XXIII in *Mater et Magistra:*

The demands of the common good on the national level must be considered: to provide employment to the greatest number of workers; to take care lest privileged classes arise, even among the workers; to maintain an equal balance between wages and prices, and make goods and services accessible to the greater number of citizens; to eliminate or keep within limits the inequalities between sectors of agriculture, of industry and of services; to bring about a balance between economic expansion and the development of essential public services; to adjust, as far as possible, the means of production to the progress of science and technology; to regulate the improvements in the tenor of life of the present generation with the objective of preparing a better future for the coming generations.

Nevertheless, the Pope adds that this concept of the social question is still too narrow. If we are to respond adequately to the possibilities of our time, it must be raised in relation to the whole of mankind. On this subject we read in *Mater et Magistra:*

There are also demands for the common good on the world level: to avoid all forms of unfair competition between the economies of different countries; to encourage with fruitful understanding collaboration among these national economies; to cooperate in the economic development of communities, economically less advanced.

All this is involved in what we call *"la grande politique"* on the level of both the state and the individual. This *"grande politique"* consists above all, in ensuring that all men have access to those vital necessities without which they cannot develop normally their subjective culture.

Primary stress must be laid on the need for a policy of full employment. In the developed nations, problems of the regional economy are being studied in an effort to ensure that all who are capable of working can do so. On the international level, it is becoming increasingly clear that in order to attain its real goal, assistance to developing countries must aim above all at enabling them to share in worldwide collaboration.

Similarly, social legislation is guided, to a large extent, by the concern to redistribute the national income as better to meet the real needs of all. From the international viewpoint, we speak of an economy that will serve the whole of mankind; this means that the abundance of production in the rich countries must supply the lack in the poor countries.

Obviously, health is one of the most vital of the good things of life. All people need the health protection made possible by scientific and technical advance. This raises the question of the measures to be taken to make good medical services available to everyone. This is one of the points of *"la grande politique"* that is constantly on the agenda in the developed countries, and that on the international level takes the form of medical aid to the developing countries.

Another essential of the good life is the education of youth. Distributive justice demands that as far as possible, all children shall receive an education suited to their aptitudes. In the prosperous countries there is an insistence on the democratization of education. Every form of assistance must be extended to developing countries, not only to ensure that every child receives what is called "basic education," but also to introduce gradually all the stages of specialized teaching.

These are only the most urgent and essential requirements of man. In responding to them, the leaders who hold responsibility for *"la grande politique"* on the national and on the international level must remain loyal to the dynamism of distributive justice, and to the ideal of ensuring the widest possible participation in the values of the objective culture.

# PART III

## THE FUNCTION OF THE CHURCH IN CHANGING SOCIETIES

# FROM TRIBALISM TO NATIONHOOD

by Adeolu Adegbola (Nigeria)

THE areas that are passing from tribalism through colonialism and racial conflict to nationhood virtually coincide with the areas of the so-called "younger churches" where Christianity has been planted during the past century, primarily by the missionary activities of preachers and evangelists from the lands of the ruling colonial powers. In these same areas evangelism was interpreted mainly in terms of spreading the gospel, preaching the faith, making converts, building churches and establishing schools primarily to swell church membership by gaining access to the parents and wielding influence over the children in their early years. Either because of preoccupation with these evangelistic tasks, or of indifference or theological prejudice, the gospel was not clearly interpreted in terms of society and social responsibility. To raise the question of the function of the church in nation-building would have been tantamount to heresy, and many a missionary who would have tolerated the question being raised in his own country would have frowned upon the idea of a "native" Christian presuming to think that he had a social responsibility arising out of the impulse of his faith, not to speak of taking an active part in the political development of his country.

In practical terms, Christians were discouraged in the days of Lugard's "indirect rule" from accepting "native chieftaincies," and so in the period of anticolonialist nationalism they considered it unchristian to engage in party politics. In Kenya, to take another example, it was never made clear whether the Christian who stood outside the Mau Mau rising was protesting against the use of violence and brutality in the achievement of political ends or against the very idea of political interest and action. There is strong evidence to show that the majority of Christians in this situation simply did not appreciate why a Christian, being what he is called to be, should take an interest in the affairs of society. The Christian's hope and goal were in heaven, and this is what he should fight for, rather than for the things of this world which in any event will pass away. The world was regarded as belonging to the Evil One and, if so, the Christian should not become involved in it at all. The temptation was to conclude that because the church is not of this world, therefore it is not for this world; or that although the church needs to build up believers in the faith, this is for the sake of church growth and not for service to the world in the name of him who called the faithful out of darkness into his marvelous light. The controversy in Ghana as to whether a libation should form part of the program of the ceremony for the inauguration of national independence suffered under the same dilemma: whether the Christian who belongs to the *ekklesia,* called out of the tribal structure, should ever dream of using a custom which grew out of and had become a preservative of the tribal social system.

This dilemma was due in no small measure to the fact that tribal political structures were seen to be bound up with pagan ritual practices. Political involvement of Christians in tribal societies was thus treated as apostasy. The effects of this situation have been, first, to give an ethical sanction to the attitude that a Christian is one who refrains from participation in the political organization of his society and, second, that political practices have only pagan religious sanctions or do not depend on any spiritual sanctions other than "the will of the people as expressed through their elected representatives."

It is easy to correct the first error, but the second is more difficult to control. The task of theology in this situation is not discharged when Christians have been exhorted to come out of the dug-out of personal pietism and bring their faith into the turbulent and more demanding arena of government administration or the intricate business of economic planning. The basic theological task is rather to proclaim the divine initiative and total engagement in man's historical situation, and to encourage a social acknowledgment of the primacy of God's action, whether in industrial organization or in political relationships.

When the Christian reflects on the function of the church in a changing society, his thinking ought to be determined by this understanding of *God's activity in the world*. This is, for the Christian, the context in which he analyzes social events, and the process by which he discovers his responsibility. The function of the church cannot be laid down finally for all possible occasions. Each emerging situation will need to be studied separately as the sphere of the activity of God and as the context in which his will can be known. This is how we become coworkers with God. In the same verse in which Paul refers to Christians as coworkers with God (*sunergoi Theou*), he speaks of them as "God's husbandry, God's building." We are not only God's coworkers: we are God's household, God's "extended family" wherein behavior in interpersonal relationship is dictated not by laws and codes but by the impulse of life together in a common Head, the Great Ancestor who, though dead, ever keeps awake and active for the good of all.

Canon M. A. C. Warren tells in *The Christian Mission,* the story of a young university student from Uganda, a girl, who sought to convey to an audience in England the dilemma of African Christians in the present revolutionary change. She said: "Many Africans are seeking answers to their questions, but the church is not playing its full part in helping young people to face the problem of society. To them God is the God of the church: He is not the God of politics and social life. They need to see him as one God: to see that the church is concerned with the whole of life."

### The Need to Relate the Sacred and the Secular in Modern African Life

This warping of Christian thought in Africa concerning the relation of God to the world is in opposition to the biblical insight of our day and to the best traditions of the people of Africa. Man in traditional African society never separated the sacred from the secular as he was later taught to do. Life to him was completely under the control of God. The routines of daily life, the momentous crises of human experience, both individual and public affairs, have all been seen as realms over which the Almighty reigned supreme. Unfortunately, conversion to Christianity has meant, among other things, acceptance of the view that life can be divided into spiritual and material, worldly and heavenly; and God has been thought of as being in control only of the spiritual. Society has been viewed as if it were only in the control of man. Catechumens have been led to repeat the Apostles' Creed, "God the Father Almighty, Maker of heaven and earth," and at the same time to behave as if the earth were outside God's sovereign control and better left in the hands of "the princes of this world." We must ask how this dualistic approach to experienced and apprehended reality came to be a Christian category of thought commonly held among Christians.

It can be said that Christianity, though seeking to displace a polytheistic system in Africa, has actually substituted a new polytheism. Thus it came about that the God who controlled Sunday did not seem to rule over the weekdays; the God who presided over church worship was regarded as having little to do with market trading; and the God who was met with in the Bible study group in the weekday church class meetings was not recognized as having sovereignty over the counsels of the political party's caucus.

Christian monotheism needs to be recovered today if the church is to make a true witness in African society. Just as the first lesson in theology taught to the Hebrews is the Shema: "Hear, O Israel, the Lord our God the Lord is one . . . ," so the restoration of a Christian monotheism should form the basis of the theology of the church in Africa for witnessing to a society which is pervaded both by traditional religion and by an aggressive Islam. The distinctiveness of the Christian faith to the adherents of polytheism or to people who have learned from Muhammad to assert the unity of God with the simple statement, "There is no God but Allah," has to begin with the affirmation of monotheism based on a pragmatic trinitarian view which stems from the theology of the incarnation. Pragmatic trinitarianism as a theological concept makes trinitarian pragmatism an ethical imperative.

By trinitarian pragmatism I mean:

1.  The grateful acknowledgment that in whatever structures of society or of economic development we find ourselves, the Almighty has been there before us. He always goes ahead of us, already involved in the creation and redemption of life's tangled relationships, even in technical development where we do not immediately discover personal categories.

2.  That it is exactly in these realms of family, industry and political affairs that the Christian is called upon to offer to God the life of ethical obedience and service.

3.  That since God is a God of history, man must constantly be ready for change and for the challenge which new social situations bring, not assuming that his ethical responses can be laid down once and for all, but knowing that they need to be rediscovered anew under the impulse of the ever-acting Spirit of God.

In other words, trinitarian pragmatism is an approach to life in which man seeks to do the will of God in every calling and human relationship, accepting the purpose set for Christ's mission in the world and the objectives that inspired his relationships with men, knowing full well that we are not on our own but that we have at our disposal the inspiration of the Holy Spirit and the strength of his fellowship.

Present-day biblical theology has rightly laid emphasis both on the Old Testament belief that "the earth is the Lord's and the fullness thereof," and on the New Testament proclamation of the lordship of the risen Christ over the whole of creation and the purpose of God to gather up all things (*ta panta*) in Christ. The whole of Christ is lord over the whole of creation. All life is under the rule, love, judgment, wrath, mercy and grace of God. Faith in the risen, ascended Lord makes man heir of all things: "For all things are yours, whether . . . the world, or life, or death, or things present or things to come; all are yours" (I Corinthians 3 : 21–22). Man's interest and engagement in social, political, economic and cultural affairs is to be submitted to his rule, for "ye are Christ's; and Christ is God's" (I Corinthians 3 : 23).

Professor Paul Lehmann of the Union Theological Seminary in

New York, commenting, in *Ethics in a Christian Context* [1] commenting on the distinction between the "God of the church" and "the God of politics," asserts that the "God of the church" *is* "the God of politics." This is what it means for God to be sovereign over the whole of life. The Christian may become aware of his presence and rule first within the church, in the reading and preaching of the word, in the administration of the holy sacraments, in the quiet peace of mind which he bestows upon those who have communed with him through the open word, the broken bread and the poured wine. But it is a mistake to confine him within the community of the church, as so much of Christian worship and understanding does. Thus, Professor Lehmann explains:

When we say that God is a "politician," and that what God is doing in the world is "making or doing politics," it is the Aristotelian *definition* of what is going on that we have in mind. According to the *definition*, we may say that politics is activity, and reflection upon activity, which aims at and analyzes what it takes to make and to keep human life *human* in the world.

In the Bible, man is addressed by God, "Where art thou?" and ultimately responds, "Whither shall I go from thy Spirit?" Man knows no existence without God, for he has been made in the image of God and cannot know any existence except existence in God, with God, in the presence of God (*coram Deo*) and for God. At the same time, God asks man, "Where is Abel thy brother?" and even though man's first reply is "Who is my neighbor?" thus indicating that he has assumed an existence apart from his neighbor and his brother, he learns to say "Though I speak with the tongues of men and of angels and have not love, I am nothing." At this point lies self-discovery, conscious awareness, the beginning of responsible selfhood. Apart from these, he is "nothing." But with these, he becomes something, not just a thing, but a subject. Even in the dealing of the transcendent divine with the human self, this subject identity is significantly respected.

The study of man has not always taken this viewpoint into serious consideration, and the treatment of man in Africa has not

---

[1] London: SCM Press, 1963.

always been an outworking of this truth. It is just this view of man which is much needed in Africa today.

Man is to be studied not primarily by an analysis of his nature (physical or even spiritual), but by an analysis of his history, a study of his socio-historical behavior, which in the New Testament is to be understood as his response to divine activity through the Holy Spirit. When man is dealt with by the Spirit of God, he is breathed into; and that act of breathing into him makes him a living soul, a self-determining creature who behaves not only with reference to himself, but also with reference to others in society and to God. This is what it means to be "a living soul." When grace is infused into the soul, it inspires. It leads to repentance and to conversion. And hence, conversion is not a static experience over which one merely rejoices in retrospect. It is a divine inbreathing which is expected to send a man to live at a higher level of relationship. Conversion is not complete until one joins the church. Joining the church is not meaningful until one joins in Christian action.

The Spirit's powers which are known to be at work in the individual become operative because the individual has become a part of the society of believers. This is important to note in the New Testament teaching of the Holy Spirit, and it should lead to a better appreciation of the meaning and significance of the corporate personality and of its contribution toward making the individual what he is. The Christian is a Christian because he shares in the Holy Spirit. It is this sharing that creates the church (Acts 2). The Christian is a Christian because he shares with others the fruit of the Holy Spirit.

The Holy Spirit is given to man as a member of the new society in the fellowship of the Holy Spirit. The reason that the Spirit is given is to enable the individual to exercise his responsibility to the Body, that is, to the rest of the community. It is this functioning, this responsibility, that gives the member his place in the Body. This is what makes a member. Apart from this functioning, it is not of the Body. What is not of the Body is then cast off like a branch, and it withers, and it becomes fit only for burning. So, to quote Paul Lehmann again:

According to the *description*, what it takes to make and to keep human life human in the world is "the unsearchable riches of Christ . . . the plan of the mystery hidden for ages in God who created all; that through the church the manifold wisdom of God might now be made known to the principalities and powers in the heavenly places . . . until we attain . . . to mature manhood to the measure of the stature of the fullness of Christ (Ephesians 3 : 1–12).

It is when we relate this view to the ethical problems of contemporary social change in Africa today that we see the way through certain present difficulties.

### The Spiritual Problem of National Democracy in Africa

Two issues illustrate the moral uncertainty and ethical dilemmas of the social situation in Africa, whether it be the plural society strongly influenced by traditional religion, custom and morality, as in East and West Africa, or the racialist situation of South Africa and Rhodesia. The first is the concept of democracy and the second is the question of race.

A common search is going on all over Africa for indigenous values in all realms of social organization, including politics and government. There is a quest for a political system that will maintain the balance of law and order, freedom and justice in a newly created nation. To what extent can the traditional political institutions of the different countries be fused with the new structures that result from the process of modernization, and what will be the shape of a democracy that can maintain the balance between unity and autonomy, between freedom and fellowship, between tribal self-determination and national self-fulfillment?

Most countries have made a deliberate choice for welfare democracy, since economic justice was one of the promises of electioneering campaigns and of the earlier movement for independence. The details of welfare democracy have still to be worked out, and party leaders have still to spell out what they mean by "democratic socialism," "conscientious socialism," or "African socialism."

Most of the newly independent countries quickly settled for democracy as opposed to totalitarianism. Since it is now recognized that certain areas of traditional society contained remarkable measures of democracy there is little conflict here. But with the granting of independence the politician has inherited a constitution that has written into it the western-type parliamentary procedure. Parliamentary democracy involves the existence of an official opposition. Even though, in practical experience, there have been instances of the electorate returning a one-party government, those who insist that parliamentary democracy necessarily involves an opposition have had to resort to the alternative of arousing minority tribal feelings to provide such an opposition, a tactic that involves some dubious ethical judgments. Indigenous governmental procedure in precolonial African societies knew no official opposition, but provided for checks upon government in other ways; hence, an official opposition is an alien institution in traditional African societies, though democratic government as such is not.

The debate about political life in Africa has concentrated so far on the defense of this official opposition as a guarantee against the threat of dictatorship or totalitarianism. Nevertheless, the emphasis need not be put there; and it is wrong to believe that there is only one possible solution, especially where this is known to be dependent on so many other preconditions. With or without an official opposition, the basic requirement of orderly and just government is respect for law and acceptance by all the rules of the game.

Traditional democracy as practiced in most African countries before the assumption of national sovereignty did not lay the emphasis so much on the will of man as on the will of God, the will of the gods and the will of the ancestors. Once that had been discovered, by divination or otherwise, no one attempted to remain in opposition. We can imagine the surprise and confusion in rural communities where administration by local councils has recently been introduced and where the new method of reaching social and political decision is by "raising up a finger and putting a fingerprint on a piece of paper," a strange departure from the previous practice where, even in the cut and thrust of the debate in the village council of elders, what each and all were reaching for was the will of the divine or of the ancestors. Man in traditional society has been able to relate Jesus' attitude, "not as I will but as thou wilt," to his processes of making social decisions. From the standpoint of tribal man, the problem of democracy is how in social and political groupings the will of God can be discerned.

Man's vocation is to know and do the will of God. The man, Jesus Christ, came both to reveal this in his own person and to perform the same in action. In the Epistle to the Ephesians, Paul essays to show that the purpose of God according to redemption is to sum up all things in Christ and to make *all* men heirs of the heritage of Christ, to make the society of men achieve perfect humanity as we see it in him. Christ's mission in the world provides the double imperative for the Christian in society: first, to seek the restoration of true humanity to mankind, and second, to work toward the realization of human unity in Jesus Christ. The kingdom of God is to be understood as the realm in which these two ideals are perfectly realized, where man becomes truly human according to the pattern of Jesus Christ and where humanity realizes itself as one by nature and by love.

When God became man in Jesus Christ, the will of God was brought within human reach and within human possibility. No longer can man complain of the impossibility of perfectionism, either for the individual or for society at large. What God requires of man is not what is impossible of attainment, because the will of God is the good of humanity. But the attainment is *sola fide;* that is, it depends upon the faith of those who, with single-eyed earnestness, make it the end of life to fulfill the holy will of God.

For society to be able to do the will of God, it first has to put itself in this attitude of faith; of readiness, that is, to know the will of God and readiness to perform it when it has been known. No man can do the will of God unless he has first known it and unless he has made himself ready to accept it. Similarly, the rule of life for organized society is that alternative possibilities of action or systems should be evaluated in the light of the revealed purpose of God for man and society. Human societies stand judged according to whether the whole bearing of man in community is self-preservation, cultural glorification and the maintenance of the status quo, or whether interpersonal relationships are geared unitedly toward the search for both the restoration of humanity and the achievement of spiritual unity to which we have referred above as being the purpose of God for the society of man.

In his famous essay on "The Responsible Society," Dr. J. H. Oldham [2] listed the provision of "ethical guidance for collective decisions and actions" as one of the insistent tasks confronting the church in modern society. "Without such guidance," he added, "the relations between groups must degenerate into a struggle for naked power." The wind of political change, which has brought sovereignty and nationhood to African countries, has brought again to the fore this ethical problem of collective action by groups. Ethical decisions are required not only from the individual acting in a responsible way, but also from social, industrial and political communities that are not exempt from knowing and responding to the will of God. Group decisions must constantly be subjected to the test of group morality. Modern society has produced a multiplicity of small groups where joint decisions have to be taken; and most people have to live their lives executing crucial decisions or being affected by those decisions taken by groups of executives, politicians, party leaders, economic or military advisers, technical consultants, market combines; and the problem of the moral content and the ethical method of collective decisions becomes crucial.

The idea of chairs of Christian ethics in theological colleges that would give special attention to questions of group morality, as Oldham had suggested, has not been taken up in any adequate manner. Yet the problem remains. The churches in developing nations will do well to attach high priority to the work of establishing Christian study centers and lay training centers where this problem can be tackled with earnest concentration. Such centers should not be ivory towers in which to indulge in abstract thought and mere theoretical formulations, but should, rather, constantly provide opportunities for competent and dedicated laymen involved in industry, trade unionism, the civil service, politics or race relations to come together and bring with them practical experiences of the complexities and dilemmas of the ethical demand for collective morality in the structures of the societies within which they live. A profitable dialogue could thus begin between Christian laymen involved in the world and non-Christians equally or even more deeply involved, between Christians living actively amid the dilem-

---

[2] *The Church and the Disorder of Society.* Amsterdam Assembly Vol. III.

mas of our race-divided and technologically organized society and other Christians who normally spend more of their waking hours in meditation and theological reflection. A fellowship based on a better understanding of the technicalities of the situation and of one another's positions might then emerge, a fellowship of prayer and faithful responsiveness to the revealed word of God. Such a group thus becomes a microcosm of the church, the waiting, communing and communicating fellowship of the Holy Spirit, a society open both to God and to the world.

## Race and the African Search for Self-Identity

Of all the forces that deny or negate human values in the society in which we live, racial bigotry, to which incidental reference has been made, is undoubtedly the most vicious and the most virulent. Unfortunately, the racial issue has formed a significant part of the story of the emergence of the African from tribalism to nationhood. It was part of the colonial ideology that tribal societies in Asia and Africa were made up of people who were inherently primitive, that African culture was debased, lower in standard and quality than the European and that no achievement in history could be credited to the Negro or the nonwhite. This inspired the concept of the "White Man's Burden" and the "civilizing mission" of the European powers and administrative personnel. Not until recent times has it been carefully attested by competent historians, with the support of archeological and documentary evidence, that the Negro past has solid foundations in history. The African nationalist believes that colonialism was supported by particular ideological props, the chief of which is that racial and postcolonialist Africa cannot be a genuine society unless it acquires particular ideological foundations, not only in refutation of its own past but also as a basis for the more positive and creative community that must emerge. This discussion involves the most exciting development that is emerging in Africa today: the search for identity.

It is impressive that this debate continues with so little bitterness, so little hatred. The Martinique poet, Aimé Cesaire, speaks for many in his prayer: ". . . my heart, preserve me from all hatred, do not make of me that man of hate for whom I have but hate, you know that it is not through hate of other races that I make myself a digger. . . ."

Yet, an increasing number of people believe that the *apartheid* situation in South Africa has so worsened that the question of violence versus nonviolence no longer remains a theoretical problem for the Christian. "Ethics," they argue, "is a matter not of logic but of life, a certain kind of reality possessed by the concrete."

It is an awkward thing to be called a "moderate" or a "liberal" in South Africa, or in any situation that requires nothing less than militancy to redress wrongs done to any section of a people. I am neither a moderate nor a liberal. A liberal in an African context is a white man who believes in redressing political wrongs by constitutional means . . . liberal gradualism.

This is the confession of Ezekiel Mphahlele, noted essayist of South African origin. It is expressive of the frustration and loss of patience with a humiliating situation that shows no appreciable sign of improvement or of eventual redemption. At this stage the dangers of communal confusion and chaos, arising from the rejection of previously accepted nonviolent methods, are real.

Even if race pride were not fraught with the dangers of conflict and social disorder, the Christian would be bound to set his face resolutely against it; for, in any event, racial prejudice is the product of a wrong interpretation of God's purpose in creation. The full meaning of this awaits some basic theological investigation of the racial issue. True enough, Christian theology sees each man as made in the image of God and therefore as having an intrinsic worth, value and dignity as a human person in the economy of God. It is also true that whatever appears to deny this truth and to treat an individual, either because of his color, configuration, birth, class or education, as less than he actually is, is blasphemy and a travesty of the divine purpose. But how did it happen that the missionary movement for so long tolerated the popular racial theories? Praise or blame for the past is not the question now. What is needed is an inquiry that will produce some fresh theological understanding of the issues involved. How is it that the Dutch Reformed Churches of South Africa, which support *apartheid,* are at the same time ardent supporters of missionary work among the Bantu? When we interpret "Jew" and "Gentile" in the

New Testament, to what extent does "race" enter into our interpretation? What are the limits of racial involvement in the biblical use of the concept? To what extent was this due to particular traits in Hebraic or hellenized anthropology and to false ideas of soteriology? What exactly was the force of the corrective contribution made by the revealed soteriology of Paul, and of his subsequent concept of the Christian mission? The question of mission is raised here with that of anthropology because both were certainly related to the issue. The fact is that the concept of mission is not so narrow as our term "missions" would convey. Some investigations in this direction may provide sobering insights for us all, including both those who confess the name of Christ yet live these convictions in terms of social ideologies that are based on fear, prejudice or self-interest, and those whose social behavior is based upon some wrong applications of the doctrine of "orders of creation." The church owes to all these, as well as to those who are going through spiritual agony about the use of methods of violence, thoughtful pastoral care.

In the search for identity, such terms as "pan-Africanism" or "African personality" are emotionally loaded, since they tend to emphasize by implication the racial difference of African people and the conflict with persisting structures of colonialism and exploitation. So also is the francophonic alternative "negritude." In place of these, Africa needs to evolve an ideology other than racialism or anticolonialism to guide the direction of national efforts and give purpose to its cooperation in international affairs. There are serious doubts whether this can be provided by the economic objectives—necessary as these are—that are generally outlined as the goals of national planning. Less articulate voices have hinted at freedom, order and unity as the yet indiscernible spiritual values that lie unconsciously behind Africa's latest commitment in history. It may be that ultimately freedom will emerge as a positive spiritual concept, that unity will assume forms other than that of militaristic action in a passive nonalignment policy, and that order will be the outcome of mutual trust and mutual respect for one another in a common endeavor to realize among men the ultimate purpose of God for mankind. To help in assuring the openness to the word of God needed for this enterprise, to cooperate in the persistent struggle of obedience to the will of God and to provide opportunities for the practical resolution of the ethical problems of group decision may well be the richest contribution of the church in this generation to Africa's endeavor to enter fully into the realization of the purpose of God.

# II

# THE CHALLENGE OF THE LATIN AMERICAN REVOLUTION

by Gonzalo Castillo Cárdenas (Colombia)

THE factors that condition the function of the church in Latin America are the union of church and state, which characterized the past and which still survives in a few countries; the anticlerical revolt against this association; the arrival of Protestant Christianity in recent history; and the process of "rapid social change," which now characterizes the Latin American scene.

### The Church and the Iberian Era in the New World

From the first moment when Christianity was introduced into Latin America, the church formed an inextricable part of a political and cultural whole. It is well known that at the time of the conquest, Iberian Catholicism, in spite of its universal vocation, was to a large degree an extension of the Spanish or Portuguese crown.[1] The christianization of the Indians was accomplished as an integral part of the establishment of the Iberian dominion in the new world. The Crown financially supported the "Catholic missions" and, in matters of faith, enforced obedience to the religious authorities. The state prohibited the church's enemies from enter-

---

[1] This situation was duly formalized by a series of concessions and privileges (Royal Patronage) granted to the Iberian kings by certain popes, especially Alexander VI. On the other hand, the church enjoyed the patronage of the state. Within this framework, the Catholic missions operated in the entire American continent south of the Rio Grande.

ing the continent and, in order to protect it from any heretical infection, the Inquisition was established, first in Peru and Mexico (1570) and later in Cartagena, Colombia, in 1610.

For its part, the church inspired in the Indians respect for and obedience to the peninsular magistrates, and helped effectively to calm the people when they were provoked by injustices. On various occasions the church served as mediator between the natives and the officials of the crown. The church struck down the enemies of the state with its severest weapon—excommunication.

Despite this close relationship, many Catholic missionaries managed to maintain their religious independence of the state. Against the arbitrary actions and excesses of the European officials, the missionaries carried out an apostolic and humanitarian task in the defense of the indigenous peoples (Bartolomé de las Casas) and of the Negroes brought from Africa (Cisneros). In this respect, undoubtedly, a humanizing function existed within the process of the conquest and colonization of the new world.

Thanks to the patronage of the state, the church was able to establish important social service and educational institutions, through which it exercised a decisive cultural and humanitarian influence. It profoundly penetrated the life and customs of the native people by developing a "folk-Catholicism," resulting from the combination of Christianity and indigenous pagan elements. It also managed to establish a delicately poised equilibrium between concern about the "after life" and attachment to this world. An additional, and perhaps principal contribution, has been to create a strong spiritual and cultural unity throughout the continent. This influence, however, did not result in the development of a deeper faith or in the formation of a more just and humane political and social order. Nor was it able to form a new type of man whose private and public life was a product of the gospel. It seems that the church, in spite of its position of privilege, was able neither to penetrate the heart of the Latin American man, nor to mold his character on a Christian basis. On the contrary, the church was no doubt involved in the historical causes of the present crisis of the continent.

## The Anticlerical Revolt

The early decades of the nineteenth century marked the end of the Luso-Hispanic dominion in Latin America. The Creoles (descendants of the Iberian colonists) who led the liberation movements were inspired by the French and American revolutions. The fine-mesh net spread over the entire continent by the crown and the Inquisition failed to prevent the infiltration of the liberal and revolutionary ideas of the period. *The Rights of Man* was published in New Granada at the beginning of the century. The philosophical ideas of Voltaire, Renan, Rousseau and Bentham, which had begun to make themselves felt before the independence, flooded the continent with all their revolutionary force immediately after liberation was achieved. Very soon this ideological ferment grew into a general revolt against the marriage of church and state, of religion and politics. In Luso-Hispanic America this reaction took the form of a violent anticlericalism, in the same way as in the Latin countries of Europe during this period. The patronage that the church had enjoyed during the colonial era, and that almost all the new nations received as a legacy after separation from their mother country, became a dangerous weapon in the hands of the new anticlerical governments. The church suffered the expropriation of the immense properties that it inherited from the colony. The Jesuits, who completely controlled education, were expelled from most of the countries in Latin America. The priest was forced to retire to his church, and the monk to his monastery. When the church attempted to resist relegation to the margin of society and demanded its former rights and privileges, it was oppressed by new laws and, when necessary, by force. But the church never surrendered. On the contrary, it maintained a fierce and dogged struggle against the vanguards of "laicism," who were also the champions of the freedom of conscience. In this battle the church established a solid alliance with the most traditional forces in society, the landowners and the political and military oligarchies, upon which it has been obliged to depend for protection, in some instances right down to the present day. The close of the nineteenth century witnessed the triumph of the anticlerical crusade in countries like Uruguay, Chile, Brazil and Mexico. Elsewhere, however, the church managed to retain a large part of its former position by means of treaties and concordats which were negotiated to its advantage, thanks to the international prestige of the Holy See. In some cases, as in Colombia, the concordat meant the triumph of the clerical forces over their "laicist" enemies. But throughout the continent a residue of anticlericalism survives, repudiating any form of ecclesiastical intervention in public life, especially in politics, and maintaining a persistent agnosticism and religious indifference.

## The Arrival of Protestantism

Protestantism came to Latin America during the nineteenth century, with the approval of the liberal and Masonic movements, which saw in it yet another ally in their struggle against clericalism. In these circumstances Protestantism inevitably assumed the role of contradicting, rectifying and providing an alternative to Iberian Catholicism. The Protestant missionaries, a majority of whom were North Americans, and the numerous "converts" whom they soon gained, favored the separation of church and state, liberty of conscience and universal public education as a means of spiritual liberation and social progress. Thus, Protestantism represented, for that great portion of society that was already imbued with liberal ideas, an authentic Christian alternative to the traditional socio-religious integration. But the form of Christianity introduced by the Protestant missionaries, a product of the age, also revealed dangerous weaknesses that have become still more apparent today. Its ethic, based on the puritan virtues, was excessively individualistic. Evangelism was conceived almost exclusively in terms of an other-worldly "salvation," the cultivation of personal character, spiritual edification. Though some missionaries saw this personal transformation as an indispensable first step toward the total improvement of society, this conviction never became a conscious factor in Protestant preaching or education. The restriction of religious expression to public worship and personal piety was stimulated not only by the hostile environment, but by the fear that still prevails of "falling into the Catholic error": of establishing an overclose relationship between "the world" (politics and the state) and "the church." As a result, an attitude of indifference toward the huge human, social and political problems, which today constitute the decisive crisis of these countries has emerged. We must, nonetheless, acknowledge that by introducing and distributing the Bible, preaching a more "evangelical" and less "Spanish" Christ and emphasis on inward transformation, Protestantism has filled a deep spiritual vacuum in some segments of the emerging middle class, as well as in the lower classes. This explains its rapid propagation in almost all the Latin American countries in a manner which many have termed phenomenal and dramatic.

## The New Situation of Revolutionary Change

Today the whole Latin American continent is in a dynamic and revolutionary situation, characterized especially by the explosive demographic growth, the internal mobilization of human masses, the formation of social groups pressing for reforms (workers, students, peasants), the incipient, but accelerated, process of industrialization and the disintegration of the traditional grouping of communities. The revolutionary character of the situation arises from the radical opposition of the forces in conflict, the explosiveness of the conditions of misery, hunger, disease, ignorance, dereliction and anxiety in which the great majority of the people live, and the absence of normal channels of social mobility that would give some hope for a better future. All this urgently requires fundamental changes in the social, political and economic structures, which the powerful governing groups are not prepared to permit, in spite of the fact that the masses demand it every day with greater resolution. This indicates that the collective conscience is awakening to the realization that an unjustly organized society, like Latin America, which requires the sacrifice of millions of human beings for its preservation, is not only unjustifiable, but calls for radical and rapid change. With regard to the churches, a realistic summary of the present situation would indicate the following:

a. The Roman Catholic Church has definitely lost its cultural monopoly in Latin America. A secular system of values now serves as the basis and orientation for the masses in their struggle for human dignity and social transformation.

b. Protestantism, being a small minority with a strongly spiritualistic emphasis, has remained on the fringe of the great problems that are the principal concern of the Latin American population.

c. Communism, socialism and other groups of the political left have gone ahead of all other groups in preaching a new system of values, which has as its motivation and goal a social justice that would satisfy the immediate necessities of the people for education, food, shelter, material goods, opportunity for social advancement, just remuneration for work and social security.

d. The movements that are leading the struggle for social justice do not regard religion as an appropriate means of achieving this end: rather, they see it as one of the causes that produced the injustices of today. Therefore, very few see the need for a religious awakening.

e. Ideologically, Marxism presents itself to the uneasy conscience of the new intellectual generation as the only ideology that explains in a comprehensive manner the present situation, and offers appropriate incentives and instruments to change it.

## The Efforts of the Churches Today

A. *Roman Catholicism.* If there is one thing that has characterized the Latin American religious scene over these last few years, it is the awakening to the harsh realities of the continent. This has been a severe shock, especially to the more sensitive individuals, and it is beginning to have the same effect on the ecclesiastical structures. The conviction is growing that there is no time to lose, that the church is awakening too late and that consequently the formulation and application of a strategy adequate to the new situation is the priority of the moment. The alternative could be a violent revolution, of antireligious and Marxist inspiration, of which Cuba, a "country no less Catholic than Brazil, is the sad symptom and example." [2]

In the last four years, under the example and inspiration of

---

[2] Emergency Plan of the Bishops of Brazil, CIF Monograph Number 2, p. 18.

Pope John XXIII, and upon the basis of the famous encyclicals *Mater et Magistra* and *Pacem in Terris,* the hierarchy itself has taken the initiative in various countries (Brazil, Chile, Peru) by means of courageous official documents.[3] The following common points reveal the unity of focus, analysis, emphasis and solutions proposed in these documents:

1. The total situation of the continent in its social, economic, political and ideological aspects is taken as the necessary starting point. The understanding and realization of the mission of the church should be built "upon the basis of a rigorous knowledge of the sociological realities." [4] These realities are obvious in the extreme: "Misery, ignorance, dereliction and desperation stare everybody in the face," say the Bishops of Chile.[5]

2. The Catholic Church sees itself, in these documents, as a "minority force" in spite of the nominal catholicism of the entire continent. ". . . Christianity constitutes a minority, not only in the number of the faithful, but also in the real influence on diverse social structures and in the national community as a whole." [6] Pastoral action, according to these documents, should proceed, not on the basis of a "Christendom," but of a "mission field." This distinction is of fundamental importance, since it recognizes that the situation of yesterday, in which Latin American society, along with its economic, political and social structures, was integrated on the basis of the Roman Catholic religion, has gone for good. This age has given way to a society which is secularized at least in the nature of its structures and in the mentality of a great part of its population. It has become impossible to continue to take for granted that Latin America is a Christian continent.

3. These documents insist on the urgent necessity for certain

---

[3] I refer here principally to the following:
1. Pastoral Plan of the Bishops of Chile (July, 1961; March, 1962)
2. Emergency Plan of the Bishops of Brazil (April, 1962)
3. Pastoral letter on social problems (Chile, 1962)
4. Pastoral letter on social reform (Brazil, 1963)
5. Pastoral letter on social reform (Peru, 1963)
Comprehensive extracts from these documents appear in *Recent Church Documents from Latin America,* Monograph No. 2, published by the Center of Intercultural Formation (CIF) Cuernavaca, Mexico.
[4] Pastoral Plan of the Bishops of Chile, p. 4.
[5] *Ibid.,* p. 26.
[6] *Ibid.,* p. 3.

basic reforms, particularly in the agrarian, educational, administrative and political spheres. The church has resolved to participate actively in this transformation, and it finds itself, therefore, aligned at times with the conviction that revolutionary changes are inevitable, be it with, without, or in spite of, the church. Nevertheless, these pastoral letters stress that the reforms should be promoted, with humanitarian and spiritual motives, because they constitute a Christian obligation.

Our labor of transformation [say the Chilean bishops] ought to be sincere and undertaken with a view to real and true economic, social, cultural, political and spiritual promotion and elevation of the working world, and not guided toward a negative anti-communism, to defeat and eliminate the enemy for the purpose of the better maintenance of the present social and economic order; nor should it be limited to a paternalism more inclined to charity than to justice. . . .[7]

How is this labor of transformation to be carried out? The main emphasis is laid here on the Christian layman, whose task is not limited—as it appears traditionally to have been—to collaboration with the hierarchy, but consists mainly in building up the new world on the basis of a Christian inspiration. "To be a true Christian one must take up a position regarding these reforms. . . ." [8] Thus, the layman fulfills "an indirect apostolate" for which he assumes full responsibility.

These approaches to the problem have already begun to show results in nearly all our countries. They are stimulating a conscious Catholic activism that constitutes a new phenomenon in Latin America, but one which is already receiving strong international support.

Efforts such as these provide a good proportion of leaven within the continent. But are they enough to leaven the entire mass? Will the clergy be able to comprehend and assimilate, with profound human and Christian sensitivity, the realities of the situation? Will they be capable of experiencing that transformation of mind and heart that true pastoral action requires?

The efforts of the Catholic Church toward renewal are encountering serious obstacles. The first, and perhaps the most formi-

[7] *Ibid.,* p. 30.
[8] *Ibid.,* p. 27.

dable, stems from the intimate relationship of Catholicism with that Latin American society which must disappear, and which is already beginning to crumble. We do not refer only to the historic marriage of the church to the "factors of power," the rich and the powerful. It is a question of the hierarchy of values—the ideology which made it possible to develop an unjust and dehumanized social and political organization. Can the church not only disengage itself completely from the traditional structure, risking the fury of its old associates, but also arrive at a new interpretation of its own social ethic? Can the church develop a new system of values, based upon justice and love, that will permit it not only to secure a place of influence in the new Latin America which must inevitably emerge, but also—and more important—to keep it faithful to its reason for existence, that is, to the gospel? In the words of an eminent Brazilian priest who has lived intensely through the drama of his people:

The problem is not a tactical one—will the church manage to survive in Latin America? It is far more a question of truth and justice. If a conflict were to arise between continuing church control of Latin America on the one hand, and truth and justice on the other, we should not hesitate for a moment in choosing the latter hypothesis ... the church can defend the common man without financial, political, or prestige concessions to the political groups that are at present entrenched in power; nor can it flatter these groups, preach only a portion of its social doctrine, defend the people only verbally and lose Latin America.... The problem consists of remaining faithful to a testimony which is our "reason for being" as Christians in the world.[9]

A second series of obstacles to Catholic efforts toward renewal concerns the traditional passivity of the laity. Roman Catholicism lacks its own tradition of religious activism. When called to reconstruct society with a Christian inspiration Catholic laymen are confronted with the task of overcoming centuries of inertia. Because of this inertia and of the tradition of being regarded and of regarding themselves, as mere "helpers" of the hierarchy, lay organizations are always in danger of simply becoming instruments of the clergy. But the most fundamental difficulty concerns theology. Can

---

[9] *CIF Reports.* Cuernavaca, Mexico: Center for Intercultural Formation, Vol. III, No. 15, p. 4.

the church develop a theology of the laity upon which solidly to base its challenge to the laymen to commit themselves to reconstruct the world with a Christian inspiration? It will have to be a theology that gives the layman coherent doctrinal support for his public activity. Here, it seems, lies the principal challenge to the priest, requiring him to set the faithful on the right course to enable them to accomplish their mission in the world.

Finally, we must recognize, as another formidable obstacle, the absence of a religious tension between ritualistic activities and the social and political realities. All the efforts in the church today toward liturgical renewal represent an attempt to cope with this problem. The Catholic Mass, the common worship of the faithful, certainly represents the participation of the believers in the sacrifice of Christ, made in the name of all mankind; it is their participation in the perfect worship that the Son has rendered to the Father through the Holy Spirit. But it implies an identification with the human situation, both personal and social, that made this sacrifice necessary; and it is also a participation in the firstfruits of the new humanity. Worship, that is to say, becomes meaningful only within the context of political, social, personal and human realities. What does this mean for the renewal of worship? [10]

B. *Protestantism.* For their part, the Protestant churches are making similar efforts. The newer "sects," more recently arrived in Latin America, seem to be discovering effective ways of carrying the gospel to the masses. Such groups begin by recognizing a reality that Catholicism is only now discovering: the total ignorance of the great mass of the people regarding the bare rudiments of Christianity. In general, Protestantism in Latin America begins by preaching the gospel in its simplest form, and this has been an important reason for its growth. It is especially true of Pentecostalism, which is creating, all over the continent, congregations that are marked by great religious fervor, strong social cohesion and profound mutual solidarity. This has been accomplished through a combination of doctrinal authoritarianism, simple and

---

[10] Among the most notable efforts to face these obstacles theologically, it is important to mention those of the Center of Intercultural Formation in Cuernavaca, Mexico.

expressive ritual, lay leadership and a radical concept of salvation. Furthermore, the Pentecostal denominations have discovered, at least in a partial and elementary manner, how to relate the gospel to some of the most pressing necessities of the poor, such as health and social solidarity. Yet the almost total absence of theological reflection and, above all, the lack of a theology of Christian social responsibility, has made the social influence of these churches very weak.

The older, more adult Protestant denominations, with their settled traditions and ecclesiastical forms, find themselves, to some extent, in the same situation as the Catholic Church, and, like the Catholics, they are hoping to bring about the reforms and to make the changes of emphasis that the situation requires. But they are beginning to understand that it is not only a change of strategy but, as in Catholicism, a profound spiritual and theological renewal that is needed. Only such a renewal can provide an adequate base for drawing the Protestant churches nearer to the Latin American man of today, enveloped as he is in the process of rapid social change. One might imagine that the Protestant denominations would find themselves in a better position than Catholicism to achieve this goal, because they are not bound to the traditional structures and culture and they possess their own tradition of religious activism and lay participation.

But Protestantism encounters equally formidable obstacles: the fact of its being a very small minority; its exaggerated individualism; its lack of indigenous forms of life and organization; its being too closely linked to outside mission organizations, sometimes to the point of dependency—especially from the United States—its immense deficit in theological and biblical reflection and its underdeveloped social ethic. Common to all Latin American Protestantism, and especially to that part of it which has grown out of organized missionary endeavor, is the individualistic concept of salvation, with its pietistic ethic that glorifies the traditional, puritanical virtues centered in the individual. These obstacles hinge heavily upon the crucial problem that confronts the church: What does it mean to be Christian in the situation in which Latin America lives today?

Latin American Protestantism has begun to confront this problem in study conferences at all levels.[11] Officially, however, the ecclesiastical bodies continue to fall victim to the defects outlined above. Yet we find in its midst growing groups of young theologians, both laymen and pastors, who are beginning to point the way to the renewal that the church requires.

## The Function of the Church in Today's "New Situation"

Accompanying the efforts toward renewal and serving as their foundation, is a series of theological reflections fostered by young theologians, both Protestant and Catholic. These reflections do not yet form a coherent whole that would serve as the basis on which to reformulate the Christian social ethic. Nor do they offer, as yet, the criteria that must set the course for the concrete action of Christians in the turbulent social and political situation which is Latin America today. Nonetheless they form the beginning.

1. *In the world but not of the world.* We must begin with the fact that the church is "the elect of God" (Colossians 3 : 12), "the Body of Christ" (I Corinthians 12 : 27). The structural changes required of the church in today's dynamic and revolutionary situation ought always to express the profound relationships, of a transcendent nature, which link the Christian community to God the Father and to his Son Jesus Christ, making of it a community of the Spirit—that is, a community of faith, love and hope. The church must certainly be orientated toward man, having as its aim the enrichment of all humanity. It does not live for itself, apart from, nor in opposition to, the world. On the contrary, the church is "in the world," and its mission is directed toward the world. Yet the church has an "ex-centric" dimension in that the center of its life, power and mission is not found within itself, but in God. Its head is Jesus Christ.

This is precisely what the evangelical churches of Latin America, with their emphasis on "being different" and "separated from

---

[11] I refer to such gatherings as the Second Latin American Evangelical Conference (Lima, 1961), the Latin American Presbyterian Conference (Bogotá 1963); the Latin American Methodist Conference and, above all, the Consultation on Church and Society at Huampani, Peru, in 1961, which marked the beginning of a movement of growing influence, one of the focal points of which is ISAL the Latin American Junta on Church and Society.

the world," are trying to underline. Unfortunately, however, this has often happened at the expense of the incarnational dimension of the gospel and of the church.

The life of the church must be lived in a continual tension between this world and the coming age, between its incarnational and its ex-centric or transcendental dimensions, between history and eschatology. It is a true tension, in constant danger of disequilibrium, because the church finds itself still on the way toward its own fullness, toward the perfect harmonization of divinity and humanity which is found in Jesus Christ, the God-Man.

In Latin America, as in many other societies, the church seems to have lost its equilibrium, as it comes to identify itself almost totally with the socio-cultural structures, and thus to obscure its true nature. At times, the church has seen itself as coexistent with the political community, embracing and integrating within itself the entire life of society (as Latin American Catholicism has done?). At other times, it finds itself identified with an ethnic and cultural minority within the total community (as has happened to Protestantism?). Or else the church has often engaged in an effort to identify itself with a certain subculture, regarded as Christian and artificially created by the means of "Christian institutions" (which is as much a Protestant as a Catholic phenomenon).

Today the church must reclaim the inherent tension of its own nature, showing the world its true character, both ex-centric and incarnational. It must reveal itself, both as a *koinonia* that lives in faith and hope, trusting neither in man nor in the world, and as a community to which nothing human is alien, that lives in and for the world, expressing within itself the firstfruits of the new humanity.

2. *Justice and Love.* Though the New Testament clearly places "this world" ("the present age") under the judgment of God, acknowledging its vanity and its impending disappearance, it also affirms that its preservation as an opportunity for the church to proclaim the gospel, is due to "the patience of God" (I Peter 3 : 20; 3 : 9; 15; Acts 17 : 3, 31; Mark 13 : 10; Matthew 24 : 14; 28 : 18; Acts 1 : 6–8).

Order, justice, the measure of peace that can be established in this world through social and political structures, are necessary conditions for that proclamation. They are "orders of preservation" that permit man to survive as a responsible human being who can listen to and respond to the message of the Gospel (I Timothy 2 : 1–4).[12]

Upon this foundation is based the responsibility of the church and of individual Christians to search for social conditions in which the gospel can be freely preached, listened to, and accepted. Such conditions do not include only personal security and freedom of speech. They embrace all those conditions of justice that make possible a dignified human existence. It is difficult for man to understand spiritual truths when hunger requires his total dedication to the struggle for daily bread. "The psychological barriers imposed by misery, disorder and insecurity to the reception of the Gospel are as real as the supression of free speech." [13]

On the other hand, the New Testament also characterizes the present age (between the first and the second coming of Christ) as the age of the church, the time when the church fulfills its mission by sharing in the sacrificial service of Jesus Christ. Like its lord, "who came not to be served, but to serve" (Matthew 20 : 28), it is sent into the world on a mission of love (Colossians 1 : 24). "The same mind" of Jesus Christ that led him to make himself one with humanity, carrying our infirmities and pain, also inspires the church. Nothing human can be alien to it. It cannot be indifferent to the slavery to which men are subjected by the demonic powers which rule this darkness (Mark 3 : 14–15; Luke 9 : 1–6). In fulfilling this mission the church, like its lord, does not refuse the company of sinners (Matthew 9 : 13; Luke 15 : 2).

## Practical Implications for the Program of the Church

The church has thus a clear task of love and justice to perform a mission equivalent to that of the Old Testament prophets. Taking into account the specific characteristics of the Latin American situation, the church's function must include the following:

---

[12] JOSÉ MIGUEZ BONINO, "Biblical and Theological Basis of the Social Responsibility of the Church," *Encounter and Challenge* (*Encuentro y Desafío*), Report of the Consultation at Huampani, Peru, p. 22.
[13] MIGUEZ BONINO, *ibid.*, p. 23.

1. It must itself be convinced, and proclaim with conviction, that Jesus Christ is sovereign over the Latin American situation. It must reject the comfortable divorce between faith and society, affirming that life in its entirety is under the judgment and mercy of God. Because of its extracultural nature and its spiritually based theology, much of Latin American Protestantism finds it difficult to take this doctrine seriously. As a result, an attitude of indifference toward the fate of society has developed, along with a belief that Jesus Christ is interested only in the "little flock" which is the Evangelical community. Latin American society is seen, therefore, as being only "under the judgment of God" (corrupted, lost) while the Evangelical church is "under the mercy of God" (transformed, redeemed).

2. Like the prophets of Israel and like Jesus himself (Luke 4 : 18–19) the church must take the part of the poor and the humble. "Seek justice, correct oppression; defend the fatherless, plead for the widow" (Isaiah 1 : 17). This means that it must speak loudly and clearly and even become actively involved in the struggle against the present political, social and economic organization that keeps the majority of the people in virtual slavery and deprives those who do not belong to the privileged elite of the full opportunity to live responsibly before God.

In order to fulfill this function, the church will have to renounce every privilege derived from its association with the groups at present entrenched in power and to demonstrate its complete independence of the ideological and economic blocs which divide the world today. "Complete independence" poses other problems that the Protestant churches in Latin America are only now beginning to discover: What should be the relationship between church and state? In what areas should there be constructive cooperation between the two? How can the churches express their unity and interdependence with their sister churches in other countries without giving the impression that they are "foreign agents"?

3. On the basis of love and justice as the ethical imperatives of the church, and according to the theological significance of the present age as the "era of the patience of God," in which the right conditions must exist for the gospel to be proclaimed, listened to and accepted, the church must understand its mission in terms of

the humanization of secular society. By this we mean at least the following:

a. Through its way of living, as a community of faith and hope, and through the proclamation of the gospel, the church will be "a voice crying in the wilderness," that points beyond the material, beyond the immediate necessities, beyond human resources, beyond the possibilities of the state and beyond itself, toward a transcendent reality, apart from which the human quality of man is reduced and stunted, and the desire of God that man "might have life and have it more abundantly" is frustrated.

b. This function, however, can be realized only by means of a responsible Christian presence in the midst of all the situations in which men are fighting for their liberation and their dignity. Christians cannot be "absent." But their presence is a responsible one only when they participate in efforts toward this end. This implies participation in equivocal situations in which the dividing line between good and evil is not clear-cut, and in which decisions will have to be made in obedience to the imperative of love and justice, of forgiveness and reconciliation. Is there a theological basis for cooperation between Christians and non-Christians? We believe that it does exist in the fact of our common humanity, the fact that all men have been created in the image of God and are seeking, whether they realize it or not, their own liberation, their consciences bearing witness to their Creator. Service to mankind implies collaboration and some identification with all men of good will, though they may ignore or deny the sovereignty of Jesus Christ over the world. This collaboration implies, in practice, cooperation for the achievement of certain short-term goals with persons who may profoundly differ from us regarding fundamental questions and ultimate aims.

c. Finally, Christians must demonstrate their presence in the revolutionary process by a concern for the integrity of men. They must refuse to allow them to be manipulated and used as mere instruments when in reality they are the object and end of the whole process of social transformation. The demolition of dehumanizing structures in society is plagued with contradictions and frustrations, which in turn tend to dehumanize and destroy its own victims. The fight against the privileged groups, the vested interests, the powerful organizations that benefit from the misery of others is a struggle in which the deception and exploitation of the masses by their pseudorepresentatives can easily let in a whole series of revolutionary injustices. The destruction of an entire social system implies, moreover, that those who carry it out find themselves outside the moral and legal codes which are a product of the very system that they are attempting to destroy, and a situation of inner anarchy can develop in the life of the revolutionary which tends to degrade his personality and corrupt his character.

In this situation the Christian presence, in its concern for human integrity, must be as the salt of the earth and as the leaven of the mass. The right forms and methods with which to fulfill its function become apparent only in the reality of each concrete situation, as the result of spiritual communion with Jesus Christ and of the determination to follow him wherever love and justice require.

# 12

# WHERE OTHER RELIGIONS DOMINATE

## by J. RUSSELL CHANDRAN (India)

HARDLY a country in the world today has escaped rapid social change. Historical and sociological studies provide ample evidence of the part the church has played in transforming these societies. But the churches have themselves been influenced and molded by changing society. We must therefore ask: What, in the purpose of God, is the distinctive function of the church in society? This chapter attempts to answer the question with special reference to a society dominated by another ancient religion, such as Hinduism.

### The Indian Church and Social Concern

The Christian community in India numbers about eleven million in a population of over 450 million. It is not easy for such a small community to believe that it has a creative function in the country's struggle for a new society, and on the whole its history reveals an absence of concern for social and political change. Christian concern for man and the humanitarian services organized by the Christian missions in the fields of education, medical aid and rural reconstruction had radical results for the reformation of Indian society, but the church showed little interest in the movement for political independence. The situation has been described as follows:

While Christians have done much in the way of social service, they have not, on the whole, seriously considered the larger questions of social, economic and political order which face the entire nation. They have trained men to be honest, considerate and just in personal relationships, but they have not usually thought through the consequences of this political life. . . . As a result, those who are concerned with social justice look to movements other than Christianity for the insights and principles which the church has failed to declare.[1]

A dominant, and continuing, factor has been the pietistic background of many of the Christian missions and the revivalist and otherworldly interpretation of personal salvation. But since political independence, many churches in India have shown a growing concern to play a more active role in social change. A similar change of outlook is to be observed among the Roman Catholics, in their life. A very active Roman Catholic Social Action group has a program of education in social concerns through institutes and publications. The National Christian Council of India has in recent years given special attention to the study of subjects like "Economic Life" and "Social Witness." The Church of South India had as the main theme for the 1962 meeting of the Synod, "Church and Society," and a resolution passed at this Synod declares: "The Synod believes that the social revolution now taking place in India is a manifestation of the eternal purpose and judgment of God in human history. . . ." [2] But the spearhead of creative Christian thinking is represented by the Christian Institute for the Study of Religion and Society, founded by the late P. D. Devanandan and now directed by M. M. Thomas, which is stimulating the churches and particularly the educated Christian laity to consider the relevance of the Christian faith for society and to give attention to the theology of social witness.

The institute is building up a body of literature on the church's social concern: the quest for democracy, religious freedom, community development, changing pattern of the family, nation-building and so on. In *Christian Participation in Nation Building* (1960), which surveys the result of four years' work on these problems, the focus of Christian social interest is on three concerns:

---

[1] *Christianity and the Asian Revolution*, R. B. MANIKAM, ed. Madras: 1954, p. 87.
[2] Church of South India, Synod Minutes, 1962, p. 15.

(1) To work out the elements of a Christian understanding of certain crucial issues in the political, economic and social development of modern India;

(2) To enter into conversation with socially conscious non-Christians, both secularist and Hindu, in order to consider together the nature of an adequate social philosophy for the new India, and to work out the basis of Christian cooperation with them in social action.

(3) To help the church in India to rethink the pattern of her life, mission and service and to reorientate her policies and programmes accordingly, with relevance to her call to social witness in a developing nation.[3]

The Institute's efforts for Christian participation in social change and the development of similar social concern in the churches really mark the rediscovery of the intimate relationship between the ultimate concerns of the church and the goals set for society. The Christian's social mission is no mere by-product, but is integral to his faith in Christ; and redemption through God's work in Christ cannot be understood without reference to the redemption of society. Participation in the work of the World Council of Churches and of the East Asia Christian Conference and in the ecumenical discussions on Church and Society has certainly helped the Indian churches to take this rediscovery more seriously, but it would be wrong to suggest that the rediscovery has come from outside. There is a dialectical relationship between the local and the world dimensions of the renewal of the church; and the discernment of this relationship, calling for responsible involvement in India's social revolution, has been awakened by their interaction.

## Concern for Social Change in Indian Hinduism

All the great religions of the world today claim to be capable of transforming society, which raises the question whether the church has any distinctive function in society. For some modern interpreters religion has little to do with social change. K. M. Panikkar, for example, recognizes that traditional concepts of society laid down in the Hindu scriptures had ceased to be relevant. But in his twofold concern for the defense of Hindu religion and

---

[3] *Ibid.*, Preface, pp. vi–vii.

for the strengthening of Indian national life, he proposed a radical separation of religion from social concerns. For him, the changes which have come about in Hindu society have in no way challenged the universal and eternal validity of the inner truth of Hinduism, which is concerned with the union of the *atman* and the *brahman*. Social changes are guided by laws which have little to do with religion. "Regeneration of the Hindu people is possible only by emphasizing the secular character of their social institutions, and by giving them the framework of a national law which will slowly transform them from an inchoate mass of unrelated groups into a single Hindu community." [4] He is not in the least concerned about what the inner spirit of Hinduism may have to contribute to social changes. Social changes are brought about by other factors, and only secular nationalistic considerations should determine the social structures. The social institutions of Hinduism are in no way integrally connected with either the outer or inner forms of religion.[5] Though this view may be shared by many, the general neo-Hindu position is that religion rightly practiced contributes to the renewal of society. Even while adopting the *advaita* interpretation of Hinduism, Swami Vivekananda advocated that Hinduism can provide the basis for the social and political regeneration of India. Dr. S. Radhakrishnan holds the same conviction. Speaking on *Religion and Society* about twenty years ago he said:

Civilization is a way of life, a movement of the human spirit. Its essence lies not in any biological unity of race or in political and economic arrangements, but in the values that create and sustain them. The politico-economic structure is the framework intended to give expression to the passionate loyalty and allegiance of the people to the vision and values of life which they accept. . . . The character of a civilization is derived from its conception of the nature of man and his destiny.[6]

He says that religion rightly conceived and practiced will bring about a profound renewal, a peaceful revolution and the conquering of abuses for the benefit of the deeper tradition. In his later

---

[4] *Hindu Society at Cross Roads*. Bombay: Asia Publishing House, 1961, p. 27.
[5] *Op. cit.*, p. 124.
[6] *Religion and Society*. London: George Allen & Unwin, 1947, p. 22.

speeches and writings he stresses the importance of the Hindu commitment to *Dharma* as a potent force for the reconstruction of society. Another apologist for Hinduism, C. P. Ramaswamy Iyer, regards the revival of Hinduism as necessary for building a stable society in India. He writes:

And I believe myself that unless a sense of true religion is reborn and revitalized as Sri Ramakrishna and Swami Vivekananda endeavored to encourage we shall not solve the problem of our stability, because mental, moral and psychological stability is not born of formal or political proposition or syllogisms. It is born of faith in something, and of conviction and aspiration towards a lofty goal. If these be absent, then we cannot get stability in society.[7]

That certain ethical values have to be realized in social and political life is acknowledged in most of the modern religious movements in Asia. After a critical study of the ethical ideals of modern Hinduism Dr. Roland W. Scott concludes:

An analysis of modern Hindu developments shows the movement towards an ethical view of society which has some important religious aspects. The general objective of the various currents of thought was a conception of life that offered human satisfaction in terms of personal values. . . . The whole movement towards the making of a democratic society which would ensure the welfare of all its members was first apparent in the social ideals of the sects and later became more forcefully evident in the political and economic as well as social objectives of national development.[8]

It is certainly difficult to see whether Hinduism has produced a clear-cut and dynamic social doctrine based on its own religious presuppositions. It is significant that Vasant Nargolkar, in *The Creed of Saint Vinoba,* explicitly acknowledges that "the idea of selfless social service to the community as part of religion is Christian in origin." [9] But even while acknowledging the role of the Christian church in initiating social services, non-Christians do not concede any uniqueness in the continuing mission of the church in society. On the contrary, there is widespread belief that the right

---

[7] *Fundamentals of Hindu Faith and Culture.* Madras: Ganesh and Co., 1959, p. 87.
[8] *Social Ethic in Modern Hinduism.* Calcutta: YMCA Publishing House, 1953, p. 217.
[9] Bombay: Bharatiya Vidya Bhavan, 1963, p. 105.

practice of Hinduism would promote harmony, peace and justice in human relations. In welcoming and honoring Hindu religious leaders such as the head of the Sankaracharya Mutts, several political leaders have recently referred to their contribution to the strengthening of social harmony and peace. Gandhi's interpretation of a nonviolent society and its continued influence in India through the Sarvodaya movement have greatly strengthened the neo-Hindu assumption about the common goal of all religions and the equality of status of all great religions with regard to their role in society.

### Secular Movements for Social Change in Indian Life

It is also important to recognize the secular forces at work toward the achievement of a new society in lands hitherto dominated by religions other than Christianity. Much more than in any previous period of human history a radical social revolution is gaining momentum today in these countries. People are being awakened to their legitimate social, economic and political rights. They are no longer satisfied with charity, they are learning to demand justice. The national life of India certainly reflects this revolution. The Indian Constitution accepts the principles of justice, liberty, equality and fraternity. In Part IV, which deals with the directive principles of state policy, the Constitution affirms that the state shall strive to promote the welfare of the people by securing and protecting, as effectively as it may, a social order in which justice—social, economic and political—shall inform all the institutions of national life. The state shall, in particular, direct its policy toward securing that the citizens, men and women equally, have the right to an adequate means of livelihood; that the ownership and control of the material resources of the community are so distributed as best to subserve the common good; that the operation of the economic system does not result in the concentration of wealth and means of production to the common detriment. The Constitution recognizes the right of every citizen to a decent standard of life and is opposed to the accumulation of wealth in the hands of a few people. The preamble of the country's Five Year Plans envisages the same goals of raising the people's standard of living and narrowing the gap between the rich and the poor. It was this goal that was defined by the Avadi Session of the Indian National Congress in January, 1955, in terms of a socialistic pattern of society: "Where the principal means of production are under social ownership or control, production is progressively speeded up and there is equitable distribution of the national wealth." [10] Economic justice is not the only objective in India's national planning. In outlining the goal of the socialist pattern of society, it is also explicitly affirmed that the goal will be implemented only through democratic methods. Nehru, who was largely responsible for the development of the idea of a socialist pattern for India, was equally firm in his opposition to totalitarian methods. In his speech to the Planning Commission in 1956 he had emphasized "the friendly cooperative approach, rather than the approach of trying to eliminate each other." Addressing the All-India Congress Committee in May, 1958, Nehru said:

I do not want state socialism of that extreme kind in which the state is all-powerful and governs practically all activities. The state is powerful politically. If you are going to make it very powerful economically also it would became a mere conglomeration of authority.... My idea of socialism is that every individual in the state should have equal opportunity for progress.[11]

The acceptance of science and technology, in order to achieve economic improvement and to liberate the people from bondage to physical need and drudgery, is another important factor of the revolution. Equally important is the effort to bring about a national integration that will overcome the divisiveness of caste, class, communalism, provincialism and linguistic loyalties. The progressive features of the growth of the secular humanistic outlook that undergirds the social revolution in India raises the question whether and how far the church should discern the sovereignty of God or even the presence of Christ in the secular revolution.

---

[10] Quoted by MICHAEL BRECHER in *Nehru: A Political Biography*. London: Oxford University Press, 1959, p. 528.
[11] MICHAEL BRECHER: *op. cit.*, p. 532.

## Social Change and National Heritage

Even those who champion revolutionary social change are concerned about continuity with the cultural heritage of the country, and no one more so, in recent times, than Jawaharlal Nehru. But in spite of his radicalism and of his open rejection of many traditional beliefs and practices, he was accepted as standing within Hindu culture because his radicalism did not involve a complete break with the past. His will, written in 1954 and published soon after his death, illustrates the spirit in which he sought to change Indian society. He said:

And though I have discarded much of past tradition and custom, and am anxious that India should rid herself of all shackles that bind and constrain her and divide her people, and suppress vast numbers of them, and prevent the free development of the body and the spirit, though I seek all this, yet I do not wish to cut myself off from the past completely. I am proud of that great inheritance that has been and is ours and I am conscious that I too, like all of us, am a link in that unbroken chain which goes back to the dawn of history in the immemorial past of India. That chain I would not break, for I treasure it and seek inspiration from it.

Other reformers before Nehru, like Ram Mohan Roy, Rabindranath Tagore, Ranade and Mahatma Gandhi, had also insisted on continuity with the cultural heritage while fighting for social change and created a dialectical relationship with the past which gave strength and vitality to their movements. What does this mean for the church's task? How far can the church identify itself with the past heritage of India?

## Confessions of Christ and Social Concern

In the church's task in society today the basic source of inspiration is the Apostolic testimony to the incarnate life of the Son of God, to the prophetic proclamation of the kingdom of God and to the Suffering Servant who was crucified for our redemption. But what does this mean in India today? The church there has no clear answer, but certain lines of thought are being developed which seem to offer the best guides for Christian thinking in the future.

a. *Contextual Ethics*. It is in the Word become flesh that we have seen the glory of God. Jesus lived and fulfilled his mission in a particular historical context. We know the universal love of God only because Jesus manifested it in a particular context and met the needs of the men and women whom he encountered. He addressed himself to the problems of the society in which he lived, relating them to his vision of the new humanity that he came to inaugurate. The church's task can be understood only in the light of concrete situations in society. Society keeps changing, and the church's task will vary accordingly. The church's mission in society cannot be the same in communist, Islamic, Hindu, Buddhist and dechristianized secular environments. Christian ethics and particularly Christian social ethics does not consist in absolute moral precepts. Recognition of their contextual dimension is most important for the church in India.

b. *Involvement in the Ambiguities of Changing Society*. It is not easy to define exactly what identification with society means for the church in India today. Obviously the church cannot simply stand aloof from the problems of our society; and any form of self-righteous judgment will lead only to its further isolation and separation, as a small minority body. Our church has to learn ways of speaking from within society rather than from outside it. It must become aware of its own involvement in the sin and ambiguities of social life. In all humility we should recognize that in many situations the church shares the moral weakness and failure characteristic of our social relations. In Asia, there are many examples of the invasion of the divisive forces of caste, race, class and the like into the life of the church. The first meeting of the East Asia Christian Conference expressed its awareness of this problem thus:

Instead of being concerned with Christ's redeeming mission to the whole community they (the local churches) are preoccupied with the preservation of their own life, as an exclusive community among many communal groups. This may be attributed to such factors as their economic backwardness, the predominantly non-Christian or even hostile environment, the apparent need to defend their own social, economic or political rights, or identification with a particular class or linguistic group.

The church's awareness of its involvement in sociological compromises should make it very humble in its prophetic pronouncements. It speaks to society not because it has become righteous but only because of its participation in the power of the new creation in Christ.

c. *Identification with Creative Movements Within Society.* The church seeks involvement in society at the points at which it discerns the operation of the sovereignty of God. Jesus discerned in the ministry of John the Baptist a movement that represented a special response to God's sovereignty and a significant preparation for the kingdom of God which he himself was to inaugurate. Is it possible for the church in India to find patterns of identification and cooperation with social and political programs as an essential part of its mission in society? In the studies and discussions on Christian participation in nation-building in India (jointly led by the National Christian Council of India and the Christian Institute for the Study of Religion and Society), it has been recognized that there are many movements and programs for national development that need to be strengthened, and for this the church is to cooperate with the government and other agencies. Special mention is made, for example, of the country's commitment to parliamentary democracy, to the goals of the welfare state, the socialistic pattern of society and to the Sarvodaya movement.[12] A special problem is that of the Christian interpretation of secularism. India is increasingly concerned to develop an open secular society, free from the unhealthy and reactionary influences of religious attitudes that tend to keep people under the bondage of fear and superstition. It is a secularism that seeks to reorder society, making the fullest use of science and technology. It may not be easy to isolate completely this secularist outlook from secular humanist philosophies; and the dogmatic antireligious movements, such as communism and Dravida Kazhagam, have made it difficult to get religious support for secularism. There are strong movements, such as the Hindu Mahasabha, which are opposed to a secular society. The pietistic interpretation of the Christian faith also militates against the development of an open secular society. Though admitting the grave dangers and limitations of secularism in any form, the reports of

---

[12] *Christian Participation in Nation Building.* Bangalore: 1960, pp. 3–5, 74–100, 245–265.

the Christian Institute for the Study of Religion and Society have affirmed that secularism has a creative role to play in India.[13] It has become "inevitable because science represents a basic living law and masses of people can enjoy the values of freedom and community by more and more technological advance. . . . Secularism has become necessary since it provides the basis for common humanity and citizenship in our culturally heterogeneous and class-conscious society." [14]

d. *Prophetic Role of the Church.* The church's role is not merely to discern the creative movements and to cooperate with them, but to fulfill its own prophetic ministry. In Christ's earthly ministry he confronted people with the message of the kingdom of God. He taught his disciples to seek the righteousness of God, which far exceeds the righteousness of the "scribes and the pharisees." In witnessing to Christ the church's task will include the ministry of constantly reminding the people of the righteousness of God revealed in Jesus Christ, a righteousness the substance of which is his universal love for every person. Hunger and nakedness, poverty and disease are contrary to the will of God and so they are to be removed. "Publicans and sinners," the socially and morally outcast, are to be restored to fellowship with others in society through forgiveness and repentance.

If the church today is inspired by the same concern for people, there can be no room anywhere for complacency about living conditions. Society needs to be constantly reminded that revolutionary social and economic changes are called for which aim at nothing short of the liberation of every single person from the consequences of an unjust order. The church cannot rest until every person for whom Christ died has been enabled to have his rightful share of resources for living and of responsibility for the ordering of his society. This prophetic task cannot be fulfilled merely by expressing the ultimate goals in terms of pious religious language. The ultimate demands of God's concern for man must be interpreted in terms of specific proximate goals to be striven for imme-

---

[13] *Op. cit.,* p. 249.
[14] *Problems of Indian Democracy,* P. D. DEVANANDAN and M. M. THOMAS, eds. Bangalore: 1962, p. 89.

diately, in the form of programs for which the appropriate bodies can work.

(1) *Economic and social justice.* There are many areas of life in India where, in terms of God's concern for the universal restoration of human dignity, the revolution is not radical enough. For the reordering of economic life the goal adopted is the socialist pattern of society. Its formulation appears to be quite radical, but are the methods adopted sufficiently so? The gap between the rich and the poor continues, and the rate at which people are able to move from substandard living to a decent standard, with adequate food, clothing, housing and education, is extremely slow. For this reason the structure and the motives of economic life need special scrutiny.

(2) *Concern for democracy.* Democracy is not a self-evident fact in India, and many factors threaten its healthy functioning. The illiteracy of the vast majority of the electorate and the absence of a sufficiently strong political opposition are serious weaknesses of Indian democracy. The tendency on the part of dissatisfied groups to resort to direct action or *satyagraha* instead of responsible political discussion has come under criticism by Christians as well as others.[15] But there have also been occasions where the failure of the government to give sufficient regard to the wishes of large minorities left no alternative. Another problem, though by no means peculiar to India, is that of corruption in public life. A Christian study of the issue has pointed out that "new ethos and social disciplines, able to control the self-seeking tendencies of men in a free society are not yet sufficiently developed; and to develop them is the only answer to corruption in the long run." It then goes on:

The sense of frustration becomes so deep-rooted that people begin to suspect the integrity of political leaders without reason and exaggerate the incidence of corruption. This saps the moral nerve of our politicians and of our political life. Undue utopianism and undue cynicism, moralism and frustration, are threats to democracy. . . . A good part of the political education of the people should be education in moral realism. Indeed, democracy is built on the belief that power corrupts

---

[15] *Christian Participation in Nation Building,* p. 35.

and corruption needs to be checked; and that parties in power, when corrupt, need to be changed.[16]

Though one of the most progressive movements in India, Sarvo-daya also has certain underlying beliefs which might ultimately weaken rather than strengthen democracy. Jai Prakash Narain, one of its leaders, has outlined a nonparty system of grass-root democracy that rejects parliamentary democracy as unsuited to the cultural heritage of India (*A Plea for Reconstruction of Indian Polity*, 1959). Christian reflection on this subject makes an important contribution to the discussion:

It is unfortunate that both secularism, whether liberal or socialist, and Sarvodaya are too utopian in their understanding of man and their interpretation of political history.... Underlying it is the shallow view that man is essentially good and that egoism is no more than a natural or historical accident which will disappear with a change of social or moral environment. This is the basis of the Sarvodaya belief that legislation is not only unnecessary, but is also undesirable because of its implicit coercion.... Similarly the Sarvodaya ideal of a casteless and classless society is no doubt a dynamic to social change. But this idealism has produced an optimism which refuses to recognize the inevitability and necessity of status differentiation in dynamic society. Only a recognition of it can help control the development of such a structure and produce social mobility and equality. Otherwise the formation of classes will be uncontrolled and the danger of class domination and exploitation is enhanced.[17]

(3) *Sex, marriage and family.* Sex, marriage and family constitute a special area of concern for the church. Under the auspices of the Christian Institute for the Study of Religion and Society and the Christian Home Movement in India several helpful consultations have been held on the problems that relate to the family. The traditional pattern of marriage and family in India has been associated with caste, joint or extended family, the dowry system and the practice of arranged marriages. All these factors have contributed to much injustice. Moreover, under the pressure of urbanization, modernization and industrialization, the joint-family system is rapidly breaking down. The caste pattern also is seriously challenged. Unfortunately, the Christian church has not been free from

[16] *Ibid.*, pp. 36–37.
[17] *Ibid.*, p. 261.

the practice of caste and has not found ways to give any creative lead on this question, even though from time to time Christian groups have, in statements, condemned caste. The church must help the Christian community to transcend caste and other forms of sub-Christian groupism in its concept of marriage and family. With regard to the concept of the family itself the far too common assumption that the western type of nuclear family is the Christian ideal needs to be radically re-examined. The family is not an end in itself. Responsible relationships within the family and the responsibility of the family to society are both equally important, and therefore it is necessary to discover how to combine the values of the nuclear family with the sense of social solidarity and joint responsibility implied in the joint family system. In India today a new pattern of arranging marriages is evolving which may be described as one of "guided choice." It combines the responsibility of the family and the right of the individual to choose his or her partner. This development should certainly be encouraged. In the interest of perfect mutuality of relationship between man and woman in marriage, the church must also continue to expose the injustice of the double standard of morality implied in the concepts of chastity and in the attitude to remarriage by widows. There is no doubt that the church should fully participate in the efforts taken to control population, a crucial economic problem. But the church should also help to sharpen the concern for meeting the moral and spiritual problems raised by the indiscriminate use of birth control appliances and the practice of sterilization. In relation to the problems of marriage and family, one essential point to remember is the interaction between the pattern of the family and the pattern of national life. As Christian study groups have said:

It is imperative that the pattern of relationship within the family be conducive to the development of democratic attitudes, such as respect for individual rights, the encouragement of initiative, the development of a sense of social responsibility and equal opportunity for social participation. In family life this implies a new concept and practice of authority and freedom, in which members of the family become aware of their individuality and at the same time of their responsibility to one another, and to the total family.[18]

---

[18] *Ibid.*, p. 174.

e. *Theological Basis for Cooperation with Others.* In expressing these and other concerns in society the church cannot simply stand over against the rest of society. The church should make its prophetic witness in the context of its identification and involvement in society. This raises the question of the theological basis for cooperation with men of other faiths in social action. Gandhians and other leaders of neo-Hinduism would suggest cooperation on the basis of recognizing that all great religions have the same goal, an impossible view for the church. The traditional Roman Catholic answer has been in terms of natural law. But this does not seem to express adequately the concerns which have arisen through faith in Christ. The suggestion put forward in a Christian Institute study might well form the basis of further theological discussion on this point:

Christian faith affirms that the common humanity of all mankind is the gift of God in Christ in creation and redemption. What is the relation of this unity of all men in Christ to the unity of the church, the people of Christ? In every locality it reduces itself to the problem of the relation between the Christian fellowship based on a common acknowledgment of the lordship of Jesus Christ, and the community of the whole neighborhood, the secular community, based on a common acknowledgment of their common humanity irrespective of religious creed. . . . The uniqueness and historical particularism of Jesus Christ are essential to make the church a universal community open to all men. The Christian exclusiveness is integral to the Christian inclusiveness. It is necessary, however, to clarify to Christians and non-Christians how the unique Christian truth affirms and reinforces the idea of the secular community based on common humanity.[19]

f. *In the World but Not of the World.* A warning given in the Indian study is also very relevant:

Christian participation in activities whose presuppositions and goals are conceived in ignorance or denial of Christ is as necessary as dangerous. It is necessary because God has set us in this world, and because his purpose concerns the whole of creation and all men. It is dangerous because even activities which are good in themselves could very easily become corrupted and confused, and can develop a kind of satanic dynamism of their own. It is of the essence of the Antichrist, as portrayed in the New Testament, that he appears as the Christ, and seeks to deceive even the elect. Therefore there has to be a place kept in-

---

[19] *Ibid.,* p. 303–304.

violate at the heart of the Christian community, where God is worshipped through Christ, in whom alone he is perfectly revealed, and who is alone the true and living way to the Father. If there is confusion in this central activity of worship, if for the one revelation of God in Jesus Christ there is substituted at this point any construction of the human religious imagination, any other alleged revelation, any idol in fact, then the end can only be a fatal loss of the one truth upon which we stand.[20]

In considering the church's mission in society, the significance of the faith that the church is not of the world even while it is in the world is also to be taken seriously. What does this mean? How is the church a colony of heaven? How does the church participate in the suffering and the death of Christ? What does it mean to participate in the resurrection of Christ? Is it possible for the church to regard itself as a forward post in the redemption of society without the danger of self-righteous exclusiveness? How does the church point to goals beyond the secular? Often the Hindu and Buddhist apologists have regarded the Christian concern for man and society as rather naïve and this-worldly in comparison with their ultimate quest for *Brahman-atman* mysticism or *Nirvana*. This is certainly a misunderstanding. But the real answer can be given only by the church being a worshiping community, whose central act or worship is the celebration of the drama of redemption culminating in the Cross and the Resurrection of Christ. Through the Holy Spirit the church lives in the constant participation of the self-offering of Christ on behalf of the world. The church understands itself as the new creation of God in Christ and not simply as an agent of society. It is a community brought into being as the Body of Christ, sharing the ultimate concerns of God; and as the firstfruit of the new humanity in Christ it faithfully serves Christ and waits for the fulfillment of the new humanity and the summing up of all things in Christ.

---

[20] *Ibid.*, p. 302.

# 13

# THE SERVICE OF THE CHURCH
# IN A SOCIALIST SOCIETY

by J. M. LOCHMAN (Czechoslovakia)

THE world has changed: This is a universal experience that—in the face of a progressive secularization—is being felt and expressed by Christians in almost the whole ecumenical world, but that applies in a more radical sense to the churches in the socialist countries. In recent decades our churches have gone through a radical change of the temporal order. The changes are far-reaching and almost unprecedented. Their main emphasis has naturally been in the economic and social fields; their aim is reconstruction toward the socialist society. But they affect other levels too, for example, the sphere of the church. This reconstruction is based on the sharply defined presuppositions of an ideology that claims to be the sole authority in all essential social spheres. It is the ideology of Marxism-Leninism, consciously materialistic, which has never had a positive relationship to religion. Consequently the life of the church, too, finds itself in a changed situation. We may formulate that change by using an almost notorious slogan: We have come to the end of the "Constantinian epoch."

By the "Constantinian epoch" we mean the era of the powerful *corpus christianum,* of the political and cultural power of Christianity, of "Christian civilization," the epoch of concordats between state and church, an arrangement whereby the church is either patronized by the state or at least protected, and where the state is regarded by the church as *"defensor fidei"* and exalted by her. For centuries Christendom in Europe belonged to this epoch and received its distinctive character—even in the depths and heights of its theological and ecclesiastical existence—through all the typical facets of this epoch. Christendom built its historical "house" in this epoch, dwelt in it and got accustomed to it. The churches of the Reformation did indeed fundamentally rebuild it—but nothing more. They too—apart from the radical movements which have always remained a small minority—firmly maintained its foundations.

As far as men can judge, this era, which covered nearly the whole of church history until now, is at an end for us. The residue of the "Constantinian order" still survives into the socialist epoch—the weight of a thousand years of European history still makes itself felt in it—for example, in the fact that in the CSSR (Czechoslovakian Socialist Republic) the church still receives financial support from the Marxist state, or in the cultural and historical context, when certain decidedly Christian movements and traditions of the past—as, for example, the Hussite movement—are maintained by public opinion even in a society that is avowedly atheist. In all essentials, however, the Constantinian solution for the relationship between church and society is over. The church is no longer one of the official pillars of society. The opposite, rather, is true: in the context of the fundamental aspirations of this society the church is ultimately regarded as a relic of a past epoch, which for pragmatic political reasons is to be tolerated but which (at least in its original, religious form) is intrinsically foreign to the future of a socialist society. To the individual Christian this means that he is no longer protected and privileged by his society, that his public prestige is not increased on account of his being a Christian, that he no longer conforms to a desirable rule, but that he is an exception, not the "householder" but, rather, "a stranger and sojourner."

At this point the urgent question arises: how is the church to react to this deep change in the temporal order? This is the question that has confronted our congregations most urgently in recent decades—both in the context of the problem of a fundamental theological orientation, and in respect of the important practical question of the proper function of the church in the new society. How is this question to be answered?

If we attempt shortcuts in responding to this situation, we shall, I believe, risk entering two *culs-de-sac* on this road:

1. There is the danger that faced with this change, we shall be overcome by a spell of "theological giddiness." By this I mean that we shall lose theological independence, that the gospel will simply become adapted to the new situation and ideology. Confronted with this temptation we should not be too ready to assume a self-righteous attitude. This, after all, has been the notorious danger to the church throughout the whole course of its history. It has always been tempted to adapt itself to its surroundings. One look at the history of the church shows that fact. Consider the extent to which Christianity in the feudal age became feudalized—even to the most subtle problems of theology! And in the bourgeois epoch Christianity became simply—bourgeois! Why, then, in a socialist epoch should a "socialist Christianity" not come into being? Why do people only then, as so frequently happens, get frightened and sound the alarm? Yet it is, and remains, a temptation.

2. But there is the opposite danger: the temptation to say a clear-cut "no" to this development, to see the threat to the Constantinian era simply as a threat to the cause of Jesus Christ, and consequently to oppose this development to a greater or lesser degree. This temptation is, so to speak, "natural," particularly so for the Roman Catholic Church, or at least for her conservative wing, for whom rejection of the Christian (and this generally means the medieval-feudal) civilization is identical with rejection of Jesus Christ. But the other Christian churches—including the churches of the Reformation—are equally faced with this temptation, especially where a form of society as clearly defined as in the socialist society is replacing the "Constantinian society."

### Two Temptations Confronting the Church

Both these possible positions are theologically false—and for a faithful church they are indeed "impossible." The error of the former position is obvious: using the important formulation of the Confession of Barmen which, in its marvelous actuality, proved to be a prophetically testing and strengthening word in our situation too—the "one Word of God" is made a relative entity with which other historical entities are associated. The Word of God loses its sovereignty, it is made to conform. The error of the other position is less obvious, yet it is—in spite of the opposed practical attitude—surprisingly like the error of the former position: for here, too, the one Word of God is in a similar way associated with a historical entity, this time perhaps an ecclesiastical one, yet, even so, an entity which is no less human and historical. This is the temptation to identify "Christian civilization" with the cause of Jesus Christ, and this means in our case the negative attitude in the face of the threat of the "Constantinian epoch." Here, too, one becomes a victim to human and historical prejudices. Here, too, God's Word loses its sovereignty and becomes conformable.

Both these positions are therefore equally impossible. Both these ways lead astray. Both are to be avoided. Yet as soon as we leave principles behind and turn toward factual Christian existence, it is necessary to add that these temptations are not equally real or equally dangerous. The first of them is relatively less so, both in the ecumenical world and with us. The temptation to assimilate the church to the "post-Constantinian order," particularly in its most pronounced form of a "socialist Christianity," of an ideological blending of Marxism with the gospel, is only slight. Neither the church nor the Marxist state encourages it. We may say, perhaps, that the changed climate of post-Constantinian society in regard of religion—for example, the atheism of Marxist ideology—in a way benefits Christian existence in the socialist system. The danger of an ideological assimilation on the part of the church is undoubtedly less than if it were confronted by a religious or idealist ideology of the state.

The second temptation, on the other hand, is much greater—and for the same reason: faced with atheism the church is being tempted by its own presuppositions and on principle to assume a hostile attitude and to extend this hostility to other components of the *Weltanschauung* (or the system), especially if they are not to the taste of its traditional bourgeois position.

It has been the task of our theological work to withstand precisely this second "reactionary" temptation—without losing sight of the first. This has been done mainly through the pioneering work of J. L. Hromadka. His creative "one-sidedness"—frequently misunderstood and criticized in the ecumenical world—must be understood precisely in this connection: as the attempt to defend the freedom of the church against the temptation of an unfruitful negativism in the light of the revolutionary breakup of the Constantinian order. We attempted this—in the context of the ecumenical biblical theological renewal chiefly represented by the theology of Karl Barth—by a return to the foundations of the biblical message. Is not the gospel of the kingship of Christ the center of that message? But if Jesus is lord—lord of the church and lord of the world—then the church is neither simply forsaken nor lost in any historical change. On the contrary, it may confidently set out on unknown and hitherto unexplored paths. And, according to the New Testament, is not the community of the disciples, obediently following this lord who was nothing but a servant, sent into the world as a servant church? If so, then its mission can never come to an end at the moment when it is losing its privileges. On the contrary, again, such a moment may well offer a genuine opportunity of seeking new ways of service. And does not solidarity with, and understanding of, the poor and oppressed correspond to the impulse of the prophetic and apostolic message? Should not the church, then, be showing understanding for socialism which, in its social experiment, is taking the part of the oppressed and underprivileged?

All these questions and the biblical answers to them offer a fundamental assurance for the church's way into the post-Constantinian society: *this way is open.* The mission continues. The service is being done. It is not superfluous to stress this statement, for it is not an obvious truth which faith is stating here. Even in our congregations, faced with an estranged and secularized environment, people are often heard asking: has the church any future at all? And in our ecumenical relationships we are obliged to listen to the questions so frequently raised by Christians who live under different and still largely "Constantinian" conditions: can the church exist at all in a fundamentally atheist society? And can it discharge its commission in that society?

One slogan emerges frequently in this connection: the slogan of *totalitarianism.* The doubts concerning the possibilities of the socialist society, and especially the possibilities of the Christian witness in it, are often justified by referring to its "totalitarian tendencies." We cannot discuss the full problem of totalitarianism in this context. Sometimes, this term has been used simply as a tool of the cold-war propaganda to support the argument that communism and fascism are only two branches of the same totalitarian tree. We emphatically reject this argument. There is a basic difference between communism, with its constructive and humanistic possibilities and destructive and nihilistic fascism. Yet the term totalitarian can be used in a more sober and less biased way, in denoting the tendency of a society to proclaim one ideology— and possibly one political party—as the only legitimate power within that society. We cannot deny that there is such a tendency in our society and that it poses serious human problems, especially for those people who do not profess that ideology—for example, for Christians within a Marxist society. Still the problem should not be exaggerated and "metaphysically absolutized." There are two basic reasons for this warning: (1) An ideology is never the whole of human reality. It is an important and influential—therefore by no means indifferent—element of social life. But the real life of men is always much richer and more complicated than its ideological pattern. Concretely, an atheistic ideological program does not create an atheistic society, just as a Christian program does not create a "Christian society." (2) A socialist society is by no means a static but, rather, a dynamic society. It may have had its days of rigidity, but those days are gone and the creative changes are not only a possibility, but a decisive reality, and bring with them a growing range of responsible participation and effective social action. To see the basic situation of man—and the situation of the church—in this society as captured within a "totalitarian structure" is totally inadequate.

From this pragmatic point of view, the skeptical doubts about the possibility of a Christian existence and mission in a socialist society are not justified; and, from the *theological* point of view, they must be dismissed, recalling the fundamental biblical assurance: The way is open. In the light of this promise, such doubts may frequently manifest a spiritual inertia that, consciously or unconsciously, links the cause of Christ with a historical "Constantinian" opportunity which is incapable of thinking imaginatively of the creative possibilities of the Holy Spirit, or even with a latent "atheism," which does not take seriously the sovereign freedom of God. That is why, in answering these well-meant but sometimes slightly petulant questions, we say emphatically, as Christians in a socialist society: The way remains open, the mission continues, the service is being fulfilled. No false cares—the cares of unbelief! Rather, the true care of faith. How, in fact, are we to go this way and walk in it straight and upright? How may the church in our society serve in obedience, and what is it to do? To this question we now turn.

### A Worldly Interpretation of the Function of the Church in Society

I shall try to consider some of the thinking and reasoning on the problems of the church's witness in the post-Constantinian society, which in our actual situation is a Marxist-socialist one, under the motto "worldly proclamation" (*zivile Verkündigung*). This motto has been coined in our congregations during recent years of intensive inquiry into a more credible and effective way of service for our church. In English it sounds slightly enigmatic. It points in a similar direction as the ecumenically inspiring program of "nonreligious interpretation" of Dietrich Bonhoeffer, with the difference that with us the ethical-social component rather than the hermeneutical is in the foreground. We try to denote by it the search for new ways of the church's witness in a world that, on account of the general secularization and of its official ideological basis, has to a large extent become estranged from the church, so that the customary "Constantinian" opportunities—like the customary media of mass-evangelization—have become spiritually as well as technically inadequate. The motto itself is of no importance. We use it merely because it contains many shades of meaning and thus brings out clearly some of the implications with which we have been concerned.

We are concerned with these assertions, particularly as regards the consequences for the church's function in society: (1) Proving the freedom of the gospel: reducing traditional "uniforms" (rules of life); (2) serving the movement of the church toward the world:

an ex-centric congregation; (3) witnessing the interhuman relations: an unconditional humanism.

1. We begin with an external, almost banal, aspect of "civilian
witness" which, however, has a certain significance, because it is
the presupposition of Christian service in a society where traditional ecclesiastical forms and institutions are no longer socially
relevant. There is, first, a *civilian mode of life* for Christians—
a *witness without religious uniform,* "without long robes," without the traditional solemn ecclesiastical "dress." In many people's
minds Christianity—as one looks back to the Constantinian form
of the church—is at first related to a certain "dress," a "uniform"
in the sense of a distinct mode of life. Thus, Christianity may be
understood, for example, as an institute for cultivating religious-
liturgical or ascetic laws and customs. To be a Christian, then, implies to take part in religious ceremonies, liturgical actions, pious
usages or self-denying exercises. Or one interprets Christian faith
in a moralistic, puritanical sense: the Christian "does not smoke,
or drink, or dance. . . ." Or, again, Christianity is assigned to
cultural-political categories: to be a Christian is to belong to a
certain party, generally a "party of the pious against the 'godless'."

The Christian church bears a large part of the guilt for these
misinterpretations. In the course of its history it has seen itself in
these "uniforms" and shown itself in them to Christians and non-
Christians alike. How often has the church succumbed to the temptation to understand itself—or to let itself be understood—as a
religious institute, as a society for the cultivation of a religious style
of life! In this way all kinds of prejudices were implanted and developed, so that the gospel became identified with religion both in
the minds of its friends and then, consequently, in the minds of
its foes. This, above all, may have been the danger of the Roman
Catholic Church. But the Evangelical church too, for its part, has
cultivated distinct, if perhaps different, prejudices. We may think,
for instance, of the "puritanical uniform" so dear to the Reformed
(Calvinist) or the pietistic type of the Reformation. Allegiance to
Jesus Christ was frequently mistaken for allegiance to a puritanical-
moralistic style of life. And do not large numbers of Christians
today—both Roman Catholic and Protestant—fall victims to the
third form of misunderstanding by linking Christianity with the

cause of a distinct civilization—that, for instance, of the "Christian Occident"?

In all these "uniforms" a terrible temptation assails the church: the gospel of the free grace of God becomes a law; the redemption of the whole of life a fragment of life; salvation for all becomes salvation only for those who are near, which in turn is all too easily misunderstood as disaster for those who are far off. All this results in a separation that is bad because it is superficial, self-chosen, not justified by the gospel. Thus, the gospel is considerably reduced. There are, admittedly, many and diverse laws of human behavior and style. Many of these laws also apply to Christians and control their lives. But the gospel must on no account be confused with these laws, for it is not they that characterize and distinguish the Christian. The distinctiveness of the Christian is not a program which could be realized through these outward means; it goes much deeper: it is rooted not in a style of life but in faith itself.

"Civilian proclamation" attempts to withstand these temptations to legalize or to make wrong distinctions. It tries to lead the congregations away from cultivating a certain style, a "Christian manner," a code of conduct, from being different on principle, and to lead them to what is simply human, natural, even worldly. The Christian is first and foremost simply a man, a man of his age, a man among men. And this means today: a modern man. He is not fundamentally different from others. "To the Jews he is like a Jew and to the Greeks like a Greek." He is not living a deliberately distinct existence. In his "dress," that is, in his style of life (in the outward forms of his demeanor, in his interests) he is a man of his time. He is not a keeper of ancient monuments, not an exponent of the Middle Ages. He is not a person who on principle always draws lines and guards them—one who is always different, a man whose heart beats to a different rhythm from that of his fellowmen. On the contrary, he is, in the full meaning of the phrase, a *"con*temporary," a man among men—a *civilian*.

This civilian state of the Christian is certainly not an end in itself and not the last word. It is not in itself the testimony, but a means of promoting it: this civilian man is now being called to bear witness to Jesus Christ. He stands where his neighbors stand. But he stands there as one who tries to remain faithful to his lord. Here, then, begins the way of the Christian—in following Jesus, in believing, hoping and loving. In the midst of unbelief— faith. In the midst of despair—hope. In the midst of hatred—love. Where this is happening, the true distinction and the real witness come to pass, yet not through any self-chosen differentiation, but through the fundamental direction of existence. To guard this direction, to defend it from shallow legal limitations, and to distinguish the true witness to Jesus Christ from the substitute wares of a religious style of life, this is the intention of the "civilian proclamation" as implied in our motto.

At a time of social change, when a certain social order (a "law") is being replaced by another, this proclamation may be of particular significance. At such a moment there looms the danger of the church being identified with the "old law." It appears to be the exponent of the past order, and the gospel is seen as the ideology of the former society. And even worse: the church is tempted to understand itself within these categories. This is attractive because at first it seems promising: some people are joining the church for cryptopolitical reasons and out of resentment. And yet, every step in this direction is fateful, for it endangers the true witness of the gospel—and makes it particularly inaccessible to the representatives of the new society. This is the point at which, for example, the theology of "anticommunism" becomes disastrous: it turns the free gospel—which must also be understood as the gospel for atheists—into a law of bondage. Thus, in striving after a "civilian proclamation" we seek to maintain the freedom of the gospel in the very age of social change.

2. Here the second dimension of the worldly testimony becomes evident: evangelical service within a worldly, social and therefore civilian life. We understand this service not merely as a demand for decent behavior as a citizen. This, too, is important. But more is at stake in our aspect of civilian proclamation: it is the understanding of and witnessing to the gospel in its movement "from the church to the world"; it is the direction of the Christian life which corresponds to this encounter.

Movement from church to world: from the point of view of the church this may of course seem dubious. Do not these words sum up precisely the program of secularization, eliminating the influ-

ence of the church from one department of public life after another? Of course we have to distinguish: there is a theologically
exaggerated version of the movement "from the church to the
world"—if this is understood to mean, with R. Rothe, the "merging
of the church into the state," or if a thoroughly justified criticism
of eccelesiastical institutions is magnified into a desire to destroy
these institutions. This almost looks like a manichaean attitude.
The historical burden—and the historical guilt—of ecclesiastical
institutions is immense. But the institutional aspect of church life
is not only a menace but also a need and a necessity: life in the
flesh—in history—also needs this support of spiritual life.

And yet the movement from the church to the world is a legitimate way for the church—and its duty. Perhaps that process of
secularization "from the church to the world" is but a response to
the guilt which the church itself has committed by notoriously cur-
tailing its movement toward the world. Church history is full of
evidence: Again and again the church has yielded to the temptation
to replace the legitimate movement of its service—and this is what
matters in this movement—by one in the opposite direction: from
the world to the church. This assumed different forms: the form
of a domineering clericalism in its Roman-medieval version, or in
the Protestant-modern version of a "purple church." This tendency
was also at work in much more subtle, more spiritual guises—
even within the structure of the church's work. We see it, for
example, in the customary superiority of "Sunday" over the "working day" (that is, the unquestioning concentration of attention
almost exclusively on solemn, festal, religious occasions); in the superiority of the priest over the layman, which, in spite of Reformed
principles, keeps its ground even in the Evangelical churches—at
least in the form of a questionable sovereignty of the religious
"professional" over the "amateur" (or in the minister's one-sided
claim on the interest of the laity without, as a rule, any real interest on his part in questions which occupy the laity). This is in line
with typically religious attitudes: a hierarchical movement in worship, in theology, in social structure. The priest likes to be at the
head of the community: *Ecclesia praecedit*. The movement of the
gospel is diametrically opposed to this typical movement of religion: According to Philippians 2 : 5–11 it is service, sacrifice,

humanity that matter. In this movement the church is being constituted, not as an autocratic institution but as an ex-centric community, a community, that is, which does not have its center within itself. Here is the paradigm of its discipleship: from the church to the world.

A "civilian interpretation" tries to do justice to this movement. It stresses the theological honor of the "working day." This does not detract from the true sovereignty of "Sunday"—the lord's day. But this day is indissolubly linked with the "working days": "The sabbath was made for man and not man for the sabbath" (Mark 2 : 27). A church which remains true to its constitutive movement can therefore never be content to be the church of a single day. It will always claim the "whole week." The theme of the weekday must also be taken much more seriously in the liturgical activity of the church, so that the worship of the church does not become a sacred reserve, but is offered in dedication to the world, to the actual joys and sorrows, labor and suffering of man. And this applies also to the scope of parochial life. It is the purpose of the Christian congregation—particularly of the churches of the Reformation to which it was committed as a special *charisma* and a special obligation—to grow not merely into a ghetto-like community centered on a cult, but into a community of all life, into a fellowship that prays, works and suffers together. This implies a much more serious participation of the laity in the work, for where the church understands itself in this way, it becomes obvious that the church is maintained not only by the clergy but by every member. Indeed, where the movement "from the church to the world" is taken seriously, there it is precisely the layman who becomes the true exponent of this legitimate movement of the church. It is precisely the revolutionary changes of the Constantinian order which make it unambiguously clear that the laity constitutes the proper "apostolic existence" of the church of Jesus Christ in the post-Constantinian world.

And it is not only the layman: The atheist, estranged from the church is caught up within the true movement "from the church to the world." In a certain sense even those who perhaps have never set foot on the floor of the church belong to its sphere—namely the sphere of its prayer and its work. They, too, should be its concern, even in their absence—and perhaps for that very reason. They, too, have the right to have their say even as regards the sermon—they, too, should be included in its message, and not merely as the "dark background" of the lost from whom those present in church are so nicely set apart as children of light from the children of darkness (how often the church has preached in this way—and still does!), but as those with whom we are united in sin and in hope through Jesus Christ. Thus the world becomes present in the church—and the church in the world.

This "civilian testimony" has not only a human and individual dimension, but also a social and collective one. Ultimately our service is concerned with real persons. But the development of modern society has shown with absolute clarity that there are no real persons without wider social relations. These relations—in particular the economic and the political—therefore concern the church. It cannot practice political abstinence and offer as a reason for it that "the political song is a nasty song." It has to join in singing it—with a genuine and pure intention in the light of the gospel, without any opportunism or resentment of the prevailing fashion. Where this is done, this song—care for better justice, truer freedom and a really just peace of the world—is part of divine service. And inversely, divine service—the perspective of the gospel—belongs to the center of the life of society in the civilian expression of faith.

This civilian participation of the church in the life of the world forms an important basis for a credible witness. It seems that it is only from this serving presence in the world, from an undemanding engagement of Christians in the burning problems of the time, that a witness is evolving which makes their neighbors prick up their ears. At a time of immense inflation of all words through the mass media of advertising and propaganda, the mere religious word is more powerless than ever. And the same may well apply to the customary means of mass evangelization and mission, even if from time to time their success—apparent or real?—is great. "Mature," "worldly" men will hardly be reached by these methods. A credible testimony will be developed only from out of the depth of real life, not hastily and superficially. It is in this sense that a true civilian mode is a presupposition of Christian witness in the modern world.

And it is not only a presupposition. In a sense this civilian presence in the world is already the witness—even if it is not yet considered or labeled as such. Dedication to the world in following God's way to men is meaningful in itself—quite apart from any results achieved by the church's standards. "Results," "successes" in the church's activity are, of course, by no means a matter for indifference. The missionary point of view in the church is justified. But it is not the only point of view—not even the first or the last one. Only service itself ranks so high. We do well to remember this in regard to the church's activity—also in regard to new ways of this activity, in regard, for example, to the attempts at a "civilian proclamation." These experiments might also be understood as another "new strategy," "method," as a clerical "gimmick"— as the last attempt of the church to conquer the world. Some of the new ways of the church's work could be so interpreted. But this is ultimately a misunderstanding—and no true help for the church or for the world. For the promise of Jesus Christ to the church is given only in the way of guileless, simple service. A genuine turning of the church to the world will be based not on clever calculations, but on following the way of Jesus. Only by following him can the true dimension of a civilian witness be perceived and faith be tested in the world.

3. We come now to the third "level" of the civilian service of the church in our society: witnessing to the gospel in interhuman relations, striving after an evangelical proexistence. It was mainly in this sense that our congregations understood the concept of "civilian interpretation" as one of the most urgent tasks and as one of the opportunities for Christian service in our society. And rightly so, for the quest for the neighbor is one of the most burning questions of our time. Indeed, this question is an ancient human question, one of the few basic questions of man. Today, however, it is being asked with particular urgency. This urgency is implicit in the structure of modern life: in the rise of "technical civilization," of "mass society" in the world. The Christian need not deplore this development. He knows in sober fact that it has unlocked unheard-of possibilities and realities for man. Foundations have been laid for effectively overcoming some of the fundamental evils of past epochs: we cannot sufficiently stress what it means that

from large parts of the world hunger, epidemics, unemployment have disappeared and are still disappearing. We have much reason to be proud of our present age. Yet it, too, has its dangers and troubles. And one of its deepest needs is the need of man for his fellowman. Amid the incalculable entities and numbers of this technical civilization and its mass society, man is always in danger of becoming a cog in a vast machine, of representing a function rather than a person. He is easily ignored as a personality. Lonely people in the human masses of great cities, men forsaken by the welfare state, neighbors in close physical proximity unknown to one another—these problems are well known. In this situation man is in danger of losing much that is essential: personal relations, mutual understanding and interest, individual assistance. Men's hunger for personal humanity, for their fellowmen, is not being stilled.

Here, then, is an important opening for the "civilian testimony" of a Christian in the modern world. It is precisely here that he is being called and demanded with particular urgency. The gospel itself sends him on this way, the way of fellow humanity; for ultimately the gospel is God's search for man. We need but to recall the hymnological summary of the way of Jesus Christ in Philippians 2, with its key sentence "and was made in the likeness of men," or the saying in Titus of the appearing of the "love of God toward man" (3 : 4). And we may remember Matthew 25 : 40 where, following this "divine humanism," men's turning toward their neighbors is made the touchstone of their Christian faith: "Inasmuch as ye have done it unto one of the least of these my brethren, ye have done it unto me." Here the scope of the Christian witness is indicated: proexistence, existence for others. Only in this movement toward one's neighbor can Jesus Christ be obediently followed; only in this movement can we tread the Christian way.

This way, then, leads to an unconditional humanity. I emphasize the "unconditional" of man's turning to his neighbor, for it is here that Christian humanism is distinguished from general philanthropy. We appreciate secular forms of solidarity with men in the numerous humanist efforts of our days. We gratefully share part of the way in common with these efforts. At times we are put to shame by the resolve and willingness, on the part of non-Christians, to make sacrifices in this cause. We do not separate from them prematurely and rashly. And yet—there is a legitimate parting of the ways. Current humanism is all too fond of drawing lines. Its first and often exclusive concern is for the "neighbor" in the literal sense of the word: for him who is "nigh," for those who belong to the same nation, race, class or religion. Sooner or later the open windows are shut. But the Christian is called to his fellowman even when every natural or ideological sympathy has ceased; when he can no longer see any natural or historical reason for it; where only walls or chasms of traditional enmity may be distinguished. It is difficult indeed to demonstrate true humanity in such conditions. But this, precisely, is the mission of the Christian: to seek and to see the face of Jesus Christ over every man. There is a beautiful saying by Luther: "to receive Jesus Christ in every man and to be Jesus Christ to every man." This means that for the sake of Jesus Christ none may ever be excluded from our common humanity. To look for our common humanity even when we are defending ourselves, when we are contradicting, when we are facing the opponent—and to love even the enemy—this is the witness of the Christian.

Let us finally mention two examples and results of this unconditional Christian service within the framework of human relations. Right from the start Christian solidarity has tended with particular devotion those for whom nobody cares, the poor and the sick, the forgotten and oppressed, those who from a utilitarian point of view are considered unproductive and superfluous. Let us remember the place of honor in the Old Testament for the "orphans and widows" or in the gospel for those who "labor and are heavy laden"! Here is the point at which both the temptation and the honor of Christian philanthropy arise. I speak of the temptation of philanthropy, namely, of the temptation for the church to express its responsibility for man, for the neighbor, exclusively in categories of personal welfare, of charity. This is a harmful limitation of Christian brotherly love. It is a judgment on our faithfulness that a movement outside the church—in particular, socialism—has recognized this state of things more clearly than the majority of Christians. To help a person effectively demands a purposeful, organized and planned system of welfare for the whole sphere of men's social life, a reconstruction of society, not only the dealing with crying individual needs. Here is the reason, based on the gospel, for our saying "yes" to socialist reconstruction, to its principle and to many of its results, such as the generous provisions of our health services. Yet precisely here where the church gratefully acknowledges this national welfare, it will underline again the honor of philanthropy in the sense of turning to those who need personal understanding, personal care, personal interest, in particular the "orphans and widows" of the modern age—people who are lonely and half-forgotten. Philanthropy in the church—which becomes a stumbling block when it claims to do everything—thus acquires a new meaning where a broad framework of solutions and opportunities has been realized, but where the personal turning of man to man is still necessary. "The poor ye have always with you"— this sentence (which in the history of the church did much harm because it was understood as a general doctrine of the impossibility and ineffectiveness of social reconstruction)—is true here. It is here that there is scope for our congregations and for every Christian, scope for our "civilian interpretation" of the gospel.

The task of a civilian interpretation in the sphere of human relations does not, however, end at the level of personal, individual relations. The light of the unconditional philanthropy of God (Titus 3 : 4) also shines on international relations, that is, on the search for a peaceful order of a world threatened by atomic annihilation. How often has the church at this point hidden its light under a bushel? How often has it strengthened the barriers between nations and power blocs rather than destroyed them? Often it has spiritually justified or even kindled the spirit of the "cold war," instead of energetically opposing it. Here is the sphere where Christianity has failed again and again. Yet here there is still an almost unlimited opportunity for new service. Never before, it seems, have we been shown as clearly, now that we are faced with the atomic danger to mankind, that the gospel of God's unconditional will for peace is of direct actuality even in the sphere of "high politics": There is no other way for the future of mankind than the will for reconciliation and peace. In our present situation this means the unconditional will for peace in the world. This is the point at which those who are aware of this will and of its grounding bear an immense responsibility. The witness of brotherly solidarity in a restless and divided world—for instance in the work of the ecumenical movement or of our Christian Peace Conference—is gaining great importance amid the rising tension of these days. It belongs to the most precious experience of our ecumenical relations in these recent years, especially at meetings of Christians from East and West, that again and again we have been able to discover: notwithstanding all our weaknesses and all our helplessness, the pure service of reconciliation, the service of peace is being accomplished in some small part through our ecumenical work. Thus, the witness of the gospel for this world is being borne through its "civilian interpretation" in the modern world.

Wherever this is done, wherever in torn human relations—of a wider or narrower range—a little island of genuine humanity becomes visible within our churches, there witness is being borne to Jesus Christ, even where his name has not yet been expressly named. Witness to Jesus Christ is not borne only where he is named. This witness is already borne where the thirsty are given a "cup of cold water" in his name. His witness is not at work only where he is acknowledged and named as such, where he stands his ground, where he is successful. We are learning afresh that in the biblical term for witness, "martyr," an abiding undertone is clearly discernible. The testimony of Jesus Christ gives light even where its witness seems to be failing, where he is not standing his ground, where he is not being recognized and acknowledged, but where he is serving in simple faithfulness to man and thereby to his lord. Here is "civilian interpretation" in the deepest meaning of this phrase.

### Renewing the Credibility of the Christian Witness

We have outlined a pattern of Christian witness for a post-Constantinian society. It is a narrow way: the church as an institution is of no decisive significance for the public life of society. The opportunities for a direct, organized, institutionalized claim on society are few and isolated. In this sense too the church—compared with its possibilities in an unbroken Constantinian order

—has become poor. Therefore, the way is narrow. And yet—it remains open. And it does not remain without promise. Our Christian witness is, on this narrow way, given the chance of a new credibility.

It cannot be denied that the credibility of the Christian church in the world today—in East and West alike—has been largely undermined. The history of modern secularization is also a history of the shrinking credibility of Christianity. And Constantinian Christianity is not without blame. The interpenetration of ecclesiastical institutions with the institutions of the society of the day, which was particularly obvious in the various forms of the union of "throne and altar," provided not only an opportunity to exert a dominating influence but for an unevangelical capitulation—and this unfortunately even more so. How often did the Constantinian church stand in its own way—fettered by false considerations of its own interests as an institution of the given order! And so the gospel was frequently hidden under the bushel—hidden from those very people who, travailing under a heavy social load, had been waiting for the justice of the kingdom of God by word and deed. Notwithstanding some outstanding achievements of a christianly inspired philanthropy, the church and its message lost all credibility, especially through its failure to meet the social needs of modern industrial society. How many then arrived at the bitter conclusion: the church speaks of God—but it means its privileges and those of its society. It is a community of conscious or unconscious hypocrites.

The burden of this failure lies on us all. Yet now that the Constantinian opportunities have been lost we may be offered a new chance. It may be that a church which has no longer any privileges, and therefore need no longer defend itself, need no longer stand in its own way or in that of others: for in the post-Constantinian society the Christian has nothing more to gain by being a Christian. The one ground for becoming and remaining a Christian in that situation is the ground of faith. Thus the shadow of hypocrisy grows less. And here is the chance of credibility. The mere existence of the Christian church can then already be true witness. A community of pilgrims, of civilian men who do not seek to preserve any social privileges or to maintain any political "anti"- conceptions; who consciously live in the new society and take it seriously—but who try to do so unequivocally as Christians: is not this already—this presence of the Christian community within the Marxist-Socialist world—a basic witness to this society?

There were times when it seemed that this presence was the only possibility of action left to the churches—because of the deep distrust of the revolutionary society toward the church and because of a certain ideological and administrative rigidity of the system. I think of the "Stalinist era." Yet there was nothing passive in this presence: the patience and the loyalty of the church—loyalty to Jesus Christ and loyalty to the people of our society—helped to shape the spiritual basis for a new and fresh service. And when the rigidity lessened, melting away, the Christians received a new chance to participate in the spiritual ferment of their country. A new relevance of the anthropological and ethical quest made many of our countrymen—including the Marxists—more attentive to the possible relevance of a Christian contribution. What is man— can he be understood and explained in economic categories only? Where is the final criterion of his humanity? The history of the past years and the role of Christians in the socialist society has proved that Christians cannot be dismissed simply as reactionary partisans of the past system, and a new dialogue became possible. As Professor Hromadka says, we are "at the threshold of the dialogue," nothing more. But we hope it will go on. We participate in it not as the "ideological masters" of our society, but as real servants. We try, by way of "civilian interpretation," to open the perspective of the gospel of God's way to man for the issues of our lives and of our society. We try to do so through a type of "Socratic evangelism," in which the evangelist is "midwife rather than preacher," to use an illuminating expression of Dr. Visser 't Hooft's. Even in this sense our way is and will be a narrow one— and there is no guarantee of success. But this may be the right way for the Christian church in the post-Constantinian era and may offer a real chance of credible and hopeful service for men in our society.

\* \* \* \* \*

*Postcript:* Comments
by Professor WOLFGANG SCHWEITZER (Germany)

1. What is the relation between gospel and law in Professor Lochman's paper? Certainly it is theologically unsound if the gospel simply becomes a law. It must remain the gospel of God's grace, the gospel which makes man free and opens new ways in every situation. But as the Word becomes flesh, so the gospel, when it reaches man, and especially when it is accepted by man, affects his behavior toward his fellowman and toward society. In the second half of his chapter, Lochman himself gives many examples under the heading "civilian proclamation" (or testimony) of the gospel. In the second half of the paper he speaks about this in a very concrete way, and I should like to subscribe to what he has said there. I would hesitate to call this a new Christian law. Non-Christians are often very good humanist "philanthropists" too. But should we not say that the gospel—and the faith of the Christian who accepts the gospel—gives existing humanistic aspirations a certain definite direction? This includes its influence upon the "laws," the moral standards, the conduct of a given society. If that is true, the trouble with the Constantinian period was not that Christians had such influence, but that they were unable to move forward with the history of man; the church became a relic of the past. I agree that the Constantinian period has ended, and this has many consequences for all of us, not only for those who live in socialist countries. Our social teaching must be radically transformed. But we should not pretend to be able ever to preach the gospel alone. We should accept the fact that Christians at least to some extent can be recognized by a certain attitude or behavior— namely in the direction which Professor Lochman himself has described under another heading.

2. Biblical ethics is always an ethic of concrete decisions in concrete situations; the main question is always: Which way of conduct is in harmony with my faith in Jesus Christ—and which is not? To accept Christ as lord surely implies following him into the world, and I fully support Professor Lochman's concern at this point. But should he not indicate where Christians may be forced to say "no" under certain circumstances?

In this connection it should be made clear that there is indeed a remarkable difference between a church "showing understanding for socialism" and the assimilation, which Lochman so well describes in the early pages of the essay. It is very important, though very difficult, to make this difference as clear as possible.

# 14

## WHERE THE CHURCH NO LONGER SHAPES THE COMMON LIFE

by HARRY ARONSON (Sweden)

THE church *in* Sweden became, through the Reformation, the Church *of* Sweden, Evangelical and Lutheran, and over the centuries it has been bound up with the history of the Swedish people. It was shaped as a national church in close connection with the state, and reshaped as a national *state* church about 1520 after a war of liberation against Denmark, led by Gustaf Wasa. He favored the new religious ideas from Germany for various reasons, and as king was eager to diminish the influence of the Roman Catholic Church. To that end he encouraged the leading Lutheran personality, Olavus Petri, a scholar of Uppsala and Wittenberg. We know, however, that the king had certain difficulties with Olavus Petri, who preached law and gospel in a most personal way, even to the king, taking an attitude toward the authorities that was to become a tradition. Later, in the seventeenth century, when the monarchy had become absolute, a priest is said to have preached against the king. When told about it, the king asked, "Did this priest have the Word of God before him?" The answer being in the affirmative, the monarch decided, "In these circumstances we can do nothing against him." Thus the king, head of both state and church, bowed to the authority of the Word of God.

It was inevitable that in the course of history the interests of the state or of the king should frequently be incompatible with the preaching or wishes of the church; and the problem was all the more striking because the king, in his own person, represented the highest authority in both state and church. But for centuries this situation went unquestioned.

Indeed, in the seventeenth century, a century of Lutheran orthodoxy, the union between state and church was consolidated. The Lutheran confession became the undisputed spiritual foundation of the whole people, a belief and conception of life and world that penetrated the political and social structure as a whole. The sociological categories of Luther's Small Cathecism, an expression of belief and a guide to life which everybody knew by heart, reflected an agrarian and patriarchal world, in which everybody could identify himself (father and son, married and unmarried, master and servant, and so on). Everyone had his privileges and duties, motivated by words from the Bible and interpreted through the theological categories of law and gospel.

This was a unified culture, patterned on the Lutheran belief in God, both as creator and ruler of the world and as redeemer and forgiver of sins. This religious and national unity was also manifested through Sweden's development into a leading power in seventeenth-century Europe. Gustavus Adolphus, who died on the battlefield in Germany in 1632 as a militant Protestant, was for centuries the symbol of readiness for sacrifice, even to death, for the evangelical faith.

This unitary culture was collectivistic, and its piety was of the "church-type." But new religious trends from the European continent—Pietism and Moravianism—reached Sweden. Pietism, which stressed personal commitment and was therefore individualistic, won its adherents mainly among the townspeople and the educated. Moravianism, on the other hand, became a popular movement and prepared the ground for the great nineteenth-century revivals. In the middle of that century several popular movements—religious, political, and temperance—arose which are now looked upon as forerunners of democracy.

Through the ideas and activities of the popular movements, the average man became conscious of himself and learned how to deal with various problems of human life. Traditional propositions about man and society were questioned as fundamental changes occurred in economic, social and cultural life. These and the popular revivals in turn affected the religious situation. Some of these revivals arose within the church; others, like the Baptist mission, were the result of foreign influence. The whole conception of union between state and church was questioned in the dissenter groups and in the political and social movements. Religious orthodoxy and civic loyalty, until then virtually synonymous, were no longer regarded as obligatory for the citizen. Increasing numbers of people came to look upon religion as a matter of personal decision, private in character, with no civic consequences. This argument harked back to the order of the early church as a result of emphasis being laid on the New Testament rather than on the whole Bible. But it was also connected with a new view of man in society. The growing dissenter groups, as well as the liberals and the labor movement, pleaded for the idea of the free and responsible citizen over against the traditional idea of the subservient subject.

These new ideas ran parallel to and grew with the development of industry and trade. Changes in the economy produced new groups that had no definite place in society and that did not feel at home in it. Estrangement from society meant estrangement from the national church, which was built into society and functioned within its framework. Quite naturally institutions had to be changed to bring them into accord with the social structure. In the 1860's, for example, new legislation was enacted to provide for popular representation in government. The medieval order, no longer sociologically relevant, was replaced by a parliament, elected through political parties. As a consequence, the church was no longer directly represented through the clergy. Instead, a church synod was established. It initiated ecclesiastical laws and had a power of veto in these matters, over against the government and the parliament. This establishment of the church synod meant a recognition both of the specific character of the church over against the state, and also of the historical union between church and state.

Later legislation has taken into account the growing demand for full religious freedom (granted in a law of 1951). A commission on future relations between church and state, appointed in 1958, is still at work; and the 1960's will see important decisions and probably changes. Some politicians challenge the veto power of the church synod, which has been exercised cautiously. What is certain, however, is that the state will be vitally concerned in how religious life is formed. We may expect some form not only of coexistence but of cooperation between church and state, a cooperation built on the historical presuppositions, but fully acknowledging the new situation and the demand for religious freedom including freedom from religion altogether.

### Einar Billing's Conception of the Folk Church

Even today a good many Swedes maintain that the national Church of Sweden is a reasonable historical form of organized religion. Some even hold that it not only is a product of historical necessity and chance, but is of genuine theological significance. This view was first expounded by Einar Billing (1871–1939), Bishop of Västeras and before that a professor at Uppsala. Beginning his academic career with a dissertation on Luther's view of the state, he continued with a broad presentation of the Hebrew and Greek view of history and its ethical implications. Almost all his subsequent writings are dedicated to the problems of a national church. Billing won substantial agreement for his conviction that the national or "folk" church, which serves all people within a certain territory and lays down no specific religious or ethical requirements for membership, does express the genuine biblical and reformed principle of grace.

This doctrine seems at a first glance to be a mere rationalization of a given historical situation. Billing himself, in his discussion with the Free Churches, admitted that the organization of the early church might seem the only ideal form, if it could be assumed that this should or could be imitated. This assumption, however, he immediately and firmly denied. Church organization could not, he affirmed, be derived directly from the Bible. The central message of the New Testament is not imitation but justification. God acts through creation and history. The scene of God's actions is history, and the character of his actions is revealed by the redemptive work of Jesus Christ. Through the church man is offered this redemption as forgiveness of sins. The ultimate character of the

Christian message is grace. God's grace is administered through each local congregation within the organization of the Church of Sweden.

Billing focused his interest almost entirely on the local parish. He paints a picture of a romantic landscape, with farms, green meadows, lakes, and on the horizon vast woods and blue mountains; and the white parish church, with its spire, to give the scene its key motif and to strike a specifically theological note. The church is thus seen as a ministry of grace to all who live within the borders of the local parish. Although Billing regards the order of the church as rather arbitrary, and not as prescribed in the New Testament, the organization of the national church expresses for him the ultimate meaning of the gospel. Through this very worldly and historically charged medium, God offers his universal grace.

Billing presupposes the agrarian society of the first decades of this century, when the parsonage itself was often a farm. But fifty years later these parishes have been largely abandoned by the younger generation, who are now in the towns, working in industry and trade. The whole economic and social structure has changed; and we must ask to what extent Billing's conception of the folk church was bound up with the agrarian society and the socio-political and cultural structure of earlier days.

Billing himself was progressive in his approach to change. His feeling for the national church was based on a belief in the dynamic function of grace and forgiveness—that is, on a theological assumption—and not primarily on a historical and social premise. This gives his thinking a remarkable flexibility. The fact that as early as 1929 he had proposed legislation on free secession, twenty years before Parliament gave attention to the question, illustrates his foresight. In his efforts to describe the function of the church, he frequently used the term "service." The church should serve the people as long as the people desire it. This service is a ministry of grace with a theological motivation. It is equally evident that his sensitive mind must have realized that a pluralistic culture was on the way, and that he must have foreseen the demands that would be made on the folk church in the new situation.

Billing's view of the Church of Sweden is by no means the only one, although it is probably the most influential. Some regard it as too much linked to the old society. A commission on social ethics of the church office for diakonal affairs (Diakonisty-relsen) is seeking a new approach to "the people" via the labor organizations, with the emphasis on "democracy." It is argued that like society at large the church should function democratically and not hierarchically. Thus, various and sometimes conflicting efforts are being made to understand the institution of the folk church and to make it function.

## The Character and the Spirit of Modern Swedish Life

In Sweden today we need to clarify the social situation of the average citizen and the conditions in which the church must work. Modern Sweden is a product of evolution, rather than of revolution; it has developed the "middle-way" pattern. Old traditions and new attitudes live side by side and often appear contradictory. What is said here, therefore, will necessarily be hypothetical and oversimplified.

The common man has moved into control of democratic institutions. He has taken over much of the responsibility and authority formerly exercised by the king and his officials. The political goal of the Social Democratic Party, in office for almost three decades, has been to make Sweden a good home for all citizens. The social democratic dream of the welfare state is approaching realization. The characteristic feature of the Swedish welfare state is public responsibility for some of the fundamental aspects of human life. The social security program includes unemployment insurance, old age pensions and a health service. The individual's life-cycle is the concern of legislators and the state institutions. The responsible citizen is aware of his contribution to this system, economically through high taxation, democratically through his right to take part in political activities (and this includes those who oppose the system). His image of a democratic way of life is thoroughly "western."

From the point of view of *personality structure,* the political development suggests a coming of age. The "ideal" worker is a man of dignity, humanitarian in his outlook, conscious, perhaps, of his power, but ready at any time to talk with his employer, who may be a "capitalist" with a free enterprise ideology. When these two men meet to discuss common problems of work and business, they may admit to conflicting interests, but fundamentally they see themselves as coworkers for the good life. Such employer-worker relations portray the middle-of-the-road ideology at work.

The welfare ideology, with its compulsory characteristics accepted by the vast majority, is one side of Swedish life. The other is to be seen in the realm of culture and "way of life" in the broader sense. In this area, as in that of consumption, the individual has free rein; and cultural pluralism prevails. Just as the social democrats have accepted the market economy, so they also have an unideological attitude toward culture. But this does not imply unconcern. Society has to provide education, leisure activities and, to some extent, cultural opportunities for the individual's free choice. But fundamentally this is a "free" area within a rational political and social system. There are limits to the state's competence.

### The Theological Approach to the Contemporary Situation

"To preach the Word of God is the trade of the preacher, just as smithing is the trade of the blacksmith," Olavus Petri, himself the son of a blacksmith, once wrote. It is the specific vocation of the preacher and of the church to teach the gospel purely and to administer the sacraments rightly. This reformation principle was kept in mind, even at times when the national church was responsible for large areas of the life of society. Conformity with the gospel, not conformity with the world, has been "the trade" of the church. Billing, though vigorously defending the national church, insisted on a religious motivation.

At the same time, Lutheran theology has been able to interpret "the world" in a positive and meaningful way. Luther's view of the world as ruled by God (and of the heathen as being under God's protection and guidance, even before they have heard of Christ) provided a theological platform on which a religious understanding of the nonreligious world could be directly based. Society from the beginning was built into theology, as God in the beginning created the heavens and the earth. The Lutheran pastor's main task has been described as properly to distinguish between law and gospel. Through these dialectics Lutheran theology has both gained its dynamics and taken its risks. The established church has certainly lived amid the hazards of the world. Its mission has been to interpret God's world in such a way that the world felt the need for salvation.

In accord with the character of Lutheran theology the law must be reinterpreted in any approach to modern man. This is due to the understanding of the revealed law as God's word, but spoken directly to his people at Mount Sinai. The ten commandments are words of eternal truth, but they were given in a historical situation. Our historical situation is a different one. Our life, given to us by God, has its own law; man has to listen to God as he speaks and guides in each place and in each historical situation.

This approach to man has the advantage of making the experience of God, as creator and ruler of the world, very real. All mankind is included in God's work, even where man does not listen to his word. There is no escape from God. For centuries, this sense of God as sovereign and preserver of the world was the self-evident and theologically indispensable presupposition for the folk church. At the same time this theological position requires that human life be interpreted in such a way that man senses both the moral imperatives that are inherent in it and an authority that transcends it.

At this point we come close to the main difficulty of the present folk church situation: the gospel is not being understood, because there is no understanding of the law, either revealed or inherent in human life. Sin and guilt, which are indispensable elements of a theology of justification, have no meaning where there is no sense of divine law. Widespread relativism hinders the identification of an individual's life experience with universal principles or with the works of a personal God. This is particularly true in the political and cultural situation in Sweden, characterized as it is by welfare ideology and cultural pluralism.

The goal of the labor unions and of their political equivalent, the Social Democratic Party, was the welfare state. The established church of half a century ago, incorporated in an agrarian political and social system with a monarchical, bourgeois and hierarchical superstructure, was slow in defining the new issues. Socialism at the beginning of this century was revolutionary and definitely atheistic; and it is understandable that the church authorities paid more attention to this side of the labor movement than to its emphasis on human rights. When the social democrats finally gained political power, they developed the positive side of their program. They have now been in office for some thirty years and have become managers rather than politicians. Although most church people are still likely to be conservative in outlook, a more positive evaluation of the way in which modern organizational society functions has developed. Organized society, with its roots in the idealistic popular movements of the last century, has even been described as the realization of God's law. Labor unions and other organizations which have spontaneously appeared are seen as instruments of love and justice.

This theology of organizational society has developed as a result of a proposition concerning the function of the established church that was submitted to the church synod in 1958. Its main concern was with a better adjustment to democratic society. The church synod made some favorable comments on the proposition, but no specific measures were adopted. Various suggestions contained in the proposition were, however, taken up by a church commission on social ethics, which initiated research and study, concentrating on labor problems. As a church reaction to the apparatus of the welfare ideology, and as an attempt at theological reinterpretation of the law, this venture is of considerable interest.

The advocates of this program pointed out that democratic society had revealed in the people previously unknown potentialities. Quite ordinary people, through their spontaneous and devoted work in democratic institutions, had manifested a remarkable creativity, which should be used within the church as well. But the church had first to become a real folk church, to identify itself with contemporary life and with the people whom it was serving. Its hierarchical structure and way of functioning had to become democratic. Then all those who were honestly seeking guidance in ethical and religious matters would feel at home and could be allowed to take part in and to influence church activities, including voting on confessional questions. The fundamental argument of this rather radical social theology is that the conception of natural law must be reconsidered. The content of natural law and revealed law is in fact the same; the demand for justice and love.

It is argued that democratic society functions through interest-groups, basically inspired by egoistic motives, but that through compromise, which is necessary in all negotiations, this element of egotism is reduced. The democratic "rules of the game" thus afford evidence of the regulating principles of the law. The labor union, for example, arises out of the necessities of life and cares for the needs of the individual. The union is a guarantee against arbitrariness and is therefore ethically and religiously legitimate. Ethics is thus derived primarily from the law, with human reason playing a substantial part. Since reason is universal, it is assumed that the church has no special truth to offer about the social-ethical function of the law. The church has to accept the organizational apparatus as an expression of God's law in our time.

With this social theology an attempt was made to reinterpret Luther's understanding of the law, and to lay foundations for contacts between labor organizations and the church. Established church and institutionalized society were to get on speaking terms.

As long as the theme is ethics, morals or even concrete social questions, people are willing to enter into a dialogue with the church. Traditional labor representatives still hold a humanist view of man as the idealistic core of welfare ideology. A dialogue on "justice and love" on a humanist basis, is, however, far removed from Luther's belief that God rules the world through his law. Even Luther's view of civil justice as executed also by heathens takes as its starting point a belief in God ruling through "the worldly regiment." What could be taken for granted in Luther's century—a general belief in God as creator and ruler of the world —no longer applies in the twentieth century, which means that "the law" is a matter of belief. We do not reach the full meaning of the law, as understood in Lutheranism, by reasoning or compromising in a certain socio-political situation.

In our cultural situation the trade of the church to preach the Word of God includes preaching the law. Since man is unable to experience God in everyday life, it is precisely there that the church has to witness to him. It has to make a specific contribution to everyday life including the political and social sector. It would be unrealistic and somewhat naïve to assume that the Christian understanding of man *sub lege* (man as created and fallen) and current ideas of the welfare state should be identical. There are certainly common ideas that should be emphasized and that can serve as the starting point for continued conversation. But in all ideologies their dynamics, their goals, arise out of very real conditions. These presuppositions and goals, bound up, as they are, with human needs, give them consistency and a relative "truth." In the field of social action the church stands beside other forces, to some extent as an ideological factor, advocating its controversial interpretation of the nature of man. It may be argued that the church has the same goals as social forces of humanist origin, but it must not be forgotten that it has a very special contribution to make.

A dialogue between church and people on the subject of creation and law is then possible and fruitful for both. The difficult problems arise when specific issues and objectives of social action are transferred to the realm of law and gospel—that is, when the church speaks as church, as an assembly of believers. Then the relationship of man to man is not the main theme, but that relationship in the light of man's relationship to God and to his righteousness and love. It is through God's revelation of his love in Christ and in personal commitment to him that human love and justice are finally to be understood. That is the message of the church. But this takes us out of the realm of reason into the realm of revelation, and not many people will follow us that far.

### Christian Witness in a Pluralistic Society

In conclusion, let us return to the problems of social and cultural pluralism. We have seen that welfare politics, in Sweden, have been rather undogmatic and pragmatic, with a minimum of ideology. Large areas of cultural life have been left to the individual's free choice; in fact, the welfare society is even called the "society of free choice," and this refers to both economic decisions and cultural values. What is chosen depends essentially on what is felt to be needed.

Swedish culture is not traditionally pluralistic, in the American sense. It could rather be described as a synthesis, built on Christian traditions that are now disintegrating. Old traditions have lost their meaning and strength, and new ones with sufficient vitality have not appeared. Confusion and a tendency toward *laissez-faire* in the spiritual and moral field are obvious signs of this development. A pluralistic society of the American type has incorporated factors that work against both *laissez-faire* and extremism. It functions through polarities, dualities and contradicting opinions: when an extreme phenomenon appears, a reaction will always be provoked. A capacity to produce one's own defense mchanisms would seem to be essential in a society where government restrictions and regulations are at a minimum.

Generally speaking, we have a good many government regulations in Sweden, but in the cultural field we have an island of pluralism. However, the mechanism of protection and production is still largely lacking. We live in a society of free choice, cultural and moral, but we are very much at a loss how to choose.

The Church of Sweden has to face the challenge of a welfare ideology and cultural pluralism, which easily becomes ethical and religious relativism. (As an established church with deep roots in folk traditions, it still has considerable influence on the majority of the people—85 per cent are baptized and confirmed). But in a situation of rapid change we cannot rely on traditions.

There is, of course, a connection between pluralism and relativism in our specific historical situation. Pluralism is a natural consequence of the breakdown of values. But it is primarily a practical political way of solving the problem of diversity. It manifests freedom of belief. We should in fact find no difficulty in working simultaneously for this freedom and for our belief. But the problem of ethical relativism remains.

What we need is a thorough theological rethinking and a reinterpretation of the biblical and Reformation understanding of the law. That is where the church can meet secularized man. The Bible as a book of eternal truth is no longer a reality for most people. Modern man is living in a closed pattern of production and consumption and finds himself tied to those modes of living. The biblical text must be transferred into this context, if it is to be ethically relevant. The law must be derived from real life. Each man in his everyday life has to sacrifice part of his life for others, from whom he desires love in return. Thus, love is always asked for, and an ethical demand is inherent in human life. This line of thought (worked out by K. E. Lögstrup, of Denmark) seems to offer a promising starting point for a reinterpretation of the law that would be especially useful in a situation of ethical relativism.

There is one feature of everyday life that, although it affects especially young people, is in a broad sense becoming everyman's philosophy of life: the new standardized culture, distributed by mass-media (cinema, radio, television, weeklies, records, and the facilities of the advertising industry). The characteristic feature of this "popular" culture is that it is produced for mass consumption, and its quality is dependent upon the qualities of the consumers. This standardized production reflects an image of the average man, his supposed wishes, dreams and needs. It is basically a-ethical: the image of man is presented without his deeper motivations: themes such as sin, guilt, responsibility, anxiety, aging, sorrow, and death are being eliminated, and we are left with a superficial description of happiness and prestige.

Here we encounter the commercial superstructure of modern technology, as it offers superficial substitutes for real experience. From the viewpoint of both social philosophy and psychology, mass culture appears to be essentially materialistic, a reflection of an economic system and of physiological materialism. In the social context it is being transformed into a forceful philosophy of life.

Against this presentation of man through commercialized images, the church must take its stand. Theologically the process must be labeled as idolatry. The church should not hesitate to offer its criticism and at the same time to present the biblical image of man as created by God and restored in Christ. If it fails to do so it functions only weakly within modern society.

# 15

# THE CHURCH IN AN AFFLUENT SOCIETY

by ROGER L. SHINN (United States)

A momentous economic revolution is at work in the world today, loaded with promise and with portent. A new technology has increased fantastically the possibilities of economic productivity. The revolution shatters the patterns expected by traditional capitalism and Marxism. It faces men with ethical opportunities and challenges never before anticipated. It reorganizes the institutions of production and of government, changes man's relation to nature and to his fellowmen, transforms the hopes and fears of vast populations and among its many consequences is "the affluent society."

A significant part of mankind and of the Christian church lives in this new kind of society. It is most evident in the United States of America and parts of western Europe. The Soviet Union is acquiring some of its characteristics. Japan, with the most phenomenal record of economic growth in the current world, is moving toward affluence. In this chapter, the American experience will furnish the primary example of the affluent society.

Although some social historians think that Christianity has been one of the several forces that have brought this new society into being, it is unanticipated in the Bible and in most of the theological tradition. Hence it calls for a rethinking of ethics, even of some aspects of theology.

The Christian church, in its centuries of history, has lived through many revolutionary eras. It has learned, or should have learned, not to ally itself too closely with any specific social environment. St.

Augustine, referring to the many types of human societies, wrote of the city of God: "It therefore is so far from rescinding and abolishing these diversities, that it even preserves and adapts them, so long only as no hindrance to the worship of the one supreme and true God is thus introduced." [1]

However, the church obviously does not remain a static community in the midst of a shifting landscape; the changing environment inevitably affects it. Its people are part of their society. They talk the language, make their livings, dwell in buildings, communicate and travel, use social institutions—all in ways provided by society. If the church is to serve a living God who reveals himself in history, then it must become even more attentive to change in that society. Its task is to respond to the leading of a God who often calls a pilgrim people to get up and move, as he surely calls today.

### Characteristics of the Affluent Society

The affluent society is an exceedingly complex social organization, often misunderstood by those who live in its confusion and by those who look at it from outside. We must avoid being deceived by terminology: it is certainly not a society in which everybody has all he wants, because human wants are insatiable. It is possible to raise the standard of living so that everybody participates in the general prosperity. But human nature craves more than a share—most people want greater wealth and status than their neighbors. Since it is impossible for everybody to live in the upper tenth or even the upper half of society, many are bound to feel that they are not affluent.

Furthermore, the affluent society creates poverty as it creates wealth, because it develops ways of living in which luxuries become necessities. It brings a metropolitan style of life in which high production and consumption become requirements for survival. Consider a few typical attainments of the affluent society: electric refrigeration, elaborate plumbing, central heating, elevators, automobiles and intricate road networks, telephones. Through-

---

[1] *The City of God*, XIX, 17.

out most of history mankind has lived without these symbols of wealth. Now cities are built that would strangle without them. They have become necessities for many, many people.

Another side of the story is that some of the common gifts of life, once available to everybody, have become expensive luxuries. As the affluent society offers electricity to everybody, it makes unpolluted air a rarity. Green grass and flowing brooks become costly. People make frantic efforts to enjoy quiet, to escape from the tyranny of the telephone, or to enjoy a simple stroll in the countryside.

For a variety of reasons, therefore, the economic strain upon the family in the affluent society is often as great as the strain upon its ancestors in impoverished societies. To enjoy mammon without serving mammon is not easy for the society or its members.

The affluent society can be defined in terms of several characteristics, some of which are important to its self-understanding and to its ethics:

1. The most obvious characteristic of the affluent society is its high production and widespread distribution of goods. It has learned to use technology to produce huge quantities of commodities which are distributed among the majority of the members of society. The economy is able to produce an abundance of the traditional necessities of mankind—food, clothing and shelter; and there is certainly no economic need for anyone to die of starvation or exposure.

2. Instead of persuading men to restrict consumption in order that limited goods may go farther, society works to stimulate consumption in order to sustain economic activity. In the new culture-ethic, the man who does not spend is not doing his duty to the system. Poverty becomes a social offense, not simply because of compassion for the poor, but because they cannot do their part in maintaining a market for commodities and employment for other poor people. The affluent society may come to the point of valuing man-the-consumer above man-the-producer. Some of its members enjoy good incomes, but never find the satisfaction of contributing anything to the society. The results for human dignity and morale are crushing.

3. The nature of work changes significantly. Fewer and fewer

people earn their living by the sweat of the brow.[2] Perhaps more and more make their income by strain on the nerves. The affluent society needs more white-collar workers than blue-collar workers —that is, more people to work in offices and sell products than to manufacture and transport them. The most obvious change is in agriculture: fewer and fewer farmers raise greater and greater crops. The distinguished economist, Kenneth Boulding, estimates that at the height of the Roman Empire seventy-five per cent of the population engaged in farming. Now in the United States of America only a small minority farm—and produce agricultural surpluses. Boulding continues:

It is by no means impossible to suppose a world at the end of this process in which we can produce our whole food supply with one per cent of the population; in which we can produce all basic commodities such as clothing, housing and so on with perhaps another two or three per cent or perhaps even at most ten per cent.[3]

Obviously the traditional definitions of work and social usefulness must change.

4. The change in work means a change in the role of persons. High productivity requires a high degree of specialization of labor. Even Marxist societies recognize this fact, despite Marx's own polemics against the division of labor. In modern industry persons become as interchangeable as parts of a machine. The affluent society is possible only because of the interdependence of millions of people who do not know each other. The meal on the table, the auto in the garage, the utilities that serve the home—all these involve the work of vast numbers of people whom the consumer never sees. He usually becomes aware of them only if something goes wrong. The result is that society is tempted to value its members more as *functions* than as persons. It does not care whether the person finds meaning in his work or even whether he disappears, so long as the function continues.

5. The affluent society gives man a seeming mastery of his environment. He tends to become less grateful to nature and to

---

[2] Gen. 3 : 19. This is only one of many examples in which the affluent society robs biblical language of its power.

[3] KENNETH BOULDING, "The Death of the City: A Frightened Look at Post-Civilization." *Ekistics,* Jan., 1962.

God than to the human systems in which he lives. He is more aware of what he can buy than of what he is given. Although he knows vaguely that all energy comes from the sun and that water comes from clouds and oceans, he deals more directly with electrical switches and faucets. His dominion over nature is a valid achievement—the fulfillment of a biblical command beyond biblical expectations. But it sometimes deceives man as to his real powers and limitations. Often it tempts him to substitute self-congratulation for gratitude.

## Two Christian Traditions Concerning Wealth [4]

The Christian church is confused about how it should approach the affluent society. It can adapt itself uncritically to the norms of the new culture, abandoning its prophetic ministry. Or it can indulge in caustic condemnation, as though it were somehow superior to the culture. Both answers are common among churchmen, but neither is an authentic service of God or men. The fact is that the church has no preconceived set of solutions for problems never before experienced by mankind. Its ignorance is no reason for shame. It should confess its guilt for its share in the injustices and idolatries of the affluent society, but its uncertainties are not shameful. The church's confidence is in God's gospel, not in its own wisdom for every situation.

Christian faith brings to the affluent society certain traditional teachings and attitudes that arose out of quite different situations. Old injunctions, woodenly applied to new circumstances, are often irrelevant and unrealistic. Neither the pastoral-agricultural practices of the Bible nor the tradition of natural law nor the casuistries of Catholicism and Puritanism tell us precisely how to live faithfully in the new world. Yet the church can too easily write off the past without appreciating the faith that lived in it. As we look at two inherited traditions, we need both to recognize the authentic elements in them and to see how our time requires its own formulations.

---

[4] A few paragraphs in this section are adapted from an earlier study that I prepared for the Department of Church and Economic Life of the National Council of Churches of Christ in the U.S.A.

The first tradition, with its deep rootage in prophetic faith and in the Christian gospel, shows a deep distrust of wealth and a glorification of poverty. Amos and Isaiah criticized the predatory rich, not only for their injustice toward the poor but also because of their deluded self-sufficiency and pride. Jesus Christ came to preach "good news to the poor." [5] He upset the normal attitudes toward wealth and poverty: "Blessed are you poor, for yours is the kingdom of God. . . . But woe to you that are rich, for you have received your consolation." [6] For centuries the church has puzzled over one of his warnings and tried to take the sting out of it: "It is easier for a camel to go through the eye of a needle than for a rich man to enter into the kingdom of God." [7]

In the early church most Christians were poor. But gradually men of affluence joined the church, and reinterpretations of Jesus' teachings seemed advisable. Within two centuries, Clement of Alexandria wrote his rather cheerful essay on the question, "Who is the rich man that shall be saved?" Much of it is clearly valid: it is not the quantity of wealth that is important, but the attitude toward it and its use that are important, says Clement. But Clement misses the point of Scripture when he says that since the rich man need not worry about his livelihood, he may be less greedy than the poor man, and therefore closer to salvation.[8]

As the church grew, wealth looked increasingly good to many Christians. But there were always those who worried about easy accommodation to the world. The monastic movement protested against dilution of the Christian ethic and re-emphasized the ideal of poverty. The Benedictine Rule ordered the "vice of private ownership" to be "cut off . . . by the roots" and prescribed utmost simplicity in food and dress.[9] But monasteries too grew wealthy. Although monks took vows of poverty, the orders acquired lands and money. In resistance to this movement St. Francis of Assisi again renounced luxury. "Married to Lady Poverty," as he put it, he demanded complete rejection of wealth in his mendicant

---

[5] Luke 4 : 18.
[6] Luke 6 : 20, 24.
[7] Matt. 19 : 24.
[8] *The Ante-Nicene Fathers,* Vol. II.
[9] *The Rule of St. Benedict,* Ch. 33.

order—an ideal that future generations of Franciscans quickly compromised.

The modern world, including both affluent societies and those striving to become affluent, is uncomfortable with this traditional praise of poverty. It sees the Manichean heresy that lurks in much asceticism, and prefers to emphasize the goodness of God's creation and man's right to subdue and enjoy it.

The vocation of voluntary poverty persists today in occasional impressive forms, less as a deliberate rejection of wealth than as part of a ministry to the poor. Most Christians, however, are unlikely to seek poverty. If they moralize about the temptations of wealth, usually they set the boundary of dangerous wealth somewhere beyond their own resources.

A second, more recent, Christian tradition has given higher regard to productive work. Although the Weber-Tawney thesis [10] on the relation between Calvinism and capitalism is strenuously debated, it is at least clear that Protestantism has often supported the virtues that had a useful function in the period of an expanding economy. If feudalism was occasionally romantic and usually paternalistic toward the poor, the Calvinists were more likely to ask, "Are you poor because you are lazy?" The question did not prejudge the answer. Calvin knew that men were poor for many reasons, but when laziness was the cause, Calvinists were not eager to say, "Blessed are you poor," or to offer alms.

An expanding industrializing economy—whether within a capitalist or a socialist framework—requires that considerable effort be directed to producing capital equipment (such as factories or machinery) rather than consumer goods. The society, or at least some within it, must accept the discipline of deferred enjoyment. The Puritan heirs of Calvin were willing to do that. For religious and moral reasons, they praised the virtues of diligence, frugality, honesty and thrift. Since such virtues frequently led to accumulation of wealth, the Puritans could often provide the capital needed for developing industry. Some of them happily accepted their wealth

---

[10] See MAX WEBER: *The Protestant Ethic and the Spirit of Capitalism,* translated by TALCOTT PARSONS. New York: Charles Scribner's Sons, 1930. Also R. H. TAWNEY: *Religion and the Rise of Capitalism.* New York: Harcourt, Brace and Co., 1926.

as evidence of God's approval, although Calvin had warned against such attempts to fathom the mysteries of providence.

Puritan moral injunctions have been preserved throughout American history even though their basis has shifted from religious to economic grounds. Benjamin Franklin, for example, poked fun at Cotton Mather, but turned many of Mather's moralisms into witty aphorisms. To this day some Americans are not sure whether their favorite sayings come from the Bible or from *Poor Richard's Almanack*.

At about the same time John Wesley was teaching his followers to "gain all you can, save all you can, give all you can." [11] This exhortation did not mean to England's impoverished workers what it did to later generations; but some of Wesley's followers distinguished themselves by following the first two-thirds of his advice. Wesley himself remembered the biblical warnings against wealth and frequently worried over the results of his own movement.

Puritan and Methodist piety have been highly important in shaping some of the societies that eventually attained affluence. In the process, Protestantism sometimes came to stand for middle-class respectability, for reliability and for a confusion of bourgeois with Christian virtues. The "pillars of the church" have often been the "pillars of the community." To this day, any political appeal for economy in government, the balanced budget and practice of the old-fashioned economic virtues is likely to stir deep responses among churchmen.

These two traditions of Christian economic ethics clearly differ from each other. The one praises poverty; the other inculcates habits that often lead to wealth. Nevertheless the two agree on a central contention: they condemn extravagance. Spending for display or for luxurious living is regarded as sinful, and waste is a religious offense.

Thus traditional Christian ethical formulations clash with the spirit of the affluent society. Frugality, once a religious virtue, has become a social threat. Debt for the sake of indulgence, once sinful, is now the basis of prosperity. Where once greed was regarded as detrimental to human welfare, we now hear that it contributes

---

[11] JOHN WESLEY: "The Use of Money," *The Standard Sermons of John Wesley*, E. H. SUGDEN, ed. London: The Epworth Press, 1921, Vol. II.

to public good. Jesus taught, "You cannot serve God and mammon"; [12] propagandists today tell us, "You serve society best by serving mammon." The New Testament said, "The love of money is the root of all evil"; [13] popular doctrine today announces, "The love of money is the root of prosperity for all."

Seeing this clash, the Christian church must ask once again the meaning of its faith. It cannot simply succumb to the blandishments of the affluent society, forget its heritage and get on with the enjoyments of reckless consumption. It may—and on rare occasions does—resist the current economic changes, attack affluence as a snare and seek ways to adhere literally to one or another of its traditions. Such attempts are usually halfhearted, and are likely to substitute the culture-ethic of a past generation for the prevailing culture-ethic of the present.

Surely our era calls for a more daring answer. D. L. Munby, the British economist and lay theologian, has written: "God is in process of transforming our economic order.... We can, and should, participate in that activity." [14] We can, in the spirit of Dietrich Bonhoeffer, seek a Christian worldliness for our time. These enterprises are not easy. Forces opposed to God and indifferent to him are at work in modern economies, and the church must learn to distinguish these. Talk of Christian worldliness easily becomes the pretext for pagan worldliness. Yet, recognizing the dangers, the church knows that it must answer to its vocation in the modern economy. This does not mean adapting in all respects to the affluent society. It means serving the God of Jesus Christ in the present age.

### Christian Responsibility in the Affluent Society

If the church is to maintain a faithful witness in the affluent society, it must carry out four tasks. These will call both for theological understanding and for sensitivity to the needs of the society.

---

[12] Matt. 6 : 24.
[13] I Tim. 6 : 10.
[14] D. L. MUNBY: *God and the Rich Society*. London: Oxford University Press, 1961, p. 179.

1. *The church needs to understand the affluent society and to appreciate the opportunities it offers.*

At first glance such appreciation may seem easy. Who does not enjoy wealth? Yet men often resent change, and Christians resist the passing of the culture in which they have been at home. Protestants have frequently found their affinities in rural culture, have made a fetish of work and have nourished a false piety that disdained economic processes. Some Christian criticisms of the affluent society arise more out of nostalgia than out of faith. It is easy —and not very helpful—to deplore the materialism of modern society. Christians should know from their Scriptures that God is concerned for the whole life of man and that no spirituality can release the church from material concerns. They should realize also that the material gains of the affluent society make possible the liberation of the human spirit from many forms of bondage.

Education is an example. Throughout most of human history education has inevitably been a luxury. Most children had to become wage earners as early as possible. Most adults had to work long hours with little access to the information and ideas that are basic to education. The affluent society makes it economically possible—even advantageous—to prolong the years of education for youth. The laborer on a thirty-five to forty-hour week has time for learning. Books, periodicals, television and educational institutions provide the means. Where there is a will to learn, the opportunities are there.

Leisure is another example. No doubt the increase of leisure presents problems. Affluent societies are full of bored people, jaded with every form of entertainment, unable to find meaning in their work or their leisure time. Protestantism, with an energetic ethic rather remote from Scripture, has not equipped its members for leisure. David Riesman in a famous book has written: "The inner-directed person, if influenced by Protestantism, is . . . unable to waste time." [15] The Protestant churches have been acutely aware that "Satan finds mischief for idle hands to do"; they need to learn also the creative possibilities of leisure. The high culture of most past civilizations has depended largely upon a small leisure

---

[15] DAVID RIESMAN: *The Lonely Crowd.* New York: Anchor Books, 1953, p. 184.

class; in the affluent society most of mankind can be admitted to that class. As a matter of fact, the traditional class distinctions may be reversed, as laborers enjoy more leisure than professional people.

A final example is health. It may be that some of the gains of the affluent society in this field are illusory, as its wealth barely enables it to treat the illnesses that it produces. But improved diet, research, sanitation and facilities for treating diseases have reduced infant mortality and prolonged life expectancy. A sign of the success is the population explosion, which brings a new set of difficulties. Evidently man is capable of few attainments that do not pose new problems. But improved health is a substantial gain. It not only reduces human misery: it brings an authentic ethical achievement, as it enables society to show a concern for the individual that is hard to realize in societies ravaged by epidemics and starvation.

2. *Against this background of appreciation for the opportunities of the affluent society, the church has the privilege and obligation to call men to responsibility in the midst of their prosperity.*

The church's call will not be a command. In pluralistic, secularized societies, the church cannot demand obedience. But when the church speaks truthfully and lives faithfully, men inside and outside its membership may respond to a prophetic word. An adequate call to responsibility includes several specific notes.

The first and most obvious is the elimination of poverty within the affluent society itself. For centuries the church has quoted—and often misinterpreted—the saying of Jesus: "You have the poor always with you." [16] The church might have compassion on the poor, but poverty was an economic necessity. Today in many societies this is no longer the case. The persistence of extreme poverty is not an inevitable fateful evil but an offense against God and man.

In the most affluent of societies, the United States of America, the relation between wealth and poverty is extremely complex. In some respects the United States has utterly refuted the Marxist expectation that the few rich would increasingly dominate the many

---

[16] Matt. 26 : 11.

poor. The majority of the population share in the benefits of high productivity. The rich and powerful corporations have wide ownership. Many of the great corporations have more stockholders than employees; and the owners include philanthropic foundations, pension funds, labor unions and individuals. But in this affluent society the lowest twenty per cent of the people live in dismal poverty. The Scandinavian countries have shown that affluence does not require neglect of the poor. But the United States stands judged by the words from Isaiah: "What do you mean by crushing my people, by grinding the face of the poor?" says the Lord God of hosts.[17]

Curiously the causes of poverty in this society are not primarily economic. In some regions, economic changes have brought poverty, and increasing automation may bring unemployment and new poverty. But at present most of the poor are not unemployed, and many skills are in great demand. The deepest causes of poverty are cultural rather than economic. The United States is a vast country of diverse peoples. In many cities there is no language that all the residents share. Where there is no common ethnic inheritance, religious belief or cultural tradition, many people live in marginal subcultures. Some of these subcultures barely participate in the main currents of the economy or culture.

The difficulties inherent in the situation are exaggerated by the vicious evil of racial prejudice, although most of the poor, contrary to some opinions, are white; in fact, the biggest impoverished area, Appalachia, includes some of the most racially "pure" Anglo-Saxon stock in the country. But Negroes, Spanish-Americans and Indians have far more than their share of poverty. Hence the answer to poverty will require a major reshaping of society. Limited answers like increased economic activity and better housing programs will help. But the United States will not solve its problem of poverty until it moves a long way toward eliminating racial discrimination, improving education, discovering motivation for frustrated persons and generally relating the various subcultures more effectively to the main culture. The church is called to a difficult and comprehensive ministry in so complex a society—a ministry that it sometimes accepts and sometimes avoids.

[17] Isa. 3 : 15.

A second responsibility concerns the society's decision as to how it will use its wealth. The very abundance of consumer goods may provoke a hunger for more. The advertising which helps maintain high production and employment deliberately stimulates some of the worst motives of pride, greed and envy. Arnold Toynbee has this to say about advertising:

It has made a fine art of taking advantage of human silliness. It rams unwanted material goods down surfeited throats when two-thirds of all human beings now alive are in desperate need of the bare necessities of life. This is an ugly aspect of the affluent society; and, if I am told that advertising is the price of affluence, I reply, without hesitation, that affluence has been bought too dear.[18]

The phrase, "the affluent society," owes its popularity in large part to a book by the economist John Kenneth Galbraith.[19] This book maintains that the United States pampers the private sector of the economy while starving the public sector. Prosperous families consume more and more, at the expense of public services in education, housing, transportation and health.

A large part of the economy of the United States—about ten per cent of the gross national product and about half of the federal budget—sustains its military program. By stimulating research, production and employment, these expenditures promote prosperity. But they also rob other areas of life. The miracle of Japanese economic growth shows what a society may do when it devotes its technology and production to civilian ends. The most public-spirited political leaders in the United States are seeking to cut military expenditures and to shift the effort to other needs. The trouble is that people are usually more willing to pay heavy taxes for military purposes than for schools and housing.

A third responsibility of the affluent society is the redefining of the meaning of useful work. We have noted above how the nature of work is changing. Machines do much of what people have done. This does not mean that people have nothing left to do. But if they are to do worthwhile things, the society must change some of its attitudes.

---

18 ARNOLD J. TOYNBEE: "Why I Dislike Western Civilization." *New York Times Magazine,* May 10, 1964.
19 *The Affluent Society*. Boston: Houghton Mifflin Co., 1958.

It is sometimes proposed that when few men are needed to produce the necessities of life, the society will detach pay from work and offer all its members a salary or an income on investments. But a possible alternative is to reconceive work and its compensation. A society usually distributes the fruits of its productivity to its members with some recognition of their social usefulness. Those who make visible, tangible, saleable objects are obviously useful— even if the objects are of dubious value to society. As technology increases productivity, industrialists reap the rewards. So does skilled labor—unless automation makes the labor unnecessary. But the nurse, the teacher and the artists do not increase their productivity proportionately, and the affluent society is likely to deprive them. As industry produces more with fewer workers, society will have to re-evaluate the contributions of its members. It may decide that a nurse is as valuable as an engineer, that a mother at home is as useful as a mother in an office, that a student is as productive a worker as a salesman of unnecessary luxuries.

3. *The church, an international community of faith, is a reminder within each society of the wider world.*

We have been considering responsibility *within* the affluent societies. But this is not enough, because these societies are islands within a world of want. Poverty and need remain gnawing concerns for most of humanity. The church, worshiping the God of all mankind, has the vocation of calling the affluent societies to their responsibility within this needy world.

Christians in many lands may read an essay like this with justified bitterness. It describes a situation so different from their own that it must seem smug and satisfied. Those Christians have an obligation to blast the complacency of churches in more prosperous societies. And the latter have the task of calling their own societies to a world responsibility.

This is not to say that the answers are simple. To talk about rotting food surpluses in one land and starvation in another is easy. To do something about the disparity is harder. The bare logistics of getting the food to hungry people far from seaports is itself hard enough. But this is the simplest part of the task—a part that can be carried out. Thus, on a single day in 1964 the United

States Department of Agriculture set aside $398 million worth of foods to meet famine in one country. The point of this example is not to claim credit for generosity—such acts should be taken for granted among humanitarian people—but to point to beneficent possibility and a limitation of affluence. To offer alms to the hungry is one thing; to strengthen the economy of a hungry land, so that alms are unnecessary, is something else.

Since the Second World War the experience of the more or less affluent societies in helping each other had been remarkable. For example, the Marshall Plan enabled European economies to rehabilitate themselves. But the attempts to strengthen economically poor societies have had no such success. The gap between rich and poor nations has grown greater, despite costly attempts to reduce it. One reason is that many of the efforts have been niggardly, compared with the need. But even the more generous attempts have frequently failed, leaving a sense of disillusion. Apparently the world lacks the skill and imagination for the task.

In this *impasse* there is no reason to expect the church to provide the skill. But it can attack one aspect of the problem. Part of the difficulty is the lack of *rapport* between the affluent world and the impoverished world. People of power look at history differently from those who are on their way to power. The wealthy may have a benign wish to do good, but they do not feel the sting of poverty. Usually they badly misread the dynamics of history. The Christian gospel speaks directly to this blindness, as it tells of the God who loves the poor and powerless:

He has shown strength with his arm, he has scattered the proud in the imagination of their hearts,
he has put down the mighty from their thrones, and exalted those of low degree;
he has filled the hungry with good things, and the rich he has sent empty away.[20]

The United States is often described as a conservative nation in a revolutionary world. That description is not quite accurate. The United States is carrying on its own revolution. It is not conservative in its exploration of space, its automation of industry, its re-

---

[20] Luke 1 : 51–53 (RSV).

shaping of the countryside. But one characteristic of this society—not necessarily inherent in affluent societies—causes specific problems: the United States enjoys its high production partly because of and partly in spite of a devotion to free enterprise. It is out of tune with the majority of mankind in its ritualistic deference to a traditional economic ideology. It wants to make its own experience (which worked in the industrialization of an underpopulated land with rich resources) the model for other societies (which may need to industrialize in quite different ways).

In some respects the fear of socialism in this country is ridiculous. The United States has led the world in socialized education. It has considerable socialized housing, socialized parks, socialized water systems, socialized road nets, socialized dams and power plants. (In the rules that govern public discussion these are not normally called socialism.) When in 1964 a right-wing clique maneuvered its way into control of a major political party, the voters gave its candidate the soundest spanking in any election in this century. But within the United States the traditional dogmatism still inhibits the pragmatic effort to meet problems with a combination of personal freedom and public control. Beyond the water's edge the inhibition is far greater. Far too often this society chooses its friends and enemies by ideological labels rather than by recognition of what they are actually accomplishing.

Surely the church has a special responsibility at this point—to criticize not simply a particular ideology but all the ideologies (leftist and rightist; political, economic, and ecclesiastical) that enslave men. No church can do this job perfectly, because the men in the church are historical men, influenced by the ideologies of their time and place. But the church knows a gospel, which constantly reminds it that the test of any social proposal is not loyalty to treasured traditions but concern for the welfare of persons who are loved by their Creator and Redeemer.

4. *Finally, the church is called to understand and use faithfully its own affluence.*

In prosperous societies, the church may participate in the general wealth. Today the church does not come close to dominating the economy of any major country, as churches in past history have sometimes done. But in several areas an affluent church must pon-

der the meaning of its Lord's blessing upon the poor and his warning to the rich. The church today can spend large sums on construction of buildings—about a billion dollars a year in the United
States. It invests endowments, which it uses largely for educational
and missionary purposes. It employs large numbers of people,
conducts research, sends representatives on international journeys
to ecumenical meetings. In some countries the church still gets support from public funds, raised by taxation. But more often its
wealth comes from the contributions of its own members.

It is good for Christians to support the church with their gifts.
In this sense, the church, far from apologizing for its resources, has
the right to ask for more. But then it must face the critical question: how does a prosperous church live out its vocation of suffering servant, pouring its life out for mankind? At this point the
study of church budgets is not encouraging. Most local churches
spend a minor part of their income on community service and on
work beyond their own boundaries. The major part of the contributions might be designated as voluntary payments to the church
for services rendered to the donors.

Of course the issue is not solely a financial one. The affluent
church shirks its responsibility, even though it contributes generously to missions and works of mercy, unless it enters into the
struggles and sufferings of men. The prosperous church of prosperous members may be rather generous with its gifts, yet still be
primarily a pleasant haven for nice people who seek peace in the
midst of the world's confusion. It can avoid the issues of the mar-
ketplace and the slums, of juvenile delinquency and community
discontents, of politics and the clash of ideologies. Such a church
—and there are many of them—needs to hear the words of the
angel, addressed to the church at Laodicea: "For you say, I am
rich, I have prospered, and I need nothing; not knowing that you
are wretched, pitiable, blind and naked." [21] The problem is not
that the church is too rich, but that the church lets its prosperity
betray it into contentment. Its comfort dulls the sharpness of
the Word of God. It seeks security in itself rather than in its God.

During the era of Stalinist persecultions, American Christians

---

[21] Rev. 3 : 17.

often expressed concern for churches in communist lands. Reinhold Niebuhr reminded them that they might worry equally about threats closer to home:

There are signs that Christianity is being subtly corrupted into a glorification of the "American way of life." Sometimes this glorification takes place under social pressure, which our demagogues know how to apply in defiance of our cherished traditions. Sometimes it is merely due to a dissipation of the Christian faith and its corruption by the mood of self-congratulation and complacency to which a rich and powerful nation is tempted, particularly when it is forced to engage in a long conflict with a foe, whose vices seem to prove our virtue. Such a situation breeds self-righteousness, unless there is an actual encounter between man and God, in the pattern of biblical religion; in which encounter even the most righteous men and nations are convicted of their sin. . . .

Actually the freedom we boast sometimes develops into an idolatrous collective self-esteem. . . . Fatness, ease, and complacency are greater perils for our faith than lean years and the threat of martyrdom.[22]

Some affluent churches are escaping, or at least beginning to escape from this predicament by facing up to an authentic ethical crisis. The racial issue, terrible though it has been for many of God's children, has in one sense been an awakening for some American churches. It has stimulated churches to ask themselves what is their real purpose, to face the meaning of their ministry, to use some of their wealth for a just cause, to identify with the victims of injustice, to accept the hostility of respectable people. The affluent church can emulate the Lord who, though he was rich, became poor for our sakes.[23]

## Conclusion

A church that shares the sufferings of the world must also share some of the world's perplexities. Often it must abandon the oracular voice of an authority that knows all the answers and adopt the questioning voice of a people eager both to challenge and to learn. In the face of injustice, greed and the idolatry of systems and privileges, the church may respond with a "Thus saith the Lord."

[22] " 'Favorable' Environments," *The Messenger,* Aug. 18, 1953. This essay was published a few months after Stalin's death.

[23] II Cor. 8 : 9.

But when confronted with the need for moral imagination and wise decision, the church must acknowledge its needs.

The intricate problems of ethical responsibility in the modern world are complicated by the fact that the dynamics of an affluent society—like the dynamics of societies in other kinds of revolutions —seem to acquire a momentum of their own that operates almost independently of the human beings within the society. Of course persons keep making decisions. But the big decisions, it may almost be said, are made by the impersonal system. Every act of industrial automation, for example, is the choice of some person or committee, but in each separate case the decision has a kind of inevitability. The system demands it, progress calls for it, the competitors are doing it and this specific corporation obviously has to automate. Nobody has looked at the whole society, assessed the gains and losses involved and decided how to proceed. This fateful quality of the system has been described by one economist: "It is not mere rhetoric to ask if Things are not already in the saddle, riding Man. . . . Man will surely never ride Things unless he is prepared to ask questions which today do not often seem to occur to him." [24]

One calling of the church in the affluent society is to ask those questions. Christian faith has always been concerned with the meeting of the ultimate with the concrete. It can be content neither with visions of eternity nor with purely pragmatic judgments that see decisions only in their immediate contexts. A major part of its calling in our day is to keep questioning society—asking for the purposes, the values, the effect upon persons of the processes the society takes for granted.

This task may be less satisfying, humanly speaking, than providing answers. Yet Jesus himself often met a situation with a searching question. His church may readily grant that it cannot always tell the society the right thing to do. The technical knowledge needed to make wise decisions in the social process comes from many sources. Helpful guidance often comes from stubbornly secular men, who have no interest in the church or its

---

[24] ROBERT L. HEILBRONER: "The Impact of Technology: The Historic Debate," in *Automation and Technological Change*, John T. Dunlop, ed. Englewood Cliffs, N.J.: Prentice-Hall, Inc., 1962, pp. 7, 25.

message. Such men too can serve God. The church has the vocation of declaring its faith, exercising its ministry of reconciliation and ceaselessly confronting society with the questions and challenges that rise out of that faith and ministry. Surely there is no refuge from the task in a nostalgia for the good old days when life was simpler.

One of the great texts of the New Testament reads: "I have learned the secret of facing plenty and hunger, abundance and want. I can do all things in him who strengthens me." [25] People usually turn to that text when they are in want, for life is obviously hard then, and they need support. But the text is equally important when people live in abundance. It tells us that there is a secret of living in plenty, that a person can live faithfully in prosperity.

So it is with Christ's church. Probably wealth is more dangerous to the church and its members than poverty. But an affluent church can use its resources, as a poor church can use its poverty, in obedience to God.

---

[25] Phil. 4 : 12–13.

# PART IV

ISSUES OF CRITICAL IMPORTANCE

# 16

# NATURAL LAW AND
# SOCIAL ETHICS

## by N. H. Söe (Denmark)

THE following passage from David Hume's *Treatise of Human Nature* (III, I.1) is frequently quoted in our day:

> In every system of morality, which I have hitherto met with, I have always remarked, that the author proceeds for some time in the ordinary way of reasoning, and establishes the being of a God, or makes observations concerning human affairs; when of a sudden I am surprised to find, that instead of the usual copulations of propositions, *is*, and *is not*, I meet with no proposition that is not connected with an *ought*, or an *ought not*. This change is imperceptible; but is, however, of the last consequence. For as this *ought*, or *ought not*, expresses some new relation or affirmation, 'tis necessary that it should be observed and explained; and, at the same time that a reason should be given, for what seems altogether inconceivable, how this new relation can be a deduction from others, which are entirely different from it. But as authors do not commonly use this precaution, I shall presume to recommend it to the readers; and am persuaded, that this small attention would subvert all the vulgar systems of morality, and let us see, that the distinction of vice and virtue is not founded merely on the relations of objects, nor is perceived by reason.

The French mathematical physicist, Henri Poincaré, stated exactly the same view, in *La moral et la science* (1913), in saying that for purely grammatical reasons it is impossible to deduce commandments from statements of experience, to go from indicatives to imperatives; and that therefore science, in the broadest sense of the word, can not prove moral propositions to be either valid or invalid. According to several philosophers this is also what G. E. Moore was arguing when, in his *Principia Ethica* (1903), he coined the now famous term "the naturalistic fallacy." John Ladd has briefly defined this concept as "the fallacy of deducing a prescriptive term from a non-prescriptive statement." To many this fallacy seems to be *the* mortal sin in this area of thought.

Is not this precisely the error which those who adhere to the doctrine of natural law commit? If we read modern Roman Catholic social ethics, such as the German Ludwig Berg's *Sozialethik* (1959), we pass with no hesitation from "metaphysical" statements of the social order to rules for right human action. "The law of the essence of social structure (*das Wesensgesetz des Sozialen*) is also the law of social action." "Become what you are, is the fundamental commandment of social ethics." Berg even goes so far as to applaud a Spanish commentator of St. Thomas, the highly thought-of Franz von Vitoria, when he says:

We can therefore argue in the following way: something is contrary to natural inclination, therefore it is immoral. Something is according to natural inclination, therefore it is morally obligatory. . . . Therefore we rightly deduce from this principle that those things towards which man by nature is inclined are good, and those which man by nature fears are bad. If, however, otherwise I deceive myself, then God who gave me this inclination is the deceiver. Reason prescribes for me what is true and will inclines accordingly.

Tendencies and statements like this were in Karl Barth's mind when, in his *Kirchliche Dogmatik* (II . 2, 1942, pp. 586ff.) and certainly without influence from either Hume or Moore, he vehemently attacked Roman Catholic social ethics for deriving an "ought" from an "is," a commandment from a given order of the created world, a procedure which can never lead to that "ought" with which we are confronted in meeting the lord Christ. We are here led to "the deity of being, the concept of God in ancient philosophy" (*das Gottesbild des Seins, der Gottesbegriff der antiken Philosophie*). And Barth continues: "This idol may, as befits these kind of demons, be able to do many things. But it cannot really command. . . . What has this metaphysics of being to do with that true God who is the foundation and lord of the church?" It comes from the epoch when Christian ethics based on the orders of creation flourished. Barth points out that this type of Roman Catholic ethics has its near parallels in the Protestant world; but in this area the Roman Catholics are masters, whereas the neo-Protestants are displaying no more than dilettantism.

We might add that Sören Kierkegaard, independently again of Hume, has called attention in *Works of Love* to the same "fallacy" and mocks those very "deep-minded" thinkers who show their truly deep thinking, their real deep-mindedness, in conveying decision in knowledge and knowledge in decision. Several other thinkers might be mentioned, but Hume has stated the point most clearly of all.

Does this line of argument suffice to remove the whole problem of natural law? Are the adherents of this doctrine simply guilty of an obvious fallacy? Sometimes this seems to be so. But some philosophers would not even admit that it is logically unpermissible to go from a statement of fact to an imperative. From the times of Greek and Roman philosophy, when the foundations of this whole doctrine were laid, it has been the course of practice to seek a parallel in the medical field. Does not a physician every day, in the most legitimate way, pass from an indicative statement about the sickness of his patient to the imperative obligation to do this or that? Why, then, should not a philosopher of social ethics be permitted, in much the same way, to prescribe necessary action or remedy for social ills?

## Some Interpretations of Natural Law Ethics

But this is not the whole truth. If we read the Roman Catholic philosopher, the German-American Dietrich von Hildebrand, we find that he directly opposes this parallelism. He even states that this equation has been the source of many errors, and he clearly sees why: Over medical problems we are in the happy position of being able to agree on what we regard as a healthy human body. In psychology, and especially in sociology, there is no such universal agreement. Hildebrand (*Christliche Ethik*, 1959, pp. 229f) clearly affirms: "No examination of the sources of moral goodness or badness can start with the question: what is in conformity with human nature? The elementary impulses or the imminent logic, which is accessible to a neutral analysis, either of a psychologist or a psychiatrist, are never able to unveil to us the foundations of ethical behaviour." And so (p. 226) he explicitly, and very helpfully, says: "We know that to be righteous is according to nature (*secundum naturam*) because we know that it is good. We do not derive our knowledge of the goodness of righteousness from its being according to nature. . . . Not because it conforms to our nature is righteousness morally good, but because it is good, our nature is called upon to take possession of it."

But what then? Do we liquidate the concept of natural law, at any rate in its traditional sense? The commonest form of deriving an "ought" from an "is" is certainly eliminated. But there are other forms. For the present, we leave Hildebrand, who is an outstanding exponent of the philosophy of values, and return to the more usual way of clarifying what we mean by natural law. We have not yet discovered the secret which seemingly makes the whole doctrine acceptable. The philosopher who defends this concept thinks not only that he can see that which, from a merely superficial point of view, exists, but that he can see through the surface of human beings and social order into the very essence of it all. He can, as he imagines, see what is true, real, essential, and can distinguish this from what simply exists. He penetrates the very core of what humanity is. And thus he imagines that he can claim that the "existentia" of man and of society can be made to conform to their true *essentia*. As far as this true and real being has not yet been realized, it stands over and against any existing form as an ideal for which to strive. Reason teaches me not only what actually is, but what is the true nature of created beings and what, therefore, fulfills their essential nature.

This rather strange way of thinking can perhaps be illustrated by the teaching of a philosopher who differs in many respects from those with whom we are dealing here: Spinoza. Spinoza has been accused of a lack of logic when, on the one hand, he teaches that the different "modi" of the divine and the perfect "substance" through nature are striving to persevere in their own being and claims that this is the first and only foundation of virtue; and then, on the other hand, two pages later, he proclaims that the striving for knowledge is the first and only foundation of virtue. There is, however, no contradiction in Spinoza's mind. The *conatus intelligendi* is the realization of the very essence of a human being and thus the only right way of that *conatus conservandi* which is the nature of any modus. This "transition" from what actually is to what ought to be, the "transition" which makes it possible for Spinoza to write on ethics, is, in his view, no *metabasis eis allo genos,* but only a statement of what "to be," and therefore "to conserve being truly," rightly means.

We should add that behind this most central part of Spinoza's philosophy, and behind that type of Roman Catholic doctrine of natural law with which we are now dealing, lies the Platonic philosophy according to which a being has much more "reality" when it has "goodness," that is, when it realizes its true essence. The doctrine of "degrees of reality," well-known to modern scholars through F. H. Bradley, but unfamiliar to many people in our day, must here be kept in mind.

Having arrived thus far, we must now ask by what means a philosopher like Spinoza or a Roman Catholic scholar is able to penetrate the surface and reach the true essence of a human being. Spinoza had his view of the very "idea" of a man. Hegel differed. Others, again, have other ideas and ideals. What enables a Christian philosopher to believe that he has arrived at the truth and penetrated to the very essence of humanity?

Here we approach a philosophy of values such as Roman Catholic scholars like Max Scheler, and especially Hildebrand present. Certain "values" reveal themselves to every sincere and unsophisticated human being, in such a way that they claim our acknowledgment and obedience. We know that we are obliged to strive for their realization. In modern terms we may call this view moral intuitionism. More traditionally, we speak of conscience as the "place" where the moral obligation is felt. (The Roman Catholic distinction between *conscientia* and *syntersis* may here be left out of account.)

If this brief sketch is correct, we see that the distinction between the different views is only one of emphasis. And yet it will be understood that some Roman Catholic scholars, like Bernhard Häring in his much discussed *Das Gesetz Christi* (5 ed., 1959, p. 260), can speak of two different lines of thinking, the one more Aristotelian, emphasizing the rational understanding achieved through our examining the created world and its "orders" ("die Schöpfungsordnungen") and the other more platonic-Augustinian, in which we speak of our being able to view the eternal "ideas." But in Thomas Aquinas these two "lines" were already combined. In spite of his "Aristotelian" philosophy, he retained in his conception of natural law much of the Augustinian heritage, as Ernsf Wolf has pointed out in his article "Zur Frage des Naturrechts bei Thomas von Aquin und bei Luther" (*Peregrinatio,* 1957, pp. 183ff.).

A discussion of these somewhat differing views or of the whole intricate question of "a philosophy of values" would take us too far from our main theme. Nor is it necessary, because the central problem is much the same in all cases: what entitles a Christian philosopher to think that his *ratio* is able to penetrate to the very essence of humanity? What leads him to conclude that he is able to perceive and acknowledge the true values and distinguish them rightly from the false? We who are familiar today with the different ideas and ideals of humanity in different cultural and historical settings, see this question as a very urgent one. It was nothing less than a crisis in our European culture when it became evident, from about the time of John Locke, that moral ideals which had hitherto been regarded as the given content of natural law could no longer claim a *consensus omnium,* but were a product of a definite historical development in which elements from Greece and Palestine, from Roman stoicism and Roman law, had been combined. Why the more or less Christian ideals of humanity, and not those of Buddhism or Confucianism or the so-called primitive society?

Roman Catholic scholars are not entirely clear and unambiguous in answering this question. They certainly appeal to *ratio,* but they are fairly definite in emphasizing that they are speaking of *recta ratio, ratio* restored to its created integrity, *ratio* cured by divine grace of the consequences of the fall into sin. Even the great Aristotle was unable to use his *ratio* in a perfect way. *De jure* he could, but *de facto* he could not. Nevertheless, it is maintained that the conception of natural law is "rational," so that it is possible to argue satisfactorily for its tenets; and those who oppose this aspect of Roman Catholic teaching are to some extent deliberately opposing true human reason.

But this position is unsatisfactory. Either the rational character of natural law is underlined in such a way that we simply cannot understand why all non-Christians go to some extent, and often very far, astray, or the need for divinely imparted grace to remedy the defects of sinful man's *ratio* is emphasized to such an extent that we can only wonder why appeal is made to reason and not to the so-called special revelation in Christ. But Roman Catholic tradition, with its clear distinction between the natural and the supernatural sphere, is far from the latter solution. *Ratio* is competent in the natural sphere, but this means *recta ratio* with all the ambiguities which that term involves.

## Natural Law and Biblical Thought

Sometimes the conception of natural law is criticized from an entirely different angle, which sees it as betraying its origin in Greek thinking and as foreign to biblical views. The Greeks had a static concept of the phenomena of this sensible world. They had, at least in Platonism, rather imperfect images of the eternal and unchangeable ideas. The task was to understand their nature, their given order. It was for the word, *logos, ratio* (to refer now especially to Stoicism) to express this given nature, to understand in their essence, and notwithstanding all changes, the fundamental, unchangeable givenness of these phenomena. Biblical thinking, on the contrary, is dynamic. The world is not just a fairly well-ordered *kosmos,* but the field of God's ever new, creative activity. Mankind has its history, the world in a process where God is always acting. If biblical thinking can speak of a continuity, and it certainly can, it is not because of the stability of a given order of the world, but of the faithfulness of God, who never forsakes his creation. In the Bible, therefore, the word is something spoken from one person to another—an I-Thou relation, to use a modern phrase. The concept of natural law has, it is argued, been unable to incorporate this historical dimension. It is, and it remains, Greek, and therefore it must be removed (see, for example, W. Pannenberg's article, "Zur

Theologie des Rechts" in *Zeitschrift für evangelische Ethik,* 1963, pp. 1ff.).

There is much truth in this criticism. But we have still to remember that leading modern thinkers, say of the neo-Thomist school, like Jacques Maritain, are aware of the problems here involved and seek to meet them without giving up the doctrine of natural law. In his important book, *Humanisme intégral* (1936) Maritain tries both to retain the fundamental elements of the social teaching of St. Thomas and to admit that the fact that we are living in a new era makes it impossible for us simply to reproduce his social doctrines. In modern times we have to use "analogical" thinking when we acknowledge our indebtedness to the great schoolmen of the thirteenth century. The teaching of that time must be translated, as it were, to suit the demands of new social problems. We need not elaborate this further. We now know that the Roman Catholic Church is not as static or inflexible as we have been apt to think.

It has surprised some people to find that since the time of Pope Leo XIII we have been able to speak of a revival of the Roman Catholic doctrine of natural law and that even a progressive Pope like John XXIII explicitly and several times appeals to this conception in his famous encyclical letters *Mater et Magistra* (1961) and *Pacem in Terris* (1963). But here there is no hesitation. Pope John quotes with approval the radio message of his predecessor at Pentecost, 1941, where "the great pontiff" speaks of the papal right to "decide whether the bases of a given social system are in accord with the unchangeable order which God our creator and redeemer has shown us through the natural law and revelation." There is "a fundamental principle of social philosophy, unshaken and unchangeable, a principle that to some extent safeguards private property and private enterprise, just as there are laws inviolable and immutable that are to be recognized and observed" and that deal with the problems of sexual life.

We notice, however, that the word "revelation" was added (*Mater et Magistra,* p. 10 in the English translation). And in *Pacem in Terris* (p. 42) we find a threefold authority: "the principles of the natural law, the social doctrine of the church and the directives of ecclesiastical authority." This is explained by the statement "that the church has the right and the duty not only to safeguard the principles of ethics and religion, but also to intervene authoritatively with her children in the temporal sphere, when there is a question of judging about the application of those principles to concrete cases."

This, perhaps, is only what we might expect. And yet, what is the point of appealing to "the unshakeable and unchangeable rock of moral law, made manifest in the order of nature by the creator himself and by him engraved on the hearts of man with letters that may never be effaced" (*Pacem,* p. 24), when this "unshakeable rock" has to be consolidated by an appeal to revelation and even to ecclesiastical authority? And practically speaking, how much of the whole doctrine in fact remains, when Pope John (*Mater,* p. 47) can say: "Man separated from God becomes inhuman to himself and to those of his kind, because the orderly relation of society presupposes the orderly relation of one's conscience with God, fount of truth, of justice and of love"? The emphasis on ecclesiastical authority is, of course, entirely different from the approach of Karl Barth. But leaving out the "dogmatic" problems here involved, how far are we, in fact, from a christological foundation of social ethics? How far are we from substituting "gospel and law" for the traditional "law and gospel," when it is only by entering into "the orderly relation" with God that an "orderly relation of society" can come into being?

A Roman Catholic scholar would probably answer that his doctrine of natural law enables him to tell his non-Christian neighbor that his ideas of a just society and his corresponding behavior are contrary to the innermost core of his being and to his own reason (*ratio*) rightly understood. But if this can be made evident and obligatory only to a Christian, it does not seem to have much practical importance. Are we to understand the late Pope to mean that the non-Christian who has become "inhuman to himself and to those of his kind" obstinately opposes the dictates of his own reason and conscience? Such an interpretation would not seem possible. And, if it were, it would surely in many instances do injustice to the non-Christian partner.

The Roman Catholic Church, in its conservative mood, retains the doctrine of natural law and can even revive it when it seems obsolete. But what does it mean, even at its most emphatic, when confronted with modern man, with his entirely different mental and moral attitude?

Karl Barth and those thinkers who join him here are usually regarded as the most radical opponents of the whole conception of natural law. Rightly understood, this view is correct. Barth is convinced that natural man, man fallen into sin, can know God only when God in Jesus Christ reveals himself to him. He opposes every kind of "natural theology" as an enemy of grace. And as God is known only in Jesus Christ through the Holy Spirit, when and wherever God in his sovereign grace so wills, it is only through the (falsely) so-called special revelation that man comes to learn what it really means to be a human being, what are the purpose and the aim of God's creative activity, and therefore to what kind of behavior and moral activity man as man, created in Christ and for Christ, is called and in Christ regenerated. Christian ethics therefore depends upon God's revelation; and the ethical part of Christian teaching is consequently an integral part of "Christian dogmatics," in a way that is secondary to what is commonly called dogmatics, because it is the God-given human answer to God's redemptive grace. We love because he first loved us and because this divine love creates in those who receive it a new life, and an obedience born of thankfulness.

This does not imply that we should now be able to derive from the Bible a complete set of moral prescripts. The Bible is not a handbook in casuistry. But we come to know God and his will. We are reborn into a new existence. We come to know that God is *agape* and what that means. We learn that we are called upon to live a life with our fellowmen and toward God in *agape*. And in the prophetic and apostolic writings we find ample illustration of what that means. This is not to say that in all respects we should try to follow exactly every guidance that, say, Paul gives the Christians of the early church. But we trust that the Holy Spirit through these and other guidances of Scripture will help us to find our way of *agape* in the circumstances and problems that happen to be ours, and which in some respects differ from those of the apostolic age.

As we know, Barth himself takes one step further. He thinks

that in applying his doctrine of *analogia fidei* and *analogia relationis,* the believer should be able to discover the structures and orders of God's creation and therefore what true humanity, according to God's purpose, rightly means. What true fatherhood means we learn from the fact that God from eternity is the father of his only begotten son and in him the father of those who are redeemed to his kingdom. What true matrimonial love involves, we learn from the fact that Christ so loves his church. . . .

I shall not try to elaborate this further. The majority of scholars have their criticisms of such publications as *Rechtfertigung und Recht* (1938) and *Christengemeinde und Bürgergemeinde* (1946). But even the more carefully and broadly worked-out statements in *Kirchliche Dogmatik* (III. 4, 1951) do not, in my opinion, satisfy.[1]

The important question is what is sometimes called Barth's "christological" approach to Christian ethics and to social ethics. Is he right? At first sight it must seem obvious that he cannot be entirely in error. Our attitude toward ethical problems depends largely on our conception of the world and of human beings ("das Menschenbild"). And if, in Christ, we gain a new understanding of God having created the world and the human race and therefore each individual, this of necessity seems to involve a change in our ethical doctrines and reactions. Non-Christians often find this obvious. It is only a matter of knowing how fundamental the change must be. And a Christian who is convinced that Christ alone is the light of the world is apt to think that compared with that light, everything else is darkness.

Here we are confronted with serious problems and must face somewhat violent opposition. We can take up only a few of the main questions.

First, there is the objection that if we eliminate the concept of natural law, no common ground remains on which Christian and non-Christian can meet for a fruitful discussion of ethical questions. A debate, we are told, leads nowhere, if one party to it

---

[1] I have given my criticisms in a review of that volume in *Theologische Zeitschrift* (Basel: 1952, pp. 443ff.), and I shall not repeat them here. Nor is it necessary to do so, because this "prolongation" of Barth's central position is, as it were, an unnecessary "addition" to his doctrine of "gospel and law."

thinks that he alone knows the truth, and supposes his opponent to be in error or in ignorance. We all know, too, that Christians and non-Christians are often able to meet and agree on ethical questions and practical issues, and that even when they disagree they can talk on equal terms and perhaps reach agreement or at least understand and respect the position of the other. Finally it is an unquestionable fact that even anti-Christian thinkers have made Christians aware of ethical truths which they had not seen or not envisaged clearly before. Did not Voltaire do much to make Christians aware of the duty of religious freedom? Was not Karl Marx an instrument in arousing a lazy church to see more clearly its social responsibility? Are not the Christians indebted to men like Nietzsche or even Freud? And does not all this prove that on ethical questions a common ground exists on which all decent human beings can meet and mutually help one another to clearer insight? We may, it is said, call this common ground natural law or find some other term for it. This does not affect the fact that this common ground is a reality. Christians sometimes think that this fact indicates that Christ, being the lord of the whole world and of all mankind, is active also beyond the borders of his church. Whether they use the old term, *logos spermatikos,* or more modern terminology, they gratefully acknowledge the fact to which we here allude.

It is claimed, furthermore, that if natural law did not exist and the revelation in Christ were only the valid foundation of true ethics, humanity outside the Christian church would be a moral chaos where the only reason for preferring one ethical attitude to another would be individual likes or dislikes. And this certainly is not so. Much has been said since the days of John Locke against the easy phrase of a *consensus omnium* in ethical questions. We certainly recognize differences in moral attitude. But are not these seemingly impressive differences unimportant compared with the fundamental agreement behind them? Can it not be proved that the so-called "Golden Rule," in its negative form, has been defined and accepted in the most remotely separated areas of the world? And, to take one particular example, although the five commandments that mean so much to Buddhism certainly differ from Christian formulations, they are nevertheless quite reasonable. Could we imagine a religious leader or a nation adhering to commandments that were in direct opposition to them?

It is a fact, we are rightly told, that Christianity enters a world which already has some generally fixed structures. Some kinds of matrimony, for example, and certain types of state and political order already exist. And human beings have always known the necessity for work and for some form of cooperation. To a large extent the world was already structured before the Christian gospel was proclaimed. And as this is not possible without some kind of morality, some moral rules for human behavior, there must of necessity be some ethics independent of Christian revelation. Christian teaching does not completely change these given structures or abolish them, though it does, perhaps, to some extent transform the manner in which they are maintained. But they are there as a given necessity, and human life would not be possible if they were radically abused or were removed. It is not surprising that some theologians, especially German, used to speak of divinely given "orders of creation" and that now, when this terminology has become impossible because of misuse by the "German Christians" of Hitler's time, modern scholars speak of given "institutions" or "mandates" which simply exist and must remain. Christianity, then, enters into something already given; it does not create new forms of social life (the church may be counted as an exception), but it may—or it may not—fill those given "mandates" or "institutions" with a new spirit. *Gratia perficit naturam,* to quote a well-known phrase from Thomas Aquinas.

What are we to say to all this, if we believe that we must uphold the main points in Barth's position regarding these questions?

## A Christological View of Natural Law

The first and perhaps the most important point to emphasize is that God has not given mankind over to perdition. He upholds his created beings in order that in the fullness of time he may gather together all things in Christ (Ephesians 1 : 10). Sinful men are not turned into demons. Human society is not a nest of robbers, a *bellum omnium contra omnes.* Man is endowed with faculties that enable him to gain the means of existence. He does not need the revelation in Christ to teach him how to cultivate the soil and invent technical ways of making life richer and easier. And man has the ability to create human communities where people behave toward one another in such a way that common life is not only tolerable but fairly happy and prosperous. Fallen man can reach high standards of morality. He can attain wonderful levels of unselfish love, come to know the "Golden Rule" and to a large extent behave accordingly. Life without Christ is not hell, but may, in a lofty sense of the word, be filled with human dignity and with love for one's neighbor, even with willingness to sacrifice one's own life for others or for society. Christians, including those of the Barthian school, should willingly, gladly, thankfully acknowledge all this. We do not honor God, or his revelation in Christ, by speaking slightingly of what man in his pre-Christian state can achieve in the ethical sphere.

It is in the light of such considerations that we must understand the famous passage in Romans 2 : 14–15. Paul does not say that the law, but that the work of the law, is written in the hearts of the Gentiles. The apostle here addresses the Jews and reminds them first of the fact that it is not enough to have the law; one must be "a doer of the law." And he goes on: Do not be too haughty; the Gentiles also sometimes perform works that deserve our praise and admiration. This is true today. Not many can join Karl Barth when he tries to interpret this text so that "Gentiles" means Christians of Gentile origin.[2] Passages like Philippians 4 : 8 and I Peter 2 : 12 also, as far as I can judge, prove that it is assumed by the apostles that heathen judgment on ethical questions is not completely corrupt. But we make a great mistake if we imagine that Christians should seek to conform themselves as far as possible to Gentile concepts of "virtue." Paul exhorts his readers (Philippians 2 : 9) to remember what they have "received and heard and seen in me." Paul's opinion on these questions is clearly stated in Romans 12 : 2, where he speaks of a renewal of the minds of the believers, "that they may ascertain what is the will of God, his good and acceptable and perfect will." Apostolic teaching is given,

---

[2] I admit that J. B. SOUCEK, *Antwort: Karl Barth zum siebzigsten Geburtstag am 10. Mai 1956* (pp. 99ff.), has argued skillfully for this interpretation. But I do not find his arguments convincing.

in an extremely condensed form, in I John 3 : 23: "And this is his commandment, that we should believe on the name of his son Jesus Christ, and love one another, as he commanded us." This is certainly not the content of what might reasonably be called natural law, if there were a reasonable way of using this most unhappy term.

Some scholars may find that in emphasizing a passage like this from I John, the dogmatic and ethical aspects are confusingly mixed. Such an objection, however, suggests remoteness from biblical thinking. Neither in the Old nor in the New Testament is this distinction made. Dogmatics and ethics cannot be separated. And something fateful happened when this separation took place in Christian theology. Christian theology ought, surely, to be forever grateful to Emil Brunner when, in his famous *Das Gebot und die Ordnungen* (1932),[3] he pointed this out. That he was not able himself to carry this insight through is of minor importance.

But Christian ethics does not strain to underline and defend its uniqueness. On the contrary, Christians should be happy when they find themselves in fairly deep agreement with non-Christians on ethical issues. To cooperate as far as possible is an obvious Christian obligation, and the Christian should not constantly emphasize the fundamental difference. But it is there. The Christian idea of humanity and of mutual love is based on the fact that Christ died for us all. We are always "ambassadors of Christ," even where his name is not mentioned and where we work for purposes like international peace or social justice and relief for the down-trodden.

But Christians have then to argue for their aims at such a level that the argument may appear reasonable, perhaps convincing, to others; and it ought to be no problem at all. We should be happy if we could make some headway by such arguments. But points are constantly reached at which the Christian partner clearly operates from another conception of what it really means to be a human being, and of what is required in defending true humanity; he proclaims loyalty to his only Lord and to his teachings. And when

---

[3] *The Divine Imperative* (1937).

"ethical" questions are at stake, we are called upon not to be "ashamed of the gospel of Christ."

Whenever this is said, the defenders of a christological approach to ethics are accused of teaching "a special Christian ethics." The most violent and determined protest has come, in our time, from Lutheran theologians. They appeal to Luther's famous doctrine of "the two realms" and interpret this doctrine, I think rightly, in such a way that in "the worldly regiment" or "realm" there is no need for special Christian guidance. We cannot take up this hotly debated question here in full. It must suffice to refer to the book of Professor Franz Lau of Leipzig, *Luthers Lehre von den beiden Reichen* (1953) in which he called upon Lutheran New Testament scholars "in careful research work to discover whether Christ has not given materially new commandments, relevant for the actions of Christians and Christendom in this world." "The Lutheran Church," he goes on, "knows of no infallible Luther" (pp. 91ff.).

There is more that should be said. But those who know something of modern Lutheranism will understand how important it is that this be noted. But if we turn, say, to Karl Barth, with the objection that he is teaching "a special Christian ethics," he would no doubt answer: "I know of no 'special' Christ. The world was created in him and for him. Why, then, should we take the 'no' of the 'unbelievers' so seriously? They also are *de jure* his redeemed children." It is probably against this background that Heinz Horst Schrey (in his article "Naturrecht" in *Weltkirchenlexikon,* 1960) affirms that we might here speak of a "christological natural law," a strange, but quite acceptable, phrase.

How far may we speak of an activity of the risen Lord (or of *logos spermatikos* or even *logos asarkos*) independently of the proclamation of the gospel? We cannot do so, primarily, I believe, because high ethical standards in non-Christian cultures do not seem, as a rule, to make people more ready to listen to the gospel. Here, I think, we must keep silent. To the surprise of many, Karl Barth has recently called attention, in *Kirchliche Dogmatik* (IV. 3, 1959), to the possibility that God, even outside the walls of his church, may enable man to speak "true words" ("wahre Worte"), to which his church has to listen and from which Christians can learn. Barth does not make it clear how he is able to combine this with the famous christocentricity and exclusive appeal to Scripture which is the content of the Barmen thesis I of 1937, a thesis which, moreover, is the text of that paragraph (69), where this view is set forth. Nor does he give examples of what he has in mind. But he may be thinking here of the fact that the Christian church could learn much from Karl Marx and his modern disciples.

Here, then, we touch the problem, mentioned above, of how far, as Christians, we can and must learn from anti-Christian thinkers like Voltaire, Marx, Nietzsche or Freud. I would not venture to state that these thinkers have spoken "true words," to which we simply must listen. But they have been instruments in God's hands to make his church aware of truths which Christians had hitherto overlooked or misinterpreted. Their teaching has to be "translated" or remodeled into biblical doctrine. These thinkers can help us only insofar as they recall our attention to what we ought to have been able to discover in the Bible. We cannot learn true Christian tolerance from Voltaire. His tolerance is founded in skepticism. But he has been an instrument in God's hand to help us see more clearly what religious freedom means.

Here, moreover, we encounter a curious fact. A much-quoted phrase from Spinoza runs, "Truth is the criterion of both itself and of that which is false." (*Veritas norma sui et falsi est*). This seems so obvious that no proof is considered necessary. And yet this adage is strangely misleading. Karl Marx rightly and truly saw that the structure of the society of his time was terribly false. His criticisms are to a large extent valid. But he was unable to see the true solution of the problems of reshaping society. His conception of man and humanity, and therefore of society, was not nourished —or at any rate not sufficiently—on biblical sources.

Many problems have been left out or only just touched upon here. English-speaking readers will, no doubt, especially deplore the omission of reference to C. H. Dodd's studies on these questions, especially to his appeal to the rabbinical doctrine of "Noachian precepts," in which he finds "the Jewish equivalent for the stoic doctrine of the law of nature." [4]

---

[4] See his article on natural law in the New Testament in his *New Testament Studies* (1953).

Nor have I discussed those passages in the Old Testament to which the champions of natural law usually appeal; nor examined all that might seem relevant in the New Testament, although I have taken up some of the most controversial passages.

I have sought only, in brief outline, to indicate what seem to be the main problems. I might conclude by quoting a passage (John 1 : 17) to which Emil Brunner so often calls our attention: "Grace and truth came by Jesus Christ," or I might simply quote the title of one of Brunner's most famous works: *Wahrheit als Begegnung* (*Truth As Encounter*) and take this title so seriously that it would prove to provide an answer to the main problem of this paper.

\* \* \* \* \*

## Postscript by Professor Söe

I have had the privilege of seeing two papers by eminent scholars, Professor Paul Ramsey, Department of Religion, Princeton University, and Professor Langdon Gilkey, Divinity School, University of Chicago, criticizing my article rather sharply. I shall try to state some of the main objections and to answer them as briefly as possible. As my opponents and I come from rather different theological positions, I feel by no means certain that I can make the differences quite clear, not to speak of convincing my critics. Nor am I arguing that I am right, but simply that my view is tenable.

The quotations given under points 1 and 2 below are from the paper by Professor Ramsey, whereas the quotations under point 5 are from the paper by Professor Gilkey.

1. I am reminded that philosophers like Hume and Moore also think that Christians are guilty of the fallacy of pronouncing "a prescription on a nondescriptive statement." We love because he has first loved us, certainly "contains or presupposes the following *normative* judgments: you *ought* to love him who first loves you, or as he loves." *My answer:* To meet Christ in the sense in which Christians understand this term is to submit one's self entirely to him, acknowledging him as lord and savior. It can rightly be called an act of obedience. So the question how my obligation

to obey him can be deduced from the fact of his loving me simply cannot be put without completely misunderstanding what conversion to Christ means. A satisfactory answer to this objection is given in a very fine way in Luther's Small Catechism where he explains the second article of the Apostles' Creed.

2. A further objection is posed: the *fact* that Christ commands and lays a claim upon you, coupled with the *fact* that he loved you and gave himself for you—these theological statements cannot by "imperceptible transitions become ethical statements. If it is ethics you are engaged upon, and not metaphysics or theology, then you must begin by showing that obedience to this command of Christ is good, and that therefore our nature is called upon to take possession of it." *Answer:* I certainly am not venturing upon ethics as something different from theology. If I were to understand that Christ's command is good before I gave my assent to it, it must mean that previous to my giving myself over to Christ, I must know what is good. Then I (my conscience) should be the supreme judge in these matters, and "revelation" so far would not be revelation. The Holy Spirit opens our blind eyes to see what until then was hidden. Christian ethics is certainly not a special kind of philosophical ethics.

3. Then I am asked why we should be invited to argue rationally against the concept of natural law, since all rational argumentation ceases when appeal is made to the lordship of Christ. *Answer:* Sometimes it is helpful or even necessary, or at any rate worthwhile, to try to show that certain answers are unsatisfactory. This I have tried to do with regard to natural law. But it can never be possible to prove that an answer which is an appeal to the lordship of Christ is the right one. This would amount to the task of proving that Christ is the lord.

4. And on a similar point: if it is considered a valid argument against an appeal to natural law that there is certainly no universal consensus as to ethical issues, why should not the same argumentation hold true against a christological ethics, seeing that even among Christians there is much disagreement as to what the ethical teaching of the Bible involves? *Answer:* We all, I think, agree that "now we see as in a glass, darkly." We have only a *theologia viatorum.* We can, of course, point to the fact that there is much

more agreement on ethical questions among Christians than in mankind as a whole. But the same holds true of Buddhism or Hinduism. If there were a consensus of all Christians, it would amount to something like a proof of the divine origin of Christianity. And such proofs are not accorded to us. An appeal to natural law can be convincing only when this "law" makes itself felt, causing something like a *consensus omnium*. To a Christian the fact of the regnant lord needs no proof. And he does not wonder that Christ never reveals the whole of his truth to us sinful beings. Natural law is problematic and needs proof. The regnant lord can never need to give proof to a Christian.

5. An essential objection to my position is that I fail to show how it comes about that human beings are able to behave decently and even in unselfish love to one another. I have been accused of saying that this is "solely because of Christ": "The author must ask and answer how the risen lord effects this 'moralization' of non-Christian man—otherwise his explanatory principle remains a *deus ex machina* and not theology at all." Or the question is put: "Is there some kind of 'hidden,' extrascriptural, extraecclesiastical communication by the Christ of the truth to all men? . . . Is this regnant lord not more aptly referred to as the *logos* of God, the pre-existent son of God, who, according to the apologists, is universally present with creation as its principle of order and goodness and so formed a 'covenant with the Greeks' thus revealing to them the divine wisdom and goodness?" *Answer:* This objection has very much surprised me. To defend a christological Christian ethics certainly does not involve being a disciple of Marcion. Nor does it involve a doctrine of the risen lord or a *logos spermatikos* being present wherever God in his gracious providence provides for his created world. Here certainly are no "great problems" raised "for a Barthian position." God (that is, the triune God) created the world in and for and in view of Christ incarnate, crucified and risen. And he preserves the world for this his purpose, endowing human beings with the faculty of establishing and maintaining in a fairly decent way human societies and communities. But when we look at all this, we can never find divine will, divine providence, divine commandments in their purity. We are only in an inextricable mixture of creation and sins ("Schöpfung und Sünde," to

make use of the title of a well-known book by Emanuel Hirsch). Why this divine preservation could be made only through the risen lord or the regnant lord or a *logos spermatikos,* I fail to understand. I have never said that this is done only through the instrumentality of Christ. How an appeal to God's gracious preservation of his own creation for the fulfilling of his purpose, "that everything in heaven and on earth should be unified in Christ," could mean the introduction of a "deus ex machina," I am unable to discover. Has not the so-called "Barthian" position here been completely misinterpreted?

6. Finally I have been asked how I can explain the striking similarities between the best examples of non-Christian ethics and Christian ethical teaching. *Answer:* To me it seems sufficient, if my answer must be brief, again to point to I John 3 : 23: "His command is this—that we are to believe in his son Jesus Christ and to love one another, as he has commanded us to do." An intolerable confusion of "dogmatics and ethics"? Perhaps it looks like that. But this is not my fault. Here, at any rate, we are very near the cornerstone of Christian ethics.

# 17

# ANGLICAN THEOLOGY AND
# THE ETHICS OF NATURAL LAW

by JOSEPH FLETCHER (United States)

THE natural law theory's storied and continuous role in the development of classical Christian ethics and moral theology has
nonetheless always failed to win it immunity from attack and out-
right repudiation. Yet never has it suffered as much skeptical
criticism, from within as well as without the camp of those who
live by the *depositum fidei,* as right now in the twentieth century.
Indeed, it seems most unlikely that it can survive conceptually in
any recognizable guise.

In the fifty years since the First World War the most creative
and compelling work in both "theological" and "special" Christian
ethics has taken shape out of ecumenical dialogue and intercon-
fessional confrontation, especially in the study commissions of the
World Council of Churches—*yet the natural law doctrine has been
given practically no attention in any of this work.* Has this been
because Protestantism has been so indifferent or antagonistic toward it and perhaps in need of the stimulus of recent encounter
with the Roman Catholic theologians to give this discusssion the
urgency and sophistication it requires? Possibly. But this view does
not do justice to the question, for there have always been some
exponents of natural law in the non-Roman churches from the
very beginnings of "Life and Work" and of "Faith and Order."
Among these, Anglicans have been both numerous and influen-

tial. Their views therefore call for a closer scrutiny, if we are to analyze the "natural law issue" in Christian ethics today, especially in relation to church and society.

## Anglicanism and Natural Law

In ecumenical circles there is a widespread but erroneous impression that the natural law doctrine is a fixed feature of Anglican theology. Every student of the history of ideas is familiar with the role of the concept in the English common law tradition and jurisprudence, and how it began to lose its force and tenability as early as the seventeenth century. It managed to keep its hold upon English theology for a somewhat longer time and, after the "Catholic revival" under Pusey and Newman, even regained its vigor and acceptability for a while, particularly in the "Christian sociology" circles of the Anglo-Catholic wing of the Church of England. Soon after the Reformation, Anglicanism's tie to the natural law was plainly put by Richard Hooker in his *Ecclesiastical Polity,* where he declared with bland confidence that its (natural law's) "general principles are such that it is not easy to find a man ignorant of them." [1] English Christianity has always kept a place for "natural theology" (the religious perception of natural reason apart from special revelation), and like Hooker 250 years earlier, Archdeacon Paley stated its view bluntly: "Now, there are two methods of coming at the will of God on any point. I. by his express declarations, when they are to be had, and which must be sought for in Scripture. II. by what we can discover of his designs and disposition from his works; or, as we usually call it, the light of Nature." [2] Bishop Butler, Paley's contemporary, was of the opinion that "almost any fair man in almost any circumstance" would know the right course to follow, but rationalist though he was, he made his own system stand on other grounds than natural law precepts.[3]

However, there has always been a measure of ambiguity in the Anglican treatment of natural law. The Caroline divines—Puritans,

---

[1] I. viii, 9.
[2] WILLIAM PALEY: *Works,* D. S. WAYLAND, ed. 1837, I. 41.
[3] Sermon 3, *Sermons.* New York: 1858.

such as Richard Baxter, William Ames and William Perkins, and churchmen such as Robert Sanderson, Joseph Hall, John Sharp, Jeremy Taylor and Thomas Barlow (all bishops)—were more or less in the "following" of the classical doctrine. But it is wise to use such qualifiers as "more or less" since they were inclined to trace with (the then uncanonized) Thomas Aquinas the sequence from eternal law to natural law to "right reason," yet as Reformation theologians they took sin and its blinders seriously and constantly "hedged" the classical doctrine of natural law in such a way that it was never the clear-cut theory the schoolmen (and later neo-Thomists) made it. Jeremy Taylor twisted and squirmed in an effort to follow the line, yet he confessed that though "all men talk of the law of nature," they differ as to its precepts and how they are discovered, "whereas if the law of nature were such a thing as is supposed generally, these differences would be as strange and impossible as that men should disagree about what is black, or what is yellow." [4] Taylor could foresee that natural law would be "used" comfortably by Nazis and anti-Nazis, Thomists and humanists, naturalists and theists.

From the start, English Protestants, taking their more independent and indigenous line of approach to theological doctrine and ethics, have had more trouble with the "discernment" of natural law than with belief in its objective reality. They had no difficulty in believing that God wills what is right and good, whether he wills it because it is good (the realists) or it is good because he wills it (the nominalists). Their belief that his will infuses his creation was like the *anima mundi* of the Stoics from whom early Christians took the natural law idea and baptized it. But they were uneasy about the *epistemology* of the classical doctrine, for reasons we shall shortly discuss. On the one hand, they sympathized with Aquinas' theory of analogy whereby they could assume that there is enough in common between the minds of God and man so that the latter may discern something of God's will (eternal law) naturally and without revelation. Yet they were troubled by the Reformation conviction that human sin and finitude set too great a

---

[4] *Ductor Dubitantium*, II.i.1.

distance between the divine mind and the mental capacities of fallen humans, to say nothing of their moral or volitional powers! They never quite shrugged off Isaiah's warning, "For my thoughts are not your thoughts, neither are your ways my ways, saith the Lord." [5]

At the same time, the English tradition in *social* ethics has fairly consistently adopted the heuristic notion that certain of what Luther, with the schoolmen, regarded as created "orders" (*die Ordnungen*)—Bonhoeffer's term "mandates" denotes the same thing —are God-given or "natural" institutions. Anglican thought focused especially upon the family and the state; work or vocation was less readily recognized as such. Yet quite as many Anglican theological treatises, perhaps most of them, "derived" their defense of and demands upon these orders of life and society from the Bible and revelation as from any alleged "natural" or "self-evident" principles.

A brief inspection of Archbishop William Temple's treatment of the natural law concept will show the ambivalence, the ambiguity and the subordination which it has encountered in Anglican theology all along. The plain truth is that Temple never developed an explicit *method* of social-ethical analysis. Most of what he wrote about moral values and social policies was constructed by dogmatic derivation (drawn by logic out of Christian doctrine, in the manner described by Barth as "analogy.") [6] Temple tended to use "natural law" and "natural order" interchangeably, although he preferred the latter phrase. Significantly, he never once used the term or the concept in his Gifford lectures, *Nature, Man and God* (1934). By "natural order" he meant nothing more than a logical relation between appropriate means and "true" ends—for example, subordinating private profit to social need. The natural law ethics of Aquinas, in Temple's view, tried to fix Christian norms in the feudal and medieval culture-pattern. [7] At the same time, he was influenced by the heuristic idea of Aristotle's "final cause"—a *phusikon dikaion* in which "true ends" are simply given or ordained in the nature of things.

---

[5] 55 : 8.
[6] *Church Dogmatics*, II/2.8.
[7] *Thomism and Modern Needs*. London: Blackfriars, 1944.

Furthermore, Temple was inclined to assume in traditional fashion that "natural order" can be discerned through (a) "universals" or what men generally hold to be good, and (b) the use of reason to figure out the "true" purposes of life. His principles of "natural order" were, abstractly expressed in terms of obedience to God, respect for human dignity, freedom, fellowship and service. Except for the first of these, the motivational principle, they are all ideals that any humanist could adopt or any cynic reject. Indeed, as already noted, he founded them not on natural law, but rather on the "implications" as he saw them of such doctrines as creation, the trinity, the incarnation, resurrection and atonement, the church and the sacraments.[8] Temple's peripheral and opaque use of natural law analysis confirms him as a representative of modern Anglicanism.

But certain serious efforts have been made to revive or rehabilitate the concept. A dramatic attempt was made at the wartime conference at Malvern on "The Life of the Church and the Order of Society" (in 1941), which Temple called together to discuss a coherent Christian scheme of war and peace aims.[9] One of the groups participating was "the Christendom group"—a company of rather Anglo-Catholic clergy and lay people devoted to the intellectual tasks of "Christian sociology." Because he obviously hoped to get from them a set of working formularies, based on their deductions from the natural law, Temple had several of them read papers (W. G. Peck, Maurice Reckitt, Dorothy Sayers, V. A. Demant and T. S. Eliot). Little or nothing crystallized. Donald Mackinnon, now a philosopher at Oxford, took issue with natural law, declaring that "to specify the content of the natural law, as it affects men, is a task of appalling difficulty." He opted instead for a dogmatic-analogical approach combined with pragmatic reasoning. Temple himself spoke of "derivative maxims worked out by theologians," but they were to come from *doctrine,* not nature. Demant wanted churchmen "to *develop* a theology of the natural Law" for social criteria, but he himself produced none.

---

[8] Cf. JOSEPH FLETCHER: *William Temple—Twentieth Century Christian.* New York: 1963, esp. pp. 147–163 and notes.

[9] *Malvern 1941,* Proceedings of the Archbishop of York's Conference. London: 1941.

In *Prospect for Christendom,* a symposium by the Christendom group published in 1945, Canon Demant again pled for a natural law ethic, joining "natural law" and "natural order" in a way which would have been familiar to Temple (who had died in 1944). And in his *Theology of Society* he argued again that "only a theological conception of a natural order can identify the permanent central data"—without indicating what those data were or might be.[10] Theologically regarded, this is an interesting inconsistency; it demands that natural law be theologically supported and presumably made a part of *theological* ethics, thus abandoning the classical doctrine that natural law ethics are a part of God's providence known by human reason, rather than a part of God's redemption known by divine revelation! Anglicans have always been blandly evasive of the problem of knowledge in natural law, and have never made the frank admission of the First Vatican Council (1870), that the church's *magisterium* is in the end needed to decide what "nature" requires—thus, in effect, abandoning the natural law's epistemological assumption, and leaving only its ontological assumption (an objective divine will or intention)![11]

Demant's conclusion that earlier written natural-law ethics are needed is like the yearning conclusion of a group of English Protestant and Roman Catholic churchmen, which met periodically for several years in the hope of finding "a guiding principle for social life equivalent to the traditional conception of 'the law of nature' (while realizing) the impossibility of simply recalling to life any ancient or medieval form of the conception."[12] Needless to say, after their years of labor they concluded only that good is to be done and evil avoided. Beyond that they could only leave every problem of justice to "theonomic thinking," since "there is no ready-made or text-book method of settling what is good or evil in every situation." Their conclusion, which is entirely sound but for reasons altogether different from that stated below, stands in sharp contrast to the explicit and integrated *system* of social ethics, for example, in a Roman Catholic treatise like that of the

---

[10] London: 1947.
[11] J. Fuchs: Le Droit Naturel. Paris: 1960.
[12] *Natural Law: A Christian Reconsideration,* A. R. Vidler and W. A. Whitehouse, eds. London: 1946.

Viennese theologian, J. Messner, *Social Ethics: Natural Law in the Modern World* (1949).[13] Almost all the English natural-law works are, and always have been, of the indeterminate and prospective kind—this and that "will be" or "could be" or "should be" or "needs to be" worked out! They have wrestled helplessly with the dozen different meanings of the term "nature" and the equivocations it introduces into all discourse in which it is used. This confusion is found, of course, in all the historic versions of the natural law—Stoic, Roman, Augustinian, Scholastic, Calvinist, Rationalist (as in the French and American "rights of man" declarations).

## Growing Disaffection

In 1921 Kenneth Escott Kirk, who became, some twelve years later, Regius Professor of Moral and Pastoral Theology at Oxford and who was subsequently bishop of the diocese, wrote a very complete, systematic and learned Anglican treatise on moral theology, and in it he gives only one-and-a-half pages out of 413 to natural law! He says rather blandly that it is "the accepted Christian belief" even though moral standards among cultures "vary almost indefinitely." As to its content, he says merely that its precepts may be *deduced* from the "cardinal" virtues.[14] In *The Threshold of Ethics* (1933), Kirk developed a phenomenology of moral experience without a single reference to the natural law! In 1947, his successor in the Oxford chair, R. C. Mortimer (who is now Bishop of Exeter and who was succeeded in the Oxford chair by Demant), also wrote a treatise on moral theology in which we find the most positive affirmations of natural law in formal Anglican treatises, but it ends in the usual style by admitting that it "may seem there is little of value" in natural law. He then identifies it with the *jus gentium,* while allowing that the latter could just as well be accounted for by positive law theory!

Another *inter belllum* leader in the Christendom group, W. G. Peck, made vigorous claims for the natural law, but in actual practice, like most Anglican ethicists, he followed the method of Karl

---

[13] Eng. trans. St. Louis, 1957.
[14] *Some Principles of Moral Theology*. London: 1921.

Barth ("analogy" or logical inference from dogma) and Temple ("inference" drawn from doctrine), rather than the neo-Thomist method of "analogy" by logical deduction from the "natural law." Striking examples of Peck's work are *The Divine Society* (1925) and *The Social Implications of the Oxford Movement* (1933), the latter being lectures given in America. In the same way but more recently, an Anglican layman and economist, D. L. Munby, has, in *Christianity and Economic Problems*,[15] called upon natural law while ignoring it in practice. Munby confesses that the concept is so murky that he risks the *odium theologicum* in referring to it (he calls his own version "descriptive" rather than legal or moral), but claims to find in it "proximate norms" such as that material things are good but subordinate, men are to work, they may own privately but should avoid pride in wealth, they are to live in social groups, and there must be government. Obviously these maxims do not need either scripture or natural law to suggest them; and, in fact, Munby proceeds thereafter in a quite rational and pragmatic way to deal with economic questions. He *refers* to Christian ideas and church writers, but has no constructive need of them to validate what he says!

Anglican philosophical theologians in the last quarter of a century have exemplified this sketchy and peripheral treatment of natural law. It was true of Lionel Thornton's work and of Eric Mascall's, as of Norman Pittenger's in America, to mention only three. This should not be surprising to anybody who is familiar with official or semiofficial formularies in the Church of England. There is no mention of natural law in the Thirty-nine Articles of Religion in the prayer book.[16] In *Doctrine in the Church of England* (1933) the phrase occurs only a single time, properly enough under "providence"—but even here it carries the scientific, *non-ethical* meaning, and is never mentioned once in connection with creation, revelation, love-justice, sin or conscience! [17]

---

[15] London: 1956.

[16] There are a few elliptic references in the two Books of Homilies associated with the Articles.

[17] A joint statement based on a 15-year statement by the Convocations of Canterbury and York.

For the past decade-and-a-half there has been little or no talk of natural law, until quite recently. In 1964 there were three English Anglican treatises, but with none of the grandeur and scholarship of Kirk, which *revive* the notion. They are generally conservative on most of the issues of the times. The first of these is Canon Herbert Waddams' *New Introduction to Moral Theology,* with a section on natural law containing more skepticism than affirmation. In effect, he bows to the views of Professor J. A. Boorman, of McGill University, Canada, that the classical Christian (Catholic) doctrine is a two-story ethic with Aristotle on the first level and the Bible on the second—a "prudential ethic" bearing little resemblance to that of the New Testament.[18] The second is Lindsay Dewar's *Moral Theology in the Modern World.* Canon Dewar's defense of the idea is equivocal: even though "there be no doubt as to what *are* the agreed principles of the natural law—and the doubt has been magnified by some recent writers—there is, to say the least, no less doubt as to the exact interpretation of the Sermon on the Mount."[19] As we shall see, his remarks upon the problematic character of the Protestant scriptural law ethic are well enough founded, but they do not strengthen the natural law position (and there is an alternative still open to Christian ethics). The third work, *The Right and Wrong,* by J. H. Jacques, is a brief and very traditional affirmation of natural law, lacking any concrete "'precepts." Jacques wants politics formed "according to the precepts of the natural law" (p. 112), but these never emerge—only "searching" questions. Nevertheless, he actually calls natural law (p. 117) "a bridge from reason to belief."

Anglican moralists are not alone, of course, in this stubborn but equivocal "loyalty" to the tradition of belief. We should recall that even Ferdinand Toennies in his *Gemeinschaft und Gesellschaft* (1887) tried to find a "sociological basis of natural law," even though it had little ethical connotation. Nathaniel Micklem, a distinguished Congregational theologian, principal of Mansfield College, Oxford, 1932–1953, took the same loyal stance.[20] Americans

---

[18] *Canadian Journal of Theology,* I.3 (1960), cited p. 60.
[19] Cf. p. 44.
[20] *Law and the Laws.* London, 1952.

and Englishmen looking toward the Continent are intrigued by the spectacle of Jacques Ellul, in France, vaguely and ambiguously defending the natural law in a Christian legal treatise,[21] while Paul Tournier of Switzerland, prefers a personalistic ethic for medicine.[22]

In America, there are persistent champions of natural law philosophy, of whom Robert M. Hutchins, of the Fund for the Republic, is a leading example. Many of those who lean upon it appear to use it politically, as Origen did long ago, to justify civil disobedience, especially in relation to dictatorships and on behalf of civil rights.[23] John C. Bennett, the editor of this volume, is a leading American ethicist in social questions who refuses to "break with" the natural law concept, even though his obvious attraction to it is formally disclaimed by such statements as this one in *Christians and the State:* "Whether or not it is wise for Protestants to avoid the use of the phrase 'natural law' (I am not sure about it)," they ought to make clear "that Christians and non-Christians do have much in common in their moral awareness and moral convictions." [24] There is something strange in the persistent notion that natural law still provides common ground with nontheological social thought, when in fact it has just the opposite effect. Walter Marshall Horton once asserted the doctrine for this reason, in the American ecumenical journal, *Christendom* (Winter, 1944, IX. 1), and traces of the same *penchant* are to be found in the work of a Methodist theologian, Walter G. Muelder.[25]

But in Anglicanism generally for the past twenty years, as well as in English and American Protestantism, natural law has suffered the same scant treatment it was given in 1950 by the group appointed by the Central Committee of the World Council of Churches to re-examine it in relation to international order: they quickly by-passed the natural law ideal altogether. After much hesitation most non-Roman theologians, Anglicans included, are in-

---

[21] *The Theological Foundation of Law.* New York, 1960.
[22] *The Whole Person in a Broken World.* New York: 1964. (*Désharmonie de la Vie moderne.* Neuchatel: 1947.)
[23] *Contra Celsum,* V. 37.
[24] New York: 1958, p. 16.
[25] *Foundations of the Responsible Society.* New York: 1959.

clined to agree with Canon Ronald Preston (of Manchester) on traditional moral theology:

There is too much law in it, too many hair-splitting legal distinctions, too little attention to empirical evidence (for instance in psychology and sociology), too simple a notion of the term "natural," and too little concern for perfection as against minimum obligations.[26]

## The Issue: Ethical Knowledge

In America the "conservatives" among Christian moralists cling halfheartedly to the natural law, or at least to the *term,* while "liberals" reject it. It is rarely mentioned, and even more rarely treated constructively. In the World Council, most of the ethics have been based on what a Roman Catholic analyst—making use of a distinction first suggested by J. H. Oldham [27] has called "inspiration" rather than ends. By "inspiration" he meant the motivation of neighbor-love, *agape,* and by *"ends"* the teleology of the Aristotelian-Thomist natural law doctrine. As Father Duff makes clear, the former is Protestant, the latter Catholic, and hence inevitably "the ethic of inspiration" has prevailed. Natural law received no serious attention in the social ethics of the Oxford conference on Church, Community and State in 1937, nor at Amsterdam in 1948, Evanston in 1954, New Delhi in 1961. It was to be expected that evangelical ethicists would ignore it, but what is significant is the absence of any vigorous or committed support even from Anglicans.

Even Emil Brunner's influence among Continental thinkers has not advanced its cause—perhaps because his support is only half-hearted.[28] (We may take note, as an example of *Natur-Recht* analysis, that Brunner rests the case for private ownership on it, whereas Melancthon in his *Loci* of 1521 took it to favor common ownership!) Brunner's predicament is the one in which any Christian finds himself when he tries to build social ethics on the natural law. He analyzes the problem more thoroughly than any

---

[26] *Theology,* Jan., 1961.
[27] EDWARD DUFF, SJ: *The Social Thought of the World Council of Churches.* New York: 1956, p. 93.
[28] *Justice and the Social Order.* London: 1945, pp. 80ff. Also *The Divine Imperative (Das Gebot und die Ordnungen).* London: 1937, esp. note p. 269.

Anglican has ever done. In *Justice and the Social Order* (p. 88), he says that St. Paul embraced the Stoic notion, and that the Reformers likewise "unanimously and unhesitatingly applied the concept of the natural law presented by the church fathers and the schoolmen, as an integral part of their social ethics." But a critical examination of his treatment shows that he accepts only *half* the concept—namely, that right and wrong are objectively real as God's will; *he does not accept the claim that by natural reason men can know what "nature" teaches.* In brief, he accepts its ontology but not its epistemology—its substantive but not its cognitive claims. Its first part fits the Christian faith, but its second part clashes with the fact of finitude. Yet surely the natural law doctrine includes both.

The year 1932 was important as the *emergence-point* of three most influential works: Brunner's *Das Gebot und die Ordnungen*, Reinhold Niebuhr's *Moral Man and Immoral Society* and William Temple's *Nature, Man and God.* Temple and Niebuhr completely ignored natural law, but in Niebuhr's case this was more definitely due to a fundamental insistence on human limitations and the relativities of knowledge and of history. It is this *relativism* which is our era's birthmark. All three approaches, however, were relativistic or "contextual" or "situational." Brunner spoke of "the occasionalism of love" and his method-principle was: "The basis of the Divine Command is always the same, but its content varies with varying circumstances." Niebuhr's very similar approach is well known. Temple put it: "There are no moral laws that are absolute except the law to love one's neighbor as oneself." [29]

Although C. H. Dodd showed in a scholarly way that the natural law idea, in the ontological or substantive sense of the term, had been implicit in the Bible, English or American writers betrayed no interest.[30] In Europe, Werner Elert has been undecided about its utility and validity and therefore has made no use of it.[31] Helmut Thielecke (*Theologische Ethik*, 1955) introduces still another variation on the theme by separating the "order of nature" from the "order of creation," the former being "fallen" enough to come into

---

[29] *Church and Nation.* London: 1915, p. 134.
[30] *Theology*, May-June, 1946.
[31] *The Christian Ethos.* Philadelphia: 1957.

ethical conflict with the latter! [32] This challenges Luther's "orders" and Bonhoeffer's "mandates" and doubles the difficulty of discerning what it is that is "ordained."

A neat and succinct repudiation of natural law, which voices the opinion of most of us, is that by James Pike, the Episcopal Bishop of California.[33] He calls it a "holy noise" and "color words." He gives four main grounds for rejecting it: (1) its "universal precepts," such as "avoid the evil, do the good" and "to each according to his due," are platitudinous; (2) it has been used in history to defend anything and everything—feudalism, capitalism, socialism, fascism, both the "divine right" of kings and democracy, denial of political and religious liberty ("error has no rights") and affirmation of the same ("conscience is always to be followed"); (3) cultural anthropology has made it plain that there is disagreement "on every subject" in morals—there is no *consensus gentium;* (4) its—the natural law's—conclusions are always built into its premises, and the premises are based on faith assertions, entirely legitimate but not a matter of reason at all!

Now that the ecumenical dialogue is widening to include Roman Catholic moralists and social-ethics thinkers, the discussion of natural law will almost certainly be given a depth, coherence and competence which it has not had from Anglican and Protestant theologians. Yet even in Roman Catholic circles the battle is being waged or rewaged. In 1963, in a Roman Catholic-Protestant colloquium at Harvard (attended by Cardinal Bea), Roman Catholic theologians indicated that there are those among them who minimize natural law theory and the "manualistic treatment of conscience," preferring instead such lines of approach as (1) charity and eschatological concern, (2) the particularity of decision—"every concrete situation is unique," and (3) "the demands of love." [34] Their openness to the relativity of ethical insight was expressed as a rejection of St. Bernard's view that one who in good faith follows an erroneous conscience commits sin, a view based on the "mystical" theory that conscience is the voice of God, and

---

[32] Cf. I. 1001ff., 2010ff., 2144ff.
[33] *A Time for Christian Candour.* New York: 1964, pp. 41–50.
[34] *Ecumenical Dialogue at Harvard,* SAMUEL MILLER and ERNEST WRIGHT, eds. Cambridge: 1964, pp. 264–270.

therefore any error or departure from the natural law (which is God speaking to man's reason) is due to man's *bad will!*

In the lively Roman Catholic debate about birth control centering on a *schema* of the Second Vatican Council, some theologians may still allow the phrase "natural law," but they depart radically from its conventional use—so radically that the phrase loses definition. The Dutch Dominican, Edward Schillebeeck, has proposed a personal instead of a biological interpretation, so that the "nature" to be respected becomes not the reproductive processes but "what is worthy of a human being"—freedom, planning, control of physical nature to serve human nature! [35] The American Jesuit, R. O. Johann, undergirds Schillebeeck with a personal philosophy directly challenging natural law.[36] F. E. Flynn has agreed that man's vocation is actually to frustrate nature as do medicine and technology, if rational needs and purposes require it.[37] In a different genre, the Australian Father Eric D'Arcy, in his antilegalist *Conscience and Its Right to Freedom* (1961), asserts not one but *four* reasons against the classical natural law doctrine of man's ability to know and do the right thing by an innate knowledge of the principles of ethics (*synderesis*).[38]

This is the heart of the problem—in the natural law theory of ethical knowledge we can postulate the presence of right and wrong objectively in the nature of things, *de rerum natura,* if we appreciate that kind of metaphysics. But this does not entitle us to claim that we *possess* such "values" cognitively. Such epistemological complacency has become impossible since the establishment of cultural relativism by Edward Westermarck in his *Origin and Development of the Moral Ideas* in 1912. On the basis of the "radical monotheism" in Christian theology, we may believe (heuristically postulate) "natural laws," but we cannot pretend to *know* them as universals or as universally obligatory. The natural law may persist as an ontological affirmation, but it is dead as an epistemological doctrine. This is an age of relativism in Christian terms of

---

[35] *De Linie.* Brussels: Dec. 20, 1963.
[36] "Natural Law and the Person," American Society of Christian Ethics, Washington, D.C.: Jan. 21, 1965.
[37] "Natural Law and Overpopulation," in *What Modern Catholics Think About Birth Control*, W. BIRMINGHAM, ed. New York: 1964, p. 167.
[38] London: 1961, p. 138.

humility: the old "canon" of rationality has been shaken by depth psychology; the old "canon" of the occidental perspective has been superseded by a global or even interspatial perspective; the old "canon" of logic and language has been replaced by non-discursive and symbolic reason. In the same way, the old "canon" of a hierarchy of values has been converted into a *spectrum*—a sliding scale of ethical relativities and a pragmatic temper.[39] With some this becomes *de gustibus non est disputandum* or an "absolute" relativism, but it cannot become so for Christians because of Jesus Christ, the man who is the measure of all things. As Brunner put it, the *Why* is always the same, no matter how much the *What* may vary. The point is that the *What* does vary.[40]

### Situational or Contextual Ethics

What, then, becomes of Christian ethics, social and personal? Is it now simply a matter of "intuition" or "guidance" or "spontaneity"? Certainly not.

There are three lines of approach to right-wrong, good-evil judgments. The *first* is legalism. Generally in the past Roman Catholicism has relied upon the "law" of nature, and Protestantism upon the "law" of Scripture. The legalist enters into every decision-making situation with an array or apparatus of prefabricated principles, precepts and rules, and forces the life-situation to fit procrusteanly the "relevant" rule. The *second* approach, at the opposite extreme, is antinomianism—the spontaneity or impulse of the moment, experienced as "intuition" from within or "guidance" from without. The antinomian enters the decision-making moment unencumbered but unarmed by any prevenient principles whatsoever. We see this in some Protestant groups, and the secular existentialists such as Simone de Beauvoir (see for example, her *Ethics of Ambiguity,* 1948). One American Lutheran has spoken of "conscience" as "the swoop of a gull." [41] But there is a *third*

---

[39] LYNN WHITE, ed.: *Frontiers of Knowledge in the Study of Man.* New York: 1956.
[40] *The Divine Imperative,* p. 132.
[41] JOSEPH SITTLER, "The Structure of Christian Ethics," in *Life and Community,* H. C. LETTS, ed. Philadelphia: 1957.

approach, the "contextual" or "situational" method. And it is toward this ethical strategy that Anglican and "Atlantic" Protestant
theologians lean sharply.

Whereas the legalist prefabricates his ethical choices, and the
antinomian or spontaneist acts on "the spur of the moment," the
situationist or contextualist enters into his decision making *well
armed with "principles generally valid" but prepared to modify,
suspend or even violate any principle or "general rule" if in the
situation the command to love the neighbor is better served.* The
situationist always remembers that he is commanded to love persons—not precepts nor even principles! This is Bonhoeffer's idea
of "formation"—"no abstract ethics." All things may be lawful
but they may not be constructive, upbuilding, edifying (I Corinthians 6 : 12, 10 : 23). There is nothing fixed or absolute or
"natural" about any guide line in this strategy. When the only law
is the "law of love" (understood according to the Commandment
in the Summary and in Romans 13 : 9–10) *anything* may be right
or good, depending on the circumstances. Otherwise, as Bultmann
has argued, principles are idolatrous. This brings an end to all
legalisms—natural, scriptural or doctrinal! When love is the norm,
we work with *maxims* but not with rules.

There is a widespread and erroneous idea that the situational or
contextual ethic is existentialist and utterly *undisciplined*. But only
the antinomian strategy is truly existential. When Pope Pius XII
proscribed the nonprescriptive ethic as both "existential" and "situational," he confused the two.[42] This confusion is seen in the
writings of Karl Rahner, SJ, who mistakenly believes that situation-
alists have adopted the existentialists' ontological theory of *radical
discontinuity*.[43] On the basis of this theory, the fabric of experience is denied; there is no connective tissue in events, all is unique.
There is no web of life to relate one moment of decision to another, and hence no basis for generalizing. According to the theory
of radical discontinuity every situation has only its particularity.
It would force us to the "absolute particularism" of *tout com-
prendre, tout pardonner*. On such an ontology the existentialists

---

[42] *Acta Apostolicae Sedis,* 44 (1952), 413–419.
[43] E.g., cf. his "On the Question of the Formal Existential Ethics," in
*Theological Investigations,* Vol. II, Pelican Press, Baltimore: 1963, pp. 217ff.

326 CHRISTIAN SOCIAL ETHICS IN A CHANGING WORLD

rightly reject all principles or "generally valid" ethical propositions—as well as those legalistic rules of *torah* which absolutize or
idolize maxims and fix them into rules.

On the contrary, situational or contextual ethics, the "new morality," as Bishop Robinson has called it in his *Honest to God*
(1963), is *not* existential, at least in the philosophical sense that
a Kierkegaard or a Sartre would suppose. It simply refuses to accept *any* principle, other than neighbor concern, as always binding.
It is, therefore, an ethic of tremendous personal responsibility and
initiative—and an ethic for a social policy which is nondoctrinaire
and elastic. This is seen in the thought of another English writer,
Canon Douglas Rhymes, as well as that of the "Cambridge Question Askers"—almost all of them Anglicans.[44] Even Karl Barth
allows for the *ultima ratio,* the outside chance that love will cancel
out a principle. Indeed, while situationalism is willing to operate
with principles or maxims, kept in their proper place, it nevertheless rejects precepts or rules as inevitably rigid and legalistic.

In America this alternative to legalism (natural or otherwise)
and antinomianism has its exponents: this writer; another Anglican, Professor George Easter of Philadelphia; Bishop Pike, already
quoted. There are non-Anglicans, too—Paul Lehmann of Union
Seminary; James Gustafson of Yale; A. T. Rasmussen of California; and others.[45] Alexander Miller in his *Renewal of Man* (1955)
held that "the absolute is an absolute loyalty, not an absolute principle," nearly the same language as that of Archbishop Temple's
ethical theory: "What acts are right may depend on circumstances.
. . . But there is an absolute obligation to will whatever may on
each occasion be right." [46] In his *Ethics,* Bonhoeffer put it thus:
"The question of good is posed and is decided in the midst of each
definite, yet unconcluded, unique and transient situation of our
lives, in the midst of our living relationships with men, things, in-

---

[44] Cf. ERIC ROUTLEY, *The Man for Others,* New York: 1964; Canon
DOUGLAS RHYMES, *No New Morality,* London: 1963; A. R. VIDLER, ed.,
*Soundings,* Cambridge: 1962, esp. H. A. WILLIAMS; and *Objections to
Christian Belief,* Cambridge: 1963, esp. D. A. MACKINNON; J. A. T.
ROBINSON, *Christian Morals Today,* London: 1964.

[45] Two works may be cited: A. T. RASMUSSEN: *Christian Social Ethics.*
New York: 1956; and less coherently a kind of subtype, PAUL LEHMANN:
*Ethics in a Christian Context.* New York: 1963.

[46] *Nature, Man and God,* London: 1934, p. 416.

stitutions and powers, in other words, in the midst of our historical existence."

The basic issue at stake between this situational ethic and the natural law theory is the locus of value. Wherein does the goodness or badness of an act lie? Is adultery wrong always and in itself because it breaks a law, or is it wrong only *if and when* it hurts and betrays the persons involved? The same may be asked of fornication. Is a theft wrong any time and any place, regardless of circumstances—even if by stealing we are doing *the most loving thing in the situation?* (see Matthew 12 : 3–4). Can abortion be right if it saves the mother's life? What of her health, her family's welfare, her freedom? What "makes" a personal act or a social policy right or wrong, good or evil? As the old realist-nominalist debate recognized long ago, the question is: Is the moral quality or "value" of a thing or action intrinsic or extrinsic, inherent or contingent? Is it "in" a right act or policy, or does it happen *to* it?

The Anglican tradition includes an elastic, nonlegalistic ethical method which calculates the greater good or the lesser evil—a system called compensationism.[47] But this sought only to establish that for love's sake we may sometimes do what is evil. The situational method, on the contrary, holds that whatever is most loving in the situation *is* right and good—not merely something to be excused as a lesser evil! *Agape* is its only law. The principles of the Christian *sophia* are at most maxims, never rules or precepts, and they illuminate situations but do not dictate decisions. Temple and Oldham, back in 1937, called them "middle" axioms. But in the *kairos* of decision the facts and technical data require careful calculation, *ex factis orbitur jus*—a Christian *sophrosunei*. Then, finally, as personal and responsible, *decision* must be made. This is not an ethic of "inspiration" or of "ends," but of *decision*. It is a Christian ethic, radically different from the preponderant legalism of the Christian past, as well as from its sporadic antinomianism. It is theonomic, or more carefully put, christonomic.

Tillich has shown that to have personal status means to have in some sense the power of self-determination, of *being free of one's*

---

[47] Cf. P. T. Coffee, "Moral Systems and a Defense of Compensationism," *Anglican Theological Review,* July, 1959.

*given nature, as well as of subpersonal nature.* So say situationists. Tillich holds that true theology arises where a question in the situation asks for an answer from the *message*—a "situational theology." Just so true ethics arises where a situation poses questions to principles! What Tillich calls the method of "correlation" applies to moral theology as fully as to systematic or philosophical theology. Therefore, the situational ethic is *ex casu* and thus far, at least, closer to existential decision than to natural law ethics which tries in a desperate way to decide according to precepts *per naturam.* Situational ethics declares that all qualifiers such as "always" and "never" and "perfect" and "complete" and "certain" must be thrown aside.

### Issues for Ecumenical Study

The situational ethic poses many theoretical, practical and prudential questions. We may close this chapter by pointing to three of these issues of basic theory or rationale:

1. Are "good," "evil," "right," "wrong" and so forth predicates or properties of personal and social actions? Do they *happen* or are they *given?* What of the situationist view that the Christian good, that is, responsive love to God through concern for our neighbors, is a formal principle, not substantive; and that only with God is love a property? "Why do you ask me about *what* is good? One there is *who* is good" (Matthew 19 : 17). With men and life and history, all is relative.

2. Can we divorce right from good? Is it true, as men sometimes say, that there are tragic situations in which the best we can do is evil? Is it possible to say that the *best* we can do (that is, the most loving thing possible for the most neighbors) is wrong? For example, is suicide always wrong? What about espionage? Simple affirmatives come from those who innocently and uncritically accept the intrinsicalist-realist metaphysics.

3. Since we are commanded to love the neighbor (Christian social ethics points out that *pleision* is generic, meaning the plural neighbors), and since the word "love" in most languages is romanticized and sentimentalized and personalized out of all rela-

tion to *agape,* should we not use the term *"justice"* instead? Justice is love calculating complex, pluralistic situations, using its head, distributing its services and concern. Justice is love facing the social and circumstantial dimensions of life and history. Does it not actually better express the meaning of the Summary of the Law?

# 18

# THEOLOGY AND
# SOCIAL SCIENCE

by WALTER G. MUELDER (United States)

THE problem of values and value judgments in the social sciences is rarely looked at from the perspective of Christian theology. Yet the social sciences are inescapably involved in questions of value, not only interpreting data but as an inherent element in their basic presuppositions and methodology. Theologians must inevitably be concerned with the values that emerge in the work of social scientists and the role and function of social science within the domain of truth. It lies beyond the purpose of this chapter to elaborate a theological analysis of the presuppositions of the behavioral sciences. On the other hand, it is evident that theologians must develop greater competence in the social sciences in order to understand their contribution to theology. Some of these contributions supplement theology; others raise theological questions in a fresh way; still others drive theology into a re-examination of assumed facts about man, nature and society. One of the main contributions of the functional method in social science may be to assist theology to clarify its statements and to make them more relevant to ethics and social policy. Since Christian theology involves not only ultimate perspectives and concerns, but also existential decision, it must traverse the domain of behavioral science.

Problems of value inevitably arise in the social sciences, because they deal with persons, groups and their interaction. Moreover, different scientists bring different assumptions of value and fact to their work. There is a sociology of knowledge, but, at present, no over-all theory of value (axiology) of the social sciences. Various societies and nations put their social scientists to work on distinctive problems. There are change-goals to be achieved and pressing problems—such as crime, mental health, population control, legal medicine, and racial and industrial relations—to be studied. The responses of science are of significance for theology.

Many years ago, because of church-state relations, theologians were consciously concerned with political science. But in recent times, economic theory, psychology and sociology have pressed for attention. As rapid social change has engulfed whole societies, a concern to understand cultural anthropology and to relate it to the Christian understanding of man and society has emerged. As the community has challenged the social scientist to investigate many problems, the scientist has striven for the integrity and autonomy that are required for his discipline. At times, he has attempted to eschew all normative elements in the quest for defensible empirical generalizations. At the same time, the policy makers' use of social science has raised normative questions which can be properly handled only within the context of ethics. In any event, behavioral science assumes the worth of persons and is caught up in the investigator's own evaluative situation.

The meaning of these assertions and the purpose of this chapter will become clearer if we illustrate briefly from specific situations. Before doing so, we must remind the Christian theologian and the scientist of a contextual relationship which governs the discussion as a whole. A Christian view of the relation of theology and the social sciences must recognize at least the following: (a) that man has a social setting; (b) that this social setting is cultural and historical; (c) that both society and history are lockstitched into nature through man's biophysical constitution; (d) that personality must be explored in terms of depth, decision and rational wholeness; (e) that selfhood involves self-transcending freedom and (f) that ultimate "I-Thou" relationships mean facing God personally as creator and redeemer as well as through society, history and nature.

*Representative Instances of Value Problems in Social Science*

The social sciences raise value problems the solution of which involves more than the selection and recording of meaningful data: it is inseparably bound up with interpretation and analysis. Thus, even in making a map the scientist does not include everything, but makes his selection according to some established criterion.

This is even more apparent in connection with experiments on people as dealt with in the "Nuremberg Code." As part of the Nazi war effort, criminal medical experiments were undertaken on non-German nationals, both prisoners of war and civilians, including Jews and "asocial" persons. A whole literature has developed around the value problems posed by the trials of war criminals before the Nuremberg military tribunals in 1946–47. Those who advocate medical experiments on human beings have noted that such experiments yield useful results that are unprocurable by other methods. However, the "Nuremberg Code" appeals to basic principles which must be observed in order to satisfy moral, ethical and legal concepts:

*The voluntary consent of the human subject is absolutely essential.* This means that the person involved should have legal capacity to give consent; should be so situated as to be able to exercise free power of choice, without the intervention of any element of force, fraud, deceit, duress, overreaching or other ulterior form of constraint or coercion; and should have sufficient knowledge and comprehension of the elements of the subject matter involved as to enable him to make an understanding and enlightened decision. This latter element requires that before the acceptance of an affirmative decision by the experimental subject there should be made known to him the nature, duration and purpose of the experiment; the method and means by which it is to be conducted; all inconveniences and hazards reasonably to be expected; and the effects upon his health or person which may possibly come from his participation in the experiment. The duty and responsibility for ascertaining the quality of the consent rests upon each individual who initiates, directs or engages in the experiment. It is a personal duty and responsibility which may not be delegated to another with impunity.[1]

---

[1] IRVIN LADIMER and ROGER W. NEWMAN, eds.: *Clinical Investigation in Medicine: Legal, Ethical and Moral Aspects.* Boston University: Law-Medicine Research Institute, 1963, pp. 116–117.

The main value principle of the illustration above relates to the doctrine of man and applies to other medical and general research situations. Hence, as a third illustration, we may note the tendency of the doctor-patient relationship to become a scientist-subject relationship. Since almost anything a physician does to and for a patient is to a degree experimental, the relationship may readily be transformed, however imperceptibly, from an "I-thou" to an "I-it" relationship. There is a general consensus among physicians that "the confidential relations between doctor and patient, the personal right of the patient to the life of his body and soul in its psychic and moral integrity are just some of the many values superior to scientific interests." [2] The scientific work of medicine must derive its valuational ground rules from the moral and theological context of man's relation to man.

The value problems arising in the relation of determinism and freedom in the field of psychiatry have an added nuance. Many psychiatrists assume determinism in human behavior because this seems to be the scientific view of the causal nexus. Determinism as a scientific idea is reinforced in the psychiatric field by the humanitarian idea that the patient is sick and that his displeasing behavior is to be accepted with equanimity as an expression of his illness. In dealing with the patient, however, the physician cannot maintain the completely deterministic belief about himself, because he must choose wisely how to behave in order to help the patient. Faith in freedom is a value which somehow enters into the behavioral aspects of the psychiatrist-patient working relationship.

The issues raised by the "Nuremberg Code," the "I-thou" and "I-it" relationships of physicians who are experimenting with patients and the freedom-determinism relationship in psychiatry are parts of the larger value problem which is evident in personality theory in psychology today. Psychology reflects the urgent question, "What sort of creature is man?" The current array of personality theories is vast and complex; and each is shaped by its view of science, nature, value and reality, whether acknowledged or not. In this brief survey we have space to identify only five of these: (a) positivistic formulations represent the empirical, ex-

---

[2] *Ibid.*, p. 37.

perimental, chiefly associationist and increasingly quantitative tradition. Man is regarded as a reactive, not a proactive being. The method is to find "small" facts under controlled conditions. This positivistic approach is often unaware that it is the prisoner of its specific philosophic outlook. (b) In the psycho-analytical formulations of personality, man is often presented as a quasi-mechanical reactor, goaded by the tyrannical forces of the environment, the id and the superego. Rationality counts for little. Full of defenses and rationalizations, man is doomed to failure in his search for final truth. If he claims to find truth in religion, this is viewed as an illusion and is attributed to neurosis. (c) Quite different are the personalistic formulations which agree that the individual is a patterned entity which must serve as the center of gravity for personality. Personalists are critical of positivism and see man as a creative unity, a purposive, growing individual who must be approached synoptically. (d) Existentialist formulations have some features in common with personalistic theories, such as the conviction that positivistic science alone cannot discover the nature of man as a "being-in-the-world" and the view that the approach of each special science, taken alone, is too narrow. We must know, the existentialist argues, how man feels, how he sees his world, what space and time mean to him, why he lives, what he fears and for what he would willingly die. A person is seen as a creature bent on enhancing the value attributes of his experience, and free to do this—to decide. (e) Finally, there are the interpersonal formulations. All values are *of, by* and *for* persons, but man is involved in a nexus of social and cultural systems. Many techniques have been developed to study the structural properties of groups. Groups and individual persons are entities which social science has shown cannot be reduced to each other. Thus the term "person" is concrete and communitarian. Man is a *socius* with a private center.[3]

The personalistic, existential and interpersonal theories in psychology lead naturally to yet another field of social science, in which problems of value are raised in a form that is of special

---

[3] I am indebted for the classification above to Gordon W. Allport, *Pattern and Growth in Personality*. New York: Holt, Rinehart and Winston, 1961.

interest to theology. This is the field of anthropology, particularly of persons in relation to cultural change. Anthropology lengthens and broadens the perspective in which patterns of meaning and value are considered. With its interest in cultural wholes and the interaction of changes in one part of a systematic whole with those in other parts, this discipline has provided guidance to those involved in inducing social change. Margaret Mead, whose chapter in the fourth of these preparatory volumes deals with "The Christian Understanding of Man in the Perspective of Modern Scientific Attitude," has emphasized, in *Cultural Patterns and Technical Change,* [4] that a change in any one part of the culture will be accompanied by changes in other parts, and that only by "relating any planned detail of change to the *central values* of the culture is it possible to provide for the repercussions which will occur in other aspects of life." This awareness is designated as "cultural relativity," meaning that practices and beliefs must be evaluated in context, in relation to the cultural whole. When theology attempts this evaluation, it must do so within the cultural context. This point will be developed below.

Economics can also be viewed as a behavioral science since it deals, among other things, with choices among scarce values and with economic life, as well as with economic institutions and processes. Economics notes that the basic problems of economic decisions arise from a fivefold set of functions in economic systems: (a) that of fixing standards as to whose wants and what wants are to be satisfied; (b) that of organizing production; (c) that of distribution; (d) that of economic maintenance in relation to progress; and (e) that of adjusting consumption to production. These functions involve decisions which affect the lives and relationships of many persons. All basic economic theories bristle with assumptions about the nature of man and the social good.

A final illustration is taken from the scientific study of race relations. When Gunnar Myrdal wrote *An American Dilemma,* he spelled out in an important appendix entitled "A Methodological Note on Facts and Valuations in Social Change" [5] some of the

[4] UNESCO, 1955, pp. 12, 13.
[5] Appendix 2, p. 1035. New York and London: Harper & Brothers, 1944, 1947.

methodological problems which are encountered in dealing with facts and values. His major finding deserves special notice: "The social scientist is part of the culture in which he lives and he never succeeds in freeing himself entirely from dependence on the dominant preconceptions and biases of his environment." Such biases touch the center of scientific method and procedure in terms of (a) the objects chosen for research; (b) the selection of relevant data; (c) the recording of observations; (d) the theoretical and practical inferences drawn and (e) the manner of presenting results. Of special significance for this essay are value attitudes in the social sciences and their dependence, at least in part, on the central values of the society within which the scientist works.

## A Critique of Theological Perspectives on Science

As theology confronts issues of value like those above, it does so properly from its own perspective. Theology operates from a different level or in a different dimension from that of science. One formulation says that science works with the tools of *discovery,* and that theology works from the vantage point of *disclosure.* Discovery and disclosure have a wider bearing than questions of value, but belong in a coherent unity of truth about value. We shall examine these ideas more fully, to show that the disjunction between discovery and disclosure (man discovers, God discloses), though useful up to a point, may be less tenable than is often proposed, for the disjunction does violence to the unity of man, whether approached scientifically or theologically.

By viewing man's experience as a whole, theology acknowledges that his spiritual life is a unity. There are, conceptually conceived, distinct elements in man's spirit. Yet, as Paul Tillich rightly observes in *Dynamics of Faith,* "all spiritual elements in man are within each other." [6] Thus, for example, faith and reason properly understood do not structurally conflict: they "lie within each other." If reason is used in the sense of scientific method, logical strictness and technical calculation, it "provides tools for recog-

---

[6] New York: Harper Torchbooks, pp. 74–75.

nizing and controlling reality, and faith gives the direction in which this control may be recognized." [7]

If reason is used to designate the source of meaning, of structure, of norms and principles, as it has been in western culture, it points to the humanity of man which distinguishes him from all other beings. And it is important that this designation shall not be lost amid the merely analytical, intellectualistic, formalistic and rationalizing emphases concerning reason in society in our day. Properly understood, it is reason that makes possible an integrated personal life and participation in community. Faith could not possibly be opposed to reason, for then, as both Tillich and the personalists have insisted, faith would rob man of his humanity. Faith which destroys reason or regard for reason dehumanizes man. As Albert C. Knudson has said, a theological faith based on radical skepticism will perish thereby. And Paul Tillich writes: "Reason is the precondition of faith; faith is the act in which reason reaches ecstatically beyond itself. . . . Man is finite, man's reason lives in preliminary concerns; but man is also aware of his potential infinite, and this awareness appears as his ultimate concern, as faith." [8]

Somewhat different from Tillich's position is that of John Dillenberger, who affirms that "revelation has to do with the mystery of *disclosure,* while science deals with the mystery that is associated with *discovery."* [9] This approach regards the unity of knowledge as at best an ideal which cannot at any moment in history be made a reality; it thus retreats into the uniqueness of the disciplines.[10] On this basis the unity of the mystery in God and the unity of spirit in man are lost.

Another approach is to adopt a kind of existential posture. The thrust of some existentialism has been against positivism in science and against making man an object, an "it." Similar protests have come on scientific, methodological grounds from many fronts: from Marx in economics (his doctrines of value and alienation), from many democratic and personalistic philosophers and even from an-

[7] *Ibid.,* p. 75.
[8] *Op. cit.,* p. 76.
[9] *Protestant Thought and Natural Science.* Garden City, N.Y.: Doubleday & Co., Inc., 1960, p. 283.
[10] *Ibid.,* p. 256.

thropologists. Some theologians have seen the emergence of existentialism in theology as a recovery of the concept of the nature of man more congenial to classical theology than that which saw him as the embodiment of value or as moral personality, claiming that the latter makes of him only an idea or ideal object. But theology has no twentieth-century monopoly on man as a real person, a real subject. It would be arbitrary to say that the choice lies between science and existentialism (as theology).

The values and dilemmas of existentialism must be faced in terms of the social sciences. Dillenberger properly points out that in Heidegger, Kierkegaard and Nietzsche science stands for unauthentic existence:

Science is a matter of indifference, of concern with selected objects or items, whether of nature or history. It conceals man in his totality, in his mystery, by a concern with the multiplication of knowledge essentially indifferent to himself as an existing subject. Although thrown into being, man is a mysterious being whose wholeness must be affirmed. Such affirmation constitutes history, not nature. . . . His being or his freedom is affirmed as he "stands out" from any objective thing which is "over against" him.[11]

In such a statement, theology expresses a thoroughly historical and personalistic concern for man and protests against any program in social science or society which dehumanizes him. Yet, the sources of the existentialism which some theology seems to adopt may be less a biblical disclosure than an accommodation to some strains in European culture—for example, in Heidegger. At this point, anthropology and cultural history may assist the critical work of theologians.

Theological existentialism stresses man as sinner, of course, and notes that apart from sin he is not at the level of humanity; and in opposition to some forms of existentialism and naturalism insists that "the refusal to accept sin constitutes that sin which is the loss of self, the loss of the risk to be and therefore of being at all."[12] Yet sin is a category that falls outside the social sciences (though some find it useful in psychotherapy) and that, being so universal in its relevance, tends not to be operationally or func-

---

[11] *Ibid.*, pp. 264–265.
[12] *Ibid.*, p. 265.

tionally relevant at all. But discriminate judgments are necessary both in social science and in ethics.

It is in the area of ethics that the problems are often most clearly seen. The tendency in much theology is to reject all biblical legalism in favour of a *kerygma* which affirms minimal cultural content and maximum insistence on *disclosure by* and *about* Jesus Christ, preferably about him as an act of faith. Absolute insistence on authority of revelation is sometimes linked with maximum relativity in concrete ethical judgments. When principles are rejected, the basis of discriminate judgment is highly relative, even relativistic. What is often left ambiguous is the relationship between man's sin and the idea that there are no universal moral answers because there are no common moral questions and no common verifiable theory of human nature.

There are both social scientists and theologians whose relativism rests in an ultimate indeterminism. Such relativism sees descriptive variety, uniqueness in value situations, conflicts of values and subjectivity as all in some sense ultimate, irreducible and irreconcilable. It affirms or assumes that there is no pattern or generalization of which the varied or the unique are but different expressions. Hence neither the conflicts nor the individual's isolation can ever be resolved. Indeterminacy, Abraham Edel claims, is at the heart of the relativist position.[13] A radical, irrationalist type of existentialism, whether Christian or other, would seem to leave indeterminacy in social science eventuating in ultimate skepticism, and to leave dread, anguish and loneliness unresolved.

Theological relativism often seeks to overcome the indeterminacy through an appeal to revelation. But revelation alone only postpones the problem, for it is then simply transferred to the diversity of God's interpreters. The indeterminacy here roots in the fact, not simply of actual disagreement, but of there being no mode of decision by which, in principle at least, the issues can be settled.[14] Much of the crisis in hermeneutics today is traceable to the irrationalism and subjectivism that underlie some of these theories.

---

[13] *Ethical Judgment, The Use of Science in Ethics*. Glencoe, Ill.: The Free Press, 1955, p. 30.
[14] *Ibid.*, p. 32.

The behavioral sciences do not, however, necessarily imply the indeterminacy and relativism that are suggested above. Theology and science can meet each other halfway at least in ethics through what is scientifically known about man. Edel [15] is probably correct in stating that ethical absolutism and ethical relativism in their extreme forms have tried short cuts to avoid the necessity of empirical investigation and because they have enshrined as common sense assumptions the results of earlier chapters of the history of science. The preliminary and provisional character of the work of science, on the one hand, and of *all* hermeneutics, on the other, does not necessarily imply indeterminate relativism. When, for example, guilt-feelings are appealed to in the area of ethics, it is well to explore one's assumptions about human nature, the origin and development of guilt-feelings in interpersonal processes, and the like. There are many tools in the behavioral sciences for dealing with such problems.

Rationality in science and in theology meet in the appeal to the person as a whole. Reason has, when properly approached, the authority of the whole in ethics where so many valuation issues deriving from these fields meet. Edel notes:

From today's psychological perspective it is established theory that there is a *system of forces* in the internal economy of the biological individual, even where consciousness shows the extreme of a split personality. In that sense it is a lesson of science that rationality involves the whole person. This serves to incorporate at least the whole-person perspective in ethical judgment. The history of the moral mandate of unity and system is itself one of the most striking cases of the tremendous scope of scientific knowledge that is really required to justify what on the face of it looks like an obvious injunction of reason.[16]

Any theory of ethics, theology or psychotherapy—and all existential decision making—must assume that man (as person and subject) has a degree of mastery over himself and some insight into himself and his goals. But, if this is granted, then man also has some control in relating means to ends and in reflecting about alternate ends. In principle, then, science can offer a great deal. Stated ideally, the contributions would include at least these:

---

[15] *Ibid.*, p. 36.
[16] Edel, *op. cit.*, p. 59.

It is elementary that a person's whims are to be distinguished from his stable and enduring goals, and that a rational man who is to be regarded as master of himself must have some insight into himself and his aims. But once this door is opened, the passageway leads on and on. Ideally, full advice to the person who asked for a cost estimate of the envisaged goals would include their scope and function in his life, their mode of development, intensity points, termination points, possible transformations, relation to common ends, possible interaction with others and their mutual alternation, and so forth—in short all the lessons that a psychological, social and historical perspective could offer in application to the particular case.[17]

## Ideology, Sociology and Theology

The social sciences and theology as developed in any particular historical era tend to reflect the ideologies of the day. In a world of competing ideologies, axiological issues influence both scientists and theologians. Christian faith and ethics do not constitute an ideology; yet one of the tendencies of culture is to reduce religion to an ideology. When Christianity is used to serve the interests of some social group and thus is robbed of its transcendent majesty of revelation and comprehensive reason, or when it is presented as if the kingdom of God could be identified with any particular economic, political or ecclesiastical order, it is reduced to the ideological level.

Karl Marx and Karl Mannheim have done much to develop the category of ideology. Marx insisted that in historical and political matters there could be no "pure theory." Behind every social theory lie collective points of view; class interests are involved. Political theories reflect social situations and limited-interest goals. Plausibility of argument in seeking to establish ideology is readily discernible in the thought of an opponent; it is not so easily noted in one's own. Marx thought of ideology as a taint, but the more careful study by Mannheim and his successors attributed to it a less sinister meaning.

Karl Mannheim, whose work has had wide influence, defined ideologies as "more or less conscious disguises of the nature of the situation." [18] This conception of ideology implies skepticism

---

[17] Edel, *op. cit.*, p. 54.
[18] *Ideology and Utopia.* New York: Harcourt, Brace, 1936, p. 49.

about the ideas advanced by our opponent and, even more, that if our opponent did recognize the truth, it would not be in accord with his interests. Mannheim also used ideology in another sense, that is, when "we are concerned with the characteristics and composition of the total structure of the mind of this epoch or this group." [19] In either case "the ideas expressed by the subject are . . . regarded as functions of his existence. This means that opinions, statements, propositions and systems of ideas are not taken at their face value but are interpreted in the light of the life situation of the one who expresses them." [20] Today ideologies are part of the cold war, of racial and national conflict, of the struggles of the developing nations. They belong to the arsenal of offensive and defensive weapons.

In Europe, the period of great change from the seventeenth to the nineteenth century has been called the "age of ideology," in that it saw an extraordinary outpouring of theories about the nature of man in relation to the present and future state of society. Today in the period of worldwide rapid social change—the revolutionary shift from colonialism to modern nationhood—we have another ideological surge. Despite great differences regarding the appropriate methods by which to reach their goals, the leaders of many of these new nations are united by a group of beliefs that express common feelings about the past, present and future. Paul E. Sigmund, Jr., has pointed out that these beliefs are ideologies in that they "elicit an emotional commitment by the leadership and their followers and are directed toward action—the development of a new society in a certain direction, in conformity with certain goals." [21]

Sigmund notes [22] that these ideologies cluster around the goals of modernizing nationalism: "national independence; rapid economic development; the creation of a nation-state governed by a régime based on a populist identification of leader, party and people; regional federation; and non-alignment in international af-

---

[19] *Ibid.*, pp. 49–50.
[20] *Ibid.*, p. 50.
[21] PAUL E. SIGMUND, JR., ed., *The Ideologies of the Developing Nations.* New York: F. A. Praeger, 1963, p. 4.
[22] *Ibid.*, p. 40.

fairs." It is instructive that in many of these countries there is no mention in their ideologies of the values of liberal pluralistic democracy which many social scientists in the West take for granted. This does not mean that these countries are all deeply infiltrated by communist ideologies. Quite the contrary. It may mean that the single party, democratic centralism and the emphasis on elites should be understood from a deeper dynamic perspective than is customary. Ideology has a function. It draws on various traditions to carry people through "the period of modernization of traditional society and to justify the ensuing sacrifices and dislocations." [23] The need of a developing country to establish its own sense of identity is frequently expressed in its disinterest in the ideological struggles of the great powers.

Theological self-awareness made perceptive by the critical methods of the sociology of knowledge should assist Christian social ethics in understanding such dynamic processes. These combined disciplines should also help scholars to understand how the religious beliefs of the developing nations inevitably become involved in their national ideologies. Religion (including theology) is so entwined in the integrating myth-structures of peoples that we should expect modern man to unite social criticism with the criticism of religion and to unite theological criticism with the criticism of social systems whose myth structures rival the Christian faith at all levels of expression.

Christian social ethics is itself not an ideology, because it recognizes the provisional character of all historical embodiments of great ideas and purposes. Even when the heritage of values acknowledges the great norms of traditional Christian ethics, the political, economic and educational embodiments of these norms are all provisional. Hence the Christian social ethic is able to interact with and respond to the ideologies of the time. It may do this through an enlightened church which has an ecumenical mission of evangelism; through a community of faith which is in, but also transcends, nations and cultures; through a decision not to exploit the new powers released in the revolutions, but rather to serve; and through the training of persons who make decisions in specific localities

---

[23] *Ibid.*, p. 37.

and institutions, but who as servants of Christ humbly seek to transcend ideological perspectives.

There are a number of elements in the theoretical issues involved in the sociology of knowledge as developed by Mannheim which theology should note. Do "facts" and "values" have a common ontological source, or do they arise from completely different sources? Both seem to arise out of the unitary life process in which the individual evolves a knowledge of the world—that is, life in a community of persons with a complex of values. Cognitive and valuational processes are complexly entwined, and valuation ultimately offers a basis of interpretation. Since facts and values are both integral aspects of knowing, the problem of validity in one area is affected by that in the other. Mannheim observes: "The position of the observer influences the results of thought." Some sociologists would add that *position means role* and *role* means one's *status* in action.

The relativity in the relationships of "facts" and "values" does not justify either moral or epistemological skepticism. Sociology of knowledge should provide a refinement in our understanding of human perception and an illumination of the conditions qualifying that perception. Despite Mannheim's constant emphasis upon the *social* conditioning of cognitive and valuational processes, there is in his work a pervasive stress upon uniqueness, individuality, spontaneity and self-determining conscience, and a genuine affirmation of the ultimacy of the *person*.

In "The Role of Value in Karl Mannheim's Sociology of Knowledge," [24] Warren Rempel has shown that Mannheim never fully came to terms *at the theoretical level* with the *normative* aspects of the science of human behavior. Mannheim's work shows the potential role of philosophy and theology because of the necessity of integrating, through interdisciplinary study, the *sociological* and the normative, or ethical, dimensions of the study of man, as complementary disciplines. Social science cannot finally disavow or eliminate metaphysical issues. If, as in Mannheim, they are pushed into the background, this only confirms the notion that social scientists must at some point become self-conscious in regard to the

---

[24] An unpublished doctoral dissertation, Boston University, 1962.

metaphysical and axiological assumptions that they hold and that pervade and guide their thoughts. The dialogue with theology must go on.

## Theology's Use of the Social Sciences

Many theologians today express the church's involvement in the secular order and a concern for responsible social change. A great deal of work is at present going on in the field of the sociology of religion which draws on the assumptions and methods of both theology and social science. Christian thought today amply stresses various elements of doctrine as imperatives and motives in social actions. There is, finally, in existentialism and various types of Christian ethics, an emphasis on decision in social situations. In all these ways theologians are being led to make empirical claims and to relate values to social science.

Because of this, some social scientists, like D. L. Munby, lift up "the importance of technical competence." [25] He expresses legitimate concern when he notes that theologians often do not employ empirical analysis precisely; or when they make a too simple distinction between means and ends, allocating means to science and ends to theology and, in addition, overlooking their complex interpenetration; or when they are poorly informed in economics and in their ignorance are unaware of its limitations; or when they indulge in false searches for "Christian" answers, giving a misplaced Christian concreteness to certain schemes and programs; or when they lack relevant expertise. To emphasize this latter point he says: "It is exceedingly rare that one can find sound theological insight unadulterated with economic nonsense." [26] Munby summarizes the two foundations of effective Christian social analysis and action as the theological/metasociological assertions about the nature of man and the willingness to accept wholeheartedly the facts as they are found to be. There are no shortcuts to responsibility.

If we are to understand critically theology's use of the social

---

[25] See D. L. MUNBY: "The Importance of Technical Competence," in *Essays in Anglican Self-Criticism*, D. M. PATON, ed. London: SCM Press, 1958, pp. 45–58.

[26] *Ibid.*, p. 58.

sciences, we must distinguish clearly between the intellectual processes of moving from theology to science and those of going from science to theology. Although the earlier portions of this paper voiced a warning against a too easy disjunction between *disclosure* and *discovery,* the methodological steps from disclosure to discovery are different from those involved in going from discovery to disclosure. Some thinkers wish to set up a continuum between theology and science. The unity of selfhood, the unity of God and the unity of truth support the idea of an ultimate unity between faith as response to disclosure and knowledge as verified discovery. Yet no easy schemes of continuity should blur the autonomy, the different methods, the contrasting modes of verification and the distinct functions, of science and theology. This is one side of the problem. The other side is that empirical inquiry is able to clarify the operational meaning of theological concepts and claims. Theology needs to develop functional definitions of religion and of the way in which religious believing and behaving take place in different settings and cultures. The behavioral sciences have *discovered* many things about man and human nature which biblical revelation did not *disclose,* and these findings are often important for personal and intergroup relationships. Theology, like science, should be open to some kind of truth test if it is to make some truth claim. As Frederick Ferré says: "Any proposition responsibly asserted or assented to must offer some means of 'verification,' in the broad sense that some good reason or reasons for maintaining that proposition's truth rather than its falsity must be able to be provided." [27]

It is evident, as a consequence of all that we have noted above, that man's understanding of the secular forces of society is part of his obligation to obey God, and that technical competence is also part of that obedience. Patient cooperation is required between the theologian and the social scientist, to build up understanding and develop technical competence. Empirical work requires careful scientific operation in the most diverse situations on earth. For example, there is a great deal of qualitative as well as quantitative social research in selected favorable areas of the world, but we lack a hard core of data on some of the greatest conflict areas of

---

[27] FREDERICK FERRÉ, "Verification, Faith and Credulity," in *Religion in Life,* Winter, 1962–1963, p. 52.

interpersonal and intergroup relations. There are few verified scientific models for conflict resolution. The facts are so diverse, and society is so complex, that only the bare outlines of a synthesis of Christian social thought—or of its middle axioms—are at present conceivable. But since we believe as Christians that a responsible social order will be one where men and women live as their creator intended them to live, all that can be learned about fact, value and interpretation in theology and social science will become part of responsible living in the secular order.

## 19

# CONVERSION AND SOCIAL TRANSFORMATION

by EMILIO CASTRO (Uruguay)

As pastor of a congregation in the heart of a large city in Latin America I preach a gospel of salvation calling to repentance, a change of life, an experience of "conversion." When someone is converted, I feel intense joy like that reflected in Luke 15 and rejoice when statistics show the Evangelical Church's impressively rapid growth. But a cruel doubt gnaws at me: To what extent will the fruits of these statistics be seen in real life in Latin America— in what is taking place in the countryside, in politics, in the factories? To what extent are the structural changes which our Latin America needs, if it is to emerge from its present semifeudal state, helped and encouraged or upset and retarded by this growth of the Evangelical Church? We see character change in individuals. But how shall we explain the social conservatism of many Christian leaders? How shall we understand the relation of conversion to social quietism?

Some will say that conversion and social change are two totally independent realities, the study of the one belonging to theology and the other to sociology. Or, if you prefer, the one to psychology, the other to history. This attitude cannot be quickly set aside. Has not the reality of conversion been presented independently of any social system, in the Roman Empire, in feudal times, in liberal democracy and in socialist regimes, in Eskimo tribes and in modern industrial society? The gospel works in freedom and requires no particular social system through which to reach man. Evangelists can claim that "man is the same all over the world" and that therefore "the message should be the same," irrespective of its social setting.

The same argument applies to the other end of our equation: society has been transformed independently of the religious experience of its members. Desirable social changes have been brought about by men who had no conversion-experience and who rejected even the possibility of it for themselves and denied its reality in others. We might even say that social change has been effected in the face of firm opposition from "converts," and that consequently our topic should be treated from a negative angle: the obstruction to social change resulting from conversion.

But this duality or separation of our terms is not acceptable. For very different reasons we are obliged to focus our attention on the relation between conversion and social change.

### The Link Between Conversion and Social Change

We often hear the assertion: Change man's heart, and society will change. The fallacy of the argument is immediately evident. No such thing as "man's heart" exists apart from man's relations. I am I and my circumstances, Ortega y Gasset would say. Martin Buber would say that I exist as a person only in the reality of my relation with a "thou." In plain language, I exist in a whole collection of relations that make up my being. To change my heart means in some measure also to change those relations.

Furthermore, there is a paradox in the original assertion. On the one hand, to escape from social responsibility, from the discipline of studying the techniques and relativities of society is to revert to a religious primitivism. The magic wand of the fairy godmother, "conversion," will turn us into model citizens. Thus we know nothing about the complexities of the social structures. We do not pose the problem that Reinhold Niebuhr defined so clearly in the title of his book *Moral Man and Immoral Society*. But, on the other hand, the assertion "new men, a new nation," reveals our conviction that as an integral part of its existence conversion carries with it a consequence, a social militancy. At the very moment when we simplify and superficialize the social problem, we are declaring the indissoluble relation between conversion and social structure.

We are also obliged to examine the views of sociologists (whether they call themselves Marxists or Christians) concerning the indissoluble relation between the religious phenomenon —including conversion—and the given patterns of society. For example, Karl Marx could argue that criticism of religion was unnecessary because it is merely the consequence of the order of production-relations in a capitalist society. In such a society the laborer needs religion as a comfort—it functions as an opiate— and the oppressing classes need it to justify their exploitation. Once the conditions of production are changed and exploitation is eliminated, the need for religion has gone and conversion as such will be impossible. It will have disappeared by virtue of the social revolution which eliminates classes and puts the means of production into the hands of the proletariat. Though there is general agreement today that Marx fails to do justice to the interdependence between the economic structure of society and the factors that make up what he called the superstructure—conscience, culture, religion and so on—we must ask what is the true relation between faith, culture and society, and how far the patterns of a given society condition the possibility of conversion and the forms that it will take.

Even Christian sociologists working in modern industrial areas confirm the futility of the churches' traditional methods: the church is completely ignored by the working classes, who are "sociologically predestined not to believe." In 1960, when the Roman Catholic Church carried out its great mission in Buenos Aires, mobilizing thousands of priests from all parts of the world in an unprecedented effort to rechristianize a city, it was virtually a failure. It was unable to project itself beyond the circles of those who in some form or another were already connected with the life of the parish. The social pattern that is given shapes a mental pattern that is impervious to the Christian message. The exceptional case of a conversion here or there simply proves the rule. We must ask ourselves where the problem resides—in the structure of society or in the forms and content of the church's message. And we shall have to look carefully to see how much wisdom was shown by the biblical writer when he prayed: "Give me not riches lest I forget thee, nor poverty lest I deny thee."

Our problem is present also in the current debate concerning the mission of the church. Traditionally we thought we had understood it: to spread, to gain through the conversion of the greatest possible number of individuals who thus came to be saved. Today the growth of the world population, the fact of a church that is not growing numerically as fast as the increase in population, the secularism of technical society, "the adult world" of Bonhoeffer, all cause us to look again to the problem of mission and evangelism. Does God will that all men should be converted? Scripture tells us clearly that God wills that all should be saved. This is plain. But Scripture speaks to us of a divine plan for salvation that includes the representation of all humanity on the one hand. The story of salvation is the story of the people of Israel, the messiah, the church, chosen to act on behalf of all humanity to be the witnessing people who proclaim and live in the light of revelation. Consequently, we must ask: What should be the church's immediate concern—its numerical growth, or the serving presence of Jesus Christ in the world? To seek the conversion of individuals or to seek the transformation of society, so that man can live a truly human life? Is this a real alternative?

In the New Testament integration into the group of disciples—whether those of John the Baptist or of Jesus himself—has clear consequences for social activity. John the Baptist, in replying to different questions about the way in which to manifest repentance, offers plain directions respecting relations with one's neighbor: for example, the man with two shirts must share with him who has none. Jesus shows that his new commandment is "Love one another." His call to service is clear. There is no greater measure of greatness than the capacity to serve. To draw near to Christ is to be placed in a position of service to your neighbor. It is to have a changed attitude toward society. To enter into discipleship means to follow him who identified himself with the needy.

Technical society adds urgency to our subject. The society that in the New Testament was concerned with personal relations, and in which love could be expressed directly, has been transformed today into an impersonal society in which love has to be expressed in social patterns. However much I may love my neighbor, I do not contribute effectively to helping him if I do not see to it that modern society has the social elements and mechanisms that serve to protect him. Or, if you will: The good Samaritan could look after the wounded man, treat him with oil and wine, lift him onto his donkey and take him to the inn. Any one who did that today would be indicted for "illegal practice of medicine. . . ."

The same charitable spirit toward the wounded must be expressed in the complexities of urban life, in the thousand and one social relations that determine the kind of help that the needy person is to receive. To know how the converted man expresses himself, can express himself or should do so, in this technical society, is most important for Christian testimony. To know how far a society of impersonal relations conditions, determines, hinders or aids "conversion" is important for the church's strategy. To know God's purpose as it is manifested in the patterns of society and to know the particular calling to which God summons the convert is demanded by our obedience to the lord of history who is the lord of our life.

## The Biblical Understanding of Conversion

Conversion is the word that has been applied in the church's history to different biblical episodes. In the Old Testament it is synonymous with repentance, a complete change in the whole life, taking God's word seriously. It was expected that conversion would occur in response to the prophetic word, which was admonition and proclamation of judgment and hope. In the face of God's word, a change of direction was produced in the people or in an individual. Hence conversion.

The New Testament puts the accent on the objective quality of what occurs. Jesus speaks to Nicodemus of rebirth, of a new beginning of life. But this is the work of "the Spirit that breathes where it wills." An objective condition is necessary if this rebirth is to be produced: the Son of Man must be lifted up. The metaphor of the healing of the people of Israel in the desert by their contemplating the serpent suggests that it is the contemplation of the crucified one that produces salvation and initiates the action of the Holy Spirit, toward rebirth.

In the synoptic gospels we recognize as calls to conversion the call that Jesus made to his disciples—"Follow me and I will make you fishers of men"—or to the rich young man—"Go, sell all you have, give to the poor and come, follow me." In every conversation with anyone who wishes to be his follower, Jesus insists on radical rethinking—to follow in his steps. He chooses his friends and expects them to decide to follow him conscientiously. It is hard to speak of the reality of conversion in the gospels because the events of the cross, the resurrection and Pentecost had not yet come. Nevertheless, experiences like that of Zacchaeus show us how that change (which later was to be called conversion) implied a relation to the person of Jesus that was a new orientation for relations with one's neighbor.

Paul uses the expression "a new creature." "If any man is in Christ he is a new creature." Here the objective character of conversion is safeguarded to the utmost. A new birth is not produced in an individual, making of him a being different from the others. The new creation has taken place in Jesus Christ. Being in him, bound to him, we are joined to the new creation and we become a new creature. The apostle constantly describes this union with Christ, and its sense is not mystic, but real and objective. Dead and raised up with Christ, our true life is hidden with Christ in God. In this union with Christ, our neighbor is present: we are placed in a position of service to him. In the Pauline ethic we are called to be what we already are, to let the inner reality of our relation with Christ manifest itself in our conduct.

The Acts of the Apostles stress the receiving of the Holy Spirit as the way in which the congregation in Jerusalem was established and the converts' adherence to the true faith ensured. The Spirit came down through the apostles' laying-on of hands. Objectively the church, through the apostles, extended recognition to the new brethren. But very intimately there remained in the convert the consciousness of the action of God's Spirit. This interplay of objective and subjective facts suggests to us a complementary dialectic: God's objective and subjective action, the cross and the Holy Spirit, man's subjective and objective action, our attention focused on the crucified one and the confirming testimony of the Christian community.

The relation of the Christians to the wider society was one of tolerant suffering: obedience, within certain limits. No claim was made to destroy the religious institution: the Christians worshiped in the temple. Civil authority was not disowned. When the apostles were arrested, there was no protest, no denial of the state's authority. But obedience was conditioned! "Judge for yourselves whether it is right to obey men rather than God." This attitude, expressed here in the purely religious sphere, comes to permeate the whole Christian outlook toward social patterns—respect and esteem so long as they do not threaten the Christian conscience, which is bound by obedience to God. What was still not seen very clearly was that obedience to God should be shown in all orders of life, and not only when the state directly attacked the church. There was still no clear conception of what it meant "to be the voice of those who have no voice in society." But it was already understood that those who for the world were worthless—slaves, thieves, prostitutes—were precisely those who were called by the gospel to make up the church. This world soon passed. Meanwhile, its poor received attention within the church.

From this rapid analysis of the New Testament we deduce that conversion means that we become aware of a relationship with Jesus Christ, and this means, in time, relationship with our neighbor. It means becoming part of the discipleship of those who serve. These two elements—relation with Jesus Christ and relation with my neighbor—can be distinguished, but they cannot be separated. No relationship with Jesus Christ exists that is not a relationship with our neighbor. "He who says he loves God, whom he has not seen, and loves not his brother whom he has seen, is a liar." The lack of a correct relationship with one's neighbor is authentic proof of the absence of a correct relation with God. Conversion understood as a personal advantage does not exist. It is always understood as a call to form part of the movement of God's mission of love to the world.

We are not dealing with an event that takes place in two moves —first, conversion to Christ and then, a "second conversion" from Christ to the world, to which we would hasten as servants. The preaching of two moves in this way has caused damage in the church, in that it has permitted people to remain at the first stage with a self-centered religiosity, in a self-complacent church that makes its own welfare a norm for judging the world. Readiness to serve my neighbor forms part of the essence of conversion. But conversion is always in reference to Jesus Christ. It is not a state. It is a relationship. It lives by its object. It is not a personality that is somehow different from the others. The difference is in its perspective. It wishes to see nothing isolated from the person of Jesus Christ. The convert is not a superman in either the moral or the intellectual sense. He is a man who lives in relationship with Jesus Christ, in the twofold sense of the expression: in relation with the historic Christ and in relation with the Christ who finds him as he ministers to his needy neighbor. And that twofold encounter is effected by the mediation of the Holy Spirit, who actualizes yesterday and leads in the world of today.

This is not to be interpreted only in terms of direct interpersonal relations: assistance to one's neighbor, the concrete individual, and unrelated to changes in social institutions, in forms of production, in power-relations between social groups. The call to follow Christ is not the traditional religious call of withdrawal from the world. On the contrary, it was a call that sent man back to the society from which he came. Becoming a Christian did not mean abandoning the duties that belonged to life in a pagan society.

The pagans or Jews converted to Christianity faced the structures of the empire with the same limitation of view as any pagan of that time possessed. Moreover, their eschatalogical vision could foresee the disappearance of the system, and so its sanctified and absolute character was removed. But that disappearance of existing social forms was not to be the result of man's action in history, but rather the result of the breaking in of the *Parousia*. We could also say that the Christians were laying new bases for human relations that would inevitably destroy the fromework of the society. (Slavery was not attacked, but there was a call to love the "brother slave"; Roman militarism was not condemned, but a vocational pacifism was taught.) Nevertheless we must recognize that such consequences were a subconscious fruit of the activity of the Christians and were not the result of a clear comprehension on their part. Later we shall discuss this problem in detail. It is sufficient here to affirm that the New Testament conceives neither of a Christian separated from the world, nor of a Christian life that does not express itself in interpersonal relations.

### The Social Factor in Conversion

But to what extent does the social situation condition conversion in the Bible? An initial answer, though a partial one, indicates that the prophets and the apostles utilized social facts for their call to conversion. The prophets did not hesitate to interpret what happened to the people, both internally and externally, as vehicles for God's call to repentance. The apostles used the Jewish dispersion, the *oikos* of the Roman houses, Paul his Roman citizenship. We should not interpret the expression "fullness of time" in a sociological sense, but we cannot overlook the fact that a series of social, economic and political conditions was present in the Roman Empire that favored the spread of the Christian message. We cannot know how much weight those circumstances bore in conditioning the kind of decision that the isolated individual who embraced Christianity through a "conversion" took. But at least the historical possibility that the call to conversion can reach its object is given or negated by the total situation.

We can also understand that although in New Testament times Christianity spoke to man, approaching the situation from the outside, without any involvement with the existing society, today it appears involved in the situation, since it is the result of twenty centuries of Christian history. It is logical to suppose that the social conditions today play a much more important role, favoring or hindering the proclamation or the reception of Christianity, in short, affecting the reality of conversion. Even if God is powerful in the midst of any circumstance to bring about the change in the individual's life, it does not mean that he does not work with due consideration for all the circumstances of human existence, nor that the church (which claims to be the vehicle of God's call) remains blind to these factors.

When Moses struggled with Pharaoh, God's demand was plain: "Let my people go, so that they may serve me." Liberty was a basic requisite for worship. Could God work among slaves? Undoubtedly he could, but slavery is not what he willed for his children. Liberty makes genuine worship possible. The fact is completed when, in the book of Joshua, after the conquest of Canaan, the people are faced with this choice: "Choose you this day whom you will serve." Liberty makes conversion possible. Or at least in the biblical revelation, the decision (taken in freedom) is what God seeks. And the struggle for freedom—with all its biblical components, which far exceed political liberty—is a task that belongs to the church's being, since it constitutes the human possibility of responsible decision before God.

We must focus attention now on the other term of our equation: social change.

By the transformation of society we understand those changes in its structure—its forms of production, property, class and the like—that affect the life of whole groups of people. In ecumenical circles the expression "rapid social change" has been coined to indicate areas of the world where people are rapidly abandoning the traditional society and are entering the modern industrial world. These changes can be the blind outcome of historical events, or they can be changes that are sought and guided. Without a doubt, to a greater or lesser degree, they are everywhere the result of objective factors and conscious planning. In the political struggle people speak of "revolution," where there is a radical change of those who hold power in a given society.

In traditional societies, the idea of social transformation plays virtually no role: Things are as they are, and that is the way they ought to be. The common man takes no part in decisions. He endures invasions or goes to war because of a factor outside himself. Where slavery exists, it is a given fact of his experience, as unchangeable as the natural laws that govern his whole life. Here or there an exceptional man may cross the barrier of social conformism. But it is precisely the exceptional person whose life is given an aura of legend who confirms the common man in his acceptance of the status quo. At times he is an unconscious agent of change. He joins masses that are filled with anger about an unbearable situation. But the historical possibility of a different kind of society never crosses his mind. To him the form of society is as fixed as the cycles of nature. An invasion, a war may mean a change of master but not a change of the forms of society. It is only in the past two centuries that we have begun to experience the era of the common man and to recognize that it is not only possible but necessary for the citizens to participate in the formation of social structures.

The Christian, as a citizen of stabilized societies, shared the same social quietism. In the first centuries his quietism was even greater, because of the Christians' awareness of their insignificant numbers and their expectation of an early end of the world. We can claim that the Hebrew-Christian tradition has contributed to the formation of the western conscience, with its idea of a future open to man's action, history to be fulfilled, a goal toward which to press. But it is also true that upon the establishment of the *corpus christianum* in Europe, the historical goal was regarded as having been reached, and there only remained the projection of the individual toward eternity and the geographical missionary expansion that would spread the hierarchical Christian society throughout the world.

Conversion in itself did not alter this outlook. It involved man with his neighbor. It placed him in a responsible situation toward society. But it did not exempt him from submitting to the disciplines of the study of society and of its problems.

If we understand this fact, we shall be freed from many fallacies. We shall not be optimistic as to whether the conversion of a greater number of citizens in a country solves its structural problems. We shall not ask, as is so often done: after twenty centuries of Christianity, what is wrong with the world that it is still unable to overcome such problems as war? We shall understand that conversion is not the irruption of the religio-magic solution into the problem of society. There is a relative autonomy in politics that is not affected by religious conversion. We say "relative," because logically any change in a person's spiritual orientation has some social consequence that will (at least slightly) affect social forms. But anyone who wants to take part actively in the struggles by which social changes are effected must do so without illusions, submitting to the technical disciplines of his specific field: economics, politics, culture, or whatever.

This understanding of conversion in a given social context enables us to grasp the senselessness of so many Christian centuries during which the "converts" failed to attack slavery as a social institution. It can help us to comprehend even certain segregationist attitudes of our day. We can find in this situation a horrifying mixture of personal compassion and social insensitivity.

Often, too, we have to deny that there has been a real conversion. There can be a psychological experience of "warmth," or a kind of "decision" that fits the traditional rules of conduct and experience that the church calls conversion, without that incorporation into Christ that is characterized by a regard for all life, in the light of our relation with his person and teaching, having taken place. We can be in the presence of psychic phenomena without spiritual reality or of ecclesiastical events without serving power. In either event, the word conversion will be used, but it does not correspond to the reality that the Bible calls rebirth. "By their fruits you shall know them." Insofar as there is an openness toward Christ's judgment and a responsible involvement with one's neighbor, we can judge—with all the human relativities of judgment—that a conversion has taken place. The definite judgment in this connection is left to the divine wisdom. But though we are willing to understand that social myopia is possible in persons whose Christian character and genuine conversion to Christ we cannot doubt, we ought not to recognize any spiritual kinship with those who (consciously or unconsciously) make use of the gospel to cover up their personal prejudices and conveniences.

## The Problem of Christian Conservatism

It is a historic fact that the church's tendency in social matters has been conservative. And it has been so, basically, because of ignorance of the autonomy of political life to which we have referred, and because of its desire to preserve a status quo situation within which the phenomenon of conversion occurred. The fact that conversion had been experienced within a certain social framework served to sanctify that framework as "the" framework within which conversions were possible. At the same time, to the extent that the "converts" and the church established forms of social service that expressed their responsibility for their neighbor, they moved with more confidence in familiar primary social patterns, which did not demand any great technical preparation. Hence the social fruits of pietism. Hence also the "social gospel." All were intent on being loyal to the conversion experience within the structural framework of known society. They lacked a comprehension of the responsibility to view society as a whole and to see the dynamic of love of one's neighbor expressed in action in the interest of justice in social structures. Our century offers the possibility of the common man sharing in this task of change. We still have to see whether the conversion experience, permanently the same, will today include an intelligent view of the forms of change in modern society.

The biblical idea that applies best to the concept of the convert is that of holiness. "Called to be saints—holy ones" is the title that the apostle applies to Christians. Holiness is separation for God's use. In many Christian circles, the emphasis has been on what was called "holiness of life," with insistence on the personal virtues that should make the convert. But it is necessary to go deeper into the concept of holiness to understand that those moral gifts of character are not ends in themselves, but marks of a life that has been placed at God's disposal. The saint ("holy one") is a person who is available. He awaits orders.

Such holiness includes a responsible attitude to one's neighbor: bearing one another's burdens, loving one another. Just as holiness can degenerate into an obsessive concern for the "beauty of our soul," so also the call to love our neighbor can degenerate into a sterile, sentimental idealism. But there is no reason why it should. The marks of a Christian character and the consciousness of being always bound to one's neighbor must find forms of expression, of placing oneself at God's disposal, in any social pattern. Moreover, they must find ways to make themselves effective in order to be genuine instruments, available for God's use in working for social change.

Our problem today is to discover what role the traditional virtues recognized in "converts" can play, in technical society, with its complex patterns. Then we shall ask: To what extent does conversion equip people to go ahead with social change, or is it in itself socially conservative? Lastly we shall inquire whether the struggle for social change is part of the church's mission.

1. As society becomes more complex, it becomes more impersonal. The bureaucrats' decision affects real flesh-and-blood people. Planning-measures that promise marvels for the many sacrifice the interests of the few. Bureaucratic machinery itself is becoming depersonalized. Officials at different levels of administration cannot see all the consequences of their actions. The sense of responsibility is becoming diluted. Personal interest is disappearing. Here indeed is precisely the situation in which the "convert" could best apply the traditional virtues of honesty, responsibility and interest in the individual. A complex society needs outstandingly the person who is dedicated to higher values to carry out routine tasks with a sense of fidelity to the very end. Revolutionary regimes seek to implant all kinds of moral stimuli to attain that grade of responsibility that is indispensable if the social machinery is to yield its fruits. The Christian must be concerned for justice in the patterns of society, and must learn the technical disciplines that can equip him to serve in society, but he must not lose sight of the importance of the basic moral virtues in every social situation.

2. But the technical world offers a field for more than the exercise of the traditional virtues. The simple fact of conversion, which includes a personal decision, places us like a brake on the tendency to mass men together—which is a by-product of technical society. In the measure in which we speak of genuine conversion to Jesus Christ, and of a person who has taken a decision that gives perspective to his whole life, we are speaking of an individual who maintains an island of humanity in the midst of dehumanizing tendencies. It is not that the convert remains unaffected by the collective influences of the systems of work, communication and so forth; but in the midst of a society that is molded by all those systems, he has taken a responsible decision of an ultimate character. He has resisted affection by all the "massifying" influences, and therefore he makes decisions, conditions the things in which he takes part and has an authority to which to refer—all of which surprises the multitude. He remembers that there is a sphere of personal responsibility and privacy that is part of man's nature; and simply by living on the consequences of his experience

of encounter with Christ, he becomes a personalizing influence in society.

3. Responsibility and decision are the personal values that the convert brings to society. To what extent does he participate in the revolutionary dynamic? To what extent does he understand that his conversion demands it?

We must begin by recognizing his conservative tendency. It is no use deceiving ourselves by pretending to be revolutionaries. A person who has experienced conversion to Jesus Christ goes through an initial period of revolutionary inhibition. Social changes frighten him. There is no reason why the period should last very long, but it is unavoidable until one goes deeper into the nature of conversion and into the intelligent forms of expression of the Christian life in the areas of society. An old militant communist of Dresden once said to me: "You Christians will never conduct a revolution, because you do not dare to accept the consequences of one." There is much truth in this statement. As a man relates his life to Christ, he can but hesitate when he faces what he must do in the fields of political and military action. With every concrete decision we are treading holy ground.

This sense of responsibility brings a temptation to avoid public dilemmas, thus taking refuge in an area of private irresponsibility: any participation in the political arena means dirtying our hands, so we withdraw from such areas, in order to maintain our personal purity. As though by doing so we were not just as guilty! There is no way of escape, by action or by omission.

This same sense of responsibility, this vacillation, can bring us to a practical expression that is both timorous and confident, reverent and daring. It places us in the position of pardoned sinners who fulfill their duty trusting in the forgiveness of sins. Converts' political activity should be characterized by deep humility, since it is carried on without illusions as to its purity. There is a risk that this realism may restrain such activity, but it should not, and so long as our conversion binds us to our neighbor and prevents us from forgetting the concrete injustices that must be combatted, it will not do so.

But the convert also tends to be conservative out of ignorance. We have already spoken of the failure to recognize the autonomy of political life. Here the teaching work of the church is basic. But more basic still is the fact that the convert should learn something from the events in his own country. We have said that this is the century of the common man. At least it is the century of the masses. In the measure that the Christian shares in the concerns for change that are manifest in his own country, he will find himself infected with them and obliged to ponder the relevance of his faith to the social conditions of his country.

If conversion places us in the midst of our brothers and identifies us with them, we shall thereby learn the importance of structural factors in our society. We shall understand how traditional kindness has definite limits. We shall understand how love demands knowledge in order that it may be poured out in service to society. But we must not deceive ourselves. The convert *per se* has no reason to possess a greater knowledge of the laws that govern the life and death of human societies. Conversion does not make us wise in any particular field. There is no substitute for serious and responsible study and an open mind toward society.

Conservatism, whether caused by fear of losing personal purity or by ignorance, has in it the basic ingredient of its correction in the very experience of conversion, which places a person face to face with his neighbor. Returning a number of times to my specific neighbor enables me to overcome inner hesitation and prevents my being satisfied with the tradition of "benevolent action." This is what is happening in the countries that used to be called "mission lands." The church brought them the message that called to conversion, but it also unavoidably increased their myopia toward social change. The missionary, being a foreigner, or through his tacit or explicit connection with the occupying power, or because he had difficulty in adapting himself to a completely new situation, added to the convert's legitimate hesitation illegitimate factors that tended to distract him from concern for social structures. Christian schools and institutions had, it is true, their influence on society; but it is only in our generation that throughout the world the need to draw the social consequences of the conversion-experience that brings us to see Christ in every neighbor is being forcefully brought home. The cup of cold water that we give in his name should be given through public health measures or economic planning. Inevitably the gospel has to bring us to take part in these decisive aspects of community life. As our knowledge of the laws that govern human societies increases, our discovery of specific ways of exercising our Christian responsibility will also increase. But the starting point will always be the concrete neighbor: "Thou shalt love thy neighbor."

## The Spiritual Power for Social Action

Anyone who struggles to serve in the political and economic forms of society knows how often he is tempted to become discouraged. Lack of understanding, hatreds, power factors—all combine to dissuade him. There are moments of bitter defeat, others of Pyrrhic victory, still others in which we do not know whether we are betraying the very thing we want to support. In all these circumstances a true conversion-experience is a source of power and of support. It gives a Christian a fixed point of reference for his life and work, and a dynamic in God's love for mankind whom he is seeking to serve.

Conversion, relating our life to Jesus Christ, ought to make us more open than anyone to the changes that are taking place in society. Our trust cannot rest definitely in any particular social or economic system; we cannot sanctify either private property or collective ownership. If God is behind the motivation of our public activity, we know that he is the lord of tomorrow and that he will also be present in other social forms. If God is the only lord of our life, we cannot judge changes in society according to how they affect our patrimony or personal interest; we shall look at them, rather, with an unselfish interest to judge all things in terms of the highest justice which God wills for us. In short, we shall be able to measure the reality of our conversion by the extent of our involvement in the struggle for social justice and the detachment with which we move in the midst of the prevailing social systems.

God has placed the church in the world out of love for that world of which it forms a part. Jesus Christ is lord of the world and those who recognize his lordship ought to show it by the serving spirit that characterizes such a lord. It is for the church to discern God's activity in the secular world, to cooperate with that activity and to point to Christ's presence in it. To proclaim his lordship, to point

out, to discern his presence, to be an instrument of his lordship—
all these are tasks of the church that bring it within the framework
of social change. God himself is at work in them. God himself is
concerned with them. His church cannot be indifferent without betraying the very lord which it claims to announce.

But if we wanted to limit our understanding of the church's
task to thinking of it as a simple quest for individual conversions,
we should at once discover that this is impossible. Conversion requires a neighbor, and I find my neighbor today in society. No
man is independent of his relationships. In loving God in my neighbor, I love him in the setting of patterns that—for better or for
worse—condition his life. And that search for my neighbor cannot be motivated by eagerness to proselytize. It is a search that
blossoms from love toward God. And that love is directed upon
my neighbor regardless of how many of them become aware of it.
If there is no love, there has been no conversion. If there is love,
we are neither able nor willing to avoid those areas that determine
and condition man's life on earth.

From the other extreme of the equation, we are equally led to
incorporate into the church's mission a genuine concern for the
transformation of society. The gospel requires certain historical
conditions if it is to reach people: freedom of conscience, peace,
communications. If we are to assure the conditions of orderly
life that make the proclamation of the gospel possible, we must
enter into the social struggle.

We would go further on this point: every true struggle to create
humane living conditions in which man may express freedom and
responsibility seeks to establish a situation in which the call to
conversion finds a man free to respond. The transformation of society—in itself a good thing if it involves the changing of injustices
into forms of justice—is also a positive fact from the point of view
of the preaching of the gospel, since it liberates man for the great
decision of his life: his answer to God's call in Christ.

We must safeguard ourselves here against misunderstanding. We
are not saying that conversions do not take place within every social pattern, or that you must first change society and then preach,
or that we are interested in social change so that men will accept
the gospel that is offered them. But we are saying that the procla-

mation of the gospel is not something isolated from given social situations, and that as far as human factors are concerned, social change affects the possibility of conversion. We must always respect the miracle of grace, the mystery of God. In other words, what we do for the whole man in society bears a relation to his salvation. By our responsible attitude in the transformation of society, we help to set the stage in which God's Word can speak freely to man. The rest belongs to the mystery of God, and to human liberty. "Let my people go, so that they may serve me. . . ." "Choose you this day whom you will serve."

# EPILOGUE

# 20

# ISSUES FOR THE
# ECUMENICAL DIALOGUE

by JOHN C. BENNETT (United States)

I am impressed by the wide area of agreement in this volume in a middle area of theological and ethical convictions. The ultimate theological frames of reference are profoundly different, as different as the traditions represented. Also apart from the traditional differences there are such contrasts within the same tradition as that between those who represent a Christocentric method in theology strongly influenced by Karl Barth and those who might be called "Neo-liberal" in method. In addition to these ultimate theological differences there are at least implicitly great differences in matters of immediate social policy or action. Some of these may be chiefly reflections of contrasting historical situations. For example, there is a deep difference between those who assume that they must act as Christians in a revolutionary situation and those who take for granted the continuities of a relatively stable society and look for gradual and orderly change.

Since the majority of the readers of this volume will probably come from the societies that stress stability and continuity it was decided to introduce them immediately, through Richard Shaull's chapter, to the experience of Christians who face the more revolutionary choices.

I shall give substance to what I say about agreements as I discuss the following areas of convergence.

## Areas of Convergence

1. The first and perhaps clearest common conviction that comes through these chapters is the belief that Christian faith involves responsibility for the transformation of the institutions and structures of society. This means the rejection of several views of Christian faith that have had acceptance in the churches. I refer to such views as an otherworldly individualism that avoids Christian involvement in political decisions, a conservatism that is based upon the acceptance of the status quo as providentially ordained or the assumption that the religious and moral persuasion of individuals to be good citizens is the substance of Christian social responsibility.

None of the authors have anything in common with the kind of Christian conservatism, quite common in the American churches, that identifies Christian ethics with absolute economic individualism. The American chapters reject this position, and so does the chapter by Bruce Reed, a British representative of Protestant evangelicalism of a type that in the United States is often found allied with this economic individualism.

Many of the authors emphasize the fact that the great churches have on the whole been conservative in their social influence, that they have been identified with the state and with other centers of privilege and power, that they have been inclined toward a rather static view of institutions and structures. Many of the authors criticize strongly the social inadequacies and even distortions that they find in their own traditions. For example, Professors Bartsch and Mehl make a special point of gaining freedom from interpretations of Romans 13 that exalt the authority of the state and discourage political protest. Dr. Nissiotis, as a Greek Orthodox theologian, seeks to disentangle his tradition from the tendency toward the sacralization of national institutions, calling his church to avoid conformism and to identify itself with the poor and the suffering.

The chapters by Lutherans strongly emphasize Christian ethics as law that has relevance for social and political institutions, and seek to overcome interpretations of the conception of the "two realms" which inhibit Christian efforts to transform society.

2. There is a general acceptance of contextualism as a cor-

rective of the tendency to think abstractly about social issues and
to impose laws and principles that are absolute or too rigid on the
many varied situations. As I shall say later, those who regard contextualism as self-sufficient will find many critics in these chapters,
and yet most of these critics themselves think differently because
of the barrage from the theologians who may seem to claim too
much for contextualism. The latter, represented in this volume
especially by Professor Shaull and Professor Fletcher, approach
the problem from totally different backgrounds. Professor Shaull,
following Paul Lehmann, found contextualism illuminating as he
struggled with the concrete problems of Christians in the midst
of revolutionary movements in Latin America. Professor Fletcher
writes as one who has given great attention to the dilemmas of
medical ethics for which traditional moral theology often provides
rigid principles.

3.   Throughout these chapters there is a clear avoidance of the
idea that there is any over-all Christian system. The emphasis upon
Christian social responsibility is as strong as it was in the "Social
Gospel," but it is not accompanied by the same optimistic view
of history or the same confidence that Christian solutions of social
problems are available. There is, as I have said in the foreword,
a sense of many new possibilities; there is a more hopeful mood
than has been the case in most of the ecumenical books since the
Oxford conference in 1937. But there is no tendency to identify
the kingdom of God with any social developments in history. There
remain the warnings of Christian realism concerning the finiteness
and the sin of man, and the precariousness of all human schemes.
There is no tendency to repeat the errors of Christendom in sa-
cralizing nations or civilizations. Though as a theme it is not emphasized, the eschatological dimension as the source of judgment
and fulfillment plays a part in the thought of most of these writers.

4.   One of the most striking characteristics of this volume is the
extent to which it expresses a strong Christian humanism. (The
humanism has a clearly Christian foundation, but it is about universal humanity.) This may appear in Christocentric forms, or it
may seem to have a broader empirical base, but everywhere it
shines through. This is not a dogmatic universalism about human
destiny (this issue as such is not raised), but it is a generous

and open attitude toward all humanity which the church is called
to serve. Essential humanity is divided by no iron curtains and
no ecclesiastical curtains. There is no tendency to use theology
to determine who is within and who is outside the circle of salvation. There is a strong affirmation that there are humane criteria
and goals on which there is widespread though not universal agreement, criteria and goals on which Christians and non-Christians
can often agree.

5. A final emphasis that pervades the book is the assumption
that the church should be oriented toward the world and that it
should take an affirmative attitude toward the secular. This subject as such is discussed more fully in Volume IV. There is here
no systematic position concerning the relation between Christianity
and "religion" or between Christianity and the secular, but the humanism to which I have referred involves this openness to the
human in its secular forms. Much is made of the relative autonomy
of the economic and political processes that are essential for the
existence of society and that must be studied on their own terms
and served in ways suitable to them if society is to be better ordered and more just. Dean Muelder's respect for the contribution
of the social sciences on their own terms would, I believe, be accepted quite generally, though no two authors would necessarily
state their view of the relation between theology and the social
sciences in the same way. I doubt if any of the authors would seek
to make the social sciences captive of either theology or the church;
and all agree that we cannot understand this changing world of
politics and economics and technology unless it is illumined by the
social sciences.

### Areas of Debate

1. *The role of theology.* The volume as a whole poses one question: how much difference does theology make to judgments in the
sphere of social ethics? I have suggested how great is the agreement on the ethical criteria and goals for society in spite of the
quite different theological traditions involved. I have stressed the
reality of a common ground morality that makes possible cooperation between Christians and non-Christians. One can press this

last point further and say that often Christians have learned from Jews and other non-Christians, including those who adhere to no traditional faith, much political wisdom and very necessary lessons concerning their responsibility for social justice. If these things are true what is the point of this theological discussion?

I think that there are at least two answers to this question. The first is that everyone's convictions about what is good for society have foundations of some sort whether they are recognized or not. Non-Christians have their own presuppositions about man and history, and they need to elaborate these. Christians must do the same, and it is most fortunate if it turns out that in spite of differences of presuppositions there are areas of agreement. But it would be wrong to assume that presuppositions make no difference and that no views of man exist that would fail to support in any way the kind of humanism that is widely shared. The experience of National Socialism is proof of what may come out of false conceptions of life. Marxism is more complex because it does contain elements of humanism and these may become dominant, but it has inspired political absolutisms that for a time at least have destroyed personal freedom.

This leads to the second answer to the question concerning the relevance of theology. There are types of Christian theology which are incompatible with the common convictions that emerge from the volume. There are forms of authoritarian legalism that would make it impossible for Christians to relate themselves creatively to the new problems with which all four volumes deal. There are conservative interpretations of providence or of the orders of creation that would preclude participation in the struggles for a transforming social justice. There are forms of the "two realms" view of Christian responsibility that separate the public order from prophetic Christian criticism. There are some doctrines of man that lend themselves to an uncritical affirmation of progress, and others that are so pessimistic that they encourage a kind of fatalism in the accepting of an oppressive status quo. There are conceptions of both church and kingdom that provide no adequate basis for criticism either of the church itself or of some "Christian society." These are only suggestions of the kind of theological positions that would be incompatible with most of the convictions about social responsibility found in this volume. The very absence of all these positions is another evidence of how much theological convergence there is in spite of differences of tradition among the authors, a convergence that would not have been possible without decades of ecumenical conversation. Also, there has been, beyond all conscious interchange of thought, a common openness to many of the same experiences and events. We all learn some of the same lessons from history if there are the beginnings of a theological interest in them.

2. *Revolutionary action and constitutional change.* A second difference may be largely the result of differing historical situations: the contrast between those who write out of relatively stable situations which provide hope for orderly transformations of society and those who write out of situations in which the continuities of life are broken or in which institutions for orderly transformation do not exist. It is hard to say how much these writers are opposed to each other in principle or how much they reflect roles that are quite different because they live with different possibilities. I am sure that there are differences of emphasis that would probably show up as differences of principle even in the same situation. Revolutionary situations are ambiguous, and we do find Christians with the same objectives differing radically in their estimate as to the kind of political movements they should support.

The clearest acceptance of responsibility for revolutionary action that renounces hope, in some situations, in legal changes by orderly processes is expressed in the three chapters from Latin America, those by Shaull, Castillo and Castro. All these writers see value in Marxism as a source of historical interpretation and revolutionary stimulus, though none of them accept Marxism as a consistent scheme and none of them seek support from Chinese or Soviet communism. They assume that some Christians should work with Marxists for social justice.

I do not know whether the authors from the United States or from the welfare states of western Europe would disagree with this revolutionary stance if they lived in Latin America, but many of their western colleagues would disagree even if they lived there and I expect that this may be one of the chief subjects for debate at the conference. Such authors as Shinn and Wendland and Aronson take for granted the modernization that is one of the goals of revolution in Asia and Africa and Latin America. They also take for granted the considerable transformation of capitalism by democratic processes that has already taken place. Shinn notes the need of radical change in the United States to overcome the "dismal poverty" which is the lot of one fifth of the population. Indeed, the rising to political consciousness of a new generation of Negroes is giving Americans an experience of revolutionary crises, and it remains to be seen how they will respond to future radical pressures which link civil rights with drastic measures to overcome urban poverty.

One of the most interesting contrasts, growing out of two entirely different historical situations, is in the discussion of the welfare state by Castro and by Lochman. This in no way reflects a difference of opinion between them but merely the different situations to which they are responding. Castro says: "The cup of cold water that we give in his name should be given through public health measures or economic planning." Lochman takes these for granted and then says: "Yet precisely here where the church gratefully acknowledges this national welfare, it will underline again the honor of philanthropy in the sense of turning to those who need personal understanding, personal care, personal interest, in particular the 'orphans and widows' of the modern age, people who are lonely and half-forgotten."

3. *The debate over principles and contextualism.* As I have said, there is a considerable agreement on contextualism as a corrective. It is interesting to find a Reformed theologian (Shaull) and an Anglican theologian (Fletcher) going all out in their affirmation of contextualism and to find two Lutherans (Wendland and Lazareth) calling for greater emphasis on law or at least for a clearer place for law in the theological structure. At the editorial meetings that prepared this volume no subject was more discussed than this, and I think that in general it was agreed that contextualism is not a self-sufficient system. It was accepted as a protest against absolutism and rigidity in imposing principles that have been wrought out in relatively stable societies on revolutionary situations, or on the nations that are seeking to establish new politi-

cal institutions without being able to presuppose most of the tissues of national unity.

Take two conceptions in the chapters by Shaull and Fletcher which point beyond a self-sufficient contextualism: Shaull's stress on "humanization" and Fletcher's on principles generally valid. "Humanization" takes for granted many criteria concerning what is human. Fletcher says that the contextualist is "well armed with "generally valid" principles but (is) prepared to modify, suspend or violate any principle or "general rule" if in the situation the command to love the neighbor is better served. The situationist always remembers that he is commanded to love persons—not precepts or even principles. This is doubtless true, but I believe that many others involved in this discussion would insist that when we violate one "generally valid" principle, we must know what we are doing and what we may be sacrificing. There would be few cases in which we would be unable to give reasons for making the exception that would reflect other generally valid principles. The word "principle" may itself be too static, but usually we find that in these cases there is a conflict of some sort between generally valid considerations, and moral judgments involving some weighing of these, even though this may be done so quickly that it seems to be a momentary intuition. But afterward, when what is done is defended or when it is suggested that it may bring some light to another situation, such weighing of contrary considerations is bound to become more deliberate. Love unguided by any tested considerations can be very blind and often very wrong.

In the writing of some contextualists two conceptions take the place of principles: the discernment of what God is doing to humanize man in a situation, and the idea of the *koinonia*. The first raises questions as to how we know what God is doing in the very ambiguous situations which we continually confront unless we have in our minds some criteria—drawn, it may be, from the very idea of humanization. Such criteria would be necessary protection against abberration, such as in the case of many churchmen who saw God at work positively in Hitler. The *koinonia* also raises questions that point beyond itself. If the *koinonia* is a kind of cell group of Christians working together in a revolutionary crisis (as in Shaull's conception), it may be necessary to choose between such groups. This would involve some criteria. If the *koinonia* is the larger church, it is in continual need of reformation in the light of some criteria.

4. *The discussion of natural law ethics.* The fourth issue that will continue to be debated and that may provide the clue to differences of theological method is the relationship between a Christocentric approach to ethics and an approach that allows what is known through Christ to be supported or supplemented by ethical insight derived apart from Christ. The status of the Old Testament is a problem here. All Christian teaching about justice owes a great debt to the prophetic tradition. On the other hand, a legalistic use of the whole Old Testament may seriously distort Christian ethics, and this approach is regularly rejected in this volume. The whole Bible is the source of social ethics subject always to the criterion given in Christ.

Within the New Testament itself the problem of criterion is important when we weigh the claims of such a passage as Romans 13 against those of the Sermon on the Mount. These are difficult exegetical issues, and some writers, especially Professors Bartsch and Mehl, give a good deal of attention to the problem of freeing Christian political ethics from the dominance of Romans 13. Bartsch corrects much Christian political ethics by desacralizing or demythologizing the state and putting all claims of the state under the criterion of service to neighbors. This doubtless raises new problems in relation to the responsibilities of states for the interests and security of national communities, but in some situations it is a welcome escape from a two-realms doctrine that does not allow real interaction between Christian love and the considerations of both justice and prudence that remain important for the Christian in political ethics.

The broader question concerning the status within theology of ethical insight that comes from sources outside the Christian circle occupies a number of the authors. No one doubts the existence of a common ground morality (not necessarily a universally recognized morality) on which Christians and non-Christians do cooperate. Professor Söe strongly affirms this broad base for morality, but he refuses to give the category of "natural law" theological status. The battle over "natural law" is partly a verbal debate, and

the use of that concept may raise too many confusions in ecumenical circles to be helpful. This may be all the more true at the
moment when Roman Catholics are themselves revising their conceptions of natural law. It remains true that these chapters contain
various substitutes for what has traditionally been known as natural law, and none more so than Prof. Söe's. In the context of the
Asian religions, there is the same openness to non-Christian sources
of morality in Principal Chandran's chapter. There is nowhere in
this book any sense of a Christian monopoly of moral wisdom.
Theologians who develop their own Christocentric ethic but who
recognize the important area of overlap between their moral judgments and those of many non-Christians with whom they cooperate, and from whom they may have learned important lessons
concerning their own moral responsibility, leave us with problems
that should have some fresh discussion.

## The Concept of the Responsible Society

Many of the issues that I have emphasized come to a head in
the discussion of the "responsible society" as a category in Christian social ethics. This has played a very large part in ecumenical
discussion since the first assembly of the World Council at Amsterdam in 1948. Attitudes toward this concept are influenced by three
debates that I have emphasized in this epilogue: The debate over
natural law and broadly based human wisdom; the debate over
principles and contextualism; and the debate over the adequacy
of ethics based upon stable constitutional societies for revolutionary situations and for new nations that may be obliged to give
priority to unity and order over the constitutionally protected forms
of freedom.

The ecumenical discussion on Church and Society should not
take a defensive attitude toward a concept that may have served
well in the past but that needs to be criticized rigorously today.
Perhaps it can be revised in such a way as to meet the criticisms;
perhaps it needs to be displaced. On the other hand, it has been
the bearer of ethical convictions that need to be preserved. "The
responsible society" receives considerable support in this volume,

especially in the chapters by Wendland and Mehl who represent both the Lutheran and the Reformed traditions.

"The responsible society" does reflect the common ground morality that I find generally accepted in these chapters. It need not be associated with the stereotypes of "natural law" that are most vulnerable. For one thing, it is not presented as a universal deliverance of reason; and Christians may well base their acceptance of some aspects of the responsible society on distinctively Christian grounds, for example, on the ground that nations should be open to a judgment that transcends the state so that it makes sense both theologically and politically for a person to say that he must obey God rather than men. No nation may fully understand this, but there is the possibility within the nation of institutions that point to this transcendent judgment. The fact of tension beween church and state within a nation is one sign that aspects of the responsible society are present. As the Evanston report said: "Forms of association within society which have their own foundations and principles should be respected, and not controlled in their inner life by the state. Churches, families and universities are dissimilar examples of this type of non-political association."

The most telling criticism of the adequacy of the concept of "the responsible society" is that it reflects the older and more stable constitutional societies and that it does not fit the context of nations for which order and unity are priorities or nations that must first go through a period of revolution in which socially transforming justice has priority over freedom. "The responsible society" presupposes an ordered pluralism, constitutional processes of social change, and so is able to magnify the freedom of the person from "interference with elementary human rights."

The New Delhi Assembly (Section on Service) recognized the existence of this problem and suggested that the criteria of the responsible society are still generally valid, but that they do not take account of the difficulties of Christians who see no choice in some situations except tribal anarchy or authoritarian government which has few of the marks of the responsible society; and in other situations between support of a corrupt and overwhelmingly unjust regime and support of a revolutionary movement that may involve them in cruel violence and in various ideological illusions.

In such situations the principles of the responsible society seem remote from all the possibilities, and it may also be difficult to discern what God is doing except perhaps in momentary flashes that give little guidance for political policy.

The predicament that is described here is not unlike that of the nonpacifist Christian in time of war, though war in the past has been taken by Christians as an interruption that did not undermine the general claims of the ethics of peace. Today the problem is how Christians may find a way amidst tumultuous events from which they see no escape and in which the political choices may seem morally intolerable according to all the "principles" learned in church in the past. How can units of the church live in these situations without either losing their integrity or becoming irrelevant?

These may be the hardest questions faced at the 1966 Conference on Church and Society. To ask them with full recognition of the limited alternatives that are often present does not mean that we must jettison all that has been said about better or worse political institutions under the heading of "the responsible society." When it may seem necessary to support an arbitrary government in order to prevent anarchy, this does not make its arbitrariness good. The pressure upon us to find a better alternative is always present, pressure that comes from love for the victims of arbitrariness— not only the victims of momentary action but the generations that may be denied participation in government as a part of their humanity. The pressure upon us comes also from the fact that such an arbitrary government fails to recognize any signs of the judgment of God and it tends to make itself into an idol. The external religious trappings of the worship of Caesar are not today the most common marks of idolatry. Intimidation of the human spirit by political power is always evil even though this may be done for the sake of needed national unity. Pressures from God are upon the Christian in the midst of revolution to keep what is done free from the terrible dehumanization involved in the torture of opponents in defense of the cause, but the existence of such evils does not of itself bind the Christian to withdraw from the cause.

The pressures from the love of God revealed in Christ to keep political institutions and policies human are always upon us. And the goals that guide the very participation of the Christian in the situations of greatest perplexity are still the deliverance of the people from injustice and the defense of the freedom of the minds and spirits of men against political intimidation and oppression. To make clearer the meaning of these pressures and of these goals may be a translation of much that was said in the name of the responsible society into more dynamic terms. The churches cannot live in their many situations with an absolute law from which can be deduced all that is required of the Christian who seeks to be obedient, or with a moral and political relativism that knows no criteria for the human, and no conflicts of conscience in the choice of political means, and no goals for political change with moral claims.

The experience of nations in which there has been a continuous development of institutions of political participation of all the people and of institutions which protect the rights of persons surely has meaning for the political goals of the rapidly changing societies. The churches in their desire to be open to the new should not cast off what can still be found good in the old. Though the concept of the responsible society as expressed in the ecumenical literature is a source of judgment upon all achievements, it grows out of the experience of partially won human rights and freedoms that are the deposit of previous revolutions and that are as much the work of God as anything that can be seen in the struggles and the partial victories of the present.